Seoul

> "All you've got to do is decide to go and the hardest part is over.
>
> ## So go!"
>
> TONY WHEELER, COFOUNDER – LONELY PLANET

THIS EDITION WRITTEN AND RESEARCHED BY

Simon Richmond

Contents

Plan Your Trip 4

Explore Seoul 40

Understand Seoul 143

Survival Guide 165

Seoul Maps 193

(left) Changing of the guard at Deoksugung (p69)

(above) Gyeongbokgung (p46)

(right) Royal food banquet

Northern Seoul
p112

Gwanghwamun & Jongno-gu
p44

Myeong-dong & Jung-gu
p65

Dongdaemun & Eastern Seoul
p107

Western Seoul
p76

Itaewon & Yongsan-gu
p86

Gangnam & South of the Han River
p96

Welcome to Seoul

Dive into this dynamic mash-up of night markets and K-Pop, temples and majestic palaces, skyscrapers and pulsing neon.

Design Matters

Seoul is evolving from a hardened concrete-and-steel economic powerhouse into a softer-edged 21st-century urban ideal of parks, culture and design. Following on from the disinterring and landscaping of the central Cheong-gye stream and upgrading of the Han River parks comes the sprucing up of hiking trails on Namsan, a mountain escape in the city's midst. The Unesco City of Design also offers several contemporary architectural marvels, including the Dongdaemun Design Plaza & Park and the giant glass wave of the new City Hall.

Historical Fragments

Gaze down on this sprawling metropolis of 10.5 million people from atop any of Seoul's four guardian mountains and you'll sense the powerful *pungsu-jiri* (feng shui) that has long nurtured and protected the city. Having endured the catastrophe of the Korean War barely 60 years ago, the 'Miracle on the Han' has its eye clearly on the future, while history clings tenaciously to many of its corners. You'll encounter fascinating fragments of the past in World Heritage–listed sites such as Jongmyo shrine, as well as in the alleys winding between the graceful *hanok* (traditional wooden homes) that cluster in Bukchon.

24-Hour City

Whatever you want, at any time of day or night, Seoul can provide. An early morning temple visit can lead to a palace tour followed by teahouse sipping in Bukchon and gallery hopping in Insa-dong. *Soju* (a vodka-like drink) and snacks in a street tent bar will fuel you for shopping at the buzzing Dongdaemun or Namdaemun night markets, partying in Hongdae or Itaewon, or playing online games at a PC *bang* or watching the latest Korean blockbuster at a DVD *bang*. Follow this with steaming, soaking and snoozing in a *jjimjil-bang* (sauna and spa). By the time you look at your watch, it will be dawn again.

Beyond the Walls

Public transport is brilliant, so there's no excuse for not stretching your travel horizons beyond the Fortress Walls. Most visitors are inexorably drawn to the fearsome modern-day barrier: the Demilitarised Zone, or DMZ, splitting South from North Korea. Day trips here are a must, and nearby is the charming arts and culture village of Heyri. To the west, Incheon is a fascinating port where the modern world came flooding into Korea at the end of the 19th century, while south is Suwon, home also to impressive World Heritage–listed fortifications.

Why I Love Seoul

By Simon Richmond, Author

Seoul is heaven for passionate foodies. Whether tucking into the snacks of commoners or the cuisine of kings, you just can't lose. A *hanjeongsik* (multicourse banquet) is a feast as much for the eyes as the tummy, as are the creations of chefs crafting neo-Korean dishes. Equally satisfying is scoffing down piping-hot, crispy *hotteok* (pancakes with sweet or savoury fillings) on a street corner, or delicious, fresh and fiery crab soup in Noryangjin Fish Market. And don't get me started on the wonderful universe of teas served in charming teahouses: this is where the soul of Seoul lies.

For more about our author, see p216.

For more about our author, see p216.

Top: Snack corner, Myeong-don

Seoul's
Top 10

Cheong-gye-cheon (p52)

1 A raised highway was demolished and the ground dug up to 'daylight' this long-buried stream. It transformed Seoul's centre, creating a riverside park and walking course that's a calm respite from the surrounding commercial hubbub. Public art is dotted along the banks and many events are held here, including a spectacular lantern festival in November, when thousands of glowing paper-and-paint sculptures are floated in the water. There's a museum where you can learn about the history of the Cheong-gye-cheon.

◉ *Gwanghwamun & Jongno-gu*

Bukchon Hanok Village (p49)

2 In a city at the cutting edge of 21st-century technology, where apartment living is the norm, this neighbourhood stands as a testament to an age of craftsmanship when Seoulites lived in one-storey wooden *hanok*, complete with graceful tiled roofs and internal courtyard gardens. Get lost wandering the labyrinthine streets, squished between two major palaces and rising up the foothills of Bukaksan. Take in the views and pause to pop into a cafe, art gallery, craft shop or small private museum along the way.

◉ *Gwanghwamun & Jongno-gu*

Changdeokgung
(p48)

3 The 'Palace of Illustrious Virtue' was built in the early 15th century as a secondary palace to Gyeongbokgung. These days this Unesco World Heritage-listed property exceeds it in beauty and grace – partly because so many of its buildings were actually lived in by royal-family members well into the 20th century. The most charming section is the Huwon, a 'secret garden' that is a royal horticultural idyll. Book well ahead to snag one of the limited tickets to view this special palace on the moonlight tours held during full-moon nights in the warm months.

⊙ *Gwanghwamun & Jongno-gu*

Gwangjang Market *(p110)*

4 This is one of Seoul's best markets. During the day it's known as a place for trading in secondhand clothes and fabrics. But it's at night that it really comes into its own, when some of its alleys fill up with vendors selling all manner of street eats. Stewed pig trotters and snouts, *gimbap* (rice, veggies and ham wrapped in rice and rolled in sheets of seaweed) and *bindaetteok* (plate-sized crispy pancakes of crushed mung beans and veggies fried on a skillet) are all washed down with copious amounts of *makgeolli* and *soju* (local liquors).

⊙ *Dongdaemun & Eastern Seoul*

Namsan & N Seoul Tower *(p67)*

5 Protected within a 109-hectare park and crowned by N Seoul Tower, one of Seoul's most distinctive architectural features, Namsan is the most central of the city's four guardian mountains. Locals actively patronise the park, keeping fit and taking in the cooler, sweeter air on hiking paths to the summit, including one that follows the line of the old Seoul Fortress Walls. The summit itself is highly commercial but still worth visiting; you won't just be marvelling at the view, but also at the multitude of inscribed padlocks that adorn the railings here – all signifying lovers' devotion.

⊙ *Myeong-dong & Jung-gu*

Lotus Lantern Festival (p21)

6 A week never passes in Seoul without some major festival or event. One of the most spectacular that is well worth building your travel plans around is the Lotus Lantern Festival, which happens in May in celebration of the Buddha's birthday. For weeks around this time, temples are strung with hundreds of rainbow-hued paper lanterns, a sight in itself. The highlight is a dazzling night-time parade that snakes its way through the city from Dongguk University to Jogye-sa, involving thousands of participants and every shape, size and colour of lantern.

✺ *Month by Month*

Hongdae (p76)

7 The area around Hongik University, Korea's leading art and design institution, has long acted as a magnet for young, independent and creatively minded Koreans. It's packed with quirky bars and cafes, jazzy boutiques, and cramped, smoky dance and live-music clubs where kids bop around to the latest K-Indie thrash bands and crooners. Come here to sample gourmet ice cream and artisan coffee, and pick up a cool craft souvenir at Saturday's Free Market. The vibe is infectious and has spilled over into Sangsu, the neighbourhood that's closer to the river and even more of a hipster hang-out.

◉ *Western Seoul*

6

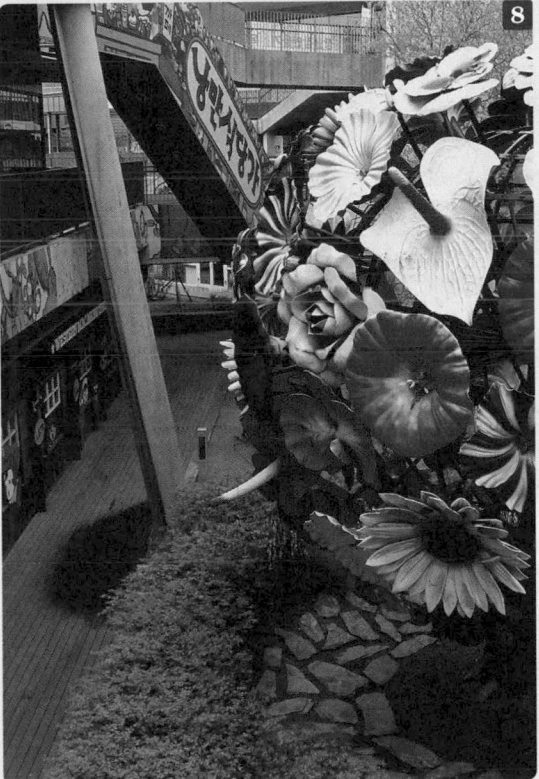

Heyri (p122)

8 So peaceful and laid-back is the arty village of Heyri that it's hard to comprehend that less than 10km north is the heavily fortified border with North Korea. Conceived as a 'book village' connected to the nearby publishing centre of Paju Book City, this low-rise contemporary community is home to artists, writers, architects and other creative souls. There are scores of small art galleries, cafes, boutiques and quirky private collections turned into mini museums. With several pleasant, design-savvy places to stay, it makes for the perfect short break from Seoul, less than an hour away by express bus.

⊙ *Day Trips from Seoul*

Cycling Beside the Han River (p80)

9 Beneath the traffic-clogged highways that shadow the course of the Han River is a string of grassy parks linked up by kilometres of cycle lanes. Joining in the pedalling fun is easy, as the city maintains bicycle-hire stations at various points along the river. One of the best places to start or finish a cycle trip is the island of Yeouido. From here you can cross over to the northern side of the Han and pedal out to the World Cup Stadium and back via Seonyudo Park, a recreation area crafted from a former water filtration plant.

🏃 *Western Seoul*

Dongdaemun (p107)

10 Historical and contemporary Seoul stands side by side in this eternally buzzing and sprawling market area. A facelift to Heunginjimum (aka Dongdaemun) has left the old east gate to the city looking grander than it has done in decades. Sections of the old Fortress Walls that the gate was once connected to have been uncovered and form part of the Dongdaemun History & Culture Park. Rising up behind this is the sleek, silvery form of the Zaha Hadid–designed Dongdaemun Design Plaza, an architectural show-stopper that could hardly be more 21st century in its conception. (DONGDAEMUN DESIGN PLAZA)

👁 *Dongdaemun & Eastern Seoul*

What's New

Dongdaemun Design Plaza & Park

Pritzker Prize–winning architect Zaha Hadid was hired to design this silvery, sinuous building that's one of the most striking recent additions to Seoul's urban patchwork. The attached park had to be modified when early Joseon-era archaeological remains were discovered on the site. These are now on view along with a couple of free exhibition halls detailing Dongdaemun's rich history. (p109)

Sungnyemun (Namdaemun)

After five years under wraps, Korea's No 1 National Treasure, the Great South Gate, has been rebuilt. Head to the bustling market area to view the grand wood and stone gateway. (p68)

Jaam Guesthouse & V Mansion

Hongdae has scores of convivial backpacker guesthouses but few as pleasant as the colourful new Jaam Guesthouse. Also check out the management's even newer operation, V Mansion, in neighbouring Sangsu. (p137)

Level 5

Visit this floor of the Noon Square mall, which is devoted to sponsoring up-and-coming fashion talent including participants of *Project Runway Korea*. (p75)

Hike up Bukaksan

The tallest of the city's four guardian mountains is now open to the public; hike the steep trail that follows the Seoul Fortress Wall. (p114)

Jung Sikdang

Chef Yim Jung-sik sets the gold standard for neo-Korean cuisine at this serene, small restaurant serving delicious works of art on a plate. (p102)

Platoon Kunsthalle

Check out this laid-back bar/gallery/events space made from old shipping containers. Drinks and eats are affordable. Thursday night is open stage for live music. (p103)

Haebangchon (HBC) & Gyeongridan

Enjoy the relaxed, foreigner-friendly vibe of the restaurants, bars and cafes that are located downhill from Itaewon. (p94)

Gilsang-sa

At this beautiful temple on a leafy hillside in Seongbuk-dong, you can sample monastic life and meditation by signing up for the overnight Templestay program. (p115)

Incheon Art Platform

An attractive complex of 1930s and '40s brick warehouses has been turned into gallery spaces and art residency studios in the historic port. (p127)

Tongin Market

Browse this traditional covered market, enjoy an inexpensive lunch-box meal, and then explore the small art galleries and artisan coffee houses scattered around nearby Tongui-dong. (p57)

For more recommendations and reviews, see **lonelyplanet.com/ south-korea/seoul**

Need to Know

Currency
Korean won (₩)

Language
Korean and English

Visas
Australian, UK, US and most Western European citizens can get a 90-day entry permit on arrival.

Money
ATMs widely available. Credit cards accepted by most businesses, but some smaller food places and markets are cash only.

Mobile Phones
South Korea uses the CDMA digital standard; check compatibility with your phone provider. Phones can be hired at the airport and elsewhere.

Time
GMT/UTC plus nine hours. No daylight saving.

Tourist Information
KTO Tourist Information Centre (☏1330; www.visitkorea.or.kr; Cheong-gye-cheon-ro, Jung-gu; ⊙9am-8pm; ⑤Line 1 to Jonggak, Exit 5) is the best information centre among many scattered across Seoul.

Your Daily Budget

Budget under ₩100,000
→ Dorm bed ₩20,000
→ Street food ₩1000–5000
→ Local beer per bottle ₩3000
→ Hiking up Namsan: free
→ Entry to National Museum of Korea: free
→ Subway ticket ₩1150

Midrange ₩100,000–300,000
→ *Hanok* guesthouse ₩70,000
→ Food walking tour ₩88,000
→ Entry to Gyeongbokgung ₩3000
→ *Galbi* (barbecued meat) meal ₩40,000
→ Theatre ticket ₩40,000

Top end over ₩300,000
→ Hotel ₩200,000
→ Royal Korean banquet ₩70,000
→ Scrub and massage at top-notch spa ₩60,000
→ DMZ tour ₩96,000

Advance Planning

Two months before Book flights and accommodation; start learning *hangeul* (the Korean phonetic alphabet) and train for hiking up mountains.

Three weeks before Plan itinerary, checking to see if there are any events or festivals you may be able to attend; book DMZ tour and Templestay program.

One week before Download coupon from BBB Korea (www.bbbkorea.org) for free phone hire.

Useful Websites

→ **Visit Seoul** (www.visitseoul.net) The official government site to everything about the city.

→ **Seoul** (www.seoulselection.com/seoul) Online version of monthly magazine with its finger on the city's pulse.

→ **Lonely Planet** (www.lonelyplanet.com/seoul) Destination information, hotel bookings, traveller forum and more.

WHEN TO GO

Spring and autumn are uniformly pleasant, while summer is sweltering and muggy, and winters nasty and long. Typhoons are a possibility from late June to September.

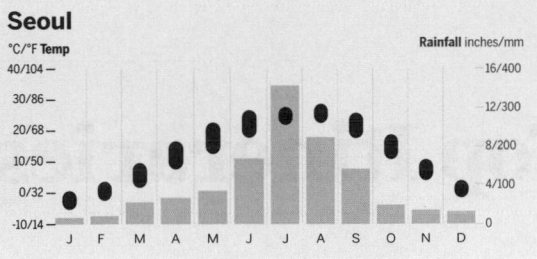

Seoul

Arriving in Seoul

Incheon International Airport
A'rex express trains to Seoul Station ₩13,800 (43 minutes); commuter trains ₩3850 (53 minutes). Bus to city-centre hotels ₩10,000 (one hour); taxi around ₩65,000.

Gimpo International Airport
A'rex trains run to Seoul Station (₩1300, 15 minutes) or take the subway (₩1250, 35 minutes). Both bus (₩5000 to ₩7000) and taxi (around ₩35,000) will be slower – around 40 minutes to an hour, depending on traffic.

Seoul Station Long-distance trains arrive at this centrally located terminal; a taxi ride to most nearby hotels will be under ₩5000.

For much more on **arrival**, see p166.

Getting Around

Buy a T-Money card (₩3000; http://eng.t-money.co.kr), which provides a ₩100 discount per trip on bus, subway, taxi and train fares.

➡ **Subway** The best way to get around with an extensive network, frequent services and inexpensive fares.

➡ **Bus** Handy for routes around Namsan; less so for other places.

➡ **Taxi** Best for short trips; basic fare starts at ₩2400 for the first 2km.

➡ **Bicycle** Hire for pedalling along the Han River and through Olympic Park.

➡ **Car Hire** Useful only for long trips out of the city; budget from ₩80,000 per day.

For much more on **getting around**, see p168.

Sleeping

There are plenty of budget guesthouses and five-star pamper palaces, but reserve well in advance especially if visiting during busy Asian travel seasons, such as Chinese New Year and Japan's Golden Week holidays (usually the end of April, early May). Rates at the cheaper places usually include the 10% government tax, but many midrange and top-end hotels quote without this amount. The top-end places also add another 10% for service.

Useful Websites

➡ **KHRC** (www.khrc.com) Online booking for a wide range of hotels in Korea.

➡ **Innostel** (http://innostel.visitseoul.net) Bookings for reasonably priced accommodation options in Seoul.

➡ **Lonely Planet** (www.lonelyplanet.com/seoul) Expert author reviews, user feedback, booking engine.

For much more on **sleeping**, see p131.

SEOUL ADDRESSES

Seoul is in the midst of moving over to a new address system of numbered houses on named streets – you'll notice numbered blue plaques on most buildings now. Confusingly, however, few people know the new street names, and old-style addresses will continue to be used until the end of 2013. For listings in this book, we've provided the address information that is the most helpful. For more on addresses, see p173.

Top Itineraries

Day One

Gwanghwamun (p44)

 Start your tour of **Gyeongbokgung** at the palace's expertly restored main gate, Gwanghwamun, where you can watch the pageantry of the changing of the guard on the hour. Explore the winding streets of **Bukchon Hanok Village** and **Insa-dong**, pausing for refreshments at a cafe or teahouse in between browsing the equally ubiquitous art galleries and craft stores in these areas.

 Lunch Dine cheaply at Tobang (p58) or in style at Min's Club (p58).

Bukchon (p49)

Join the 2pm tour of **Changdeok-gung**, which also includes the Huwon (Secret Garden). Afterwards explore the wooded grounds of the venerable shrine **Jongmyo**, housing the spirit tablets of the Joseon kings and queens.

Dinner Sample Korean street food at Namdaemun Market (p68).

Myeong-dong (p65)

Take your seat at a fun **nonverbal show** such as *Nanta* or *Jump*. Be dazzled by the bright lights and retail overload of **Myeong-dong** and neighbouring **Namdaemun Market**, where the stalls stay open all night.

Day Two

Yongsan-gu (p86)

 Survey centuries of Korean history and art by selectively dipping into the vast collection of the **National Museum of Korea**. Shuttle over to the west side of Yongsan-gu to enjoy the contemporary art and architecture at the splendid **Leeum Samsung Museum of Art**.

 Lunch Snack on tacos with a twist at Vatos (p89).

Namsan (p67)

Browse some of Itaewon's boutiques then, for a post-lunch work out, hike up **Namsan** to **N Seoul Tower**. It's not a difficult climb, but if you don't have the energy then there's a cable car or a bus. It's very romantic watching the sunset from atop this central mountain as the night lights of Seoul flicker to life.

Dinner Savour delicious Euro-style cuisine at OKitchen (p89).

Itaewon (p86)

Freshen up with a steam in the saunas and a soak in the tubs at the **Dragon Hill Spa & Resort**. Return to **Itaewon** for dinner and a fun night of hopping between cafes, bars and dance clubs.

Day Three

Seodaemun (p112)

 Reflect on the struggles and sacrifices of Koreans to overcome colonialism and create a modern country at **Seodaemun Prison History Hall**. Afterwards, hike up nearby **Inwangsan** for fabulous views of the city, surreal rock formations and the other-worldly shamanistic rituals of **Inwangsan Guksadang**.

> **Lunch** Enjoy authentic pizza at Serious Deli (p117).

Seongbuk-dong (p112)

 Keep on shadowing the **Seoul Fortress Wall** down to Buam-dong and over **Bukaksan** and to Seongbuk-dong, a hike of around two hours. Catch your breath and rest your feet in the beautiful teahouse **Suyeon Sanbang**, and the equally serene surrounds of the temple **Gilsang-sa**.

> **Dinner** Snip noodles with big scissors at Woo Rae Oak (p110).

Dongdaemun (p107)

 If your hiking legs haven't given out, it's only another hour or so following the fortress wall over **Naksan** and down to **Dongdaemun**, where the night market will just be starting to crank up (alternatively take the subway). Admire the 21st-century architectural styling of **Dongdaemun Plaza & Park**, then trawl the market stalls for a new outfit.

Day Four

Yeouido (p79)

 Both contemporary art and panoramic views up and down the Han can be enjoyed from the top of the **63 City**. Back on the ground, hire a bike and pedal around Yeouido, passing the **National Assembly** building. Also spend some time strolling **Seonyudo Park** on an island in the Han River.

> **Lunch** Get your fix of fresh seafood at Noryangjin Fish Market (p81).

Hongdae (p78)

 If you're interested in contemporary architecture, then **Ewha Womans University's** stunning entrance building and **KT&G SangsangMadang** in Hongdae are both worth seeing. Hongdae and neighbouring Sangsu are brimming with hipster hang-outs, and if it's Saturday you can shop for quirky, original craft souvenirs at the **Free Market**.

> **Dinner** Tuck into delicious *galbi* (barbecued beef) at Samwon Garden (p102).

Gangnam (p96)

 A late-afternoon visit to the atmospheric Buddhist temple **Bongeun-sa** can segue nicely into browsing the boutiques of **Apgujeon, Cheongdam** or **Garosu-gil**. After dinner pitch up at the **Banpo Hangang Park** by 9pm to see the day's last floodlit flourish of the **Moonlight Rainbow Fountain** off the Banpo Bridge.

If You Like...

Contemporary Architecture

Dongdaemun Design Plaza & Park Zaha Hadid's sleek building is straight out of a sci-fi fantasy. (p109)

New City Hall This giant glass wave is a modern reinterpretation of traditional Korean design. (p70)

Ewha Womans University Dominique Perrault's stunning main entrance dives six storeys underground. (p78)

Tangent Daniel Libeskind–designed building that's like a work of art. (p104)

Palaces

Changdeokgung The most attractive one with a 'secret garden'. (p48)

Gyeongbokgung The biggest one with extra museums and a changing of the guard. (p46)

Changgyeonggung The one with a beautiful pond and elegant greenhouse. (p54)

Deoksugung The one where Korea's last emperor lived and sipped coffee. (p69)

Major Museums

National Museum of Korea Packed with national treasures spanning the centuries. (p88)

Seoul Museum of History Learn how much the city has changed over the last century. (p52)

National Folk Museum of Korea Fascinating exhibits indoors and in the palace grounds. (p47)

MANFRED GOTTSCHALK / GETTY IMAGES ©

Changing of the guard outside Gyeongbokgung (p46)

War Memorial of Korea Masses of military-related displays and good exhibits on the Korean War. (p90)

Art Galleries

Leeum Samsung Museum of Art Three top architect-designed buildings and a stunning collection of art from ancient to contemporary. (p89)

National Museum of Contemporary Art The best reason for making the trek out to Seoul Grand Park. (p100)

Seoul Museum of Art Good exhibitions in the former Supreme Court building. (p70)

Commercial galleries Seoul has scores of them; most offer free exhibitions. (p62)

Parks & Gardens

Olympic Park Home to a 1700-year-old earth fort and over 200 quirky sculptures. (p98)

Seoul Forest Expansive park by the Han River with wetlands and Sika deer. (p109)

Seonyudo Park Beautiful park and gardens on an island in the Han River. (p79)

Seonjeongneung Park Housing the tombs of two Korean kings and one queen. (p99)

Eungbong Park Views of the Han River from the pavilion atop Maebongsa. (p89)

Mountains, Hiking & Fortress Walls

Bukaksan Start your circuit of the Fortress Walls by hiking up the tallest of Seoul's four guardian mountains. (p114)

Naksan Heading east, the lowest of the guardian mountains with the arty neighbourhood of Ihwa-dong on its slopes. (p112)

Namsan The mountain at the heart of the city, criss-crossed with hiking trails and walking paths. (p67)

Inwangsan Climb up past weirdly eroded rocks and giant boulders for brilliant views. (p116)

Suwon Hike around the World Heritage–listed Fortress Walls in this town south of Seoul. (p124)

Traditional Architecture

Hanok Guesthouses The best way to experience a *hanok* is to stay overnight in one. (p131)

Bukchon Hanok Village Around 900 *hanok* make this Seoul's largest neighbourhood of these homes. (p49)

Namsangol Hanok Village Five differing *yangban* (upper-class) houses are in this park at the foot of Namsan. (p70)

Korean Folk Village Gathering of some 260 thatched and tiled traditional buildings from around the country. (p125)

Religious Buildings

Jogye-sa Home to Daeungjeon, the largest Buddhist temple building in Seoul. (p51)

Inwangsan Guksadan Seoul's most famous shamanist shrine on the slopes of Inwangsan. (p116)

Jeoldusan Martyrs' Shrine Memorial museum and church dedicated to Korea's Catholic martyrs and saints. (p78)

For more top Seoul spots, see:
➡ Eating (p28)
➡ Drinking & Nightlife (p31)
➡ Entertainment (p34)
➡ Shopping (p36)
➡ Sports & Activities (p38)

PLAN YOUR TRIP IF YOU LIKE...

Myeong-dong Catholic Cathedral Gothic-style cathedral with a vaulted ceiling and stained-glass windows. (p70)

Bongeun-sa Join the Templelife program here every Thursday afternoon. (p99)

Gilsang-sa Former exclusive restaurant turned into a serene temple in the hills. (p115)

Quirky Museums & Experiences

Lock Museum Exhibits locks as both lovely works of art and fearsome apparatus, such as a medieval chastity belt. (p117)

Steaming at a jjimjil-bang Strip down and join relaxing Koreans for a communal sweat, steam and full-body scrub. (p95)

Seoul Yangnyeongsi Herb Medicine Museum Learn about your yin, yang and *sasang* constitution. (p109)

Watching an e-game tournament Cheer on StarCraft players on the 9th floor of I'Park Mall. (p94)

Samsung D'Light Techno-geek heaven that's a fun way to glimpse the gadgets of tomorrow. (p101)

Korean Design Museum Fascinating private collection tracing the history of modern design in Korea. (p78)

Month by Month

January

Local religious holidays and festivals, such as Seollal, follow the lunar calendar, while the rest follow the Gregorian (Western) calendar. Dates have been given for upcoming years; sometimes Seollal will occur in February.

✴ Seollal (Lunar New Year)

Seoul empties out as locals make the trip to their home town to visit relatives, honour ancestors and eat traditional foods over this three-day national festival. That said, there are a number of events for travellers in Seoul during this time, held at the major palaces as well as the Korean Folk Village, Namsangol Hanok Village and the National Folk Museum of Korea. For more information, visit www.visitseoul.net or www.visitkorea.or.kr. In 2013 Seollal begins on 12 February, in 2014 on 31 January and in 2015 on 19 February.

April

It can still be cold and wet in spring, so come prepared. Nature determines the exact timing of this event, but early April is generally when parts of Seoul turn pink in a transient flurry of delicate cherry blossoms.

☉ Hangang Yeouido Spring Flower Festival

One of the best places to experience the blossoming trees and flowers is Yeouido. Other good spots include Namsan and Ewha Womans University, and Jeongdok Public Library in Samcheong-dong. For more details of the Yeouido event, see http://tour.ydp.go.kr.

☉ Royal Wedding Ceremony of King Gojong and Empress Myeongseong

This re-enactment of the royal wedding ceremony of King Gojong, the last king of the Joseon dynasty, and Empress Myeongseong (Queen Min), is held on the third Saturday in April at Unhyeon-gung, where the original ceremony took place on 21 March 1866. See http://unhyeongung.or.kr for details.

May

Buddha's birthday (celebrated on 17 May in 2013, 6 May in 2014 and 25 May in 2015) brings a kaleidoscope of light and colour, as rows of delicate paper lanterns, lit at dusk, are strung along the main thoroughfares and in temple courtyards.

✴ Jongmyo Daeje

Held on the first Sunday of the month, this ceremony honours Korea's royal ancestors. It involves a solemn costumed parade from Gyeongbokgung through downtown Seoul to the royal shrine at Jongmyo, where spectators can enjoy traditional music and an elaborate, all-day ritual. For details see www.jongmyo.net/english_index.asp.

✪ Yeon Deung Ho (Lotus Lantern Festival)

Seoul's Buddhist temples, such as Jogye-sa and Bongeun-sa, are the focus of this celebration of Buddha's birthday. The weekend preceding the birthday, Seoul celebrates with a huge daytime street festival and evening lantern parade – the largest in South Korea; see www.llf.or.kr for details.

☆ Seoul World DJ Festival

Dozens of DJs from all over Korea and the world descend upon an outdoor arena for two nights and three days of nonstop partying. See www.worlddjfest.com for details.

June

The hot weather and period before the rains of July mean this is a great time to enjoy Seoul's outdoors.

☆ Korean Queer Cultural Festival

Seoul's LGBT community emerges from the shadows for a series of citywide events, culminating in a parade through downtown and a party at Hanbit Media Park on the first Saturday of the month. For details see www.kqcf.org.

✪ Dano Festival

Held according to the lunar calendar, this festival features shamanist rituals and mask dances at several locales, including Namsangol Hanok Village. See http://hanokmaeul.seoul.go.kr for details.

July

Pack heavy-duty rain gear and waterproof shoes, as this is when Seoul experiences a month of monsoon-like rains. It's a good job then that there are a couple of decent film festivals you can enjoy indoors.

☆ Puchon International Fantastic Film Festival

This festival brings films and filmgoers from across Asia to Bucheon, just outside of Seoul, to feast on the best in sci-fi, fantasy and horror. Theatres are within walking distance of Songnae Station (Line 1, towards Incheon). See www.pifan.com for details.

☆ Seoul International Cartoon & Animation Festival (SICAF)

Half a million animation geeks pack auditoriums in Seoul each year to see why the city is an epicentre of animated craftsmanship (fans of *The Simpsons* have Korean artists to thank). See www.sicaf.org for details.

August

The rains start to abate and are replaced by sweltering humidity. Cool off in Seoul's parks and public areas: there are free outdoor concerts most nights in Seoul Plaza and many free events held in the parks along the Han River.

☆ Seoul Fringe Festival

One of Seoul's best performing-arts festivals, when local and international artists converge on the hipster Hongdae area to flee the mainstream. For full details, see www.seoulfringe.net.

September

In this busy month for events and festivals, also check out the Korea International Art Fair (www.kiaf.org) at COEX, one of the region's top art fairs and a good opportunity to get a jump on the country's hot new artists.

✪ Sajik Daeje

Held at Sajikdan on the third Sunday of the month, the 'Great Rite for the Gods of Earth and Agriculture' is one of Seoul's most important ancestral rituals, and designated as an Important Intangible Cultural Property. The ceremonies, which include offerings of fresh meat and produce, are performed in traditional costumes to live music played by a court orchestra. For more information, go to www.rfo.co.kr.

✪ Chuseok

The Harvest Moon Festival is a major three-day holiday when families gather, eat crescent-shaped rice cakes and visit their ancestors' graves to make offerings of food and drink and perform *sebae* (a ritual bow). Begins 19 September in 2013, 8 September in 2014 and 27 September in 2015.

☆ Seoul Drum Festival

Focusing on Korea's fantastic percussive legacy, this three-day international event in Seoul Plaza brings together all kinds of ways to make a lot of noise. See www.seouldrum.go.kr.

October

Autumn is a great time to visit Seoul, particularly if you like hiking, as this is the season when the mountains run through a palate of rustic colours.

✯ Seoul International Fireworks Festival

Best viewed from Yeouido Hangang Park, this festival sees dazzling fireworks displays staged by both Korean and international teams. For more details, see www.bulnori.com.

☆ Asia Song Festival

This mega K-Pop event at Jamsil Stadium includes performances by star *hallyu* bands and singers (meaning ones that have become popular outside of Korea), such as Girls' Generation and Super Junior. See http://asf.kofice.or.kr/english for details.

November

✯ Seoul Lantern Festival

Centred along the Cheonggye-cheon, this festival sees the stream-park illuminated by gigantic fantastic lanterns made by master craftsmen. For more information, see http://blog.naver.com/seoullantern.

(top) Fireworks over the Han River
(bottom) Drummers at the Seoul Drum Festival

With Kids

Children are more than welcome in Seoul – this is a safe and family friendly city with plenty of interesting museums (including several devoted to kids themselves), as well as parks, amusement parks and fun events that will appeal to all age groups.

K-Pop Rules

The best way to cut down on child grumbles in Seoul is to mix your sampling of traditional Korean culture with things that the kids are more likely to enjoy. Fortunately, thanks to the global appeal of local pop culture, the young ones are likely to be more au fait with contemporary Korean pop culture than you are! Be prepared to search out shops stocking Girls' Generation posters, DVDs of Korean TV soap operas such as *Boys Over Flowers*, or *manhwa* (Korean comics and graphic novels). Kyobo Bookstore is a good place to start.

Educational Experiences

Not that museums and other traditional culture centres need be boring. The National Museum of Korea and the National Folk Museum have fun, hands-on children's sections, and the War Memorial of Korea has outdoor warplanes and tanks that make for a popular playground. Various events,

some involving dressing up in traditional costumes or having a go at taekwondo happen at Namsangol Hanok Village. Older kids and teenagers will likely want to visit places such as the Seoul Animation Center to learn more about local animated TV series and films, or Samsung D'Light to play with the latest digital technology. Nonverbal shows such as *Nanta* and *Jump* are great family entertainment.

Park Life

Amusement parks range from charming Pororo Park, perfect for small kids, to the theme-park extravaganzas of Lotte World and Everland, where fun comes in mega-sized portions. Easier on the wallet are the scores of free open spaces that constitute Seoul's wealth of city-managed parks – places such as Seoul Forest, Olympic Park and the string of bicycle-lane-connected parks that hug the Han River's banks. Each summer six big outdoor-pool complexes open in the Han River parks, too. If animals appeal, Seoul Grand Park includes a good zoo with pony and camel rides.

Need to Know

Sleeping & Eating

Korean-style *ondol* rooms are ideal for families, as everyone sleeps on a *yo* (floor mattress) in the same space. Children are welcome in restaurants, but few places will have kids' menus; there's no shortage of the usual fast-food franchises if all else fails. High chairs are not common.

Babysitting

A few top hotels and residences can arrange babysitting services.

Festivals

On Children's Day (5 May) there are special events for kids across the city.

More Information

➡ Lonely Planet's *Travel with Children* is good for general advice.

➡ Korea 4 Expats.com (www.korea4expats.com) has more child-related information on Seoul.

Like a Local

Prepare for Seoul's cultural divide. Bukchon (north of the Han River) is the city's historical heart, where courtly palace culture meets pre- and post-colonial commerce. South of the Han, nouveau riche Gangnam is stacked with top-end boutiques and expense-account restaurants and bars.

Round-the-Clock Shopping

Whichever side of the river they live on, Seoulites love (or is that live?) to shop. For all the city's headlong rush into the 21st century, sprawling all-night markets, such as those at Dongdaemun and Namdaemun, confirm more traditional and time-worn images of Asian commerce. This impression is further reinforced by the bazaars devoted to herbal medicines at Seoul Yangnyeongsi and to antiques at Dapsimni. A fascinating insight into local life can also be gleaned from what people sell off at flea markets, the biggest of which is the Seoul Folk Flea Market. If the old and second-hand aren't to your taste, contemporary fashions and fads can be gauged on trips to mercantile hubs such as Myeong-dong, Apgujeong, Cheongdam and Garosu-gil/Serosu-gil.

Keeping Fit

Going hiking in and around Seoul can be a frightening business. This is not so much because of the precariousness of the mountain trails (quite the opposite – these are usually well marked and seldom short of small armies of hikers), but because you will almost certainly feel under-dressed. Seoulites are super avid walkers and few would even think of venturing out without being kitted head to toe in the latest hi-tech and invariably brightly coloured gear. A trip to Dongdaemun Market or a shopping mall to purchase an outfit of local brands, such as Blackyak or The Redface, should have you breathing a little easier.

Hiking is not the only popular keep-fit pastime. The cycle lanes running alongside the Han River are also actively patronised, as are the free outdoor gyms located in many parks.

Bang-ing Around

The old expat playground of Itaewon has become a much more multicultural affair, appealing to worldly Koreans and their curious brethren. The adjacent areas of Hannam-dong, Haebangchon (aka HBC) and Gyeongridan have an equally, if not more, happening vibe.

However to really take Seoul's relaxation pulse, a nocturnal visit to hip Hongdae and Daehangno – both major hubs for students and the young – is recommended. Here you'll encounter the highest concentrations of Seoul's various versions of the *bang*. Meaning 'room', *bang* come in the shape of karaoke rooms (*noraebang*), private DVD screening rooms (DVD *bang*) and online-game rooms (PC *bang*).

Finally, if you really want to sample local life, get naked! Stripping off and sweating at a *jjimjil-bang* (luxury sauna) is a very popular way for Seoulites to steam off their stresses.

For Free

There's no need to shell out wads of won to have an enjoyable time in Seoul. In fact, many of the best things you can do – from hiking around the city's ancient fortress walls to enjoying the pageant of the changing of the guard at the palaces – cost nothing at all.

Go for a Hike

Join the legions of locals who, dressed in colourful gear and big sun visors, take full advantage of Seoul's mountainous topography, hiking up the hills with steely vigour. All four of the city's guardian mountains – Bukaksan, Naksan, Namsan and Inwangsan – have hiking routes, and less than an hour north of the centre there's Bukhansan National Park, easily accessible by subway. For the really ambitious (and fit), there's the route that shadows the remains of Seoul's Fortress Walls – the views from atop the mountains make the effort well worthwhile. The 18.7km circuit takes around 12 hours all up, but the hike is far better appreciated when broken up and done in manageable chunks.

Riverside Diversions

The city government has spent enormous sums to create pleasant waterside parks both along the Han River and in central Seoul, where the long-buried-over Cheonggye-cheon now sparkles in the light of day. Seoul Forest is another major reforestation project, as is the creation of a beautiful landscaped park from an old water-filtration plant on the Han River island of Seonyudo.

Architectural Treasures

Admission to most royal palaces is not costly and usually includes free guided tours. Additionally, it costs nothing to enjoy the changing of the guard ceremonies at Gyeongbokgung, Deoksugung and the Bosingak bell tower pavilion. Impressive religious architecture is freely on show at World Heritage–listed Jogye-sa and the Buddhist temples Bongeun-sa and Gilsang-sa. You can also view aristocratic *hanok* (traditional Korean one-storey wooden houses) for free at Namsangol Hanok Village, or clusters of still-lived-in, more modest traditional homes in Bukchon.

Museums & Galleries

The list of museums with no entrance fee is pretty extensive. You also don't need a wallet full of credit cards for the scores of free art-gallery shows in areas such as Insa-dong, Tongui-dong and Samcheong-dong, and south of the Han River in Apgujeong and Cheongdam. There are also thousands of outdoor sculptures scattered across Seoul – over 200 of them are in Olympic Park.

Festivals & Events

Not one week goes by without a free festival or event happening somewhere in the city. Seoul's government often puts on free shows in Seoul Plaza in front of City Hall, and there's the spectacular lighting up of the fountain flowing off Banpo Bridge in the warmer months. There's no cost to join in the Sunday singalong service at the Yeouido Full Gospel Church – with a cast of tens of thousands – either.

Courses & Tours

Helping you know your hansik (Korean food) from your hanbok (traditional clothing), a variety of courses and tours will put you on the fast track to understanding Korean culture. Some are very popular, so they're worth booking well in advance, particularly the USO trip to the DMZ.

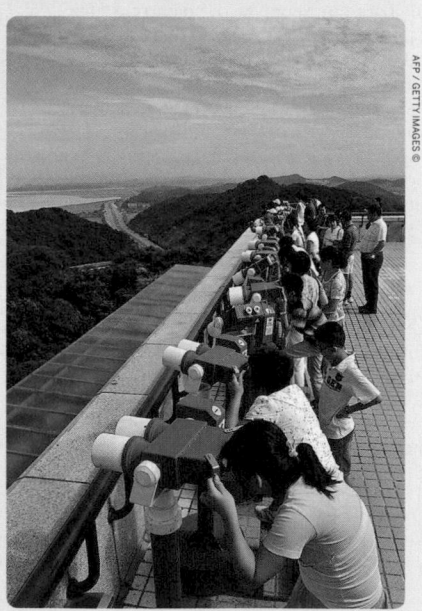

Watching North Korea from the DMZ

AFP / GETTY IMAGES ©

Courses

Templestays & Meditation Courses

Templestay (☏2031 2000; www.templestay. com; Insa-dong; ⓜLine 3 to Anguk, Exit 6) No attempt will be made to convert you to Buddhism during these inexpensive and relaxing programs, which are a brilliant way to learn a little about Korean Buddhism and meditation, as well as spend time in beautiful temples around the country. You needn't leave Seoul: overnight stays are available at Gilsang-sa (for ₩50,000), and day courses at Jogye-sa and Bongeun-sa, where you can learn about tea ceremonies or how to make Buddhist lanterns, woodblock prints and prayer beads.

Ahnkook Zen Centre (☏3673 0772; www. ahnkookzen.org; Gahoe-dong; ⓜLine 3 to Anguk, Exit 2) Offers Zen practice and English lectures on Buddhist teaching every Saturday from 2.30pm until 4pm.

Buddhist Institute English Library (☏730 0173; www.bels.kr; Yulgongno, Insa-dong; classes from ₩5000; ⊙11am-4pm Mon-Fri, 11am-2pm Sat; ⓜLine 3 to Anguk, Exit 6) Organises dharma talks, group and meditation study, and lectures on Buddhist beliefs and practice. The teachers are Korean and Tibetan Buddhist monks who speak English. They offer a wonderful opportunity to study Buddhism seriously in an Asian context at a beginner or advanced level.

Cooking & Culture

O'ngo (☏3446 1607; www.ongofood.com; Insa-dong; courses from ₩65,000, tours from ₩57,000; ⓜLine 1, 3 or 5 to Jongno 3-ga, Exit 5) Well-run cooking classes and food tours around the city are offered by Dan Grey of Seoul Eats (www.seouleats.com) and his team. The beginners' class lasts two hours and covers four dishes, while intermediate courses can cover Buddhist temple cuisine.

Hansik Experience Centre (☏772 9180; www.korea-food.or.kr; Jonggak; courses from ₩30,000; ⊙courses 10am, 2pm & 5pm Mon-Sat; ⓜLine 1 to Jonggak, Exit 5) At the KTO Information Centre beside the Cheonggye-cheon is a kitchen where you can get hands-on experience at making Korean foods such as kimchi (fermented vegetables), *bulgogi* (barbecued beef slices and lettuce wrap) and *bibimbap* (rice topped with egg, meat, vegetables and sauce).

When cooking classes are not being held, they offer free food tasting.

Yoo's Family (☑3673 0323; www.yoosfamily. com; Kwonnong-dong; courses ₩20,000-70,000; ◎Mon-Sat; ⓂLine 3 to Anguk, Exit 4) Housed in a *hanok* (traditional Korean one-storey wooden house with a tiled roof), Yoo's Family's cooking courses cover making kimchi and *hotteok* (pancakes), as well as various other foods. You can also practice the tea ceremony, make prints from carved wooden blocks and dress up in *hanbok*. A minimum of two people is required.

Korean Language

YBM Sisa (☑2278 0509; http://kli.ybmedu. com; Insa-dong; courses from ₩130,000; ◎6.30am-9pm Mon-Fri, 9am-4pm Sat & Sun; ⓂLine 1, 3 or 5 to Jongno 3-ga, Exit 15) Korean classes (maximum size 10) for all ability levels cover grammar, writing and conversation. Private tuition (₩40,000 per hour for one person) can also be arranged here.

Yonsei University (☑2123 3465; www.yskli. com; Sinchon; ⓂLine 6 to Sinchon, Exit 6) The university runs part- and full-time Korean language and culture classes for serious students.

Tours

Seoul City Tour Bus (☑777 6090; www. seoulcitybus.com; ◎Tue-Sun; ⓂLine 5 to Gwanghwamun, Exit 6) If you want to see as much as possible in a short time, this is one way to go. Comfortable and colourful tour buses run between Seoul's top tourist attractions north of the Han River. You can hop on and hop off anywhere along the two routes – downtown (adult/child ₩10,000/8000, 9am to 7pm, half-hourly) and around the palaces (adult/child ₩12,000/8000, 10am to 5pm, hourly). Ticket holders receive considerable discounts on tourist attractions. The routes cover the palaces, Insa-dong, Namdaemun and Dongdaemun markets, Itaewon and Namsan, the National Museum and the War Memorial. Buy tickets on the bus, which can be caught outside Donghwa

NEED TO KNOW

Advance Booking

Necessary for most tours; sometimes tours will only go with a minimum number of people.

Where to Meet?

Check whether the tour company will pick you up from your accommodation and if that's included in the tour cost.

Free Walking Tours

Seoul City Government offers free walking tours with volunteer guides on 17 different routes; see http://dobo. visitseoul.net/index.jsp for more information.

Duty Free Shop at Gwanghwamun. Check the website for details of night tours, which zigzag across the Han River so you can view the illuminated bridges.

Koridoor Tours (☑02 795 3028; www. koridoor.co.kr) Apart from running the very popular DMZ/JSA tour for the USO (United Service Organizations; see p121), this company also offers city tours; trips to out-of-town destinations, such as Suwon and Incheon; paragliding, scuba diving and deep-sea fishing tours; and ski trips to local resorts in the winter.

Royal Asiatic Society (www.raskb.com) Organises enlightening tours to all parts of South Korea, usually on weekends; check the website for the schedule. Nonmembers are welcome to join. The reasonably priced tours are led by English speakers who are experts in their field. The society also organises lectures several times a month.

Discover Seoul Desk (☑795 0355; www. dragonhilllodge.org/discoverseoul) Walking tours of Seoul Fortress, led by entertaining guide Jacco Zwetsloot, are offered by the tour desk at the Dragon Hill Lodge on Yongsan Army Base. Join the tours at Gate 1 of the base and make payment over the phone or via email with your credit card.

Royal food banquet

Eating

Sampling the varied and – to international travellers – generally unfamiliar delights of Korean cuisine is one of Seoul's great pleasures. Restaurants, cafes and street stalls are scattered throughout every neighbourhood with options to suit all budgets and tastes – from small, unpretentious joints serving healthy rice and vegetables or DIY beef or pork barbecue, to the overflowing abundance and delicacy of a royal banquet.

What's Hot

Seoul's international restaurants range from Bulgarian to Vietnamese. Much of the international food you get is fairly authentic (particularly Italian and Japanese), although places do tend to tweak their recipes and presentation to meet local tastes.

Crazes come and go fairly quickly. At the time of research, Mexican – particularly soft shell tacos – were the rage, often mixing in local flavours such as kimchi and BBQ pork. Gourmet burger bars are also on the increase across the city. To catch the culinary Zeitgeist, zone in on dining hotspots such as Itaewon and Garosu-gil/Serosu-gil.

Restaurants & Cafes

Korean restaurants often specialise in one or two dishes only; in some cases you'll find whole streets packed with places offering the same meal, ie *tteobokki* (a Korean pasta stew) in Sindang-dong Tteobokki Town.

Most Korean-style restaurants offer a table and chairs option, but in some traditional places customers sit on floor cushions at low tables. Few staff speak English, but most restaurants have some English on the menu or else pictures or plastic replicas of the meals.

Cafes and teahouses mainly specialise in drinks, but a few do offer decent food. Bakery chain cafes such as Paris Baguette and A Twosome Place are very common and can be relied on for things such as sandwiches, pastries and cakes. For more on different types of Korean food see p150.

Department Stores & Malls

In Seoul, eating out (like most everything else) is a group activity. A number of Korean meals, such as *jjimdak* (spicy chicken pieces with noodles) or *hanjeongsik* (a banquet of dishes) are not usually available for just one person.

Solo diners won't feel out of place at major department stores or shopping malls – both great options for casual meals.

Convenience Stores & Street Stalls

For eating on the go there's always a convenience store, such as 7-Eleven or Family Mart, near to hand. They are packed with snack foods for quick and easy meals; there's usually a small area to prepare foods, with hot water or a microwave, and tables to sit at.

Street stalls and *pojenmacha* (tent bars) are another option – Insa-dong, Myeong-dong and around the Namdaemun and Dongdaemun markets are the best location to dig in with locals on everything from spicy chicken skewers to piping-hot *hotteok* (either the sweet or savoury versions of these deep-fried dough pockets).

Vegetarians & Vegans

Although rice and vegetables make up a considerable part of their diet, few Koreans are fully vegetarian. It can be a struggle for vegetarians in ordinary restaurants. Many otherwise seemingly vegetarian dishes have small amounts of meat, seafood or fish added for flavour. The same is true of kimchi. Generally risk-free things to order include *bibimbap* or *dolsot bibimbap*, both without meat (or egg), *beoseotjeongol*

PLAN YOUR TRIP EATING

NEED TO KNOW

Price Ranges

$	less than ₩10,000
$$	₩10,000-20,000
$$$	over ₩20,000

Opening Hours

➡ **Restaurants & cafes** 11am-10pm

➡ **Convenience stores** 24 hours

Reservations

Where a telephone number is listed, reservations are recommended. For most places, it's unnecessary to book tables unless you want your own private room or are in a large group.

Guides & Blogs

➡ **Shikdang** (www.shikdang.com)

➡ **ZenKimchi** (www.zenkimchi.com)

➡ **Seoul Eats** (www.seouleats.com)

➡ **Hungry Seoul** (www.hungry seoul.com)

➡ **Tom Eats Jen Cooks** (www.tom eatsjencooks.com)

Smoking

Smoking in restaurants is permitted only if there is a separate room where smokers are seated. Not all restaurants, cafes and bars follow this rule.

Tipping & Service Charges

Not a Korean custom, and is not expected. Generally only restaurants in top-end hotels may add 21% to the bill (10% service charge then 10% VAT).

(mushroom hotpot), *doenjang jjigae* (soybean paste stew), *dubu jjigae* (spicy tofu soup), *jajangmyeon* (noodles and sauce), vegetable *pajeon,* and pumpkin *juk* (rice porridge).

Happy Cow (www.happycow.net/asia/south _korea/seoul) is a good resource for vegetarians looking for somewhere to dine, as is the blog **Alien's Day Out** (http://aliensdayout. com). Department-store basement food courts and Indian restaurants always offer some vegetarian meals.

Eating by Neighbourhood

➡ **Gwanghwamun & Jongno-gu** (p56) Insa-dong, Samcheong-dong and Bukchon are packed with places offering everything from street snacks to table-overflowing banquets.

➡ **Myeong-dong & Jung-gu** (p72) Fun street food; plenty of reliable chain restaurants; plus department-store food courts.

➡ **Western Seoul** (p79) The University districts are big on casual cafes and street eats. Seafood lovers shouldn't miss Noryangjin Fish Market.

➡ **Itaewon & Yongsan-gu** (p89) The best range of international restaurants that are used to dealing with expats.

➡ **Gangnam & South of the Han River** (p102) Expense account restaurants in Apgujeong and Cheongdam. More casual hang-outs in Garosu-gil/Serosu-gil.

Lonely Planet's Top Choices

➡ **Jung Sikdang** (p102) Neo-Korean.

➡ **Tosokchon** (p57) Chicken stew for the soul in an old *hanok*.

➡ **GastroTong** (p56) Fine dining Swiss treat in Tongui-dong.

➡ **Mokmyeoksanbang** (p72) Healthy *bibimbap* on the side of Namsan.

➡ **Samwon Garden** (p102) The classic *galbi* (BBQ beef) experience.

➡ **Gwangjang Market** (p110) Super tasty and cheap street food in a covered market.

Best by Budget

$
Joseon Gimbap (p57)

Tobang (p58)

Casablanca Sandwicherie (p94)

Myeong-dong Gyoja (p72)

$$
Coconut Kitchen (p73)

Busan Ilbeonji (p82)

Slobbie (p79)

Shim's Tapas (p79)

$$$
Min's Club (p58)

OKitchen (p89)

Gorilla in the Kitchen (p102)

Le Saint-Ex (p89)

Best by Cuisine

Korean Traditional
Harvest (p59)

Woo Rae Oak (p110)

Gogung (p59)

Chilgapsan (p59)

Bibigo (p57)

Korean & Neo-Korean Jeonsik (Banquets)
Congdu (p56)

Hanmiri (p57)

Korea House (p73)

Nwijo (p58)

Chicken
Baekje Samgyetang (p72)

Yeong-yang Centre (p72)

Andong Jjimdak (p72)

Chuncheon-jip (p81)

Dumplings
Jaha Sonmandoo (p117)

Koong (p59)

Sadongmyeonok (p59)

Cheonjinpoja (p60)

Italian & Pizza
Chung-jeong-gak (p72)

Dejangjangi Hwadeog Pijajip (p59)

Macaroni Market (p90)

Serious Deli (p117)

Mexican & Indian
Vatos (p89)

Grill5Taco (p102)

Bella Tortilla (p81)

Dhal (p58)

Potala (p73)

Vegetarian & Vegan
Balwoo Gongyang (p57)

Osegyehyang (p59)

Deongjang Yesool (p117)

Loving Hut (p81)

Dessert & Cakes
Parlour (p90)

Seoureseo Duljjaero Jalhaneunjip (p60)

Fell & Cole (p81)

Tartine (p90)

Life is Just a Cup of Cake (p91)

Sandwiches & Baked Goods
Euro Gourmet (p57)

Rose Bakery (p91)

Paul (p82)

The Baker's Table (p91)

Le Gourmet (p117)

Drinking & Nightlife

From quaintly rustic teahouses and own-roaster coffee houses to craft beer pubs and classy cocktail bars, Seoul offers an unbelievable number of places to relax over a drink. No-frills hof (pubs) are common, and don't miss that quintessential Seoul nightlife experience: soju shots and snacks at a pojenmacha (street tent bar).

Teahouses & Cafes

Korea's tea culture, which dates back centuries, can be appreciated in Seoul's many quaint and charming teahouses. These places major on herbal and fruit teas, many of which have medicinal properties, but it's also possible to sip quality green, black and other fermented teas.

In recent decades, Koreans have taken to coffee in a big way. Properly brewed coffee is abundantly available (though the quality varies greatly) at Western-style cafes, from foreign imports like Starbucks and Coffee Bean & Tea Leaf to Korean chains like Angel-in-us Coffee and Caffe Bene. Far better brews are available from artisan roasters who treat their globally sourced, sometimes fair-trade bean with reverence.

You'll quickly suss out that a quality cup of tea or coffee in Seoul is not cheap, and is often equivalent to what you can pay for a whole Korean meal. You're also paying for occupying the space, so don't feel bad about lingering all day over your drink. Many newer breeds of cafes and teahouses encourage you to do this by creating interesting environments packed with books, magazines, plants, art – even tiny songbirds flying around or cats to cuddle.

Hof & Bars

Drinking, and drinking heavily, is very much a part of Korean socialising, and an evening out can quickly turn into a blur of bar-hopping.

Many a big night out starts and finishes in a *hof*. Inspired by German beer halls, the term generally means any watering hole that serves primarily draft Korean beer, with the requisite plate of fried chicken and other *anju* (snacks commonly eaten when drinking). Always check whether a bar requires you to buy a plate of *anju* before drinking; places that don't are called 'one-shot' bars.

If you're looking for something more sophisticated there are plenty of cocktail bars, lounge bars and quirky drinking dens in places such as Itaewon, Hongdae, Sinchon and Gangnam. Western-style wine bars are springing up too, but also make an effort to sample one of the growing number of bars specialising in Korean rice wines such as *makgeolli* and Baekseju.

Tent Bars & Convenience Stores

Beloved by Seoulites are *pojenmacha* or tent bars. Usually shortened to *poja*, these humble blue-tarp shelters are scattered across the city's streets – you'll find them in places such as Nagwon-dong adjacent to Insa-dong and next to major train stations such as Yongsan. *Poja* also serve food; if you've had plenty of *soju* you may feel brave enough to order *takbal* (chicken feet).

Poja are also cheap, but not as cheap as convenience stores, which are open 24 hours and often have places to sit either inside or out to drink your can of beer or bottle of *soju*.

NEED TO KNOW

Opening Hours

➡ **Bars** Noon-6am

➡ **Clubs** 10pm-6am Wed-Sun

How Much?

➡ Local beer ₩3000-5000

➡ Craft beer ₩5000-10,000

➡ Cocktail ₩6000-15,000

➡ Coffee ₩3000-6000

➡ Tea ₩6000-9000

Cover Charges

At clubs the entry charge of ₩10,000-20,000, usually includes a free drink; charges can be as high at ₩30,000 on Friday and Saturday nights or for special events.

Drinking Water

In restaurants and cafes you'll be presented bottled or filtered water (*mul*) upon sitting down, which is safe to drink.

Drinking Etiquette

Always pour for your elders, never pour for yourself and use both hands to hold your glass when it's being filled.

Drinking Trends

Makgeolli, a milky alcoholic brew made from unrefined, fermented rice, long popular among the older generation is catching on with the young and trendy, too. Seoul has several bars now where higher quality styles of *makgeolli,* akin to the range of Japanese sake, are served and savoured.

Until recently beer (*maekju*) has been the least exciting of all Korean alcohol. Ubiquitous and cheap local brands, all lagers, include the equally bland Cass, Max and Hite. However, tastier imported beers are increasingly available, and are being supplemented by a growing number of decent craft ales from microbreweries such as Craftworks and Magpie Brewing, both in Gyeongridan.

Clubbing & Booking

Hongdae is home to Seoul's main clubbing scene, but Itaewon and Gangnam have a few decent choices, too. Most clubs don't start becoming busy until 10pm and only start buzzing after midnight. Friday and Saturday nights have a real party atmosphere. Except in the classiest of Gangnam clubs, dress codes are generally not too strict.

One of the ways Koreans hook up at clubs (and some bars) is via 'booking'. This is where a waiter will introduce you to the guys or girls that you're interested to meet – or will just push groups of people together (Koreans rarely go partying solo). There's even a chain of pub-clubs called Blue Ketchup (www.blueketchup.kr) devoted to this kind of socialising.

GLBT Scene

GLBT friendly areas of the city include Itaewon (mainly gay and transsexual/transvestite bars), Nagwon-dong and Dongui-dong near Insa-dong (gay bars) and Hongdae and Edae (mainly lesbian bars). The Rainbow Meet Market (www.facebook.com/meetmarketseoul) organised by the Butch-Hers is a semi-regular gay/lesbian party held at Club Myoung Wol Gwan in Hongdae (Map p204).

Drinking & Nightlife by Neighbourhood

➡ **Gwanghwamun & Jongno-gu** (p60) Teahouses and cafes in Insa-dong and Samcheong-dong, Bukchon and Tongui-dong; tent bars and gay bars in Nagwon-dong.

➡ **Western Seoul** (p82) Hongdae for groovy, youth-orientated bars, cafes, dance and live music clubs.

➡ **Itaewon & Yongsan-gu** (p91) Expat friendly bars and clubs; gay friendly 'homo hill'; craft beers in Gyeongnidan.

➡ **Gangnam & South of the Han River** (p103) Chic, pricey cocktails bars in Apgujeong and Cheongdam; mega clubs with top DJs.

➡ **Northern Seoul** (p118) Hang out in cool cafes and bars with the students around Daehangno; seek out charming cafes in Seongbuk-dong.

Lonely Planet's Top Choices

➡ **Suyeon Sanbang** (p118) Charming teahouse in heritage *hanok* in the hills.

➡ **Anthracite** (p82) Top independent coffee-roaster and cafe in happening Sangsu.

➡ **Dawon** (p60) Traditional teahouse in heart of Insa-dong set around a spacious courtyard.

➡ **Platoon Kunsthalle** (p103) Pop and counter-cultural events space with cool, creative vibe.

➡ **District** (p91) Stylish complex with pub, cocktail bar and dance club.

Best Tea

Cha Masineun Tteul (p61)

Et M'amie (p60)

Dalsaeneun Dalman Saenggak Handa (p61)

Yetchatjip (p61)

Chloris Tea Garden (p83)

Best Coffee

Club Espresso (p118)

Kopi Bangasgan (p60)

Dabang (p61)

Takeout Drawing (p91)

Double Cup Coffee (p61)

Best Cocktails & Wine

Top Cloud Bar (p63)

Naos Nova (p73)

Pierre's Bar (p74)

Coffee Bar K (p103)

Berlin (p92)

Best Cafe-Bars

Café Sukkara (p82)

aA Café (p82)

Grove Lounge (p73)

Café Goods (p83)

Ways of Seeing (p92)

Best Microbrew Bars

Craftworks (p91)

The Brew Shop (p92)

Castle Praha (p83)

Oktoberfest (p103)

Best Traditional Alcoholic Beverages

Moon Jar (p103)

Baekseju-maeul (p60)

Pub of the Blue Star (p60)

Mowmow (p93)

Best Clubbing

Ellui (p103)

M2 (p83)

Bahia (p83)

B1 (p93)

Best Gay & Lesbian Bars & Clubs

Barcode (p61)

Shortbus (p61)

Labris (p83)

Queen (p92)

Almaz (p93)

Pulse (p93)

PLAN YOUR TRIP DRINKING & NIGHTLIFE

Entertainment

Don't worry about the language barrier: Seoul's many performing arts centres and theatres offer an intriguing and surprisingly accessible menu of traditional music, dance, drama and comedy. It's also very simple to make your own entertainment in private rooms (bang) devoted to karaoke, playing computer games or watching DVDs.

Classical & Traditional

Seoul is the best place in Korea to enjoy traditional music and dance performances. Some shows may include half a dozen different dance and music styles including the energetic farmers' *samullori* group dances, where the dancers play a variety of percussion instruments, and *pansori,* a solo opera with one singer accompanied by a drummer. Gymnastic stand-up drumming on three drums is a crowd favourite, as is the elegant fan dance. *Gayageum* (12-string zither) and flute instrumentals also typically feature. There's a broad range of international classical offerings; top-class overseas orchestras and dance troupes frequently visit Seoul.

Jazz, Rock & Pop

Classy live jazz venues can be found in Daehangno and Apgujeong, as well as in Hongdae and Itaewon. Haebangchan has a growing live-music scene, some of it provided by expat bands, while Hongdae is the place for live indie music cutting across genres. Concerts by visiting superstars of the likes of Lady Gaga are held in the Olympic Stadium at Jamsil or **AX Korea** (http://ax-korea.co.kr; ⑤Line 5 to Gwangnaru, Exit 2) in eastern Seoul.

Bang Culture

Seoul is overflowing with *bang* – complexes of 'rooms' where you can make your own entertainment in a variety of ways:

Noraebang Karaoke rooms where you can sing along to well-known songs, including plenty with English lyrics.

DVD bang The best place to see Korean movies, as they can be shown with English subtitles. You watch the film on a big screen sitting on a comfortable sofa in your own private room.

PC bang Let the e-games begin at these rooms where fans of online computer gaming gather.

Theatre & Cinema

Theatre, except for drama festivals, is usually performed in Korean: the very lively theatre scene in Daehangno is worth a visit despite this. There's also a small number of expat theatre groups that do have shows in English, including the Probationary Theatre Company (www.probationarytheatre.com), Seoul Players (www.seoulplayers.com) and the Seoul Shakespeare Company (www.facebook.com/seoulshakespeare). Musicals and non-verbal performance shows, such as *Nanta,* can be enjoyed even if you don't understand any Korean.

Non-Korean movies are screened in their original language with subtitles. There's also a city-funded program of Korean movies with subtitles – call ☎02 120 for details.

Entertainment by Neighbourhood

➡ **Myeong-dong & Jung-gu (p74)** Non-verbal theatre is king here; see traditional shows at the Korea House and Namsangol Hanok Village.

➡ **Western Seoul (p83)** Hongdae is the hub of Seoul's vibrant indie music scene; free movies at Cinemateque KOFA.

➡ **Gangnam & South of the Han River (p104)** Home to the Seoul Arts Centre and LG Arts Centre.

➡ **Northern Seoul (p118)** Daehangno is a performing arts hub with scores of venues, big and small.

Lonely Planet's Top Choices

Nanta (p74) The first and the best of Seoul's wide selection of nonverbal shows.

National Theatre of Korea (p74) Home to the national drama, *changgeuk* (Korean opera), orchestra and dance companies.

Korea House (p73) Intimate theatre for quality variety show of traditional performing arts.

Luxury Noraebang (p84) Karaoke in style in the heart of Hongdae.

Best for K-Indie

Café BBang (p83)

FF (p84)

DGBD (p84)

Freebird (p84)

Best for Jazz

Club Evans (p83)

All That Jazz (p93)

Once in a Blue Moon (p105)

Chunnyun (p118)

Best for Theatre & Dance

Seoul Arts Centre (p104)

Sejong Centre for the Performing Arts (p63)

LG Arts Centre (p105)

Hanguk Performing Arts Centre (p118)

White Box Theatre (p93)

Chongdong Theatre (p74)

Best for Movies

Cinemateque KOFA (p85)

Cinematheque/Seoul Arts Cinema (p63)

Oh! Zemidong (p74)

Cine de Chef (p102)

Best Arts Festivals

Seoul Performing Arts Festival (www.spaf.or.kr) Starting late September and lasting a month, this fest offers a mix of top class local and international acts.

International Modern Dance Festival (www.modafe.org) Held in May and based at the Arko Art Centre in Daehangno.

Seoul Fringe Festival (www.seoulfringefestival.net) Each August this major performing arts event takes over Hongdae.

Seoul International Dance Festival (www.sidance.org) Held in October and based mainly at the Seoul Arts Centre.

Best Rock-Pop Music Festivals

Pentaport (www.pentaportrock.com) Incheon in August; attracts major international acts.

Greenplugged (www.greenplugged.com) Usually held in May; good for local artists.

Grand Mint (www.mintpaper.com) In October; another chance to enjoy a range of Korean pop music live.

Evergreen (www.evergreenmusicfestival.co.kr) Favourite singers from decades ago join forces with contemporary indie faves for this multigenerational event, held in October.

HBC Festival (www.hbcfest.com) The expat area hosts a thriving indie band scene, held in May and October.

Shopping

Whether it's with traditional items such as hanbok (clothing) or hanji (handmade paper), or digital gizmos and K-Pop CDs, chances are slim that you'll leave Seoul empty-handed. Seoul's teeming markets, electronics emporiums, underground arcades, upmarket department stores and glitzy malls are all bursting at the seams with more goodies than Santa's sack.

Always in Fashion

For clothing, shoes, accessories or fabrics you can't beat Dongdaemun Market or Myeong-dong where you'll find local brands such as Codes Combine (www.codes-combine.co.kr) and Bean Pole (www.beanpole.com). Myeong-dong is also stacked with cosmetic chains such as Etude House, Skin Food and Nature Republic.

Larger sizes in clothes and shoes, souvenir T-shirts, leather jackets and tailor-made clothing, can be found in Itaewon, where English is widely understood. Outfits by hot local designers such as Lie Sang Bong, Doii Lee and Misung Jung, are best sourced in major department stores or the boutiques of Myeong-dong, Apgujeong and Cheongdam.

Shirts or blouses made of lightweight, see-through *ramie* (cloth made from pounded bark) make an unusual fashion gift; the quality is usually high, but as with naturally-dyed *hanbok,* such clothes are pricey.

Antiques & Crafts

Antique-lovers should browse the Dapsmni arcades or Insa-dong, Itaewon and the Seoul Folk Flea Market where stalls sell antiques, reproductions and collectables. Souvenirs such as embroidery, patchwork wrapping cloths (*bojagi*), handmade paper *(hanji),* wooden masks, fans, painted wooden carvings and lacquerware boxes inlaid with mother-of-pearl (*najeon chilgi*) can be found in Insa-dong's craft shops. More expensive items include pale-green celadon pottery, reproduction Joseon-dynasty furniture and contemporary art from Seoul's multitude of commercial galleries.

Food & Drink

The many types of Korean tea are a popular buy. Brands of rice wines such as *makgeolli* and Baekseju, and local liquors such as *soju* are also good souvenirs. Ginseng, the wonder root, turns up everywhere. You can chew it, eat it, drink it or bathe in it to benefit from its health-giving properties.

Shopping by Neighbourhood

➡ **Gwanghwamun & Jongno-gu (p63)** Insa-dong and Samcheong-dong are packed with art galleries and traditional craft and antique shops.

➡ **Myeong-dong & Jung-gu (p75)** Best for department stores, fashion outlets and cosmetics. All-night shopping at Namdaemun Market.

➡ **Itaewon & Yongsan-gu (p93)** Itaewon is great for expat-sized clothing and shoes, and is developing a rep for choice boutiques. Near Yongsan station are tons of electronics vendors and a huge shopping mall.

➡ **Gangnam & South of the Han River (p105)** Luxe retail in Apgujeong and Cheongdam; more affordable boutiques in Garosu-gil; one-stop shopping at megamalls such as COEX and D Cube City.

Lonely Planet's Top Choices

Kyobo Bookshop (p63) Books, CDs & DVDs to fulfil all your Korean pop-culture needs.

KCDF Gallery (p63) Gorgeous design emporium embracing traditional crafts with a contemporary slant.

10 Corso Como Seoul (p105) Beautifully curated high-fashion and lifestyle store in classy Cheongdam.

Namdaemun Market (p68) Haggle for bargains at this sprawling city-centre warren of stalls selling all life's essentials.

Shinsegae (p75) The 'Harrods' of Seoul is the city's classiest department store.

Best Markets

Dongdaemun Market (p110)

Seoul Yangnyeongsi Herb Medicine Market (p111)

Dapsimni Antiques Market (p111)

Seoul Folk Flea Market (p111)

Noriyangjin Fish Market (p81)

Best Fashion

Doota (p111)

Level 5 (p75)

Åland (p75)

Daily Projects (p105)

Boon The Shop (p105)

Dolsilnai (p119)

Best Department Stores & Malls

Galleria (p105)

Lotte Department Store (p75)

D Cube City (p105)

COEX Mall (p105)

I'Park Mall (p94)

Best for Books, CDS & DVDs

Seoul Selection(p63)

What the Book (p93)

Purple Record (p85)

Evan Records (p105)

Pungwoldang (p106)

Best for Design

Market m* (p63)

Jonginamoo (p64)

KT&G SangsangMadang (p78)

Little Farmers (p85)

Millimetre Milligram (p93)

NEED TO KNOW

Opening Hours

➡ **Shops** 10am-9pm; some closed Sunday

➡ **Department Stores** 10am-8pm

➡ **Markets** Times vary, but some stalls may stay open even on days when a market is generally closed.

Bargaining

Acceptable at markets and some shops. If you are buying more than one item, it's also OK to ask for a discount – use your judgement.

VAT Refunds

Global Refund (www.globalrefund.com) offers a partial refund (between 5% and 7%) of the 10% value added tax (VAT) on some items. Spend more than ₩30,000 in any participating shop and the retailer gives you a special receipt. At Incheon International Airport go to a Customs Declaration Desk (near the check-in counters) *before* checking in your luggage, as the customs officer will want to see the items before stamping your receipt. After you go through immigration, show your stamped receipt at the refund desk to receive your refund.

Best for Crafts & Souvenirs

Ssamziegil (p64)

Free Market (p85)

Key (p85)

Kukjae Embroidery (p64)

Korea House (p73)

PLAN YOUR TRIP SHOPPING

Sports & Activities

Baseball and soccer are the major spectator sports in Seoul. As for activities, don't miss out on having a relaxing sweat and cleansing soak in a jjimjil-bang (communal sauna and bathhouse). Hiking is popular year-round, while skiing and ice skating take over in winter.

Baseball

Introduced in 1905 by American missionaries, baseball is Korea's favourite sport. There are three Seoul teams in the Korean League (www.koreabaseball.com) and two of them – the Doosan Bears and the LG Twins – play at Jamsil Stadium. Matches take place from March to October (except for the summer break), and are well attended, with a lively atmosphere.

Soccer

In the 16-team professional K-League (www.kleague.com), Seoul FC plays from March to November in the World Cup Stadium. Crowds are bigger and there's more atmosphere when the national team is playing at the stadium, cheered on by the Red Devil supporters.

Basketball

Seoul's Samsung Thunders and SK Knights play in the Korean Basketball League (www.kbl.or.kr). Matches play November to March at Jamsil Gymnasium; play-offs until May.

Ssireum

Ssireum is Korean-style wrestling, more like Mongolian wrestling than Japanese sumo. Competitions held at Jangchung Gymnasium during Lunar New Year and Chuseok holidays.

24-Hour Spas

The best *jjimjil-bang* offer a variety of baths (maybe green tea or ginseng) and saunas (mugwort, pine or jade). Men and women are always separate in the bath area, but saunas, napping rooms and other facilities may be mixed; in these areas wear the robes or shorts and T-shirts provided. Most spas are open 24 hours. Basic entry fee covers up to 12 hours of unlimited use of all the baths and saunas; treatments like body scrubs cost extra.

Baseball & Golf Practice

You'll find baseball hitting practice nets in several areas including Insa-dong. Private golf courses are usually for members only, but there are driving ranges in top-end hotels and elsewhere including Gangnam.

Cycling

Cycleways run along both sides of the Han River past sports fields and picnic areas; there are plenty of **bike hire stalls** (per hr ₩3000; ⊙9am-8.30pm Mar-Nov). Bring your own padlock, and leave a driving licence or other ID.

Winter Sports

From December to February a handful of ski resorts within easy reach of Seoul (an hour or less by bus) open. There can be free shuttle buses from Seoul, but you might also want to look into travel-agency package deals that include transport, accommodation, ski-equipment hire and lift passes.

During the same months, skate under the stars at the magical, inexpensive ice-skating rink that appears on **Seoul Plaza** (Map p202; www.seoulskate.or.kr/eng.php), outside City Hall. Swimming pools along the Han River are also turned into skating rinks, as are the pools at the Grand Hyatt Seoul and Banyan Tree Club & Spa. Lotte World's indoor ice-skating rink is open all year.

Lonely Planet's Top Choices

Cycle along the Han River (p80) Hire a bicycle and get some exercise on the lanes running either side of the Han.

Dragon Hill Spa & Resort (p95) The best of Seoul's inner-city *jjimjil-bang* experiences.

Takewondo Experience Program (p70) Join a practice session for this martial art at Namsangol Hanok Village.

Ice Skating on Seoul Plaza (p70) Enjoy this central outdoor rink set up each winter next to City Hall.

Watching a baseball game (p106) Head to Jamsil Sports Complex and cheer along with the crowds.

Best for Skiing

Bears Town Resort (☑031 540 5000; www.bearstown.com) Located 50 minutes northeast of Seoul. USO, the American troops' activities organisation, runs ski tours to this resort and anyone is welcome to join.

Jisan Resort (☑02 3442 0322, 031 638 8460; www.jisanresort.co.kr) Fifty-six kilometres south of Seoul and a 40-minute bus ride from Gangnam.

Yangji Pine Resort (☑02 744 2001, 031 338 2001; www.pineresort.com) Around a 40-minute drive southeast of Seoul.

Best Spas & Jjimjil-bang

Dragon Hill Spa & Resort (p95)

Silloam Sauna (p75)

Spa Lei (p106)

Chunjiyun Spa (p75)

Itaewonland (p95)

Best for Live Sports

World Cup Stadium (p85)

Jangchung Gymnasium (p111)

Seoul Racecourse (p106)

NEED TO KNOW

Contacts & Information

➡ **Adventure Club** (www.adventurekorea.com) Contact for details of caving, rock climbing, white water rafting, paintball games and other adventurous outdoor activities.

➡ **Seoul Hiking Club** (www.hikingkorea.com) Find people to go hiking with.

➡ **Korea4Expats.com** (www.korea4expats.com) Listings for community groups & different activities.

Costs

➡ Baseball/soccer tickets ₩7000 to ₩20,000

➡ *Jjimjil-bang* ₩7000 to ₩12,000 entry, depending on the level of facilities.

Taekwondo

Try this traditional Korean martial art at Namsangol Hanok Village or visit the Kukkiwon (p106).

Swimming

Outdoor pools open in July and August in the Han River parks and include **Yeouido Hangang Swimming Pool** (Map p207) and **Ttukseom Swimming Pool** (Map p212). Itaewon's Hamilton Hotel has a popular outdoor pool open to nonguests.

Explore Seoul

SEOUL'S
TOP SIGHTS

Neighbourhoods at a Glance

❶ Gwanghwamun & Jongno-gu (p44)

The centuries-old heart of Seoul revolves around these once regal quarters of palaces – there are five to discover in this area and you can get between all on foot. Between Gyeongbokgung and Changdeokgung, Bukchon covers several smaller areas including Samcheong-dong and Gahoe-dong famous for

its traditional *hanok*. South of Bukchon are the equally maze-like streets of Insa-dong, a popular spot for tourists to shop and eat.

❷ Myeong-dong & Jung-gu (p65)

Seoul's retail world achieves its ultimate conclusion in the brightly lit, packed to the gills and supremely noisy streets of Myeong-dong.

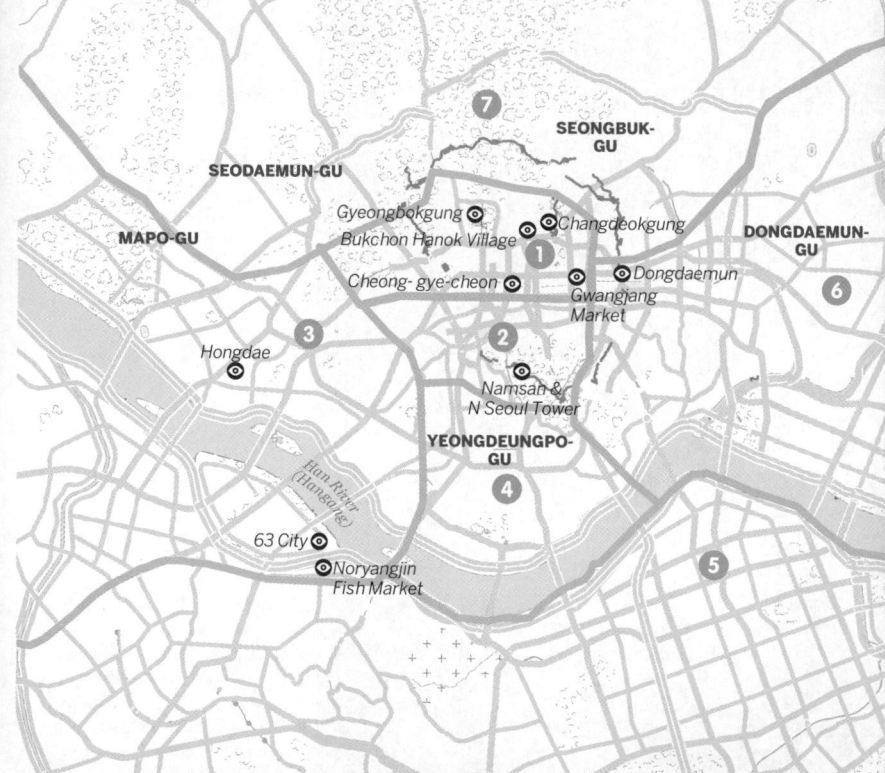

This is Seoul's equivalent of London's Oxford St or New York's Fifth Ave, with the massive, 24-hour Namdaemun Market on hand just in case you need to exponentially add to your shopping options. Looming over the commercial frenzy are the peaceful and tree-clad slopes of Namsan, a great place for exercise and city views.

③ Western Seoul (p76)

Seoul's principal student quarter is home to Hongdae (around Hongik University), Edae (around Ewha Womans University) and Sinchon (between Yonsei and Sogang Universities). These are youthful, creative districts short on traditional sights, big on modern-day diversions and sybaritic entertainments. South of Hongdae across the Han River, the island of Yeouido has several places of interest, all easily visited if you hire a bike in its riverside or central park.

④ Itaewon & Yongsan-gu (p86)

The off-limits US army base is like a giant void around which Yongsan-gu's sights and attractions revolve. You'll surely be paying a visit or two to Itaewon to sample its eating, drinking and shopping possibilities. The adjacent areas of Hannam-dong, Haebangchon (aka HBC) and Gyeongridan should be on your radar for the same reasons. The area has several major museums and a top resort-like *jjimjil-bang* (upmarket sauna).

⑤ Gangnam & South of the Han River (p96)

Gangnam (meaning south of the river) is a newly built area with high-rise blocks bisected by broad highways. There are large parks in the shape of Olympic Park, the strip of recreation areas along the Han River, and just outside the city limits, Seoul Grand Park. Luxury label boutiques are clustered in Apgujeong and Cheongdam. You'll also find several major performance arts centres across the district.

⑥ Dongdaemun & Eastern Seoul (p107)

The sprawling, high-rise 24-hour shopping experience that is Dongdaemun is the largest of several markets east of the city. You can shop for clothing here, and flea-market goods, antiques and herbal medicines further east. There's dramatic contemporary architecture in the shape of Dongdaemun Plaza & Park, while a stroll along a quieter section of the Cheong-gye-cheon is a pleasant way to see off-the-beaten-track things.

⑦ Northern Seoul (p112)

Some of Seoul's most charming neighbourhoods are clustered on three of the city's guardian mountains. Downhill from Naksan you'll find the student and performing arts hub of Daehangno. Moving anti-clockwise across to Bukaksan first comes Seongbuk-dong then Buam-dong, quietly affluent residential districts. The slopes of Inwangsan are home to the city's most famous shamanist shrine and there's a good park dedicated to the country's independence at Seodaemun.

NEIGHBOURHOODS AT A GLANCE

Gwanghwamun & Jongno-gu

INSA-DONG | BUKCHON | SAMCHEONG-DONG

Neighbourhood Top Five

1 Admire the scale and artistry of **Gyeongbokgung** (p46) the largest of Seoul's palaces, fronted by the grand gateway Gwanghwamun where you can watch the changing of the guard.

2 Discover Huwon, the serene traditional garden hidden behind **Changdeokgung** (p48).

3 Get lost in picturesque **Bukchon Hanok Village** (p49), the city's densest cluster of traditional-style homes.

4 Learn about Buddhism at **Jogye-sa** (p51) one of Seoul's most active temples and epicentre of the spectacular Lotus Lantern Festival in May.

5 Sip tea in one of **Insa-dong's traditional tea-houses** (p60), then explore the area's many **art galleries** (p62).

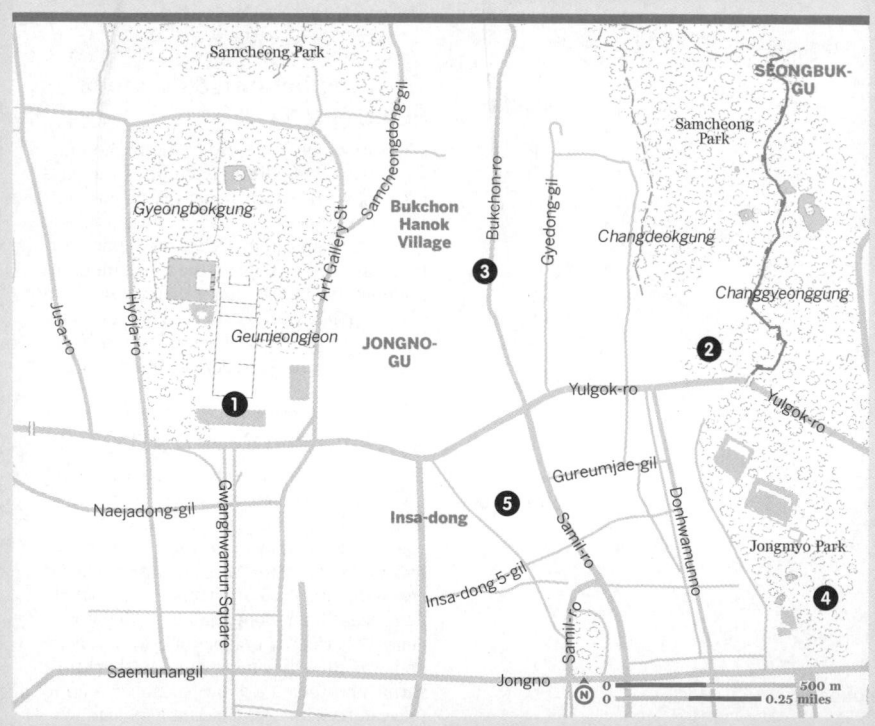

For more detail of this area, see Map p200 ➡

Explore: Gwanghwamun & Jongno-gu

Although their size and splendour have been greatly reduced from their heyday in the 18th century, Seoul's royal palace compounds, in the district of Jongno-gu, provide a glimpse of what it was like to live at the powerful heart of the old city. The area is also referred to as Gwanghwamun after the majestic gate to the main palace of Gyeongbokgung and the elongated square that has recently been created in front of it.

Save for the odd painted screen and altar, the large palace buildings are mostly empty allowing you to appreciate the Confucian ideals of frugality, simplicity and separation of the sexes in the architecture as well as the gardens.

Between Gyeongbokgung and Changdeokgung, stroll around Bukchon ('north village') which covers several smaller areas including Samcheong-dong and Gahoe-dong, famous for its traditional houses. Centuries ago this is where the *yangban* (aristocrats) lived but most estates were divided into plots in the early 20th century to create the smaller *hanok* you can now view around Gahoe-dong. West of Gyeongbokgung smaller clusters of *hanok* can be found in Tongui-dong, a popular location for small commercial art galleries.

South of Bukchon are the equally dense and maze-like streets of Insa-dong, one of Seoul's most tourist friendly areas, packed with craft shops, galleries, traditional teahouses and restaurants.

Local Life

➡ **Sunday Shopping** It's a car-free day on Insa-dong-gil making this a popular time for browsing the area's many crafts, antiques and art, and fashionable accessory shops.

➡ **Jomgmyo Square** The park in front of this venerable shrine is a daily gathering spot for Seoul's senior set who come to natter, play board games such as *baduk* and *janggi* and sometimes dance to *trot* (traditional electro-pop music).

➡ **Streamside Wanders** Stroll along the landscaped paths either side of the Cheong-gye-cheon; if the weather's fine, cool your heels in the stream.

Getting There & Away

➡ **Subway** Lines 1, 3 and 5 all have stations in this area with Anguk being the best for Insa-dong and Bukchon.
➡ **Tour Bus** The Seoul City Tour Bus has stops around the palaces and Insa-dong.

Lonely Planet's Top Tip

During the warmer spring and summer months, special events are often staged in the early morning or evening at the palaces; tickets for some are limited so plan ahead particularly for the very popular Moonlight Tours of Changdeokgung.

Best Places to Eat

➡ Congdu (p56)
➡ GastroTong (p56)
➡ Tosokchon (p57)

For reviews, see p56 ➡

Best Places to Drink

➡ Dawon (p60)
➡ Kopi Bangasgan (p60)
➡ Pub of the Blue Star (p60)

For reviews, see p60 ➡

Best Places to Shop

➡ Kyobo Bookshop (p63)
➡ KCDF Gallery (p63)
➡ Ssamziegil (p64)

For reviews, see p63 ➡

TOP SIGHTS
GYEONGBOKGUNG

Like a phoenix, the grandest of Seoul's palaces has risen several times from the ashes of destruction. Tourists have replaced the thousands of government officials, scholars, eunuchs, concubines, soldiers and servants who once thronged the palace. With its recently restored Gwanghwamun entrance, changing of the guard ceremonies and several museums, it's a place you should set aside at least half a day to see.

Palace History

Originally built by King Taejo in 1395, Gyeongbokgung (경복궁; Palace of Shining Happiness) served as the principal royal residence until 1592, when it was burnt down during the Japanese invasion. It lay in ruins for nearly 300 years until Heungseon Daewongun, regent and father of King Gojong, started to rebuild it in 1865. Gojong moved in during 1868, but the expensive rebuilding project bankrupted the government.

Four months after the assassination of his consort Myeongseong, Gojong fled to the nearby Russian legation building and never returned to Gyeongbokgung. During Japanese colonial rule, most of the palace was destroyed.

Palace Layout

Having been shuffled to various locations in the city, the palace's impressive main gate Gwanghwamun is back in its rightful place. It is flanked by stone carvings of *haechi*, mythical lion-like creatures traditionally set to protect the palace against fire; they never really did work and, appearances to the contrary, are superfluous today as the gate is now a painted concrete rather than wood structure.

DON'T MISS

➡ Gwanghwamun
➡ Geunjeongjeon
➡ National Folk Museum
➡ National Palace Museum

PRACTICALITIES

➡ Map p200
➡ http://english.cha.go.kr
➡ adult/child ₩3000/1500
➡ ⊙9am-5pm Wed-Mon Mar-Oct, to 4pm Wed-Mon Nov-Feb
➡ Ⓜ Line 3 to Gyeongbokgung, Exit 5

Moving across the palace's broad front courtyard, you pass through a second gate Heungnyemun and over a small artificial stream (for good feng shui a palace should have water in front and a mountain to the rear, which in this case is Bukaksan) to face the ornate two-storey **Geunjeongjeon**. In this impressive throne hall kings were crowned, met foreign envoys and conducted affairs of state.

Left of the throne hall Gyeonghoeru, a large pavilion resting on 48 pillars, overlooks an artificial lake with two small islands. State banquets were held inside and royals went boating on the pond.

Living Quarters & Gardens

A series of smaller meeting halls precede the king's living quarters Gangyeongjeon, behind which are Gyotaejeon, the queen's chambers. Behind that is a terraced garden, Amisan; the brick chimneys decorated with longevity symbols on the garden's top terrace are to release the smoke from the palaces *ondol* (underfloor heating) system.

On the eastern side of the grounds is Donggun, the living quarters for the Crown Prince. To the rear, King Gojong built more halls for his own personal use and an ornamental pond with Hyangwonjeong, an attractive hexagonal pavilion on an island.

Museums Within the Palace

The **National Palace Museum of Korea** (http://foreign.gogung.go.kr/eng/index.jsp; admission free; ⊙9am-5pm Tue-Sun), to the left just inside Gwanghwamun, has royal artefacts that highlight the wonderful artistic skills of the Joseon era – royal seals, illustrations of court ceremonies, and the gold-embroidered *hanbok* (traditional clothing) and exquisite hairpins worn by the queens and princesses. Note this museum closes on a different day to the palace.

In a separate section in the northeast of the grounds is the excellent **National Folk Museum of Korea** (www.nfm.go.kr; admission free; ⊙9am-5pm Wed-Mon Mar-Oct, to 4pm Wed-Mon Nov-Feb). It has three main exhibition halls covering the history of the Korean people, the agricultural way of life and the life of *yangban* (aristocrats) during the Joseon era. Among the many interesting exhibits is an amazingly colourful funeral bier.

Leave time to explore the open-air exhibition of historical buildings and structures including a street of buildings styled as they would have been in the early 20th century; you can sip coffee (for just ₩200) in a *dabang* (old-style cafe) here. There's also a separate Children's Museum (same opening times as the Folk Museum) and play area.

TOURS & CEREMONIES

An audio commentary and a free guided tour (at 11am, 1.30pm and 3.30pm) are available to learn more about the palace. At the National Folk Museum of Korea the guided tours start at 10.30am and 2.30pm, while at the National Palace Museum of Korea, the English guided tour is at 3pm. Changing of the guard ceremonies occur every hour, on the hour between 10am and 4pm at Gwanghwamun. For more information see www.sumunjang.or.kr.

QUEEN MIN'S ASSASSINATION

In the early hours of 8 October 1895, Gyeongbokgung was the scene of a dramatic moment in Korean history. Japanese assassins broke into the palace and murdered Empress Myeongseong (Queen Min), one of the most powerful figures at that time in Korea. After her body was burnt; it is said only one finger survived the fire. Later 56 individuals were arrested but not one was convicted for the murder.

◎ TOP SIGHTS
CHANGDEOKGUNG

A Unesco World Heritage property, as well as the most beautiful of Seoul's four main palaces, Changdeokgung (meaning Palace of Illustrious Virtue) was originally built in the early 15th century as a secondary palace to Gyeongbokgung. Following the destruction of both palaces during the Japanese invasion in the 1590s, Changdeokgung was rebuilt and became the primary royal residence until 1872. It remained in use by members of royal family well into the 20th century.

Visiting the Palace

You must join a guided tour to see inside Changdeokgung (창덕궁). English tours run at 11.30am and 2.30pm from March to December; if you don't care about the commentary then there are Korean tours on the hour. If you wish to gain entry to the Huwon (Secret Garden) – and you do – then you must join a special tour for an extra ₩5000; these run at 10am, 1pm and 2pm and are restricted to 50 people at a time. Also well worth joining are the monthly Moonlight Tours limited to 100 people and costing ₩30,000. Tickets can be bought online from Interpark (http://ticket.interpark.com); look under 'exhibitions and sport' and book well in advance as it's very popular.

DON'T MISS

➡ Huwon
➡ Injeongjeon
➡ Nakseonjae
➡ Ongnyucheon

PRACTICALITIES

➡ Map p195
➡ http://eng.cdg.go.kr/main/main.htm
➡ admission by guided tour in English adult/child ₩3000/1500
➡ Ⓜ Line 3 to Anguk, Exit 3

Palace Layout

Enter through the imposing gate Donhwamun, dating from 1608, turn right and cross over the stone bridge (built in 1414) – note the guardian animals carved on its sides. On the left is the beautiful main palace building, **Injeongjeon**. It sits in harmony with the paved courtyard, the open corridors and the trees behind it.

Next door are the government office buildings, including one with a blue-tiled roof. Further on are the private living quarters of the royal family. Peering inside the partially furnished rooms, you can feel what these Joseon palaces were like in their heyday – a bustling beehive buzzing round the king, full of gossip, intrigue and whispering.

Round the back is a terraced garden with decorative *ondol* chimneys. Over on the right is something completely different – **Nakseonjae**, built by King Heonjong (r 1834–49) in an austere Confucian style using unpainted wood. Royal descendants lived here until 1989.

The Secret Garden

Walk through the dense woodland and suddenly you come across a serene glade. The **Huwon** is a beautiful vista of pavilions on the edge of a square lily pond, with other halls and a two-storey library. The board out the front, written by King Jeongjo, means 'Gather the Universe'. Joseon kings relaxed, studied and wrote poems in this tranquil setting.

Further on are a couple more ponds and Yeongyeongdang, originally built in 1828 as a place for the Crown Prince to study. **Ongnyucheon** is a brook at the back of the garden where there's a huge rock Soyoam with three Chinese characters inscribed on it by King Injo in 1636: *ong-nyu-cheon,* which means 'jade flowing stream' and a poem composed in Chinese characters by King Sukjong in 1690.

TOP SIGHTS
BUKCHON HANOK VILLAGE

Bukchon (North Village), covering the area between Gyeongbokgung and Changdeokgung, is home to around 900 hanok, Seoul's largest concentration of these traditional Korean homes. Although super-touristy in parts, it's a pleasure to aimlessly wander and get lost in the streets here admiring the buildings' patterned walls and tiled roofs contrasting with the modern city in the distance. Many of the hanok have been turned into charming cafes, galleries, boutiques or guesthouses. There are also small private museums and houses that you can enter.

Bukchon Information & Events

To find out more about Bukchon Hanok Village (북촌 한옥마을), head first to the **Bukchon Traditional Culture Centre** (Map p195; admission free; ◷9am-6pm Mon-Fri), which has a small exhibition about *hanok* and is housed, appropriately enough, in a *hanok*. There are sometimes English-speaking volunteers here and you should be able to pick up the free English booklet *Discovery Buckchon* which includes a map detailing the top eight photo spots around the area.

With three days advance notice you can arrange a free guided tour of the area with a volunteer from Seoul City Government; see p27 for details. Mobile guide systems can also be rented from the **Bukchon Tourist Information Centre** (Map p195; ◷rent 10am-2pm, return by 5pm); these digital gizmos provide you with multimedia information as you stroll around.

Inside the Hanok

Given the throng of tourists and the number of *hanok* that now house commercial businesses, it's easy to overlook the fact that this region was once a residential area and still remains so in parts.

For a critical take on the contemporary history and development of Bukchon see Kahoidong.com (www.kahoidong.com). The site is run by David Kilburn, who lives with his wife in a Gahoe-dong *hanok;* they occasionally open their home to the public for art events.

In the middle of the most famous Bukchon area, 31 Gahoe-dong, the National Trust of Korea manages another residential property **Simsimheon** (심심헌; Map p195; www.simsimheon.com; admission ₩10,000; ◷9am-6.30pm Mon-Sat), meaning 'House Where the Heart is Found'. This modern *hanok* was rebuilt using traditional methods on the site of two older ones. Entry includes tea, which is sipped overlooking the internal garden.

Craft & Art Museums & Workshops

There are several places in Bukchon where you can learn about the traditional crafts still practised in this area or view private collections of arts and crafts. Search out the **Gahoe Museum** (Map p195; www.gahoemuseum.org; adult/child ₩3000/2000; ◷10am-6pm Tue-Sun) for its collection of amulets and folk paintings. The **Dong-Lim Knot Workshop** (Map p195; www.shimyoungmi.com; adult/child ₩2000/1000; ◷10am-6pm Tue-Sun) holds classes in traditional knot techniques to make tassels, jewellery and other ornaments. For details of more places see the *Discovery Bukchon* booklet.

IDREAMSTOCK / ALAMY ©

TOP SIGHTS
JONGMYO

Surrounded by dense woodland, World Heritage–listed Jongmyo houses the spirit tablets of the Joseon kings and queens and some of their most loyal government officials. Their spirits are believed to reside in a special hole bored into the wooden tablets.

Shrine Layout

Near the entrance to Jongmyo (종묘) are two ponds, both square (representing earth) with a round island (representing the heavens). In the middle of the main path you'll notice triple stone paths; one is for the king, the other for the crown prince and the raised middle section for the spirits.

The stately main shrine, **Jeongjeon**, constructed in 1395, is fronted by a large stone-flagged courtyard. Inside are 49 royal spirit tablets in 19 small windowless rooms which are usually locked. On the right-hand side of the main entrance is Gonsindang, which houses the spirit tablets of 83 meritorious subjects.

The smaller shrine, **Yeongnyeongjeon** (Hall of Eternal Peace), built in 1421, has 34 spirit tablets of lesser kings in six rooms. These include four ancestors of King Taejo (the founder of the Joseon dynasty) who were made kings posthumously. Behind this building a footbridge leads over to Changgyeonggung.

Jongmyo Daeje

On the first Sunday in May the Yi clan, descendants of the Joseon kings, enact this ceremony, making lavish offerings of food and drink to the spirits of their royal ancestors. Starting at 11.30am with a procession from Gwanghwamun Square to the shrine, the ceremony culminates seven hours later at the main shrine Jeongjeon.

DON'T MISS

➡ Jeongjeon
➡ Yeongnyeongjeon

PRACTICALITIES

➡ Map p198
➡ http://jm.cha.go.kr
➡ adult/child ₩1000/500
➡ ⊘9am-5pm Wed-Mon Mar-Oct, to 4.30pm Wed-Mon Nov-Feb
➡ Ⓜ Line 1, 3 or 5 to Jongno 3-ga, Exit 11

TOP SIGHTS
JOGYE-SA

The headquarters of the Jogye Order of Korean Buddhism is home to Daeungjeon, the largest temple building in Seoul. It was completed in 1938, but the design followed the Joseon-dynasty style. Murals of scenes from Buddha's life and the carved floral latticework doors are two of its attractive features. The temple compound, always a hive of activity, really comes alive during the city's spectacular Lotus Lantern Festival celebrating Buddha's birthday.

DON'T MISS
➡ Daeungjeon
➡ Central Buddhist Museum
➡ Temple Life programs

PRACTICALITIES
➡ Map p198
➡ www.jogyesa.org
➡ Ujeongguk-ro, Insadong
➡ ⊘24 hours
➡ Ⓜ Line 3 to Anguk, Exit 6

Buddha Triad

Inside Daeungjeon (대웅전) at Jogye-sa (조계사) are three giant gilded Buddha statues: on the left is Amitabha, Buddha of the Western Paradise; in the centre is the historical Buddha, who lived in India and achieved enlightenment; on the right is the Bhaisaiya or Medicine Buddha, with a medicine bowl in his hand. The small 15th-century Buddha in the glass case was the main Buddha statue before he was replaced by the much larger ones in 2006. On the right-hand side is a guardian altar with lots of fierce-looking guardians in the painting behind, and on the left side is the altar used for memorial services.

Believers who enter the temple bow three times, touching their forehead to the ground – once for Buddha, once for the *dharma* (teaching) and once for the *sangha* (monks), 20 of whom serve in this temple.

Other Buildings

Behind Daengjeon is the modern Geuknakjeon (Paradise Hall) dedicated to Amitabha Buddha; funeral services, dharma (truth) talks and other prayer services are held here. The statues are the 10 judges who pass judgement, 49 days after someone's death, to decide if they go to heaven or hell.

Beomjongru (Brahma Bell Pavilion) houses a drum to summon earthbound animals, a wooden fish-shaped gong to summon aquatic beings, a metal cloud-shaped gong to summon birds and a large bronze bell to summon underground creatures. The bell is rung 28 times at 4am and 33 times at 6pm.

Also within the grounds is the **Central Buddhist Museum** (adult/child ₩2000/1000; ⊘9am-6pm Tue-Sun) displaying regularly changing exhibitions relating to the religion. Attached to the museum is a tea shop and gift shop.

Temple Life Programs

Jogye-sa's **Information Centre for Foreigners** (⏉732 5292; ⊘10am-5pm) is staffed by English-speaking guides. Ask here about the Temple Life program (₩20,000, open 10am to 2.30pm Saturday) which includes a temple tour, tea ceremony, basic meditation practice, a traditional vegetarian monk's meal, making lanterns and doing woodblock printing. Mini-Temple Life programs featuring two or three activities are generally available daily for a small donation.

To find out more about Buddhism or book a Templestay program elsewhere in Seoul or Korea, the **Templestay Information Centre** (p198; www.templestay.com) is just across the street from Jogye-sa. Along the street you'll also find many shops selling monks' robes, prayer beads, lanterns and the like.

 **SIGHTS**

Gwanghwamun & Around

GYEONGBOKGUNG   PALACE
See p46

FREE **SEOUL MUSEUM OF HISTORY**   MUSEUM
Map p200 (서울역사박물관; www.museum.
seoul.kr; ⊙9am-9pm Tue-Fri, 9am-6pm Sat &
Sun; Ⓜ Line 5 to Gwanghwamun, Exit 7) To gain
an appreciation of just how much Seoul
has changed in the last century visit this
fascinating museum, which has made a big
effort to upgrade its displays. Outside you
can see one of the old tram cars that used
to run in the city in the 1930s as well as a
section of the old Gwanghwamun gate. Inside there's a massive scale model of the city
you can walk around, which includes future
development projects such as the Yongsan
International Business Development District. There may be charges for special exhibitions. Classical music concerts are sometimes staged here and there's an excellent
neo-Korean restaurant called Congdu.

GWANGHWAMUN SQUARE   SQUARE, EXHIBITION
Map p200 (광화문; Sejong-ro; Ⓜ Line 5 to Gwanghwamun, Exit 4) There are things to see above
and underground at this broad elongated
square that provides a grand approach to
Gwanghwamun. At the square's southern
end is a statue of Admiral Yi Sun-sin (1545–
98) who designed a new type of metal-clad
warship called *geobukseon* (turtle boats),
and used them to help achieve a series of
stunning victories over the much larger
Japanese navy that had attacked Korea at
the end of the 16th century. In the middle
of the square stands another giant statue,
this one of King Sejong (1397–1450). Steps
lead down to an **underground exhibition**
(admission free; ⊙10.30am-10pm Tue-Sun) with
sections on both these illustrious Korean
heroes.

FREE **CHEONGWADAE SARANGCHAE**   EXHIBITION
Map p200 (청와대 사랑채; www.cwdsarang
chae.kr; ⊙9am-6pm Tue-Sun; Ⓜ Line 3 to Gyeongbokgung, Exit 4) Much more interesting than
the tour of Cheongwadae itself is this new
exhibition hall opposite the exit from the

 TOP SIGHTS
CHEONG-GYE-CHEON

A raised highway was torn down and roads removed in
this US$384-million urban-renewal project to 'daylight'
the Cheon-gye-cheon (청계천), a stream that used to run
through northern Seoul's centre, out to the Han River.
The water that now flows for 5.8km down this beautifully
landscaped oasis is actually pumped in at great expense
from elsewhere, inciting the ire of environmentalists.
Despite this, the revitalised stream with its walkways,
footbridges, waterfalls and public artworks has been a
hit with Seoulites who come to escape the urban hubbub
and, in summer, dangle their feet in the water.

Cheong-gye Plaza, marking the start of the stream, is
spiked with the giant pink-and-blue sculpture by Claes
Oldenberg and Coosje van Bruggen entitled *Spring*.
There's also a free video and e-postcard facility here,
and the plaza is the setting for various public events,
including the Cheong-gye-cheon Festival (www.cheong
gyecheon.org) held in May.

Between the Gwang-gyo and Jangton-gyo bridges
is a 192m wall mural of painted tiles depicting King
Jeongjo visiting his father's tomb in Hwaseong (Suwon)
in 1785. Continue on past Dongdaemun and you'll eventually reach the Cheong-Gye-Cheon Museum.

DON'T MISS
➡ Cheong-gye Plaza
➡ Mural of King
Jeongjo's royal
parade
➡ Walking beside the
stream

PRACTICALITIES
➡ Map p200
➡ www.cheong
gyecheon.or.kr
➡ Ⓜ Line 5 to Gwang-
hwamun, Exit 5

presidential compound. Inside are displays promoting Korea and Seoul as well as the work of past presidents and some of the gifts they have been given by international visitors. It's all very nicely put together and in one section you can have a photo op with a digitised image of the president on Cheongwadae's front lawn. There's also a pleasant cafe.

FREE CHEONGWADAE
(BLUE HOUSE)   PRESIDENTIAL COMPOUND
Map p200 (청와대; www.president.go.kr; Ⓜ Line 3 to Gycongbokgung, Exit 5) Back in 1968 a squad of 31 North Korean commandos was caught just 500m from Korea's answer to the White House on a mission to assassinate President Park Chung-hee. Security remains very tight, but you can still see inside if you join a free 40-minute tour, which includes a five-minute film show and a walk around the palatial grounds; they are nice enough but not really worth the hassle.

Tours (passports required) run from Tuesday to Saturday at 10am, 11am, 2pm and 3pm. You must pre-book online and pick up the tickets at the ticket booth in Gyeongbokgung's car park (Map p200). A tour bus then takes you the short distance from the car park to Cheongwadae's public entrance.

FREE GYEONGHUIGUNG   PALACE
Map p200 (경희궁; http://jikimi.cha.go.kr; ◷9am-6pm Tue-Sun; Ⓜ Line 5 to Gwanghwamun, Exit 1) The Palace of Shining Celebration was completed in 1623 and used to consist of a warren of courtyards, buildings, walls and gates spread over a large area. But it was destroyed during the Japanese annexation and a Japanese school was established here. Only the main audience hall, Sungjeongjeon, and the smaller official hall behind it along with a few paved courtyards, walls and corridors have been restored. The entrance gate, Heunghwamun, has toured around Seoul, and was moved to its present site in 1988.

FREE SEOUL MUSEUM OF
ART ANNEXE   MUSEUM
Map p200 (http://seoulmoa.seoul.go.kr; ◷10am-5pm; Ⓜ Line 5 to Gwanghwamun, Exit 1) Two large, white hangar-like structures make up the annex of the Seoul Museum of Art. Periodically changing exhibitions cover

---

> ⓘ
> **TICKET TO THE PALACES**
>
> If you plan to visit all four of Seoul's palaces – Gyeonbukgung, Changdeokgung, Changgyeonggung and Deoksugung – then you can save some money by buying a combined ticket (₩10,000) valid for up to a month. The ticket is sold at each of the palaces and also covers entry to Huwon at Changdeokgung.

everything from traditional brush and ink to modern angst.

FREE SAJIKDAN   SHRINE
Map p200 (사직단; www.jongno.go.kr; Sajik Park; Ⓜ Line 3 to Gyeongbokgung, Exit 5) This impressive stone altar in a tranquil park and surrounded by low stone walls and ornate wooden gates dates back to 1395 and King Taejo, founder of the Joseon dynasty. It was used to pray to the gods for good harvests.

FREE SEJONG GALLERY   GALLERY
Map p200 (www.sejongpac.or.kr; Sejongno; ◷10am-5pm; Ⓜ Line 5 to Gwanghwamun, Exit 8) Next to the theatre and concert hall; the changing exhibitions are generally worth a look as modern Korean artists often display wonderful work in the four gallery rooms.

**DAELIM CONTEMPORARY
ART MUSEUM**   GALLERY
Map p200 (✆720 0667; www.daelimmuseum.org; charge varies with exhibition; ◷10am-6pm Tue-Sun; Ⓜ Line 3 to Gyeongbokgung, Exit 5) This gallery specialises in exhibitions on photography, design and fashion. The building, which was originally a family house was remodelled by French architect Vincent Cornu and has a lovely garden to the rear.

HAMMERING MAN   STATUE
Map p200 (Ⓜ Line 5 to Gwanghwamun, Exit 6) The moving metallic shadow of a hammering man, made out of 50 tonnes of steel by American artist Jonathan Borofsky, towers five storeys above the street. Funded by a local insurance company, the superman of a blacksmith has been silently hammering since 2002. The statue may be simple, but is also thought provoking. Is work just a meaningless ritual that dominates our lives?

Insa-dong, Bukchon & Samcheong-dong

CHANGDEOKGUNG PALACE
See p48.

BUKCHON HANOK VILLAGE NEIGHBOURHOOD
See p49.

JONGMYO SHRINE
See p50.

JOGYE-SA TEMPLE
See p51.

CHANGGYEONGGUNG PALACE
Map p195 (창경궁; http://jikimi.cha.go.kr; adult/child ₩1000/500; ⊙Tue-Sun 9am-6.30pm Apr-Oct, 9am-5.30pm Nov-Mar, 9am-5pm Dec-Feb; MLine 4 to Hyehwa, Exit 4) The Palace of Flourishing Gladness was originally built in the early 15th century by revered King Sejong for his parents. Like the other palaces, it was destroyed twice by the Japanese – first in the 1590s and then again during the colonial period from 1910 until 1945, when the palace suffered the indignity of being turned into a zoo. Only a fifth of the palace buildings survived or have been rebuilt. The oldest surviving structure is the 15th-century Okcheongyo stone bridge over the stream by the main gate.

The main hall, Myeongjeongjeon, with its latticework and ornately carved and decorated ceiling, dates back to 1616. The stone markers in the courtyard show where the different ranks of government officials had to stand during major state ceremonies. The smaller buildings behind the main hall were where the kings and queens lived in their separate households. Beyond here paths through a spacious wooded garden with an ornamental pond Chundangji lead to the Great Greenhouse, Korea's first modern conservatory built in 1909 by the Japanese.

English-speaking tours (free, one hour) around the palace are offered at 11am and 4pm from Okcheongyo. Also look out for dates when the palace is open for night viewing and illuminated, making it a romantic spot (if you can ignore the crowds).

UNHYEON-GUNG PALACE
Map p198 (www.unhyeongung.or.kr; Samil-daero, Insa-dong; adult/child ₩700/300; ⊙9am-7pm Tue-Sun Apr-Oct, to 6pm Tue-Sun Nov-Mar; MLine 3 to Anguk, Exit 4) The name of this minor palace translates as Cloud Hanging Over the Valley Palace. It has a modest and plain natural-wood design reflecting the austere tastes of Heungseon Daewongun (1820–98), King Gojong's stern and conservative father, whose policies included massacring Korean Catholics, excluding foreigners from Korea, closing Confucian schools and rebuilding Gyeongbokgung. Gojong was born and raised here until 1863 when he ascended the throne aged 12 with his father acting as regent.

Rooms are furnished and mannequins display the dress styles of the time. It's also possible to try on *hanbok* (₩1000), and various artistic events are staged here throughout the year including traditional music and dance concerts usually on Saturday afternoons; see the website for details.

TAPGOL PARK PARK
Map p198 (탑골 공원; Jung-ro, Insa-dong; ⊙9am-6pm; MLine 1 or 5 to Jongno 3-ga, Exit 1 or 5) Opened in 1897, Tapgol is a symbol of Korean resistance to Japanese rule. On 1 March 1919, Son Byeong-hui and 32 others signed and read aloud a Declaration of Independence (a copy in English can be read on the memorial plaque). Many of them were high-school teachers, 16 were Cheondogyo followers, 15 were Protestant Christians and two, including poet-monk Young-un, were Buddhists. All were arrested and locked up in the notorious Seodaemun Prison. A torrent of protest against Japan followed in Seoul and throughout Korea, but the *samil* (1 March) movement was ruthlessly suppressed. Hundreds of independence fighters were killed and thousands arrested. In the park, 10 murals depict scenes from the heroic but unsuccessful struggle.

LOCAL KNOWLEDGE

NAKED ART

On the east side of Gyeongbokgung the **UUL National Art Museum of Seoul** (Map p200; www.uul.go.kr), a new branch of the National Museum of Contemporary Art, is under construction and set to open late in 2013. The construction site wall facing the palace is decorated with comical takes on famous pieces of art, including a rather saucy Mona Lisa.

Neighbourhood Walk
Bukchon Views

Take in views across Bukchon's tiled *hanok* roofs on this walk around the area between Gyeonbokgung and Changdeokgung. Don't worry if you get a little lost in the maze of streets – that's part of the pleasure. Also note this description uses the new street names for the area; some maps and business addresses will have the old address system.

From the subway exit turn left at the first junction and walk 200m to ❶ **Bukchon Traditional Culture Centre** where you can learn about the area's architecture. Turn left at the junction and then right at Bukchon-ro. On the corner is the ❷ **Bukchon Tourist Information Centre**. Walk up this major road lined with shops; 25 years ago it was a much narrower residential street leading into the hills.

Around 250m up on the left-hand side is ❸ **11-gil**, **Bukchon-ro**; follow this narrow street uphill towards the parallel set of picturesque streets lined with *hanok* in ❹ **31 Gahoe-dong**. To see inside one of the *hanok* pause at ❺ **Simsimheon**.

Turn left and go a few blocks west to 5-gil, Bukchon-ro; just to the right is a ❻ **viewing spot** across Samcheong-dong. Head south down the hill, perhaps pausing for tea at ❼ **Cha Masineun Tteul**. Further downhill is ❽ **Another Way of Seeing** (www.artblind.or.kr) an art gallery exhibiting work by the vision impaired.

Turn left after the ❾ **World Jewellery Museum** and then right at the junction; on the corner by another tourist information booth, walk up to ❿ **Jeongdok Public Library**, where you'll find a museum devoted to education and a small quiet park; the cherry blossoms are lovely here in spring as are the ginkgo trees turning yellow in autumn.

Return to the subway station via Yun Boseon-gil which runs behind the Constitutional Court.

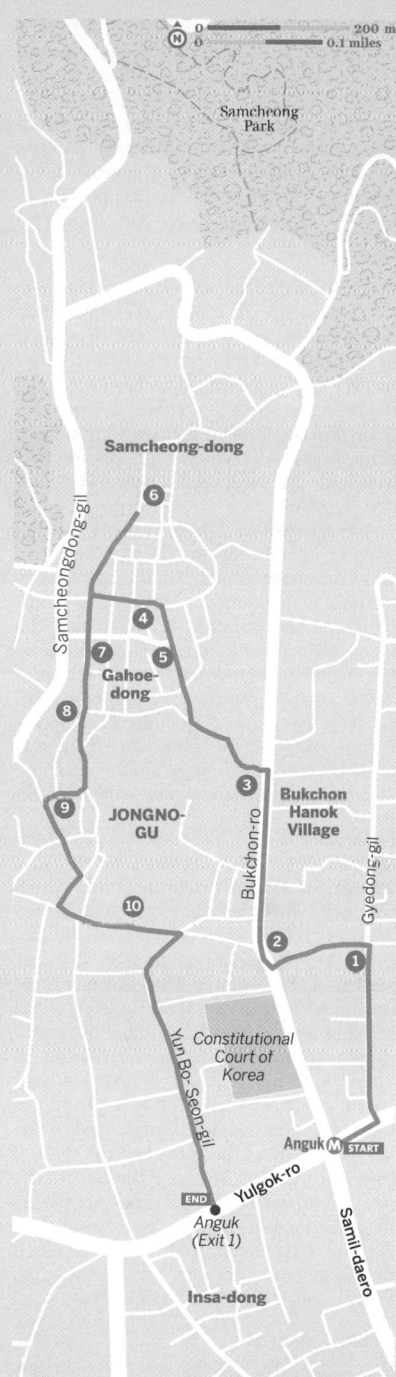

The park's other outstanding feature is the 10-tier, 12m-high stone pagoda, encased in a glass box. It once graced Wongak-sa, a nearby Buddhist temple destroyed in 1504 on the orders of the Confucian king. Buddhists were forced out of the cities into the mountains, where most of Korea's great temples still stand today. The pagoda, a treasure of Buddhist art, has wonderful carvings all over it.

CHEONDOGYO TEMPLE TEMPLE

Map p198 (천도교 중앙대교당; Insa-dong; ⊙9am-6pm; Ⓜ Line 3 to Anguk, Exit 6) Designed by a Japanese architect and constructed in 1921, this is a handsome baroque-style, red-brick and stone temple with a tower. Inside, the wood panelling, lines of chairs and plain decoration create an impression of a lecture theatre, although there are stained-glass windows.

Cheondogyo is a home-grown Korean religion containing Buddhist, Confucian and Christian elements that gathered momentum in the 1860s. Its members were key figures in the Donghak rebellion and the independence movements opposed to Japanese rule. The founder, Great Master Suun (1824–64), was executed for being a radical reformer. Followers believe that God is within everyone. Services (featuring lots of bowing) are held every Sunday at 11am. Men sit on the left and women on the right.

BOSINGAK BELL TOWER

Map p198 (보신각; Jung-ro, Insa-dong; Ⓜ Line 1 to Jonggak, Exit 4) This ornate pavilion, which contrasts with the modern Jogno Tower opposite, houses a recent copy of the city bell – the original, forged in 1468, is in the garden of the National Museum of Korea. Costumed guardsmen patrol around the bell and ring it 12 times at noon (ceremony runs from 11am to 12.20pm Tuesday to Sunday) but in the past the great bell was struck 28 times every night at 10pm to ask the heavens for a peaceful night and to signal the closure of the gates and the start of the nightly curfew. To signal the start of the new day it was struck 33 times for the 33 Buddhist heavens at 4am, after which the gates were reopened. It also sounded when fire broke out, as often happened with so many wooden and thatched buildings.

MOKIN MUSEUM MUSEUM

Map p198 (목인박물관; www.mokinmuseum. com; Insa-dong 11-gil, Insa-dong; adult/child ₩5000/3000; ⊙10am-7pm; Ⓜ Line 3 to Anguk, Exit 6) *Mokin* are carved and painted wooden figures and decorative motifs that were used to decorate *sangyeo* (funeral carriages). Carved by humble village craftsmen, they are a unique folk art drenched in Buddhist and shamanist beliefs, and this small private museum includes some prime examples of the craft. Carved flowers represent wealth and yearning for a perfect world, while birds represent messengers from this world to the next, fish symbolise life and learning (as they never close their eyes), and tigers and goblins scare evil spirits away.

WORLD JEWELLERY MUSEUM MUSEUM

Map p195 (www.wjmuseum.com; Hwa-dong; adult/child ₩7000/5000; ⊙11am-5pm Wed-Sun; Ⓜ Line 3 to Anuk, Exit 1) The well-lit displays of this private collection prove that small is beautiful. The pieces were amassed from around the world over three decades. There's a shop selling jewellery here, too – all of which is designed to appeal to the women who love to browse the surrounding boutiques.

✖ EATING

Gwanghwamun & Around

TOP CHOICE CONGDU NEO KOREAN $$$

Map p200 (www.congdu.com; Seoul Museum of History, Seamunan-ro; lunch/dinner from ₩27,000/45,000; ⊙11.30am-2pm Mon-Fri, 11.30am-3.30pm Sat & Sun, 5.30-8.50pm daily; Ⓜ Line 5 to Gwanghwamun, Exit 7; 🖥 🗎) Elegantly presented, contemporary twists on Korean classics, such as pine nut soup with soy milk espuma (foam), are what make this restaurant a pleasure along with its relaxing atmosphere: ask for a seat in the conservatory section overlooking a garden at the back of the museum.

TOP CHOICE GASTROTONG SWISS, EUROPEAN $$$

Map p200 (✆730 4162; www.gastrotong.co. kr; Tongui-dong; lunch/dinner from ₩22,000/66,000; ⊙10am-3pm, 6-10pm; Ⓜ Line 3 to Gyeongbokgung, Exit 3; 🖥 🗎) Swiss-German chef Roland Hinni and wife Yong-Shin run this charming gourmet restaurant that blends sophistication with traditional European cooking. The set lunches are

TONGIN MARKET & LUNCH BOX CAFE

With convenience stores blanketing the city, Seoul's market arcades lined with food vendors and single product shops have been dying out. One that is bucking the trend is **Tongin Market** (통인시장; Map p200; http://tonginmarket.co.kr; Ⓜ Line 3 to Gyeongbokgung, Exit 2). Some of the vendors here are part of a scheme that makes for a fun way to put together lunch. About half-way along the arcade is the **Lunch Box Café** (도시락 Café; ⏰11am-4pm Mon-Sat) where you can buy a set of 10 coupons for ₩5000. Save ₩2000 of coupons for the rice, soup and kimchi side dishes served at the cafe, then use the rest to browse the participating market vendors (marked by a sign) and select foods to put in the plastic lunch box tray the cafe provides. You can buy more coupons, if needed, and trade back unused ones for cash.

splendid deals, including appetiser, soup or salad, dessert and drinks as well as a wide choice of main courses. It's small so booking is essential.

EURO GOURMET
CAFE, DELI **$$**

Map p200 (www.eurogourmet.co.kr; mains ₩8500-13,000; ⏰10am-10pm; Ⓜ Line 3 to Gyeongbokgung, Exit 3; 🛜🦽) Handy if GastroTong is full, but also worth visiting in its own right is this delightful Euro-style delicafe specialising in sandwiches, pasta and baguette-style pizza made with premium ingredients.

TOSOKCHON
KOREAN **$$**

Map p200 (토속촌; ☎737 7446; meals from ₩15,000; ⏰10am-10pm; Ⓜ Line 3 to Gyeongbokgung, Exit 2) There's always a line of people waiting for the bubbling *samgyetang* (ginseng chicken soup) at this venerable restaurant spread over a series of *hanok*. Tip some salt and pepper together into a small saucer and use it as a dip for the chicken. Ex-presidents have dined here; it's the best restaurant of its type in Seoul.

JOSEON GIMBAP
KOREAN **$**

Map p200 (조선김밥; gimbap ₩3500; ⏰7am-8pm; Ⓜ Line 3 to Anguk, Exit 1) Behind the building site for the new contemporary art museum this quirky, tiny place is marked by a sign drawn on a T-shirt. Inside there's astro turf in the front seating area where you get a ring-side seat on the jumbo *gimbap* being made. These whoppers come with a range of side dishes making it one of the best value feeds in the city.

HANMIRI
NEO KOREAN **$$$**

Map p200 (한미리; ☎757 5707; www.hanmiri.co.kr; lunch/dinner from ₩30,000/50,000; ⏰11.30am-3pm & 6-10pm; Ⓜ Line 5 to Gwanghwamun, Exit 5; 🦽) Sit on chairs at tables for

this modern take on royal cuisine; book one of the rooms with windows overlooking the Cheong-gye-cheon. It's gourmet and foreigner-friendly. There's another branch in Gangnam.

BIBIGO
KOREAN **$$**

Map p200 (www.bibgo.com; Saemunan-ro; meals ₩10,000-12,000; ⏰11am-10pm; Ⓜ Line 5 to Gwanghwamun, Exit 6; 🦽) Traditional Korean dishes such as *bibimbap* are done fast-food style at this quite stylish operation where you can also choose the different elements of the dish, ie type of rice, topping and sauce. There's also a branch in Apgujeong.

MEMILGGUJ PILMURYEP
KOREAN **$**

Map p200 (메밀꽃 필 무렵; Tongui-dong; meals ₩7000-8000; ⏰noon-8pm) Handy for Gyeongbukgung and Tongui-dong, this simple eatery where you sit on the floor serves up big steaming bowls of buckwheat noodles, dumplings and *pajeon* pancakes.

SONG'S KITCHEN
NEO KOREAN **$$**

Map p200 (Tongin-dong; ⏰11am-11pm Tue-Sun; mains ₩6000-25,000; Ⓜ Line 3 to Gyeongbokgung, Exit 2) In an artfully styled *hanok*, interesting dishes to share are offered (such as *tteokbokki* served in a carved-out squash), alongside Western cuisine including pizza and fried-rice filled omelettes. There's a good wine and drinks list making it a pleasant spot to linger in the evening.

Insa-dong, Bukchon & Samcheong-dong

BALWOO GONGYANG
VEGETARIAN **$$$**

Map p198 (발우공양; ☎2031 2081; www.baru.or.kr; 5th fl, Templestay Information Centre, Ujeongguk-ro, Insa-dong; lunch/dinner from

₩25,000/36,000; ⊘11.40am-3pm & 6-9pm; Ⓜ Line 3 to Anguk, Exit 6) Make reservations three days in advance for delicate temple-style cuisine served here. It's all beautifully presented. For less fancy vegetarian food go down to the 2nd floor to another kitchen (open from 11.30am to 8pm) where there's a buffet (₩7000) or simple noodle and rice dishes for around ₩4000.

MIN'S CLUB
FUSION $$$

Map p198 (민가다헌; ☑733 2966; www.mins club.co.kr; off Insa-dong 10-gil, Insa-dong; lunch/dinner from ₩25,000/60,000;⊘noon-2.30pm & 6-11.30pm; Ⓜ Line 3 to Anguk, Exit 6) Old-world architecture meets new-world cuisine in this classy restaurant housed in a beautifully restored 1930s *hanok* that offers European-Korean meals (more European than Korean). There's an extensive wine selection.

TOBANG
KOREAN $

Map p198 (토방; Insa-dong-gil, Insa-dong; meals ₩5500; ⊘10am-7pm; Ⓜ Line 3 to Anguk, Exit 6) A white sign with two Chinese characters

above a doorway leads the way to this excellent value eatery, where you sit on floor cushions under paper lanterns. Order the *sundubu jjigae* or *doenjang jjigae* for some Korean home-cooking flavour and excellent side dishes that include bean sprouts, fish, cuttlefish and raw crab in red-pepper sauce, plus a soup and rice.

NWIJO
KOREAN $$

Map p198 (뉘조; ☑730 9310; off Insa-dong 14-gil, Insa-dong; meals from ₩18,000; Ⓜ Line 3 to Anguk, Exit 6) Traditional *jeonsik* meals that tend towards vegetarian Buddhist style cuisine are served on rustic pottery in this *hanok*. The food is fresh and has a pleasing mixture of textures.

DHAL
INDIAN $$

Map p195 (☑736 4627; www.dalindia.com; Art Sonje Center, 5-gil Bukchon-ro; mains ₩15,000-25,000, lunch/dinner set menu ₩25,000/35,000; ⊘noon-3pm, 6-10pm; Ⓜ Line 3 to Anguk, Exit 1; 🖥📶) Some of Seoul's most authentic and delicious Indian food is served here in elegant surroundings – it's well worth splashing out.

LOCAL KNOWLEDGE

BUKCHON'S HIDDEN TREASURES

Editor of the monthly magazine *Seoul* and author of guidebooks to Seoul and Korea, Robert Koehler has lived in Korea for over 15 years. Dressed in traditional Korean clothing, Koehler conducts Saturday-afternoon walking tours of Bukchon (see p63) during which he waxes lyrical about one of his favourite topics: architecture. We asked him for the scoop on the hidden gems of this increasingly touristed area.

Best Coffee
Kopi Bangasgan (p60) is run by an interesting character who used to work in IT but then moved into brewing coffee. I like the way he's renovated the *hanok* to make this cafe – it still looks like it's lived in, like a Korean grandmother's house. Sitting inside you can see the tiled roofs of other *hanok* outside.

Best Gimbap
Joseon Gimbap (p57) is just a hole in the wall that's right behind a construction site, but it serves *gimbap* to die for.

Best Hanok
Simsimheon (p49) Even though it's on one of Bukchon's busiest streets, hardly anyone goes here. Plus they serve wonderful tea.

Best Pumpkin Rice Cake
Cha Masineun Tteul (p61) is a beautifully renovated *hanok* with an internal garden and huge plate-glass window providing views over the area. But it's the wonderful pumpkin rice cakes they serve that I love the most.

Best Guesthouse
Rak-Ko-Jae (p134) A delightfully subtle experience, that's its own little world, a million miles from modern Seoul. The rooms don't even have TVs!

HARVEST KOREAN $$

Map p195 (747 5056; Gye-dong-gil; meals ₩13,000-35,000; noon-3pm, 6-10pm Mon-Sat; Line 3 to Anguk, Exit 3) Four friendly brothers run this super stylish, light-filled restaurant specialising in North Korean dishes from the province of Hwanghae. Try the chicken dish where you mix the rice with a thin consommé soup or *onjin bulgagi*. They sometimes hold Sunday flea markets on the courtyard in front of the restaurant.

KOONG DUMPLINGS $

Map p198 (궁; 733 9240; www.koong.co.kr; Insa-dong 10-gil, Insa-dong; dumplings ₩7000; 11.30am-9.30pm; Line 3 to Anguk, Exit 6) Koong's traditional Kaeseong-style dumplings are legendary. Enjoy them in a flavourful soup along with chewy balls of rice cake.

GOGUNG KOREAN $$

Map p198 (고궁; 736 3211; www.gogung.co.kr; Ssamziegil, Insa-dong-gil, Insa-dong; meals from ₩8000-12,000; 11am-10pm; Line 3 to Anguk, Exit 6) In the basement of Ssamziegil is this smart and stylish restaurant, specialising in Jeonju (capital of Jeollabuk Province) *bibimbap*, which is fresh and garnished with nuts, but contains raw minced beef. The *dolsot bibimbap* is served in a stone hotpot. Both come with side dishes. Also try the *moju*, a sweet, cinnamon homebrew drink.

JIRISAN KOREAN $$

Map p198 (지리산; 723 4696; off Insa-dong 14-gil, Insa-dong; meals from ₩10,000; noon-10pm; Line 3 to Anguk, Exit 6) This authentic restaurant is a great place to try *dolsotbap* (hotpot rice, ₩10,000). Various ingredients are added to the rice, and you mix it all up in a separate bowl with the sauces and side dishes – a do-it-yourself *bibimbap*. Pour the weak burnt-rice tea from the kettle into the stone pot and put the lid on, then drink it at the end of the meal.

OSEGYEHYANG VEGAN $

Map p198 (오세계향; www.go5.co.kr; Insa-dong 12-gil, Insa-dong; meals from ₩7000; noon-3pm & 4-9pm; Line 3 to Anguk, Exit 6) Run by members of a Taiwanese religious sect, the vegetarian food combines all sorts of mixtures and flavours. The barbecue-meat-substitute dish is flavoursome. Non-alcoholic beer and wine is served.

CHILGAPSAN KOREAN $$

off Map p198 (칠갑산; 730 7754; Sambong-gil; meals ₩6000-13,000; 11.30am-10pm; Line 1 to Jonggak, Exit 2) This convivial restaurant's specialty is excellent *neobiani*, a beef patty the size of a small pizza. Meant for sharing, it comes with a dressed green salad. The barley and rice *bibimbap* is original – you mix in *doenjang jjigae* rather than *gochujang*. Look for a building with a white frontage covered with ivy.

SADONGMYEONOK DUMPLINGS $

Map p198 (사동면옥; 735 7393; Insa-dong 8-gil, Insa-dong; dumplings ₩6000; Line 3 to Anguk, Exit 6) This bright and breezy eatery is hidden away, but is usually busy and has a long menu. It's famous for *manduguk* – because the dumplings are the largest you'll see (three make a meal). Also famous is the platter of *haemul pajeon* (seafood pancake, ₩10,000), known for its size, crispiness and the big chunks of octopus.

DEJANGJANGI HWADEOGPIJAJIP PIZZERIA $$

Map p195 (대장장이 화덕 피자집; 765 4298; Gahoe-dong; pizza ₩16,000-20,000; 11.30am-10pm; Line 3 to Anguk, Exit 2;) *Daijangjangi* means blacksmith and that is exactly what the owner Lee Jae-Sung is. Some of his metal creations adorn the quirky interior of this *hanok* turned pizzeria, along with Lee's epic LP collection. The pizza is authentic and the service friendly.

SOLMOE-MAEUL KOREAN $$

Map p195 (솔뫼마을; 720 0995; Samcheong-dong gil; mains ₩8000-15,000; Line 3 to Anguk, Exit 1;) Sit on the floor or on chairs on the narrow balcony to enjoy an excellent multi-course meal for ₩22,000 that includes *bulgogi*. The *gujeolpan* is a speciality with pink radish wraps, as is the *pajeon* and the sprouty version of *bibimbap*. A bit of a walk from the subway but you'll need some exercise after this generous Korean feast.

SAMCHEONG-DONG SUJEBI KOREAN $

Map p195 (삼청동 수제비 전문; 735 2965; Samcheong-gil; meals ₩7000; 11.30am-9pm; Line 3 to Anguk, Exit 1;) A no-frills, no-nonsense restaurant that's famous for its *sujebi*, big dough flakes in a mild soup of sliced vegetables and shellfish. *Dongdongju* (fermented rice wine) goes well with the meal – in fact, for some diners the *sujebi* is just an excuse to enjoy some *dongdongju*.

SEOURESEO DULJJAERO
JALHANEUNJIP
DESSERT $

off Map p195 (서울서둘째로잘하는집; Samcheong-ro; desserts ₩6000; ⊙noon-9pm; Ⓜ Line 3 to Anguk, Exit 1) Little has changed at 'Second Best Place in Seoul' a tiny tea and dessert cafe, since it opened in 1976. Apart from the medicinal teas they serve wonderful thick *danpatjuk*, red-bean porridge with ginseng, chestnut and peanuts.

CHEONJINPOJA
DUMPLINGS $$

Map p195 (천진포자; Insa-dong; meals ₩5000; ⊙10am-7pm; Ⓜ Line 3 to Anguk, Exit 6) This simple place serves tasty handmade meat, seafood or vegetable-stuffed dumplings. A few doors up the road another branch specialises in noodles.

HWANGGEUMJEONG
BARBECUEQ $$

Map p195 (황금정; Bukchon-ro; meals ₩10,000-15,000; ⊙10am-10pm; Ⓜ Line 3 to Anguk, Exit 2) Sit inside or outside at this friendly neighbourhood barbecue joint, where diners grill up pork ribs or strips to eat with salad and side dishes. Order rice or *naengmyeon* for a more substantial meal. Just a dozen steps from the subway exit.

🍷 DRINKING & NIGHTLIFE

Gwanghwamun & Around

ET M'AMIE
TEAHOUSE

Map p200 (Tongui-dong; ⊙11am-11pm; Ⓜ Line 3 to Gyeonbokgung, Exit 5) A rabbit poking its head from a lampshade, attractive print wallpaper, curtains and upholstery add to the charm of this *salon de thé* serving Mariage Frères teas and home-baked goodies. Treat yourself to their afternoon tea tray for ₩24,000 for two.

MK2
CAFE

Map p200 (Tongui-dong; ⊙11am-11pm; Ⓜ Line 3 to Gyeonbokgung, Exit 5) The name indicates the style of this cafe, which is tastefully furnished with mid-century modern pieces. It's a good pit stop for coffee and snacks while touring the galleries of Tongui-dong.

CAFÉ IMA
CAFE

Map p200 (Sejong-daero; ⊙10am-10pm Mon-Sat, 11.30am-8pm Sun; Ⓜ Line 5 to Gwanghwamun,

Exit 8) This casual, spacious cafe is on the ground floor of the Ilim Museum of Art, which is housed in the attractive 1920s building that once was home to the Dong-A Ilbo (East Asia Daily) newspaper. It's handy if you've been walking around Gwanghwamun Square or along the Cheong-gye-cheon.

Insa-dong, Bukchon & Samcheong-dong

🅣🅞🅟 DAWON
TEAHOUSE

Map p198 (다원; Insa-dong 8-gil, Insa-dong; teas ₩7000; ⊙11am-11pm; Ⓜ Line 3 to Anguk, Exit 6) The perfect place to unwind on a warm summer evening is under the shady fruit trees in this courtyard with flickering candles. In winter sit indoors in *hanok* rooms decorated with scribbles or in the garden pavilion. Small exhibition spaces surround the courtyard. The teas are superb, especially *omijacha hwachae* (fruit and five-flavour berry punch), a summer drink.

🅣🅞🅟 BAEKSEJU-MAEUL
BAR

Map p198 (백세주마을; ☑720 0055; www.ksdb.co.kr; Ⓜ Line 2 to Jonggak, Exit 4) See the website's English pages to learn more about the excellent range of traditional rice wines available at this drinking and dining outlet for brewer Kooksoondang. There are several other branches dotted around Seoul including in Daehangno, Sinchon and Gangnam.

KOPI BANGASGAN
CAFE

Map p195 (커피 방앗간; ⊙8am-11pm) Based in a *hanok*, 'Coffee Mill' is a charming spot decorated with retro pieces and the quirky, colourful artworks of owner Lee Gyeonghwan whom you're likely to spot painting at the counter. The bags of fair-trade roasted coffee beans have his cute drawings on, too. Apart from various coffees they also serve waffles.

PUB OF THE BLUE STAR
BAR

Map p198 (off Insa-dong 16-gil, Insa-dong; ⊙3pm-midnight; Ⓜ Line 3 to Anguk, Exit 6) Owned by a stage actor this rustic hang-out, plastered with posters, is a good place to sample traditional *makgeolli* rice wine served out of brass kettles into brass bowls. Order slices of their homemade tofu and kimchi to eat as you drink.

LOCAL KNOWLEDGE

NAGWON-DONG & DONUI-DONG GAY BARS

For most international visitors, queer Seoul amounts to Itaewon's 'Homo Hill' (see p92). However, for Korean *iban* (gay men and women) the most popular area of town is between Tapgol Park and Jongno 3-ga subway station, an area that supports around 100 gay bars and small clubs. Not all are welcoming of foreigners, or will expect patrons to pay a hefty cover charge for *anju* (snacks).

'One-shot bars' where you can drink without a cover charge include:

Barcode (Map p198; ⊘7pm-4am; MLines 1, 3 & 5 to Jongno 3-ga, Exit 3) Run by friendly English-speaking Kim Hyoung-Jin, this stylish place is on the second floor – look for the English sign as you come out of the subway.

Shortbus (Map p198; ⊘7pm-4am; MLines 1, 3 & 5 to Jongno 3-ga, Exit 3) A wine and cocktail bar that is appealing, spacious and mixes a mean mojito. It's on the third floor with an English sign.

Bar Friends (Map p198; ⊘7pm-4am; MLines 1, 3 & 5 to Jongno 3-ga, Exit 5) A fluttering rainbow flag outside marks this basement bar that is comfy and friendly to foreigners.

Alternatively drop by the outdoor *pojangmacha* food stalls around Jongno 3-ga to sink cheap beer, soju and snacks with the gay community. The cafe **Coffee Bean & Tea Leaf** (Map p198) at the back of the Fraser Suites is also a popular gay hang-out.

CHA MASINEUN TTEUL
TEAHOUSE

Map p195 (차마시는뜰; ⊘8am-11pm) Overlooking Samcheong-dong from Bukchon is this lovely *hanok* with low tables arranged around a courtyard. They serve traditional teas and a delicious bright yellow pumpkin rice cake that is served fresh from the steamer.

DALSAENEUN DALMAN SAENGGAK HANDA
TEAHOUSE

Map p198 (달새는 달만 생각한다; Insa-dong 12-gil, Insa-dong; teas ₩6500-9000; ⊘10am-11pm; MLine 3 to Anguk, Exit 6) 'Moon Bird Thinks Only of the Moon' is packed with plants and rustic artefacts. Bird song, soothing music and trickling water add to the atmosphere. Huddle in a cubicle and savour one of their teas, which include *gamnipcha* (persimmon-leaf tea). *Saenggangcha* (ginger tea) is peppery but sweet.

YETCHATJIP
TEAHOUSE

Map p198 (옛찻집; Insa-dong 6-gil, Insa-dong; ⊘10am-11pm; MLine 3 to Anguk, Exit 6) Half a dozen little songbirds fly around inside the 'Old Teashop'. Ethereal music, water features and candles add to the ambience – even the unique toilets do their bit. Antique bric-a-brac so clutters this hobbit-sized teashop that it's hard to squeeze past and find somewhere to sit.

DABANG
CAFE

Map p195 (다방; www.mulnamoo.com; Gyedong-gil; ⊘10am-midnight; MLine 3 to Anguk, Exit 2) Sip tea or hand-dripped coffee in this minimalist, retro-styled cafe that's part of a 1930s building that includes a gallery and analogue photo studio.

SAJINGAUN
TEAHOUSE

Map p195 (Bukchon-ro; ⊘noon-midnight Tue-Sun; MLine 3 to Anguk, Exit 2) Wine and beer are also served in this *hanok* teashop that specialises in black teas in many varieties and flavours, making it a good option for a sophisticated late night drink if you're staying in the area. Next door is a *hanok*-based dentist!

DOUBLE CUP COFFEE
TEAHOUSE

Map p195 (Changdeokgung 1-gil; ⊘8am-10pm; MLine 3 to Anguk, Exit 3;) Grab a gourmet roastery coffee and sandwich at this funky cafe while ambling around Bukchon between the palaces.

BEAUTIFUL TEA MUSEUM
TEAHOUSE

Map p198 (www.tmuseum.co.kr; off Insa-dong-gil; ⊘10am-10pm; MLine 3 to Anguk, Exit 6) As well as Korean teas you can sip teas from around the world in the pleasant covered courtyard of a modern *hanok*. Loose leaf teas and tea-making sets and implements are also sold here and there's an exhibition area.

JILSIRU TTEOK CAFÉ DESSERT $

Map p198 (질시루 떡 카페; Donhwamun-ro; www.kfr.or.kr; tteok/set ₩1500/6000; ⊘9am-9pm; MLine 1, 3 or 5 to Jongno 3-ga, Exit 6) Choose from the soft, delicately flavoured handmade gourmet rice cakes *(tteok)* on offer with all sorts of unusual flavours such as citron or coffee. Upstairs is a **museum** (admission ₩3000; ⊘10am-5pm Mon-Sat, noon-5pm Sun) with displays of rice cakes in

---

LOCAL KNOWLEDGE

GALLERIES GALORE

'Visitors to Seoul are often quite surprised by the diversity of art and number of galleries here,' says Monica Cha, owner of Gallery Cha in Tongui-dong west of Gyeongbokgung. Although some major commercial galleries are based south of the Han River, Seoul's eclectic contemporary art scene is concentrated around Insa-dong, Bukchon and Tongui-dong. Unless otherwise mentioned the galleries are free to browse. Most galleries are closed Monday. Useful resources include the free monthly art magazine *ArtnMap* (www.artnmap.com) and *Seoul Art Guide* (in Korean).

Insa-dong

The following are on Map p198. The closest subway station is Anguk, Exit 6.

Hwabong Gallery (⊘737 0057; www.hwabong.com; Insa-dong 7-gil; ⊘10am-7pm) Cutting-edge Korean art is usually on show in two of the galleries, while the third contains the smallest book in the world (no more than a dot), as well as the largest book.

Insa Gallery (⊘735 2655; www.insagallery.net; Insa-dong 10-gil; ⊘10am-6pm) Exhibitions change twice a month. They also have a branch in Cheongdam.

Sun Art Center (⊘734 0458; www.sungallery.co.kr; Insa-dong 5-gil ⊘10am-6pm) Specialises in early 20th-century Korean art.

Tong-gui-dong

The following are on Map p200. The closest subway station is Gyeonbokgung, Exit 5.

Gallery Cha (⊘730 1700; www.gallerycha.com; ⊘11am-6.30pm Mon-Fri, noon-6pm Sat) Specialises in emerging Korean artists.

Jean Art Gallery (⊘738 7570; www.jeanart.net; ⊘10am-6pm Tue-Fri, 10am-5pm Sat & Sun) Pioneer of the Tongui-dong gallery scene. Look for the metallic butterfly sculpture between the gallery's two red-brick buildings; art inside includes a 2m-tall dotted pumpkin sculpture by Japanese artist Yayoi Kusama.

Artside (⊘725 1020; www.artside.org; ⊘10am-6.30pm Tue-Sun) Regularly exhibits contemporary art by Chinese artists.

Gallery Simon (⊘549 3031; http://gallerysimon.com; ⊘10am-6.30pm Tue-Sun) Exhibitions include sculptures and interesting installations. Has a chic top-floor cafe with views over *hanok* roofs.

East of Gyeongbokgung

The following, except Artsonje Center, are all on Map p200. The closest subway station is Anguk, Exit 1.

Artsonje Center (Map p195; ⊘733 8945; www.artsonje.org/asc; adult/child ₩3000/1000; ⊘11am-7pm Tue-Sun) Supports experimental art and has an annual Open Call for new works. Also has a book cafe and art-house cinema.

Gallery Hyundai (⊘287 3500; www.galleryhyundai.com; ⊘10am-6pm) Two outlets close by each other here; their main gallery is in Gangnam.

Hakgojae (⊘720 1524; www.hakgojae.com; ⊘10am-7pm Tue-Sat, to 6pm Sun) Contemporary works in a converted *hanok;* look for the robot sculpture on the roof.

Kukje (⊘735 8449; www.kukjegallery.com; ⊘10am-6pm) There's a second gallery space off the main road. Look up to the roof to see the running woman sculpture by Jonathan Borofsky.

different colours, flavourings, shapes and sizes, plus the utensils to make them.

CAFÉ YEON
CAFE, BAR

Map p195 (Samcheong-ro; ⊘noon-11pm) The *hanok* goes global at this charming 'traveller's hang-out' decorated with colourful cushions, photos and Snoopy items. As well as beer and cocktails they also serve soft drinks and snacks.

TOP CLOUD BAR
BAR

Map p198 (www.topcloud.co.kr; 33rd fl, Jongno Tower, Insa-dong; ⊘8.30pm-midnight; MLine 1 to Jonggak, Exit 3) This candlelit bar with classy staff offers a magical night view of Seoul along with the magic of live jazz music from 7pm to 11pm. If you're hungry they do a buffet for lunch and dinner and there's also a separate swish restaurant.

☆ ENTERTAINMENT

Gwanghwamun & Around

SEJONG CENTRE FOR THE PERFORMING ARTS
THEATRE

Map p200 (세종문화회관; ☑399 1111; www.sejongpac.or.kr; Sejong-daero, Gwanghwamun; MLine 5 to Gwanghwamun, Exit 1) This leading arts complex puts on major drama, music and art shows – everything from large-scale musicals to fusion *gugak* (traditional Korean music) and Romany violinists. It has a grand hall, a small theatre and three art galleries.

Insa-dong, Bukchon & Samcheong-dong

CINEMATHEQUE/ SEOUL ARTS CINEMA
CINEMA

Map p198 (☑741 9782; www.cinematheque.seoul.kr; 4th fl, Nagwon Arcade, Nagwon-dong; tickets ₩5000; MLines 1, 3 & 5 to Jongno 3-ga, Exit 5) Catch independent and foreign films (with subtitles in Korean) at this arts cinema where you'll also find Hollywood golden oldies screening at the Silver Cinema. Some Korean films may have English subtitles but it's best to check first. Various film festivals and retrospectives are held here including the annual LGBT Film Festival in May.

SHOPPING

Gwanghwamun & Around

TOP CHOICE ❯ KYOBO BOOKSHOP
BOOKS, MUSIC

Map p200 (B1, Kyobo Bldg, Jongno; MLine 5 to Gwanghwamun, Exit 4) The flagship branch of this famous bookstore sells a wide range of English-language books and magazines, as well as stationery, gifts, electronics and CDs and DVDs in their excellent Hottracks (www.hottracks.co.kr) section. Join their membership club (it's free and easy) for instant discounts.

SEOUL SELECTION
BOOKS, DVDS

Map p200 (☑734 9565; www.seoulselection.co.kr; ⊘9.30am-6.30pm Mon-Sat; MLine 3 to Anguk, Exit 1; @) Sells new and secondhand books on Korean culture in English, along with Korean CDs and Korean movies and drama series on DVD (with English subtitles). Staff speak English and can recommend titles. Also serves drinks and has free internet surfing. The website has an excellent monthly newsletter about what's on in Seoul and they run English language walking tours of Bukchon every Saturday (₩30,000).

MARKET M*
HOMEWARES

Map p200 (www.market-m.co.kr; Tongin-dong; ⊘12.30-8pm Mon-Thu, until 7pm Fri-Sun; MLine 3 to Gyeongbokgung, Exit 2) Like a compact, upmarket version of Ikea, this market sells well-designed, simple wooden furniture and other products such as bags, storage and stationery from Korea and Japan. Their own brand leather slippers and waxed paper bags by Siwa are delightful. Check with them about rental of a *hanok* they own in the area.

Insa-dong, Bukchon & Samcheong-dong

TOP CHOICE ❯ KCDF GALLERY
CRAFT

Map p198 (www.kcdf.kr; Insa-dong 11-gil; MLine 3 to Anguk, Exit 6) The Korean Craft and Design Foundation's gallery has a shop on the ground floor showcasing some of the finest locally made products including woodwork, pottery and jewellery. It's a great place to find a unique, sophisticated gift or souvenir.

SSAMZIEGIL
HANDICRAFTS

Map p198 (www.ssamzigil.com; Insa-dong-gil, Insa-dong; Ⓜ Line 3 to Anguk, Exit 6) This attractive, arty four-storey complex built around a courtyard is a popular stop for one-off clothing, accessories or household goods. In the basement look for **Cerawork** (www.cerawork.co.kr) where you can paint your own design onto pottery for a unique souvenir.

JONGINAMOO
HOMEWARES

Map p195 (종이나무; http://jonginamoo.com; Jae-dong; ⊘10am-10pm Mon-Sat, noon-10pm Sun; Ⓜ Line 3 to Anguk, Exit 2) Selling beautiful traditional styled furniture and decorative pieces for your home including a variety of lamps with shades made of *hanji* (handmade paper).

O'SULLOC
TEA

Map p198 (www.osulloc.com; Insa-dong-gil; Ⓜ Line 3 to Anguk, Exit 6) A variety of nicely packaged teas grown at the company's plantations on Jeju-do (Jeju Island) as well as tea-making implements are on offer here. A cafe upstairs serves up the mainly green teas in all sorts of drinkable and edible ways and there's a premium tasting lounge on the top floor.

KUKJAE EMBROIDERY
HANDICRAFTS

Map p198 (www.suyeh.co.kr; Insa-dong-gil, Insa-dong; Ⓜ Line 3 to Anguk, Exit 6) Exquisite traditional embroidery pieces from Kukjae have often been presented as official gifts by Korean presidents to visiting dignitaries.

ROOM TO ROAM
SOUVENIRS

Map p195 (www.roomtoroam.kr; 5na-gil, Bukchon-ro; Ⓜ Line 3 to Anguk, Exit 1) Billing itself as a 'creative space for creative minds' this shop-cafe is worth a look while strolling around Bukchon. It sells a variety of products by Korean and international designers – unusual souvenir items such as mugs, T-shirts, bags, accessories and toys.

NAKWON MUSICAL INSTRUMENTS ARCADE
MUSICAL INSTRUMENTS

Map p198 (Samil-daero, Insa-dong; ⊘10am-7.30pm Mon-Sat; Ⓜ Line 1, 3 & 5 to Jongno 3-ga, Exit 5) Want a pink guitar or an orange banjo? Browse the vast variety of musical instruments and equipment of all kinds spread over the 2nd and 3rd floors of this large arcade in a dazzling maze of shops.

✐ MERA HATT
FASHION, CRAFT

Map p198 (Insa-dong-gil; ⊘11am-8.30pm Mon-Sat, noon-8pm Sun; Ⓜ Line 3 to Anguk, Exit 6) Apart from handmade, fair-trade womens' clothing and accessories in subtly natural shades, Mera Hatt also sells organic tea, coffee and chocolate.

MAISON DE SISON
ACCESSORIES

Map p195 (Gahoe-dong; ⊘10am-6pm Tue-Sun; Ⓜ Line 3 to Anguk, Exit 3) Designer Sison Jung's colourful reinterpretations of traditional patterns and styles on bags, blankets, pillows and other items are eye-catching.

Myeong-dong & Jung-gu

Neighbourhood Top Five

1 Climb or ride the cable car up **Namsan**, topped by **N Seoul Tower** (p67); the 262m central city peak is a leafy retreat from Myeong-dong's commercial throng.

2 Haggle day and night with the vendors at the mammoth **Namdaemun Market** (p75).

3 Learn about traditional Korean houses and culture at **Namsangol Hanok Village** (p70).

4 Go shopping crazy on the packed, neon-festooned streets of **Myeong-dong** (p75).

5 Enjoy the changing of the guard outside **Deoksugung** (p69) and wander the pleasant palace grounds.

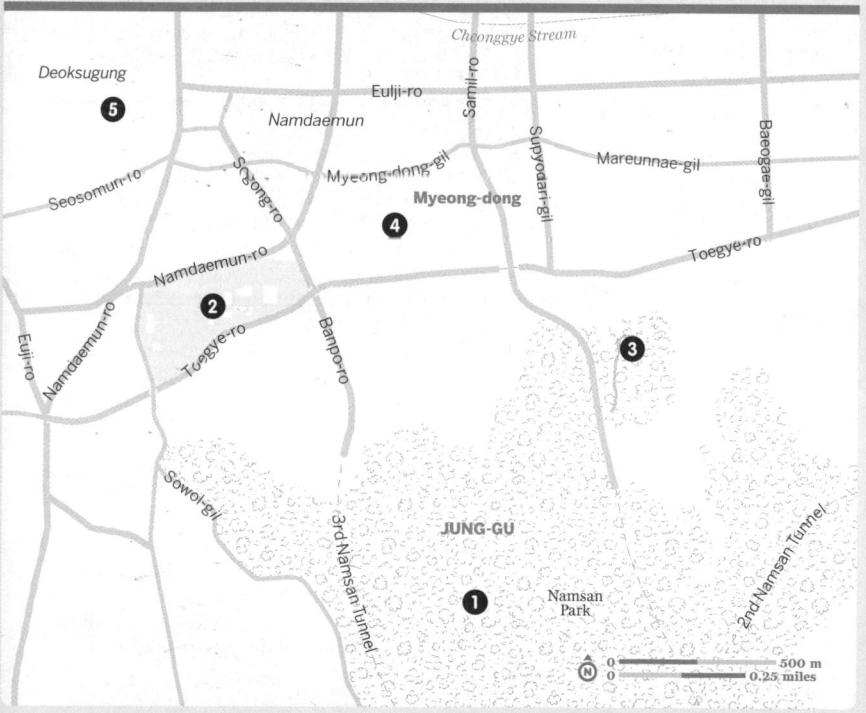

For more detail of this area, see Map p202 ➡

Lonely Planet's Top Tip

On the roof of the original Shinsegae building is Trinity Garden, dotted with sculptures by Alexander Calder, Henry Moore, Joan Miró and Jeff Koons among others; there's a cafe or you could enjoy a picnic of goodies bought from the department store's food hall.

 ### Best Places to Eat

➡ Myeong-dong Gyoja (p72)

➡ Mokmyeoksanbang (p72)

➡ Chung-jeong-gak (p72)

For reviews, p72 ➡

 ### Best Shopping

➡ Namdaemun Market (p68)

➡ Shinsegae (p75)

➡ Level 5 (p75)

For reviews, p75 ➡

 ### Best Entertainment

➡ Nanta (p74)

➡ Chongdong Theatre (p74)

➡ Korea House (p73)

For reviews, see p74 ➡

Explore: Myeong-dong & Jung-gu

Branding itself the city's belly button, Jung-gu (www.junggu.seoul.kr) stretches from the southern city gate of Sungnyemun (Namdaemun) and round-the-clock Namdaemun Market towards the eastern gate of Heunginjimun (Dongdaemun). Dominating the district's heart is the youth fashion shopping area of Myeong-dong. Myeong means 'light' – apt for an area where Seoul's commercial razzle-dazzle reaches its apogee.

They may be almost traffic-free, but Myeong-dong's streets and alleyways are invariably teeming with shoppers. Masses of boutiques cater to every youthful style tribe, along with plenty of cafes, restaurants, department stores and high-rise shopping malls with food courts, spas and cinema multiplexes. Japanese visitors in particular adore it and you'll often hear shop and stall vendors address the crowd in that language. The mass of humanity, noise and visual stimulation can become overwhelming, but don't let that put you off spending some time soaking up the electric atmosphere and indulging in retail therapy.

Tranquillity can be regained on nearby Namsan, downtown Seoul's green lung, its hiking trails, parkland and old Fortress Walls newly spruced up. Also providing a change of pace is the area to the west of Seoul Plaza and City Hall. Here you'll find Deoksugung, a lovely palace around which early missionaries built Seoul's first Protestant churches and schools, and where foreign legations were based; many old buildings have been preserved and it's a fine area for leisurely exploring.

Local Life

➡ **Sunday Worship** Attend a service at either the historic Myeong-dong Catholic Cathedral or the Romanesque style Anglican Church (Map p202).

➡ **Get Fit** Join locals stretching their legs and keeping fit on the Northern Namsan Belt Way; for an extra workout drop by the large outdoor gym behind the National Theatre of Korea.

➡ **Free Concerts** From mid-May to the end of August grassy Seoul Plaza fronting the City Hall is the scene for free performances most nights. In summer there's also a water fountain that kids love to splash in.

Getting There & Away

➡ **Subway** Line 4 connects Seoul Station with Namdaemun Market, Myeong-dong and Chungmuro for the Namsangol Hanok Village

➡ **Bus/Cable Car** Taxis are banned from going to the top of Namsan, so use one of the eco-friendly buses or hop on the cable car.

TOP SIGHTS
NAMSAN & N SEOUL TOWER

Beloved by locals as a place for exercise, peaceful contemplation and hanging out with loved ones, Namsan was a sacred shamanistic spot when the Joseon ruler Taejo ordered the construction of a fortress wall across this and Seoul's three other guardian mountains. The mountain is protected within a 109-hectare park and crowned by one of the city's most iconic features: N Seoul Tower.

Historic Structures

Sections of the original Fortress Walls still snake across Namsan (남산); near the summit you can also see the **Bongoodae** (signal beacons), a communications system used for 500 years to notify the central government of urgent political and military information. A traditional lighting ceremony is held here between 10am and 12.30pm Tuesday to Sunday.

In the 1920s the Japanese built a Shinto shrine on the mountain, removing the shamanist prayer hall Guksadang from Namsan's summit in the process (it was rebuilt on Mt Inwangsan).

Northern Namsan Circuit

Over the last few years the city has been restoring parts of the Fortress Walls and parks and trails on the mountain. Along the Namsan Northern Circuit, a pedestrian path that snakes for 3km from the lower cable-car station to the National Theatre, you'll find **Waryongmyo** (⏲8am-4pm), a Buddhist/Taoist/shamanist shrine dedicated to Zhuge Liang (AD 181–234), a Chinese statesman and general.

Further along is the archery practice ground and hall for the **Korea Whal Culture Association** (www.korea-bow.or.kr; for 20 arrows ₩2000; ⏲9am-6.30pm); *whal* means bow and Koreans have trained expert archers for centuries and you can practice firing arrows, too. Nearby, behind the National Theatre of Korea, is an excellent outdoor gym maintained by the Chung Chung Athletic Association.

Southern Namsan Circuit

The Southern Namsan Circuit has a pedestrian path and a road used by buses. It cuts through the old Fortress Wall. Accessed from the Southern Namsan Circuit or via a pedestrian bridge over the road from near the Grand Hyatt is the Namsan Outdoor Botanical Garden. Paths lead from here through more wooded sections of Namsan Park where you'll find a firefly habitat.

Modern Attractions

Riding the **cable car** (one-way/return adult ₩6000/8000, child ₩3500/5000; ⏲10am-11pm) to **N Seoul Tower** (서울 타워; www.nseoultower.com; adult/child ₩9000/5000; ⏲observatory 10am-11pm) is Namsan's most popular attraction these days. If the weather's fine, the tower's observation deck offers panoramic views. At sunset you can watch the city morph into a galaxy of twinkling lights.

The tower has become a hot date spot, with the railings around it festooned with padlocks inscribed with lovers' names.

TOP SIGHTS
NAMDAEMUN MARKET & AROUND

DAJ / GETTY IMAGES ©

At this sprawling round-the-clock market you can find pretty much anything – from food and flowers to spectacles and camera equipment. It can be a confusing place; get your bearings from the numbered gates on the periphery.

What's on Sale

Haggling is the mode of business. Different sections have different opening hours and some shops open on Sunday, although that's not the best time to visit. Look out for **Alpha** (Gate 2; ⊘8.30am-8pm Mon-Sat, 10.30am-7pm Sun), which sells toys and stationery over many floors; **Samho Woojoo** (Gate 3; ⊘hours vary) has a jaw-dropping amount of fashion jewellery. Camera shops are clustered near Gate 1.

Dining Options

Small stalls selling *sujebi* (dough and shellfish soup), homemade *kalguksu* noodles and *bibimbap* (mixed rice, meat and vegetables) for around ₩5000 to ₩6000 are clustered near Gate 6 on Kalguksu Alley. Haejangguk Alley, between Gates 2 and 3, is lined with small cafes selling Korean food – all with plastic replicas outside to make choosing easy. Next to Gate 2 is a great stall selling veggie *hotteok* (deep-fried pancakes) for ₩1000 and toasted sandwiches filled with freshly made omelettes (₩1200) or ham and cheese (₩1700).

Sungnyemun (Namdaemun)

Seoul's Great South Gate, known as Namdaemun, was destroyed by arson in 2008. Four years of painstaking reconstruction of Korea's No 1 National Treasure are nearing completion and the wraps should now be off a reborn **Sungnyemun** (www.sungnyemun.or.kr). The wood and stone gateway stands on an island amid major roads; check the website for visiting details.

DON'T MISS

→ Namdaemun Market
→ Sungnyemun
→ Kalguksu and Haejangguk food alleys

PRACTICALITIES

→ Map p202
→ ⊘24 hours
→ Ⓜ Line 4 to Hoehyeon, Exit 5

TOP SIGHTS
DEOKSUGUNG

Deoksugung (meaning Palace of Virtuous Longevity) is the only one of the four main palaces that you can visit in the evening to enjoy a quieter atmosphere and see the buildings – both traditional Korean and Western-style neo-classical structures – illuminated. The palace's main gate is also the scene of a picturesque changing of the guard ceremony three times a day.

DON'T MISS

➡ Changing of the Guard

➡ Jeonggwan-heon

➡ Junghwa-jeon

➡ Seokjo-jeon

PRACTICALITIES

➡ Map p202

➡ www.deoksugung.go.kr

➡ adult/child ₩1000/500

➡ ⊘9am-9pm Tue-Sun

➡ Ⓜ Line 1 or 2 to City Hall, Exit 2

Palace History

Deoksugung (덕수궁) became a palace in 1593 when King Seonjo moved in after all of Seoul's other palaces were destroyed during the Japanese invasion. Despite two kings being crowned here, it became a secondary palace from 1615 until 1897 when Emperor Gojong took up residence so he could be close to where foreign legations were concentrated in the city at the time. Forced by the Japanese to abdicate 10 years later, Gojong carried on living here in some style until he died in 1919.

The palace used to be three times as big as it is now. Hwangudan, the Altar to Heaven, where Gojong performed rituals related to Korea's standing as an 'empire', was inside the grounds but is now tucked behind the Westin Chosun across Seoul Plaza.

Palace Buildings

Deoksugung is a potpourri of contrasting architectural styles. Junghwa-jeon, the palace's main throne hall is adorned with dragons and has golden window frames. Behind it is the mini Buckingham Palace–style Seokjo-jeon, designed by British architect GR Harding and completed in 1910, and a western wing designed by a Japanese architect in the late 1930s. Both were closed for restoration at the time of research but should now be open as an annex of the National Museum of Contemporary Art.

Behind Gojong's living quarters, Hamnyeong-jeon, is the interesting fusion-style pavilion Jeonggwan-heon designed by Russian architect Aleksey Seredin-Sabatin as a place for the emperor to savour coffee and entertain guests. Gojong developed a taste for the beverage while holed up for a year in the Russian legation following the assassination of Queen Min. The pavilion's pillars, a veranda and metal railings are decorated with deer and bats – both auspicious creatures.

The stone mythical creatures in the main courtyard are *haechi,* which are supposed to protect the palace from fire. In 1904 they must have fallen asleep as the palace burnt down.

Daily Events

The **changing of the guards** (⊘11am, 2pm & 3.30pm Tue-Sun) is an impressive ceremony involving 50 participants, who dress up as Joseon-era soldiers and bandsmen. It happens at the Daehanmun main gate next to the ticket office facing Seoul Plaza. After the first ceremony of the day the guard marches to the Bosingak pavilion, and after the last to Gwanghwamun Sq.

Free guided tours of the palace (in English) take place at 10.30am Tuesday to Friday, and at 1.40pm on Saturday in January, March, May, July, September and November, and 1.40pm on Sundays in other months.

⊙ SIGHTS

N SEOUL TOWER VIEWPOINT
See p67.

NAMDAEMUN MARKET MARKET
See p68.

DEOKSUGUNG PALACE
See p69.

FREE **NAMSANGOL HANOK VILLAGE** ARCHITECTURE
Map p202 (남산골한옥마을; http://hanokmae ul.seoul.go.kr; Chungmuro; ⊙9am-9pm Wed-Mon Apr-Oct, to 8pm Wed-Mon Nov-Mar; ⒨Line 3 or 4 to Chungmuro, Exit 4) Five differing *yangban* (upper class) houses from the Joseon era have been moved to this park at the foot of Namsan from different parts of Seoul. The architecture and furniture are austere and plain, and conjure up the lost world of Confucian gentlemen scholars, who wielded calligraphy brushes rather than swords.

Also in the village you'll find **Seoul Namsan Gugakdang** (☑2261 0512; http://sngad. sejongpac.or.kr; tickets from ₩20,000) where traditional music and dance concerts are staged most evenings and you can also dress up in *hanbok* (traditional costumes). It costs ₩10,000 or ₩15,000 with drink at **teahouse** (⊙10-11.30am & 1-5.30pm). Displays of the traditional Korean martial art taekwondo are staged in the village at 11am, 2pm and 5pm Wednesday and Saturday; to take part make a reservation via www.taek wonseoul.org.

On the right of the entrance gate is an **office** (⊙10.30am-3.30pm) that provides free tour guides around the village and where you can also find out about various cultural programs including calligraphy, making traditional paper (*hanji*), kites and masks.

FREE **SEOUL MUSEUM OF ART** MUSEUM
Map p202 (서울시립미술관; http://seoulmoa. seoul.go.kr; Jeong-dong; ⊙10am-8pm Tue-Sun Mar-Oct, until 7pm Nov-Feb; ⒨Line 1 or 2 to City Hall, Exit 2) Hosting top-notch exhibitions that are always worth a visit, this museum has ultra-modern, bright galleries inside the handsome brick-and-stone facade of the 1927 Supreme Court building. For some special exhibitions an entrance fee is charged.

CITY HALL ARCHITECTURE
Map p202 (http://english.seoul.go.kr; ⒨Line 1 or 2 to City Hall, Exit 5) Looking like a tsunami made of glass and steel, the new City Hall is set for completion in early 2013. It is a modern re-interpretation of traditional Korean design; the cresting wave providing shade (like eaves found on palaces and temple roofs) over the handsome old City Hall which was built from stone in 1926.

Seoul Plaza fronting City Hall is the scene for events and free performances most nights during the summer as well as an outdoor ice-skating rink for a couple of months each winter.

MYEONG-DONG CATHOLIC CATHEDRAL CHURCH
Map p202 (명동 성당; ☑774 1784; www.mdsd. or.kr; Myeong-dong; ⒨Line 4 to Myeong-dong, Exit 6) Go inside this elegant, red- and grey-brick Gothic-style cathedral, consecrated in 1898, to admire the vaulted ceiling and stained-glass windows. The cathedral provided a sanctuary for student and trade-union protestors during military rule, becoming a national symbol of democracy and human rights. A new entrance plaza is under construction and set for completion in a couple of years.

PLATEAU ART GALLERY
Map p202 (www.plateau.or.kr; Taepyeongno 2-ga; adult/child ₩3000/2000; ⊙10am-6pm Tue-Sun; ⒨Line 1 or 2 to City Hall, Exit 8) Sponsored by Samsung, and formerly known as the Rodin Gallery, this unusual glass pavilion was built to house castings of two monumental sculptures by Auguste Rodin: *The Gates of Hell* and *The Burgers of Calais*. Changing contemporary art exhibitions are staged in two additional gallery spaces.

FREE **CULTURE STATION SEOUL 284** ARCHITECTURE, GALLERY
Map p202 (www.seoul284.org; Tongil-ro; ⊙10am-7pm Tue-Sun; ⒨Line 1 or 4 to Seoul Station, Exit 2) This grand 1925 building with a domed roof has been beautifully restored inside and out and made into a cultural arts space staging a variety of events under the auspices of the Korea Craft & Design Foundation (KCDF). The number 284 refers to the station's historic site number.

FREE **BANK OF KOREA MUSEUM** MUSEUM
Map p202 (museum.bok.or.kr; Myeong-dong; ⊙10am-5pm Tue-Sun; ⒨Line 4 to Hoehyeon, Exit 7) Built in 1912, and an outstanding example of Japanese colonial architecture, the old

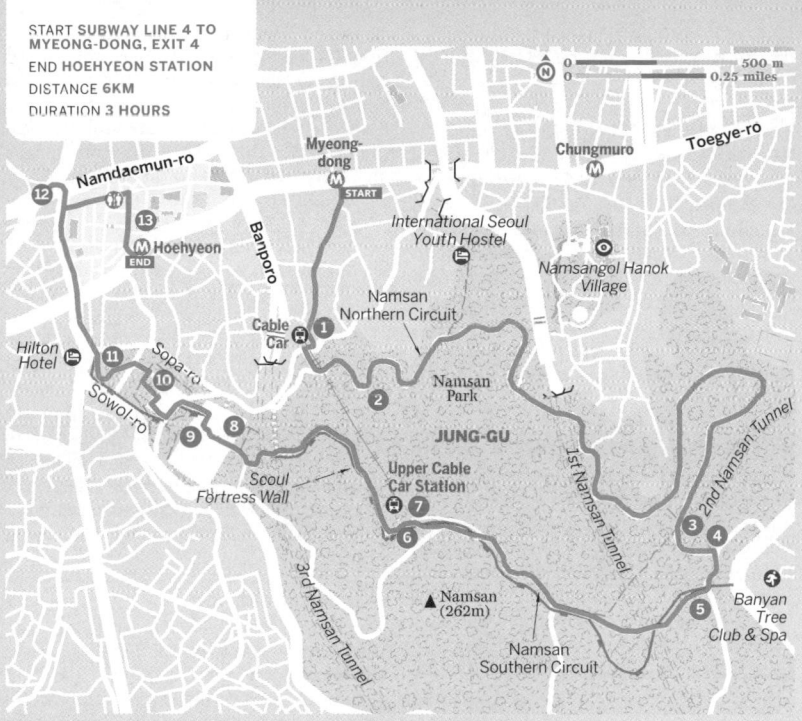

Neighbourhood Walk
Namsan Circuit

Following pedestrian pathways and parts of the Seoul Fortress Walls, this hike takes you around and over Namsan, providing sweeping city views along the way and a chance to enjoy the mountain's greenery and fresh air. It's best done early in the morning, but leafy trees do provide some shade most of the way. From the subway exit walk up to the **①** **cable car station**; just before you reach here you'll see steps leading up the mountainside to the pedestrian-only Namsan Northern Circuit.

Walk left for five minutes, and pause to look around the shrine **②** **Waryongmyo**, before following the road as it undulates gently around the mountain, past routes down to Namsangol Hanok Village and Dongguk University, until you reach the **③** **outdoor gym**, uphill from the National Theatre of Korea.

You can cut out the next bit by hopping on one of the buses that go to the peak from the **④** **bus stop** near here. Otherwise turn right at the start of the Namsan Southern

Circuit road and you'll soon see the **⑤** **Fortress Walls**. A steep set of steps shadows the wall for part of the way to the summit; at the fork continue on the steps over the wall and follow the path to **⑥** **N Seoul Tower** and the **⑦** **Bongoodae** (signal beacons).

Grab some refreshments to enjoy at the geological centre of Seoul, before picking up the Fortress Wall trail down to pretty **⑧** **Joongang Park**. On the left is **⑨** **Ahn Junggeun Museum** and on the right the tower block housing Seoul Education Research Institute.

A newly created continuation of the park over a road tunnel leads via **⑩** **Baekbeom Square** and **⑪** **Adong Square** down towards the Hilton Hotel; along the way you'll see reconstructed sections of the wall. Finish up taking a look at the reconstruction of **⑫** **Sungnyemun (Namdaemun)**, then browsing **⑬** **Namdaemun Market**.

Bank of Korea now houses a reasonably interesting exhibition on the history of local currency.

FREE AHN JUNG-GEUN MEMORIAL HALL
MUSEUM

Map p202 (www.partriot.ork.kr; ⊙9am-6pm Tue-Sun Mar-Oct, 10am-5pm Tue-Sun Nov-Feb) In a striking contemporary building on the west flank of Namsan, this museum is dedicated to Korean independence fighter Ahn Jung-guen. Ahn assassinated Ito Hirobumi, the Japanese governor-general of Korea, in 1909 at Harbin station in Japanese-controlled Manchuria, a crime he paid for with his life.

FREE SEOUL ANIMATION CENTER
MUSEUM

Map p202 (www.ani.seoul.kr; ⊙9am-5.50pm Tue-Sun; Ⓜ Line 4 to Myeong-dong, Exit 1 or 3) Up the hill on the way to the cable car you'll find this diverting museum and cinema devoted to cartoons and animation – not just from Korea. There's an extensive DVD/video library from which you can choose your favourite animation. It's a good place to distract kids with the images able to break through language barriers.

FREE AGRICULTURE MUSEUM
MUSEUM

(www.agrimuseum.or.kr; ⊙9.30am-5.30pm Tue-Sun; Ⓜ Line 5 to Seodaemun, Exit 5) A promotional exercise by Nonghyup, a national agricultural co-operative, this museum has imaginative displays that relate the history and practice of farming on the Korean peninsula. It's a worthy effort, but probably has small chance of persuading young Koreans that farming is a future career.

✕ EATING

MYEONG-DONG GYOJA
NOODLES $

Map p202 (명동교자; www.mdkj.co.kr; Myeong-dong; noodles ₩8000; Ⓜ Line 4 to Myeong-dong, Exit 8; 🅟) Their special *kalguksu* (noodles in a meat, dumpling and vegetable broth) is famous, so it's busy, busy, busy. If the place is full, there's a second branch further down the street opposite Andong Jjimdak.

MOKMYEOKSANBANG
KOREAN $

Map p202 (목멱산방; Northern Namsan Circuit; mains ₩8000-10,000; ⊙11.30am-8pm; 🅟) Order and pay at the till, then pick up delicious and beautifully presented *bibimbap* from the kitchen when your electronic buzzer rings to pick up. The traditional wooden house in which the restaurant is based is named after the ancient name for Namsan (Mokmyeok); they also serve Korean teas and *makgeolli* (rice wine) in brass kettles.

CHUNG-JEONG-GAK
ITALIAN $$

(충정각; 🅙313 0424; www.chungjeonggak.com; Chungjeong-ro; mains ₩15,000; set menu from ₩20,000; ⊙10am-11pm Mon-Sat; Ⓜ Line 2 or 5 to Chungjeongno, Exit 9; 🅦🅟) Housed in an attractive red-brick Western style building from around 1910 with a turret and white wood wrap-around veranda, this restaurant is a precious fragment of Seoul's past. The food is delicious and it's a pleasure to eat outside in the leafy garden when it's warm. The restaurant interior also serves as an art gallery which is open on Sunday. From the subway exit turn right and it's on your right.

BAEKJE SAMGYETANG
KOREAN $$

Map p202 (백제삼계탕; Myeong-dong 2-gil, Myeong-dong; mains ₩14,000-25,000; Ⓜ Line 4 to Myeong-dong, Exit 6; 🅟) This 2nd-floor restaurant, marked by a sign with red Chinese characters, offers reliable *samgyetang* (stuffed chicken) served with a thimbleful of *insamju* (ginseng wine). Put salt and pepper into the saucer and dip the pieces of chicken into it. Drink the herbal soup at the end.

YEONG-YANG CENTRE
KOREAN $$

Map p202 (영양센터; Guangian-gil, Myeong-dong; mains ₩9,500-19,500; Ⓜ Line 4 to Myeong-dong, Exit 7; 🅟) A Myeong-dong institution since 1960, this is fast-food Korean-style: the tasty deep-fried chicken comes in various size portions or there's *samgyetang*. A good set lunch (₩9000) with salad, soup, bread and pickled radish is available until 4pm on weekdays, 2pm on weekends.

ANDONG JJIMDAK
KOREAN $$

Map p202 (안동찜닭; off Myeong-dong-gil; mains ₩17,000-27,000; Ⓜ Line 4 to Myeong-dong, Exit 7; 🅦🅟) A convivial young crowd comes here for the *jjimdak* experience, a very spicy concoction of chicken, noodles, potatoes and vegetables that comes on a platter meant for sharing.

GOGUNG
KOREAN $$

Map p202 (고궁; 🅙776 3211; Myeong-dong; mains from ₩11,000; Ⓜ Line 4 to Myeong-dong,

WORTH A DETOUR

KOREA HOUSE

Scoring a hat trick for high quality food, entertainment and shopping is **Korea House** (한국의집; Map p202; ☑2266 9101; www.koreahouse.or.kr; Chungmuro; set menu lunch/dinner ₩57,200/68,200; ⊘noon-2pm, dinner 5-6.30pm & 7-8.30pm Sun; Ⓜ Line 3 or 4 to Chungmuro, Exit 3). A dozen dainty, artistic courses make up the royal banquet. The *hanok*, the *hanbok*-clad waitresses, the *gayageum* (zither) music and the platters and boxes the food is served in are all part of the experience.

The intimate theatre stages two, hour-long **dance and music performances** (shows ₩50,000; ⊘6.30 & 8.30pm) which you can see independently of eating here. Put on by a troupe of top musicians and dancers, the shows have some English commentary on a screen. The show includes elegant court dances, *pansori*, a spiritual shamanist dance, *samullori* and *samgomu* – acrobatic female drummers each banging on three drums.

Rounding out the experience is Korea House's **shop** (⊘10am-8pm) which stocks a well-edited selection of quality design goods, traditional crafts, books and cards.

Exit 10, Ⓓ) Serves authentic Jeonju *bibimbap;* there's another branch in Insadong.

SINSEON SEOLNONGTANG   KOREAN $

Map p202 (신선설농탕; www.kood.co.kr; Myeong-dong-gil; meals ₩7000-8000; ⊘24hr; Ⓜ Line 4 to Myeong-dong, Exit 7; Ⓓ) *Mandu* (dumplings), tofu or ginseng can be added to the beef broth dishes served at this inexpensive chain, but purists will want to stick to the traditional version.

POTALA   TIBETAN, INDIAN $$

Map p202 (☑070-8112 8848; off Myeong-dong-gil; mains ₩7,000-15,000; Ⓢ Euljiro 1-ga, Exit 12) Books about Tibet and colourful crafts and pictures adorn this restaurant where you can sample the cuisine of the high Himalaya plateau, including *momo* (dumplings). While not exclusively vegetarian, there are plenty of veggie options.

COCONUT KITCHEN   MALAYSIAN, SINGAPOREAN $$

Map p202 (Namsan-dong; mains ₩10,000-14,000; ⊘11.30am-11pm Mon-Sat; Ⓜ Line 4 to Myeong-dong, Exit 3; ☏Ⓓ) The English-speaking chef fell in love with Malaysian food while studying in Sydney so he came back to Seoul and opened this small cafe. He serves pretty decent renditions of *nasi goreng* rice and *char kway teow* or *laksa* noodles.

CAFÉ MAMAS   SANDWICHES, SALADS $

Map p202 (Hanbit Media Park; mains ₩8,000-10,000; Ⓜ Line 2 to Euljiro 1-ga, Exit 3; Ⓓ) Around the corner from Hanbit Media Park, where events are sometimes held, is this popular fresh juice and sandwich operation. Order at the counter first. A cluster of other classy cafes nearby includes the chain **Coco Bruni** (www.cocobruni.co.kr), which serves gourmet chocolates and drinks.

HADONGKWAN   KOREAN $$

Map p202 (하동관; www.hadongkwan.com; Myeongdong 1-ga; soup ₩10,000-12,000; ⊘7am-4.30pm Mon-Sat; Ⓜ Line 4 to Myeong-dong, Exit 8) The big bowls of wholesome beef broth and rice at this popular pit stop come either in the regular version with slices of meat or the more expensive one with added tripe. Add salt and masses of sliced spring onions to taste.

🍷 DRINKING & NIGHTLIFE

NAOS NOVA   WINE BAR

Map p202 (☑754 2202; www.naosnova.net; Sowol-ro; ⊘noon-1pm; Ⓜ Line 1 or 4 to Seoul Station, Exit 10; Ⓓ) Facing the lower slopes of Namsan, this elegant bar and restaurant occupies an angular, light-filled contemporary building. There's a fine wine and liquor list here and some very tempting food to go with it, but bring your credit card as it's not cheap.

GROVE LOUNGE   CAFE, BAR

Map p202 (1F State Tower, Namsan, Toegye-ro; ⊘11am-midnight Mon-Fri, 11am-10pm Sat; Ⓜ Line 4 to Myeong-dong, Exit 4; Ⓓ) This attractive cafe-bar is a stylish and spacious spot for a reviving coffee or draft beer while lounging in comfy, designer chairs. Their international style food is good too and includes tasty toasted sandwiches with fries.

PIERRE'S BAR
BAR

Map p202 (🖈317 7181; www.pierre gagnaire.co.kr; 35th fl New Wing Lotte Hotel; Ⓜ Line 2 to Euljiro 1-ga, Exit 8) Pierre Gagnaire's Seoul restaurant is an epicurean and wallet hammering experience (lunch kicks off at ₩84,700 including tax and service). Alternatively drop by the attached glam-to-the-max bar specialising in vodka and champagne. The plush booths are ideal for intimate liaisons.

THE STORY
CAFE

Map p202 (Namsan; ☺8am-8pm Mon-Fri, 9am-6pm Sat; Ⓜ Line 4 to Myeong-dong, Exit 1) Myeong-dong isn't short on chain cafes, but for something with more individual character hike up to this hidden gem on the lower slope of Namsan next to Literature House. Sip your coffee (which at ₩2000 is one of the cheapest decent brews you'll find around here) inside or at outside tables.

☆ ENTERTAINMENT

CHONGDONG THEATRE
THEATRE

Map p202 (🖈751 1500; www.chongdong.com; Jeong-dong; tickets ₩30,000-40,000; ☺4pm & 8pm Tue-Sun; Ⓜ Line 1 or 2 to City Hall, Exit 2) The venue for the popular nonverbal musical show *Miso,* a traditional tale about star-crossed lovers. You can also dress up in traditional costumes here an hour before the show (₩5000) or join a *janggu* drumming class (₩15,000).

NATIONAL THEATRE OF KOREA
THEATRE

Map p202 (🖈2274 3507; www.ntok.go.kr; Heung-inmun-ro, Namsan; Ⓜ Line 3 Dongguk University, Exit 6) The several venues here are home to the national drama, *changgeuk* (Korean opera), orchestra and dance companies. Free concerts and movies are put on in summer at the outdoor stage. From September to October the complex is the location of a major theatre festival. Walk 10 minutes here or hop on bus 2 at the stop behind Exit 6.

FEEL
LIVE MUSIC

Map p202 (Samil-daero, Myeong-dong; ☺8pm-3am; Ⓜ Line 4 to Myeong-dong, Exit 10) In an incredibly decorated cavelike space, eccentric owner Mr Shin (who's been running the place since 1990) and his friends cover everything from Elvis to Korean rock. Drinks are beer or whiskey. You'll find it on the raised pathway running beneath the cathedral.

FREE OH! ZEMIDONG
DVD LIBRARY

Map p202 (www.ohzemidong.co.kr; Chungmuro Station; ☺1pm-3am; Ⓜ Line 4 or 3 to Chungmuro Station) Occupying a corridor of rooms on the upper level of Chugmuro Station, this facility

---

SEOUL SHOWTIME

Running for over 15 years, with no end in sight, is Korea's most successful nonverbal performance **Nanta** (http://nanta.i-pmc.co.kr; tickets ₩40,000-60,000). Set in a kitchen, this high-octane 90-minute show mixes magic tricks, *samulnori* folk music, drumming, kitchen utensils, comedy, dance, martial arts and audience participation. It's top-class entertainment that has been a hit wherever it plays. It's staged at three venues in Seoul:

➡ **Myeong-dong** (Map p202; 3rd fl Unesco Bldg, Myeong-dong 2-ga; ☺2pm, 5pm & 8pm; Ⓜ Line 4 to Myeong-dong, Exit 6)

➡ **Ganbuk Jeong-dong** (Map p202; Jeong-dong; ☺5pm & 8pm; Ⓜ Line 1 or 2 to City Hall, Exit 2)

➡ **Hongdae** (Map p204; Yellow Stone Bldg, Seokyo-dong; ☺5pm & 8pm; Ⓜ Line 2 to Hongdae, Exit 9)

Nanta has inspired a plethora of equally fun productions that have tweaked the blueprint, replacing cooking with drumming, quick draw painting, martial arts and breakdancing (called b-boying in Korea) as the main themes. Other recommended shows include **Jump** (Map p198; www.yegam.com/jump/eng; Seoul Cinema; tickets from ₩40,000; ☺8pm Mon, 4pm & 8pm Tue-Sat, 3pm & 6pm Sun; Ⓜ Line 1, 3 or 5 to Jongno 3-ga, Exit 14), featuring a wacky Korean family all crazy about martial arts; and **Bibap** (Map p202; www.bibap.co.kr; Cinecore Bldg, B2 Gwancheol-dong; tickets from ₩40,000; ☺8pm Tue-Sat; 5pm & 8pm Sat, 3pm & 6pm Sun; 🚇line 1 to Jonggak, Exit 4), a comedic Iron Chef style contest that adds beatbox and a cappella into the mix.

run by the Seoul Film Corporation includes a free library of books and DVDs both Korean and international. There are five viewing booths but you'll need to get there early in the day to grab one. There's also a gallery.

 SHOPPING

NAMDAEMUN MARKET MARKET
See p68.

SHINSEGAE DEPARTMENT STORE
Map p202 (www.shinsegae.com; Sogong-ro, Myeong dong; M Line 4 to Hoehyeon, Exit 7) Wrap yourself in luxury inside the Seoul equivalent of Harrods. It's split over two buildings, the older part based in a gorgeous 1930 colonial building that was Seoul's first department store Mitsukoshi. Check out local designer fashion labels and the opulent supermarket in the basement with a food court; another food court is up on the 11th floor of the new building with an attached roof garden to relax in.

LEVEL 5 FASHION
Map p202 (http://level5ive.cafe24.com; Level 5, Noon Sq, Myeongdong 2-ga; M Line 2 to Euljiro 1-ga, Exit 6) No need to root around Dongdaemun's markets for the latest hot designers; visit this floor of the Noon Square mall, which is devoted to sponsoring up-and-coming fashion talent. The Lab 5 store showcases the designs of 100 rising stars including participants of *Project Runway Korea*.

ÅLAND BOUTIQUE
Map p202 (www.a-land.co.kr; Myeong-dong; M Line 4 to Myeong-dong, Exit 6) This multi-label boutique mixes up vintage and garage-sale items with new designer items to wear and decorate your home. You'll find cool indie CDs and magazines here too. Pronounced A-land, they also have a slick store and an outlet shop in Hongdae (in the same building as where *Nanta* is performed).

LOTTE DEPARTMENT STORE DEPARTMENT STORE
Map p202 (Namdaemun-ro, Myeong-dong; M Line 2 to Euljiro 1-ga, Exit 8) Retail behemoth Lotte spreads its tentacles across four buildings: the main department store, Lotte Young Plaza, Lotte Avenuel and a duty-free shop. Also here is a multiplex cinema, restaurants and an attached hotel.

UNDERGROUND ARCADES

Apart from Myeong-dong's abundance of overground retailers there are hundreds to be discovered in a series of underground arcades. The longest, stretching 4km beneath Eulji-ro from City Hall to Dongdaemun is Eulji-ro Arcade; many of the stalls here stock fashions that are a throwback to yesteryear. More upmarket vendors selling handicrafts and antiques can be found in the Sogong Arcade beneath Sognog-ro.

MIGLIORE MALL FASHION
Map p202 (Toegye-ro, Myeong-dong; 11am-11.30pm Tue-Sun; M Line 4 to Myeong-dong, Exit 6) Always teeming with young trendsetters, this high-rise mall is packed with small fashion shops. There's an outdoor performance stage by the entrance where you watch groups and brush up on your K-Pop dance moves.

 SPORTS & ACTIVITIES

SILLOAM SAUNA TRADITIONAL SAUNA
Map p202 (실로암사우나찜질방; www.silloamsauna.com; Jungrim-dong; sauna adult/child before 8pm ₩8000/6000; sauna & jjimjil-bang adult/child before 8pm ₩10,000/7000; 24hr; M Line 1 or 4 to Seoul Station, Exit 1) Across the street from Seoul Station, this spick-and-span foreigner-friendly operation (lots of signs in English), with a wide range of baths and sauna rooms, is great if you need to freshen up before or after a trip out to the airport, or get into town late and need a temporary place to stay. Rates for the 8pm to 5am session are slightly higher.

CHUNJIYUN SPA TRADITIONAL SAUNA
Map p202 (http://seoulesthe.com; Myeong-dong; admission ₩20,000; 9am-midnight; M Line 4 to Myeong-dong, Exit 8) This compact spa, popular with Japanese tourists, offers the essentials – a pinewood, jade and clay sauna as well as green tea, ginseng and mugwort hot baths. An extra ₩82,000 covers a body scrub, oil massage and cucumber facial; the website has a discount coupon. It's in the basement of the building with 'Sunshine' written on it in red letters.

Western Seoul

HONGDAE | YEOUIDO

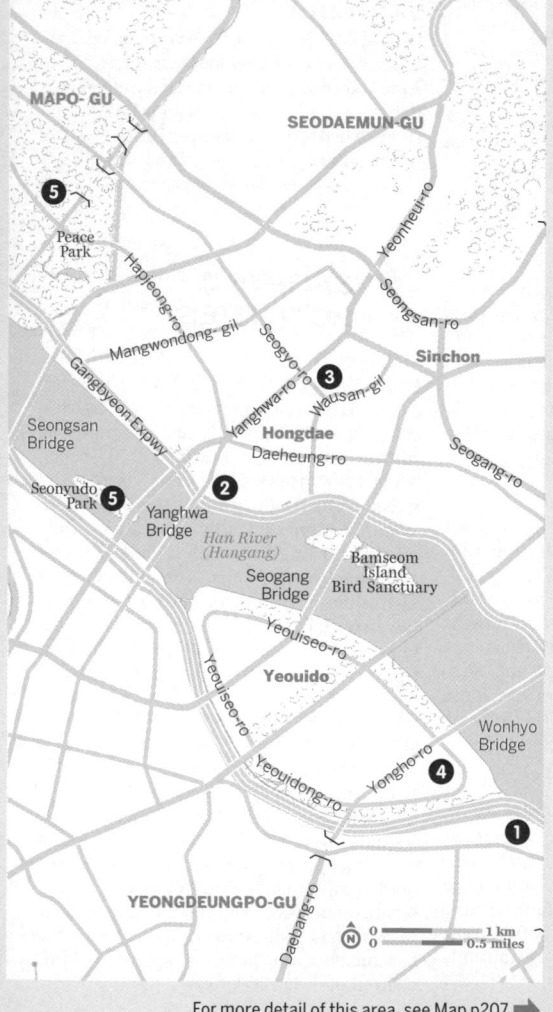

Neighbourhood Top Five

1 Sample seafood at **Noryangjin Fish Market** (p81), Korea's largest seafoods market, where you can buy everything from king crabs to sea cucumbers, and have it cooked up on the spot.

2 Learn about the sacrifices made by the first Korean Christians at the **Jeoldusan Martyrs' Shrine** (p78).

3 Catch the latest in K-Indie and mingle with Seoul hipsters in **Hongdae** (p83)

4 Enjoy the view and surrounding art at the top of **63 City** (p79)

5 Hire a bike and cycle along the Han River to **Seonyudo Park** (p79) and the **World Cup Stadium** (p85)

For more detail of this area, see Map p207 ➡

Explore Western Seoul

Home to several major campuses the areas of Hongdae (around Hongik University), Edae (around Ewha Womans University) and Sinchon (between Yonsei and Sogang Universities) are – as you'd expect – packed with places for students to be diverted from their studies. Hongik is Korea's leading art and design institution, so this is a particularly fertile patch for chaotic creativity and unbridled hedonism; it's also ground central for the K-Indie scene with scores of live music clubs and dance spots.

Hongdae morphs into Sinchon, another student area with masses of bars and budget restaurants, not to mention love motels, pool halls and DVD, karaoke and internet rooms. From Sinchon it's a skip to Edae, where female students are the predominant customers. French architect Dominique Perrault's stunning redesign of the Ewha campus centre has put the area on the archi-tour map.

In complete contrast is the no-nonsense business centre of Yeouido. This 3km-long and 2km-wide island on the southern side of the Han River used to be a sandy airfield. It's now home to skyscrapers housing media, finance and insurance companies, as well as the National Assembly and stock exchange buildings. It's not entirely devoid of tourist attractions: the aquarium and observation deck of the gold-tinted 63 City and nearby Noryangjin Fish Market are both impressive. There's also the central Yeouido Park and Yeouido Hangang Riverside Park, each lovely places to relax or go for a bike ride.

Local Life

➡ **Worship** Join in the singing with a 15,000-plus congregation at Sunday services at Yeouido Full Gospel Church (p79).

➡ **Markets** Go shopping for handmade souvenirs and listen to local musicians at Hongdae's Free Market (p85) in the tiny park opposite Hongik University; on Sundays the Hope Market here is a traditional flea market.

➡ **Blossoms** The park along the southeastern side of Yeouido is popular in mid-April when a profusion of cherry trees blossom; at its peak they're lit up at night.

Getting There & Away

➡ **Subway** Best way to get to all these areas; Hongik University also a stop on the A'REX line from Incheon International Airport.

➡ **Bicycle** Bikes can be hired on Yeouido and are the best way to get around this island and across the north side of the Han River where there are also cycle lanes.

Lonely Planet's Top Tip

Major retailers are moving into Hongdae, pushing up rents and pushing out smaller, more interesting boutiques, cafes and bars to neighbouring areas; explore the back streets south and west of Sangsu station to find them.

 Best Places to Eat

➡ Noryangjin Fish Market (p81)

➡ Slobbie (p79)

➡ Shim's Tapas (p79)

For reviews, p79 ➡

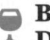 **Best Places to Drink**

➡ Anthracite (p82)

➡ Café Sukkara (p82)

➡ aA Café (p82)

For reviews, see p82 ➡

 Best Live Music

➡ Club Evans (p83)

➡ Café Bbang (p83)

➡ DGBD (p84)

For reviews, see p83 ➡

WESTERN SEOUL

 SIGHTS

Hongdae & Around

EWHA WOMANS UNIVERSITY
ARCHITECTURE, MUSEUM

off Map p204 (www.ewha.ac.kr; Edae; MLine 2 to Ewha Womans University, Exit 2) When it was founded in 1886 by American Methodist missionary Mary Scranton, the name of this all-female educational institution was Ewha Hak Dang, meaning Pear Blossom Academy. Come here to view Dominque Perrault's stunning main entrance, a building that dives six stories underground and is split by a broad cascade of steps leading up to the Gothic-style 1935 Pfeiffer Hall. Walking through here feels like going through the parting of the Red Sea. Look around inside and you'll find cafes, shops and an art-house cinema (p85).

To the left of the entrance is the university **museum** (museum.ewha.ac.kr; admission free; ⊙9.30am-5pm Mon-Sat) which contains gorgeous examples of traditional ceramics, art, furniture and clothing.

KT&G SANGSANGMADANG
ARCHITECTURE

Map p204 (KT&G 상상마당; www.sangsangmadang.com; Seogyo-dong, Hongdae; ⊙10am-11pm;

MLine 2 to Hongik University, Exit 5) Funded by Korea's top tobacco company, this visually striking building is home to an art-house cinema, a concert space (hosting top indie bands) and galleries that focus on experimental, fringe exhibitions. There's also a great design shop for gifts on the ground floor. The architect Bae Dae-yong called his design the 'Why Butter Building' as the pattern of concrete across its glazed facade resembles both butterfly wings and butter spread on toast.

KOREAN DESIGN MUSEUM
MUSEUM

Map p204 (www.designmuseum.or.kr; Chagjun-dong, Hongdae; adult/child ₩5000/4000; ⊙10am-6pm Tue-Sun; MLine 2 to Hongik University, Exit 9; ☎) About 1600 items from a collection of over 20,000 are displayed on the two floors of this small private museum that traces the history of modern design in Korea from the 1880s to contemporary times. It's a fascinating collection that spans a wide range of locally designed products from 19th century books and newspapers, to 1960s toys and electronics and posters for the 1988 Olympics. Not much is labelled in English, but the items generally speak for themselves. There's a cafe and they sell some attractive retro-themed postcards.

TOP SIGHTS
JEOLDUSAN MARTYRS' SHRINE

Jeoldusan means 'Beheading Hill', as it is here that thousands of Korean Catholics were tortured and executed in the 1860s by royal decree. The victims' bodies were thrown into the nearby Han River. Jeoldusan Martyrs' Shrine's museum (절두산 순교 성지) has books, diaries and relics of the early Catholic converts, 103 of whom have been made saints for their martyrdom. There are also mementoes of Pope John Paul II's visit here in 1984.

Steadfast early Christian converts faced waves of government persecution, but they refused to recant their new faith. Inside Catholic churches, *yangban* (aristocrat) nobles and ordinary folk sat together as equals in the sight of God, an act that challenged the rigid Confucian hierarchy of Joseon society.

Next to the museum is a stark, white memorial chapel and sculpture garden. From the car park, steps lead down to the Han River where you can stand at the foot of the cliffs that the dead bodies of the martyrs were thrown from. The shrine is less than a 10-minute walk from the subway exit.

DON'T MISS

➡ Korea Catholic Martyrs' Museum
➡ Memorial Chapel
➡ Sculpture Garden

PRACTICALITIES

➡ Map p204
➡ www.jeoldusan.or.kr
➡ admission to museum by donation
➡ ⊙museum 9.30am-5pm Tue-Sun
➡ MLine 2 or 6 to Hapjeong station, Exit 7

Yeouido

63 CITY
AQUARIUM, VIEWPOINT

Map p207 (www.63.co.kr; Ⓜ Line 5 to Yeouinaru, Exit 4) This gold-tinted glass skyscraper, one of Seoul's tallest buildings, offers four attractions plus a theatre. The best reason to come here is for the view from **63 Sky Art Gallery** (adult/child ₩12,000/11,000; ⊙10am-9.30pm), which combines a 60th-floor observation deck with good changing art exhibitions. Back in the basement, where you'll find the main ticket hall, is the aquarium **63 Sea World** (adult/child ₩17,000/15,000; ⊙10am-9.30pm), with penguin, seal and sea lion shows. If you have more time to kill there's also **63 Art Hall** (adult/child ₩12,000/11,000; ⊙10am-5.30pm), an IMAX theatre showing hourly movies with an English-language commentary; and the mini Madame Tussaud's–like **63 Wax Museum** (adult/child ₩14,000/13,000; ⊙10am-9.30pm). There are discount packages for three or more attractions, plus a further small foreigner discount (if you ask).

FREE YEOUIDO FULL GOSPEL CHURCH
CHURCH

Map p207 (yfgc.fgtv.com; ⊙services 7am, 9am, 11am, 1pm & 3pm Sun, 10.30am Wed, 9.30pm Fri; Ⓜ Line 9 to National Assembly, Exit 1) Founded in 1958, this giant Pentecostal church, with some 830,000 members, has been based on Yeouido since 1973. A visit during the Sunday services, when tens of thousands pack the circular, cathedral-sized building, is highly recommended. Huge TV screens flank the altar and there's a 150-member choir and orchestra. The foreigners' sections, where headphones provide a translation of the service, are on the 3rd and 4th floor in the balcony.

FREE NATIONAL ASSEMBLY
NOTABLE BUILDING

Map p207 (www.assembly.go.kr; ⊙9am-6pm, closed 2nd & 4th Sun of month; Ⓜ Line 9 to National Assembly, Exit 1) Home to South Korea's parliament since 1975, the interior of this green domed building can be viewed only as part of a tour (in Korean, and lasting around one hour); you should apply three days in advance via the website. The central Rotunda Hall is impressive as is the Plenary Chamber where the MPs sit. On weekends, only the separate Memorial Hall section of the complex is open. The pleasant grounds

with a fountain and an elaborate *hanok* (traditional wooden house; used for official functions) are worth a wander.

FREE SEONYUDO PARK
PARK

off Map p207 (http:/hangang.seoul.go.kr; admission free; ⊙6am-midnight) Part of the Hangang River Park, this award-winning nature space covers the island of Seonyudo, formerly the site of a water-filtration plant. The old industrial buildings have been cleverly adapted as part of the new landscaping and gardens which include lily-covered ponds, plant nurseries and exhibitions halls.

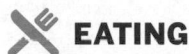

✕ EATING

Hongdae & Around

Not much fine dining in these parts, but you'll find an abundance of places serving the kind of inexpensive dishes and drinks that students love. The grid of streets on the Donggyo-dong side of Sinchon is lined with BBQ joints.

SLOBBIE
KOREAN $

Map p204 (☏2679 9300; blog.naver.com/slobbie8; Hongdae; meals ₩8000; ⊙11.30am-11.30pm Mon-Sat; Ⓜ Line 2 to Hongik University, Exit 9; 📶🍴) One of two restaurants in the Hongdae area run by social enterprise Organisation Yori, promoting a slower, healthier and more organic lifestyle; the other is **O-Yori** (Map p204; www.orgyori.com; ⊙11.30am-9pm Tue-Sun; Ⓜ Line 6 to Sangsu, Exit 1). Both help train young chefs from challenged backgrounds and provide jobs for single mothers. The food at Slobbie (pronounced Slow-bee) is simple, tasty Korean dishes such as *bibimbap,* while O-Yori offers a tasty pan-Asian menu.

SHIM'S TAPAS
SPANISH $$

Map p204 (☏3141 2386; Hongdae; tapas ₩5000-15,000; Ⓜ Line 2 to Hongik University, Exit 8; 📶🍴) Three sisters are the driving force behind this adorable tapas bar. They whip up authentic and creative Spanish-style nibbles including light as a feather tortilla and homemade anchovies. Wash them down with a sangria, glass of cava or one of their fine dry martinis.

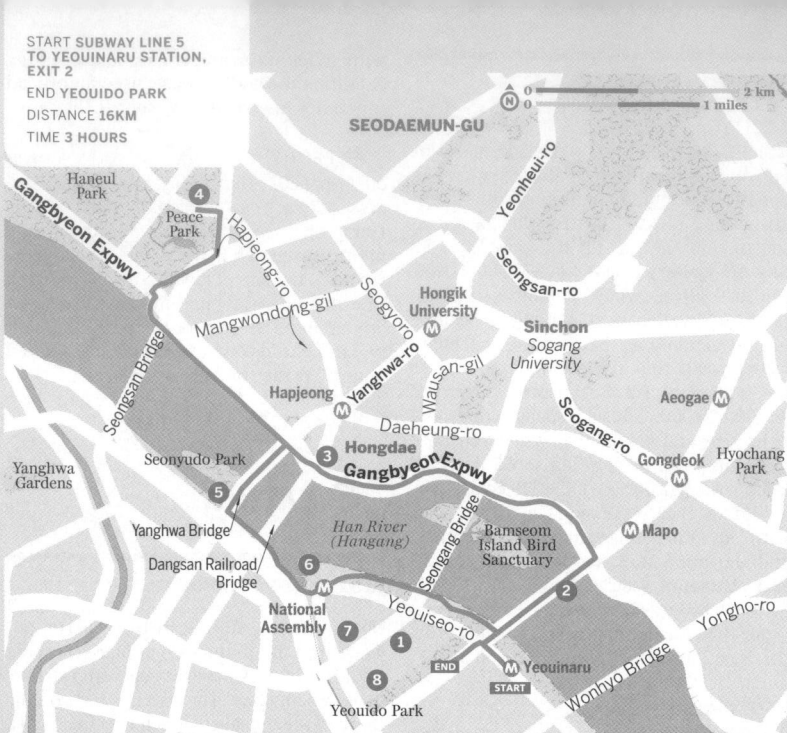

START SUBWAY LINE 5
TO YEOUINARU STATION,
EXIT 2
END YEOUIDO PARK
DISTANCE 16KM
TIME 3 HOURS

Neighbourhood Walk
Han River Cycle Ride

Dedicated cycle paths run along much
of both sides of the Han River. This
16km route loops from Yeouido across
the river to the World Cup Stadium and
back, providing great views along the way.
Walk west a block from the subway exit to
Yeouido Park where you'll find a **1** **bicycle
rental stall** (first hour ₩3000, every
extra 15 mins ₩500; ⏱9am-5pm); bring
some form of photo ID for them to keep as
a deposit.

Cycle out of the park and across the
2 **Mapo Bridge**, taking the blue ramp
down to the north bank of the river. Head
west for about 4km until you reach a steep
cliff at the top of which is **3** **Jeoldusan
Martyrs' Shrine**. Continue west under the
Yanghwa and Seongsan bridges until you
reach a small bridge across a stream. Turn
right after crossing this bridge and then left
(at the sign) to pedal uphill to reach the
4 **World Cup Stadium**.

Retrace your route back to the Yanghwa
bridge and carry your bike up the stairs to
the pathway on the west side. On an island
about halfway along the bridge is the beautifully landscaped **5** **Seonyudo Park**.
You'll have to leave your bike outside if you
wish to explore the park which has wonderful river views.

Continue from the park back to the
south bank of the Han River and pedal back
towards Yeouido. At the western tip of the
island you can pause to view the ritzy
6 **Seoul Marina** and the **7** **National
Assembly**. Before or after dropping off
your bike, have a look at Yeouido Park,
which includes a **8** **traditional Korean
garden**.

BAP
KOREAN $

Map p204 (off Wausan-gil, Hongdae; meals ₩8000-20,000; ☺11am-9pm Mon-Sat; Ⓜ Line 2 to Hongik University, Exit 9) Kindly ladies run this cosy place decorated in wood and brick with abundant plants. The *jeongsik* (banquet-style meals) come with plenty of side dishes, rice and soup, so are great value and beloved by the local student population. The *bulgogi* (₩20,000) serves two people.

BELLA TORTILLA
MEXICAN $

Map p204 (Dokmak-gil, Hongdae; tacos ₩3000-5000; ☺noon-10pm Tue-Sun; Ⓜ Line 6 to Sangsu, Exit 1; 🌐) There's a couple of counter chairs, but this is mainly a take-out kiosk. The soft-wrap tacos and tortilla wraps are the real deal and make an ideal snack or fuel stop while Hongdae bar-hopping.

CHUNCHEON-JIP
CHICKEN $

Map p204 (춘천집; meals ₩10,000-15,000; ☺24hr; Ⓜ Line 2 to Sinchon, Exit 2) The specialty is *dakgalbi,* a boneless chicken dish with chunks of cabbage, leek and carrot in a spicy sauce. The staff cook at your table, so there's nothing to do except put on the apron and wait. To find it, turn left at the lane between Starbucks and the SK Telecom store.

LOVING HUT
VEGAN $

Map p204 (www.lovinghut.com; mains ₩5000-6000; Ⓜ Line 2 to Sinchon, Exit 2; 🌐📶) A variety of slogans in English urge diners on to a more compassionate, meat-free life at this pastel shaded, pleasantly modern cafe. It serves very tasty and good-value Korean meals with rice, noodles, veggies – and no animal products.

TAMLA SIKDANG
KOREAN $$

Map p204 (탐라식당; ☎337 4877; 337-11 Sangsu-dong; dishes ₩8000-30,000; ☺5pm-2am Mon-Sat; Ⓜ Line 6 to Sangsu, Exit 3) On a cafe-lined backstreet in Sangsu, this rustic cafe specialises in food and drink from Jeju-do, the big island off the south coast of Korea. The menu is big on pork. Also try the very palatable *soju.*

FELL & COLE
ICE CREAM $

Map p204 (www.fellncole.com; Hongdae; 1 scoop ₩4200; ☺noon-10pm Sun-Thu, until midnight Fri & Sat; Ⓜ Line 6 to Sangsu, Exit 1; 🌐) Hongdae is light on gastronomic experimentation – but not when it comes to ice cream and sorbet. The fabulous flavours here are changing all the time but might include perilla leaf, parsley lemonade, burnt banana and *kalimotxo* (aka Jesus Juice)!

SINSEON SEOLNONGTANG
KOREAN $

Map p204 (신선설농탕; Sinchon; meals ₩6000; ☺24hr; Ⓜ Line 2 to Sinchon, Exit 3) A handy branch of the tasty *seolnongtang* beef soup operation.

WESTERN SEOUL EATING

TOP SIGHTS
⊚ NORYANGJIN FISH MARKET

Providing terrific photo opportunities, Seoul's Noryangjin Fish Market (노량진수산시장) supplies every kind of aquatic life form to restaurants, fish shops and the general public. Wander the tungsten-bulb-lit aisles holding some 700 stalls and peer at bucket after bucket and multiple tanks filled with crabs, mussels, prawns, flounder, squid and octopus – as well as uncommon marine life such as the dark-orange-and-red *meongge* (Korean sea squirt), very much an acquired taste.

The apron-clad vendors will happily sell you produce for consumption at home or cooked at one of the several restaurants attached to the market; for a recommended one see p82. If you want to view the market at its liveliest, get here for the auctions, which kick off around 5am.

The easiest way to reach here is to use the pedestrian bridge that goes across the train tracks from Exit 1 of Noryangjin station. The stairs down the other side lead directly into the market.

DON'T MISS

➡ Eating at one of the restaurants
➡ Early-morning auctions

PRACTICALITIES

➡ Map p207
➡ www.susansijang.co.kr
➡ admission free
➡ ☺24 hours
➡ Ⓜ Line 1 to Noryangjin, Exit 1

WESTERN SEOUL DRINKING & NIGHTLIFE

CAT & DOG CAFES

Tokyo started it with cafes where you can cosy up to cats. Seoul had to go one better, so dogs are also on offer as temporary pets. Korea may be known as a place where people eat dog meat, but at **Bau House** (Map p204; 334 5152; off parking lot alley; 2-11.30pm Mon-Fri, 12.30-11pm Sat & Sun; Line 6 to Sangsu, Exit 1) patrons are only interested in playing with the pooches. You'd have to be a dog lover, as the 5th-floor cafe is pretty whiffy.

Over in Gangnam there's the classier **Caffe Pawz** (cafe.naver.com/cafepawz; 11am-11pm; Line 2 to Gangnam, Exit 5) which is a dog 'hotel' and grooming centre with an attached cafe also serving organic dog treats.

Cat lovers are also well catered for in Seoul at the **Godabang Cat Cafe** (www.godabang.com) chain; you'll find ones in Sinchon (Map p204) and Gangnam (Map p210).

Yeouido & Around

BUSAN ILBEONJI
SEAFOOD $$$

Map p207 (부산일번지; 2nd fl, Noryangjin Market; mains ₩15,000-30,000; 10.30am-10.30pm; Line 1 to Noryangjin, Exit 1) Generous fresh fish and crab meals are a bargain. Try *kkotge* (spicy blue-crab soup), which includes side dishes such as garnished tofu, sweet red beans, green salad and grilled fish.

PAUL
BAKERY, CAFE $

Map p207 (www.paul-international.com/kr/splash-country; Marriott Yeouido Park Centre; bakery items from ₩2,000; 8am-10pm; Line 5 to Yeouido, Exit 2;) French baker and patisserie; a charming option for a light lunch or drinks and cakes while touring Yeouido.

63 BUFFET PAVILION
BUFFET $$$

Map p207 (www.63buffet.co.kr; 63 City, Yeouido; lunch Mon-Fri ₩63,000, lunch Sat & Sun, dinner Mon-Sun ₩72,000; noon-3pm & 6-10pm Mon-Fri, 11am-3.30pm & 5-10pm Sat & Sun; Line 5 to Yeouinaru, Exit 4) With too many temptations to count, this gourmet buffet is the perfect way to sample a range of Asian cuisines. Children up to 18 eat for about half price.

DRINKING & NIGHTLIFE

Hongdae & Around

TOP CHOICE **ANTHRACITE**
CAFE

Map p204 (www.anthracitecoffee.com; off Tojeong-ro; 11am-midnight; Line 6 to Sangsu, Exit 4;) Based in an old shoe factory, a short walk towards the river from the heart of Hongdae, this is one of Seoul's top independent coffee roaster and cafe operations. Drinks are made using the hand-drip method at a counter made out of an old conveyor belt. Upstairs the industrial space has been converted to an ubercool lounge and there's outdoor seating on the roof.

CAFÉ SUKKARA
CAFE, BAR

Map p204 (www.sukkara.co.kr; Sanullim Bldg, Seogyo-dong; 11am-midnight; Line 2 to Hongik University, Exit 9;) There's a brilliant range of drinks and some very tasty things to eat (try their butter chicken curry) at this shabby chic farmhouse-style cafe. They make their own juices and liquors – try the black shandy gaff, a mix of homemade ginger ale and Magpie Brewery dark beer.

AA CAFÉ
CAFE, BAR

Map p204 (www.aadesignmuseum.com; Hongdae; cafe noon-midnight, shop noon-8pm; Line 6 to Sangsu, Exit 1;) The antithesis of Seoul's usual cramped cosy cafes, aA offers soaring ceilings and space, filled with designer and retro furniture. It's a pleasure to hang out here, do some web-surfing and have a light bite – their food is very tasty (try the chicken salad). Browse more classic furniture pieces in the basement shop/museum. There's also a branch in Samcheong-dong.

THE CURE
BAR

Map p204 (blog.naver.com/thecure_bmp; Hongdae; 6pm-2am Sun-Thu, 5pm-5am Fri & Sat; Line 6 to Sangsu, Exit 1) Chris, a former professional Korean table tennis player in France (!), has an amazing collection of 1980s British music including, of course, the Cure. His spacious basement bar, lined with sofas and video screens, is a comfy place to indulge in pop nostalgia.

EUNHASU DABANG
CAFE

Map p204 (은하수 다방; Hongdae; ☺11am-1am; Ⓜ Line 6 to Sangsu, Exit 1) Tapping into Seoul's nostalgia boom is this throwback cafe |that caters to a crowd too young to remember original *dabang* (old-style cafes). No matter; it's a relaxing original-styled place playing retro K-Pop and serving drinks and food on cute painted crockery.

CASTLE PRAHA
MICROBREWERY

Map p204 (캐슬프라하; www.castlepraha.com; Solnae 6-gil, Hongdae; ☺noon-3pm & 5pm-2am; Ⓜ Line 6 to Sangsu, Exit 1) Offering one of the most extraordinary facades in Seoul, this medieval fantasy 'bohemian bistro' has an equally bizarre dungeon-cum-cellar interior. It serves up several Czech-style pilsner and dunkel brews, and has branched out to outlets in Gangnam, Garosu-gil and Itawon, too.

LABRIS
LESBIAN

Map p204 (라브리스; Wausan-gil, Hongdae; ☺7pm-2am Mon Thu, 7pm 5am Fri Sun; Ⓜ Line 6 to Sangsu, Exit 1) On the 8th floor above Uniqlo, this is a women only space that's lesbian-oriented but not exclusively so. There are three levels filled with comfortable sofas. DJ nights are Friday to Sunday when the minimum charge for a drink and compulsory *anju* (bar snacks) is ₩15,000.

WOODSTOCK
BAR

Map p204 (월플라워스; Sinchon; ☺7pm-4am; Ⓜ Line 2 to Sinchon, Exit 2) Years of scribbles have built up all over the walls, tables and chairs in this bar where the big attraction is the loud rock music selected from its huge collection.

BAHIA
CLUB

Map p204 (바히아; ☑335 1512; Saemulgyeol 2-gil, Hongdae; admission ₩6000; ☺6pm-midnight Tue-Thu, to 1am Fri-Sun; Ⓜ Line 2 to Hongik University, Exit 2) This cosy dance club, specialising in salsa, meringue and *bachata* (music originating from the Dominican Republic), has a friendly atmosphere and mirrors down one side, so you can check out your moves. Saturday always sizzles.

M2
CLUB

Map p204 (www.ohoo.net/m2; Hongdae; admission Sun-Thu ₩10,000, Fri & Sat ₩20,000; ☺9.30pm-4.30am Sun-Thu, 8.30pm-6.30am Fri & Sat; Ⓜ Line 6 to Sangsu, Exit 1) Deep underground is M2, one of the largest and best Hongdae clubs. It has a high ceiling and plenty of lights and visuals. Top local and international DJs spin mainly progressive house music.

CHLORIS TEA GARDEN
TEAHOUSE

Map p204 (www.cafechloris.co.kr; Changcheon-dong, Sinchon; ☺10am-midnight; Ⓜ Line 2 to Sinchon, Exit 3) Drunken revels may be in full flight around it, but this gentile corner of Sinchon remains forever England, offering an impressive range of black and flavoured teas, dainty cakes served on real china and comfy chairs for quiet enjoyment. They also run the similar Café de Chloris on the same street.

VINYL
BAR

Map p204 (Wausan-gil, Hongdae; ☺4pm-2am, to 3.30am Fri & Sat; Ⓜ Line 6 to Sangsu, Exit 1) This bar's neat idea – all drinks sold in plastic, IV-style bags with straws – has caught on, with other places copying it. Either drink your cocktail in this cute little bar or take it with you as you wander around Hongdae.

CAFÉ GOODS
CAFE, BAR

Map p204 (www.cafegoods.co.kr; Chagjun-dong, Hongdae; Ⓜ Line 2 to Hongik University, Exit 9; 🛜📱) Designers, artists and writers get 50% off most drink prices at this spacious, design-savy hang-out. They serve the usual caffeinated beverages plus some refreshing homemade juices and 'ades along with beer, wine and cute animal-shaped cookies. Plenty of design books and mags to browse too.

☆ ENTERTAINMENT

Hongdae & Around

CLUB EVANS
JAZZ

Map p204 (☑337 8361; www.clubevans.com; Wausan-gil, Hongdae; admission ₩1000; ☺7.30pm-midnight Sun-Thu, to 2am Fri & Sat; Ⓜ Line 6 to Sangsu, Exit 1) Appealing across the generations, Evans offers top grade jazz and a great atmosphere. Get here early if you want a seat or book ahead. They release their own label CDs, too.

CAFÉ BBANG
LIVE MUSIC

Map p204 (카페 빵; http://cafe.daum.net/cafebbang; Hongdae; ☺7pm-6am; Ⓜ Line 2 to Hongik

LOCAL KNOWLEDGE

K-INDIE SCENE

US-born singer-songwriter and cafe-bar owner Ray Kang has been in Korea since 1996. He presents Indie Afternoon on TBS 101.3FM.

What is K-Indie?

It's a hidden gem – real voices (not manufactured as in K-Pop) and real artists. It covers all genres – rock, jazz, hip-hop etc – and you really see the performers' creative lives. However, it hardly gets any exposure at all. The big record companies are not interested in picking up most artists for wider distribution, and apart from our show it's impossible to hear on the radio.

Where can you hear it?

Hongdae is the mecca of the K-Indie scene. Check out the live music clubs Ta, FF, Freebird, V-Hall (in KT&G SangsangMadang) and C-Cloud. Music festivals are another popular stage for K-Indie artists (see p35).

Recommended bands & artists?

The Peppertones (www.peppertones.net) are a two-man mod pop rock group. Their music has an electronic rock feel; they've released three CDs and are moving into the mainstream. The Yellow Monsters are a punk group who recently played at music festivals in the US. Energetic electronic rock band the Koxx (www.thekoxx.com) made a lot a waves in 2011. As for singer-songwriters, look out for Park Sae-byul (www.parksaebyul.com) and the acoustic guitarist Choi Go-eun. Big Baby Driver is also excellent – she plays slide guitar and does 1920s-'30s US blues.

Where can I find out more?

Read *Korean Indie* (www.koreanindie.com) which has grown out of a blog *Indieful ROK* (http://indiefulrok.blogspot.com) kept by a girl in Sweden. Also check CDs and digital tracks put out by the indie labels Beatball (www.beatballrecords.com) and Ruby Salon (www.rubysalon.com). K-Indie CDs are available at Evans Records and Hottracks in Kyobo bookshops.

University, Exit 8) Basement venue where you're sure to catch something interesting – apart from gigs by indie artists and bands, it also hosts film screenings, art exhibitions and parties.

FF   LIVE MUSIC

Map p204 (☎011-9025 3407; Hongdae; admission ₩10,000; ⊙7pm-6am; MLine 6 to Sangsu, Exit 1) A top live venue with up to eight local indie bands playing at the weekend until midnight. Afterwards it becomes a dance club with DJs.

DGBD   LIVE MUSIC

Map p204 (디지비디; cafe.daum.net/dgbd; Hongdae; admission ₩5000-10,000; ⊙8-11pm; MLine 2 to Hongik University, Exit 9) A legendary live-music venue where all the top Hongdae bands have played over the years. It's standing room only and there's a balcony.

FREEBIRD   LIVE MUSIC

Map p204 (프리버드; www.clubfreebird.com; 2nd fl, Eoulmadang 2-gil, Hongdae; admission free Mon-

Thu, ₩20,000 Fri-Sun; ⊙6pm-midnight; MLine 2 to Hongik University, Exit 9) One of Hongdae's longest running live music venues, offering a range of genres from death metal to *Sound of Music* out-takes. Usually a handful of acts play every evening. Wednesday is audition night, when new bands and singers take their chances on the stage.

TA   LIVE MUSIC

Map p204 (http://cafe.daum.net/liveclubta; Hongdae; admission ₩20,000; ⊙7pm-3am Tue-Thu, to 5am Fri-Sun; MLine 6 to Sangsu, Exit 1) Live acoustic sets usually run from around 9.30pm until midnight Friday to Sunday. It's free to watch acoustic busking nights from Tuesday to Thursday.

LUXURY NORAEBANG   KARAOKE

Map p204 (럭셔리노래방; ☎322 3111; Eoulma-dang-gil, Hongdae; room per hr ₩10,000-38,000; ⊙9am-7am; MLine 6 to Sangsu, Exit 1) Karaoke your heart out and be noticed: some rooms have floor to ceiling windows fronting onto the street so you can show off your K-Pop moves. Rates rise between 6pm and 7am and everyone gets a free ice cream.

FREE CINEMATEQUE KOFA   CINEMA
(한국 영상 자료원; ☑3153 2001; www.korea film.org; ⓜLine 6 to Susaek, Exit 2) Free classic and contemporary Korean films are on the bill at one of the three cinemas in this home of the Korean Film Archive. See the website for directions from the subway exit.

ARTHOUSE MOMO   CINEMA
off Map p204 (www.cineart.co.kr; Ewha Womans University main entrance bldg; tickets ₩9000; ⓜEwha Womans University, Exit 3) In the basement of the main entrance to the university is this two screen cinema, showing a wide range of international movies in their original language (with Korean subtitles).

🛍 SHOPPING

Hongdae & Around

TOP CHOICE KEY   ARTS, CRAFTS
Map p204 (www.welcomekey.net; off Dabog-gil, Hongdae; ☻noon-10pm; ⓜLine 2 to Hongik University, Exit 8) Representing 48 different artists and craftspeople, several of whom also sell their goods at the Freemarket on Saturday, this small gallery and showroom offers affordable, exclusive items, from jewellery to pottery to fabric art and paintings.

🖊 LITTLE FARMERS   ACCESSORIES
Map p204 (www.littlefarmers.co.kr; Wausan-gil, Hongdae; ☻noon-9pm; ⓜLine 2 to Hongik University, Exit 8) Eco-friendly shoes, bags and other goods, some made from recycled product, are sold at this attractive basement store. You'll also find K-Indie CDs here and other colourful accessories.

FREE & HOPE MARKETS   ARTS & CRAFT, MARKET
Map p204 (www.freemarket.or.kr/v3; Hongdae Playground, opposite entrance Hongik University;

☻1-6pm Sat Mar-Nov; ⓜLine 2 to Hongik University, Exit 9) A girl in ripped jeans selling her own hand-painted cigarette lighters; a Korean James Blunt sound-alike crooning into a microphone in front of adoring fans; hand-painted bottle tops and suitcases, hairpins that look like fruit salad, wallets made of goat leather, a caricaturist and a knitter; all can be found in this crafters market. The Hope Market that runs here on Sunday afternoons is a traditional flea market.

PURPLE RECORD   MUSIC
Map p204 (Wausan-gil, Hongdae; ☻10.30am-11pm; ⓜLine 2 to Hongik University, Exit 9) An interesting selection of music genres can be browsed in this independent CD store; you can find many Korean artists here including titles by K-Indie singers and bands.

🏃 SPORTS & ACTIVITIES

WORLD CUP STADIUM   STADIUM
(월드컵주경기장; www.seoulworldcupst.or.kr; ⓜLine 6 to World Cup Stadium, Exit 1) Built to stage the opening ceremony and matches during the 2002 Football World Cup, this 66,000-seat venue is still used as a sports and events stadium. Also in the building is a **museum** (adult/child ₩1000/500; ☻9am-6pm) about the World Cup event, as well as a cinema multiplex, the shopping store Homeplus and Spoland, a sports centre with swimming pools and 24-hour sauna. Around the stadium are large parks created from landfill sites returned to a natural state and cycling tracks.

HAN RIVER CRUISES   CRUISE
Map p207 (www.hcruise.co.kr; Yeouido; adult/child ₩11,000/5500; ☻11am-8.40pm; ⓜLine 5 to Yeouinaru, Exit 3) Take a trip from Yeouido pier to any of the Han River ferry piers or take a one-hour round trip back to Yeouido. You can also board night cruises here.

Itaewon & Yongsan-gu

Neighbourhood Top Five

1 Survey centuries of Korean culture and art at the mammoth **National Museum of Korea** (p88) and take time to explore the attached gardens.

2 Be amazed by the art and architecture of the **Leeum Samsung Museum of Art** (p89).

3 Pay homage to those who gave their lives for the nation at the **War Memorial of Korea** (p90).

4 Eat, drink and party the night away in **Itaewon** (p89) and neighbouring areas.

5 Sweat, soak and be scrubbed super clean at **Dragon Hill Spa & Resort** (p95).

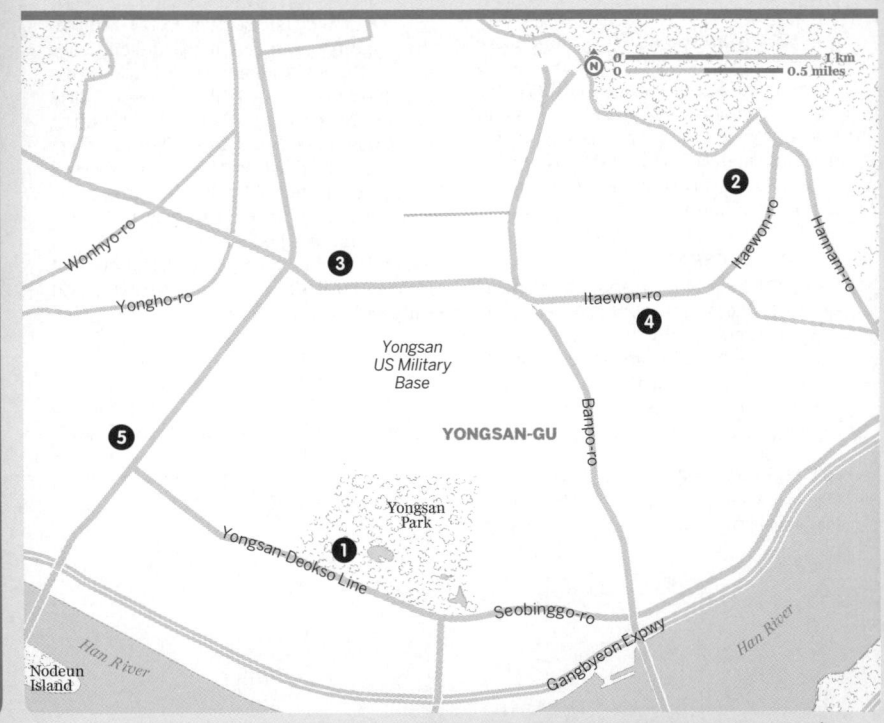

For more detail of this area, see Map p209 ➡

Explore Itaewon & Yongsan-gu

Immediately south of Namsan, Yongsan-gu has for many decades been defined by the presence of the US army base on a massive tract of land. Next door is Itaewon, ground central for army personnel and expats to shop and relax in an international mix of restaurants, bars and, umm, other places. For this reason it had a dodgy rep, but no longer. The hostess and transvestite bars of 'Hooker Hill' are still there (as is a cluster of Seoul's most foreigner-friendly gay hang-outs on 'Homo Hill'), but this is now one of Seoul's trendiest dining and shopping districts, attracting people from across the city.

The vibe is spilling over into adjacent areas. Head down Itaewon-ro, the main drag, in one direction and you'll swiftly hit classy Hannam-dong, where you'll find the excellent Leeum Samsung Museum of Art, boutiques and cool cafes. In the other direction is happening Haebangchon (aka HBC) and Gyeongridan, home to laid-back restaurants, cafes and craft beer bars. In all these areas you're as likely to hear English spoken as Korean – and not just by the expats.

Two major cultural institutions – the National Museum and the War Memorial of Korea – are area highlights and there are fine opportunities to de-stress, either in one of Seoul's most elaborate *jjimjil-bang* (sauna) complexes or by strolling along the Han River Park, which can be accessed in around a 15-minute downhill walk from Itaewon.

Local Life

➡ **Shopping** Itaewon is the best place to find clothes and shoes in foreigner friendly large sizes as well as have something tailor made. It's also now getting a rep for small fashion boutiques.

➡ **Religion** The beautiful Seoul Central Mosque, Korea's largest such house of worship, sits atop a hill in Itaewon, surrounded by hallal restaurants and shops with imported items from Islamic countries.

➡ **Online Gaming** Cheer on StarCraft players on the 9th floor of I'Park Mall where TV tapings of e-game tournaments are often held.

Getting There & Away

➡ **Subway** Line 6 is the best way to reach Itaewon and around, with Samgakji the closest station to the War Memorial of Korea; transfer here to line 4 to reach the National Museum.

➡ **Tour Bus** The War Memorial of Korea and National Museum are both stops on the City Tour Bus route.

Lonely Planet's Top Tip

The best way to reach the Banpo Bridge (p99) from Itaewon is to walk south down Pokwangdong-gil (which, incidentally, is one of the fast-disappearing areas of central Seoul to retain an old Asian shopping atmosphere) to a pedestrian tunnel that leads to the riverside park.

 ### Best Places to Eat

➡ OKitchen (p89)
➡ Vatos (p89)
➡ Le Saint-Ex (p89)

For reviews, p89 ➡

 ### Best Places to Drink

➡ Craftworks (p91)
➡ Takeout Drawing (p91)
➡ District (p91)

For reviews, see p91 ➡

 ### Best Places to Shop

➡ Millimetre Milligram (p93)
➡ Yongsan Electronics Market (p93)
➡ What the Book (p93)

For reviews, see p93 ➡

ITAEWON & YONGSAN-GU

TOP SIGHTS
NATIONAL MUSEUM OF KOREA

Korea's National Museum occupies a grand, marble-lined, modernist complex, built on the former golf course of the adjacent US military base. Set in landscaped parklands, the massive Great Hall displays a fraction of the museum's 270,000 cultural treasures from prehistoric times to the Joseon dynasty.

Exhibits & Gardens

Hour-long English-language tours leave from National Museum of Korea (국립중앙박물관) Great Hall lobby at 10.30am and 2.30pm; alternatively you can rent an audio guide or ask for the useful pamphlet *20 Masterpieces*.

Among the must-see exhibits in the ground-floor galleries are the Baekje Incense Burner, a decorative metal piece that's an extraordinary example of the artistry of the 6th-to 7th-century Baekje Kingdom; and the Golden Treasures for the Great Tomb of Hwangham, a delicate 5th-century gold belt and crown dripping with jade gems.

In the 3rd-floor sculpture and craft galleries, search out the Pensive Bodhisattva from the 7th century and beautiful examples of pottery. Also look down on the top of the Goryeo dynasty Ten Story Pagoda carved from marble. The surrounding park is best appreciated in good weather, when the Great Hall is perfectly reflected in the large Reflecting Pond. The original Bosingak Bell is in the grounds near the picturesque Dragon Falls.

Other Facilities

For picnic snacks in the park, there's a Family Mart convenience store near the main entrance, as well as several cafes and restaurants in the complex. There's also the fun Children's Museum, which provides hands-on exhibitions and educational programs (in Korean); admission is limited.

DON'T MISS

⇒ The Great Hall
⇒ Reflecting Pond
⇒ Dragon Falls

PRACTICALITIES

⇒ www.museum.go.kr
⇒ Ichon
⇒ admission free
⇒ ⊙9am-6pm Tue, Thu & Fri, 9am-9pm Wed & Sat, 9am-7pm Sun
⇒ Ⓜ Line 4 or Jungang Line to Ichon, Exit 2

◉ SIGHTS

NATIONAL MUSEUM OF KOREA   MUSEUM
See p88.

EUNGBONG PARK   VIEWPOINT
(응봉공원; Eungbong; **M**Line 6 to Hangangjin, Exit 2) For a panoramic view of the Han River looking towards Gangnam, take a short hike up to the pavilion atop Maebong-san, the hill at the heart of Eungbong Park northeast of the junction of Itaewon-ro and Hannam-ro. In spring masses of forsythia blossoms paint the park yellow. To reach the park cross the pedestrian bridge over Hannam-ro and walk north.

✕ EATING

OKITCHEN   FRENCH, ITALIAN **$$$**
Map p208 (☑77 6420; www.okitchen.pe.kr; off Itaewon-ro; mains ₩19,000-36,000; ⊙noon-2.30pm, 6-9.30pm; **M**Line 6 to Itaewon, Exit 1; 🛜🖐) Friendly service and set menus (starting at ₩21,000/52,000 for lunch/dinner) that balance price with quality make this one of Itaewon's surest bets for a quality meal. The chef hails from Okinawa and used to live in New York with his Korean food-stylist wife – the international sophistication shines through.

VATOS   MEXICAN **$**
Map p208 (☑797 8226; www.vatoskorea.com; off Itaewon-ro; mains ₩9000; ⊙11.30am-2pm & 5-10pm Tue-Fri, to 11pm Sat, to 10pm Sun; **M**Line 6 to Itaewon, Exit 4; 🛜🖐) Tacos have long been popular as a snack of choice for GIs and expats in Itaewon but these guys take their 'urban tacos' and Mexican eats to a gourmet level with delicious riffs such as tacos filled with galbi short ribs and Korean-style pork belly. The kimchi carnitas fries are good to try with the cocktails, which include a 'makgeolita', or selection of bottled US craft beers.

LE SAINT-EX   FRENCH **$$$**
Map p208 (☑795 2465; www.facebook.com/lesaintex; Itaewon 2-gil, Itaewon; mains ₩27,000-43,000; ⊙6pm-midnight; **M**Line 6 to Itaewon, Exit 1; 🛜🖐) The blackboard menu at this very French bistro with consistently good food and service is always tempting. A heater

◉ TOP SIGHTS
LEEUM SAMSUNG MUSEUM OF ART

Only have time to visit one art gallery in Seoul? Then make the Leeum – a masterful combination of contemporary architecture and exquisite art – your first choice. The hillside complex is made up of three contrasting buildings designed by leading international architects. It's fronted by a sculpture garden, containing Louise Bourgeois' *Maman* (a couple of giant spindly-legged spiders) and her surrealist *Eyebenches*, and is a great spot to relax.

The randomly flashing LED installation *Transcend Section* by Tatsuo Miyajima leads you into the lobby from where you access the three main buildings. Swiss architect Mario Botta took his inspiration from Korean pottery for Leeum's Museum 1, which houses refined traditional works – beautiful ceramics, metal work and Buddhist paintings. Korean art from 1910 and international pieces from 1945 onwards are the focus of Museum 2, in a building designed by Jean Nouvel.

Dutch architect Rem Koolhaas was commissioned for the museum's third element, the Samsung Child Education & Culture Center, a space used for special exhibitions.

DON'T MISS
➡ Museum 1
➡ Museum 2
➡ Samsung Child Education & Culture Centre

PRACTICALITIES
➡ Map p208
➡ www.leeum.org
➡ adult/child ₩10,000/free; temporary exhibition admission costs vary
➡ ⊙10.30am-6pm Tue-Sun
➡ **M**Line 6 to Hangangjin, Exit 1

and even blankets are available for the outside patio. The lunch sets are excellent, and in a sneaky move the irresistible desserts are always on display.

PARLOUR
BAKERY, CAFE **$$$**

Map p208 (📞9560 9561; Hannam-dong; afternoon tea without/with champagne ₩25,000/38,000; ⏱10am-10pm; 🚇Line 6 to Hangangjin, Exit 2; 🛜🖬) In the HQ of the company behind the ubiquitous Paris Croissant chain of bakery-cafes are several upscale operations of which this is the newest and most stylish. Offering a Fortnum & Mason–like experience, this is tea the English way (albeit with Kusmi brand teas from France). They also do 'elevenses' and snacklike nibbles for dinner. Upstairs is the swank bakery/cafe/confectioners Passion 5.

BUDDHA'S BELLY
THAI **$$**

Map p208 (📞796 9330; off Itaewon-ro; mains ₩5000-12,000; ⏱11.30am-2am; 🚇Line 6 to Itaewon, Exit 1; 🛜🖬) It's not difficult to understand why this restaurant and lounge bar is a much-recommended locals' favourite. The cooking is authentic and the ambience relaxed. The original tiny takeaway outlet is down the hill in Gyeongridan, with a few seats for dine-in customers.

SALAM
TURKISH **$$**

Map p208 (📞793 4323; www.turkeysalam.com; mains ₩8000-13,000; ⏱noon-10pm, closed 1st & 3rd Mon of month; 🚇Line 6 to Itaewon, Exit 3; 🖬) Next to the Itaewon mosque, this classy Turkish restaurant and bakery is great for a meal of hummus, kebabs and pide (Turkish pizza). If you're hungry there's a big set menu for ₩24,000.

MACARONI MARKET
FRENCH, ITALIAN **$$$**

Map p208 (📞749 9181; 2nd fl Hannam Bldg, Itaewonno; meals ₩20,000-30,000; ⏱11am-2am; 🚇Line 6 to Itaewon, Exit 2; 🛜🖬) This upscale, spacious deli, cafe, restaurant and bar is presided over by an accomplished local chef who served as one of the judges on the Korean version of the TV show *MasterChef*. The food is authentic and the big balcony windows provide a ringside seat on all the street action.

TARTINE
CAFE **$$**

Map p208 (📞3785 3400; www.tartine.co.kr; mains ₩9000-38,500; ⏱10am-10.30pm; 🚇Line 6 to Itaewon, Exit 1; 🖬) Looking for dessert?

TOP SIGHTS
WAR MEMORIAL OF KOREA

The huge three-floor War Memorial of Korea museum (전쟁기념관) documents the history of warfare in Korea, with the focus mainly on the Korean War (1950–53). Photos, maps, artefacts and black-and-white documentary films give a fascinating insight into what the war was like: the surprise 4am attack from the North (spearheaded by 240 Russian-made tanks), the build-up of UN (mainly US) forces in Busan, the daring amphibious landing at Incheon and the sweep north followed by the surprise Chinese attack.

On the 3rd floor the Combat Experience Room is just that, and lasts five minutes (every 30 minutes from 9.30am to 4.30pm). Other displays cover Korea's involvement in the Vietnam War (4700 Koreans died), North Korean attacks on the South since 1953, and Korea's UN peacekeeping roles.

Outside there's plenty of large military hardware, including tanks, helicopters, missiles and a B52 bomber, as well as monuments and giant statues. Time your visit to see the **Honour Guard Ceremony** (⏱2pm Fri early Apr-end Jun, mid-Oct–end Nov) when a military band performs, and a marching parade culminates in an awesome display of military precision and weapon twirling.

DON'T MISS

➡ Korean War Room
➡ Combat Experience Room
➡ Statue of Brothers
➡ Outdoor Exhibit Areas

PRACTICALITIES

➡ Map p208
➡ www.warmemo.co.kr
➡ Samgakji
➡ admission free
➡ ⏱9am-6pm Tue-Sun
➡ 🚇Line 4 or 6 to Samgakji, Exit 12

You won't go wrong with the scrumptious fruit pies and other confections at this charming bakery-cafe run by an American baker. So successful has this place been it's expanded its operation across the alley to a bustling brunch cafe with plenty of menu options.

THE BAKER'S TABLE
BAKERY, CAFE $

Map p208 (http://blog.naver.com/mirabakery; Gyeongridan; sandwiches ₩5000; ⊗8am-9pm Tue-Sun; ⓂLine 6 to Noksapyeong, Exit 2; 🍴) German baker Micha Richter, one of the people behind Itaewon's long-running Gecko's Terrace, has opened this cute cafe serving gourmet-style sandwiches made using his breads, as well as other freshly baked pastries, sweet treats, soups and – why not? – Irish pale ale on tap.

M BURGER
BURGERS $

Map p208 (Noksapyeong-daero, Itaewon; burgers ₩7500-10,000; ⊗11.30am-10pm Tue Sun; ⓂLine 6 to Noksapyeong, Exit 2; 🛜🍴) Joining several other appealing eating houses lined up along Noksapyeong-daero is this mini-diner-style burger bar. Cheeseburger lovers should order the 'Juicy Lucy': the cheese is sandwiched inside the 170g patty.

ZELEN
BULGARIAN $$

Map p208 (⌨749 0600; Itaewon 2-gil, Itaewon; meals ₩9000-24,000; ⊗11.30am-3pm & 6-11pm Wed-Sun, 6-11pm Tue; ⓂLine 6 to Itaewon, Exit 1) Run by a couple of Bulgarian guys, this is a warm and welcoming restaurant. Meat lovers have plenty of options, and there are wines, too. Meals like *kiufte* meatballs are served on a big white platter, while the *giuvedje* stew is smaller but packed with meats.

ROSE BAKERY
BAKERY, CAFE $$

Map p208 (Hannam-dong; mains ₩13,500-18,000; ⊗8am-9pm; ⓂLine 6 to Hangangjin, Exit 1; 🛜🍴) On the ground floor of the hip Comme des Garçon boutique (itself worth a look for its maze-like five-floor layout and super-fashionable clothing) is this relaxed cafe. There are coloured crayons are on the table for you to doodle on the butcher's paper while you wait for your tasty sandwich, quiche or home-baked treat to be served.

LIFE IS JUST A CUP OF CAKE
CUPCAKES $

Map p208 (www.cupcake.co.kr; Hannam-dong; cupcakes ₩4800; ⊗noon-9pm; ⓂLine 6 to Itaewon, Exit 2) Super-cute cafe specialising in iced cupcakes which come in many different flavours. Ask the English-speaking owner/baker Saem Lee about her special orders of mini cupcakes.

🍷 DRINKING & NIGHTLIFE

⌚CHOICE CRAFTWORKS
MICROBREWERY

Map p208 (http://craftworkstaphouse.com; Gyeongridan; ⓂLine 6 to Noksapyeong, Exit 2) Craftworks has secured a treasured place in the heart of Seoul's real ale lovers. You can sample seven types from their range for ₩9500 and then decide which one to savour in a pint. What with a full week of special dining nights plus the super-popular pub quiz on Wednesday – is it any wonder that many locals have made this their local?

TAKEOUT DRAWING
CAFE

Map p208 (www.takeoutdrawing.com; ⊗2pm-10am) Gyeongridan (ⓂLine 6 to Noksapyeong, Exit 2) Hannamd-dong (ⓂLine 6 to Hanganjjin, Exit 3; 🛜🍴) These guys want to use drawing 'to change the world' and we're not about to argue with that. Either of the two branches of this arty cafe are a cool place to hang out and enjoy graphic art, books, magazines and coffee with a twist (try the espresso with a spiky meringue topping), organic teas and other beverages.

DISTRICT
BAR, CLUB

Map p208 (www.mykinc.com; ⓂLine 6 to Itaewon, Exit 1) A department store of pleasurable intoxication, this new drinking, dining and dancing complex behind the Hamilton Hotel has a trio of appealing, fashion-conscious options. On the ground floor is the handsome gastro-pub Prost, serving a hearty pub-style meals and beers; up a floor is the dark and stylish cocktail and wine bar Glam; and up one more floor is the dance club Mute.

UNION
BAR, DJ

Map p208 (off Itaewon-ro; ⓂLine 6 to Itaewon, Exit 4) Run by DJ Conan, this three-storey *soju* and beer bar, also serving dishes such as *samgyeopsal* (barbecue streaky bacon) is a prime spot to take Seoul's musical pulse. A changing roster of local DJs keeps the vibe cool and laid-back, plus there's a breezy rooftop deck that's great when the weather's steaming.

THE BREW SHOP
MICROBREWERY

Map p208 (http://magpiebrewing.com; Gyeongridan; ⊙2pm-10am; ⓂLine 6 to Noksapyeong, Exit 2) A stripped-down outlet behind Baker's Table is where you can come to sample the real ales of Magpie Brewing, a fledgling microbrewery establishing a name for itself around town. Occasional beer-making classes (₩50,000 including lunch, beer tasting and take-home booklet) are held here as well as food parings and tastings.

BERLIN
COCKTAILS

Map p208 (☏749 0903; ⊙11.30am-2am; ⓂLine 6 to Itaewon, Exit 1) This sophisticated gay-friendly cafe, lounge and restaurant, set away from the main Itaewon drag, has an airy terrace with a view across to the Yongsan US military base; later in the evening a DJ plays. Upstairs is the restaurant Buddha's Belly, owned by the same people.

BURN
BAR

Map p208 (www.burninhal.com; Gyeongridan; ⓂLine 6 to Noksapyeong, Exit 2) All kinds of cigars including top-class Cuban ones, single malt whiskeys and other rare tipples are the poisons of choice at this convivial bar with a shabby Edwardian English club atmosphere on the main strip in Gyeongridan.

WAYS OF SEEING
CAFE, BAR

Map p208 (http://thesuninjang.com; Hannam-dong; ⊙11am-midnight Mon-Sat, 11am-10pm Sun; ⓂLine 6 to Hanganjin, Exit 3; ☏) This is as good a place as any to suss the area's pulse and hang with hipsters while sipping your latte or beer. It's down an alley that runs parallel to Itaewon-ro in Hannam-dong that's seeing a few trendy boutiques and cafe-bars opening up. They do food and host events including art shows and the Fifty Seoul (https://twitter.com/fiftyseoul) flea market.

3 ALLEY PUB
PUB

Map p208 (www.3alleypub.com; Itaewon 2-gil, Itaewon; ⊙noon-1am Sun-Thu, noon-2am Fri & Sat; ⓂLine 6 to Itaewon, Exit 1) Mixing together a friendly pub atmosphere (darts, pool, cheap chicken wings on Tuesday, a trivia quiz on Wednesday) with top-notch European-style pub grub and nine draught beers is a formula that makes this place an expat magnet, especially with the older crowd. Upstairs is another popular boozer, Sam Ryans.

ROCKY MOUNTAIN TAVERN
PUB

Map p208 (www.rockymountaintavern.com; ⓂLine 6 to Itaewon, Exit 3) On the first Thursday of the month this Canadian-themed pub hosts **Stand Up Seoul** (www.facebook.com/groups/70594819792; cover charge ₩5000) a

---

LOCAL KNOWLEDGE

ON THE HILL

Squished between 'Hooker Hill' and the Little Arabia strip by the Seoul Mosque, 'Homo Hill' (Map p208) is a 50m alley so called because of its cluster of gay-friendly bars and clubs. Most hardly have room to swing a handbag, so on warm weekends the crowds often spill into the street. All genders and sexual persuasions will feel welcome here.

At the bottom of the hill on the left is **Trance** (http://cafe.daum.net/trance; admission ₩10,000; ⊙11pm-5am), a basement club with pouting drag queens and late-night shows; the entrance fee includes one drink. Next door is the eternally popular **Queen** (www.facebook.com/queenbar; ⊙8pm-5am Tue-Sun), which offers sit-and-chat zones though it usually gets very crowded with most everyone dancing.

Flirty friendly staff, low-playing music and a cosy style mark out **Always Homme** (⊙8pm-4am Sun-Thu, 8pm-6am Fri & Sat); the same management runs **Why Not** (admission ₩10,000; ⊙8pm-6am), a dance club across the alley with lights and lasers; expect plenty of K-pop. On the same side of the street, higher up the hill is **Soho** (⊙7pm-5am), one of the roomier places on the strip and the main competition to Queen; most customers spend the night shuttling between the two. Finish up (or start) the night at **Eat Me** (⊙6.30pm-4am), a convivial joint that serves Asian nibbles all night long.

To reach here from exit 3 of Itaewon station head uphill and take the first major road right; Homo Hill is the second street on the left. For info on other venues here and nearby see http://queerkorea.weebly.com/itaewon.html.

chance to catch the variable comedy stylings of expat performers.

MADAGASCAR CAFE
Map p209 (www.madagascarlove.com; Hyochang Park; ☉9.30am-11pm; Ⓜ Line 6 to Hyochang Park, Exit 2; ☎) Around the corner from the White Box Theatre and near pleasant Hyochang Park is this spacious, comfy travel-themed cafe, its walls decorated with arresting photo images and shelves lined with books.

MOWMOW BAR
Map p208 (Itaewon; ☉11.30am-2am; Ⓜ Line 6 to Itaewon, Exit 1) There are usually a lot more brands of *makgeolli* (staring from ₩4000) to choose from than listed on the menu at this airy bar and eatery up the hill from the main Itaewon dining alley. Try one of the *makgeolli* cocktails (₩9000).

ALMAZ GAY
Map p208 (☉7am-4pm Sun-Thu, to 6am Fri & Sat; Ⓜ Line 6 to Itaewon, Exit 3) The bars of Homo Hill are not the only gay-friendly watering holes in Itaewon. Almaz, at the foot of Hooker Hill, is one of the best places to start the evening. It's a large, elegant lounge with an outdoor patio area and friendly bartenders.

PULSE GAY
Map p208 (entrance Fri/Sat ₩10,000/15,000; ☉midnight-6am Fri & Sat; Ⓜ Line 6 to Itaewon, Exit 3) There's room for upwards of 1000 punters on a busy weekend night at this popular gay club. K-pop and house music rule and there's plenty of stripper poles and flashing lights for you to shimmy around. Don't expect it to start rockin', though, until the very small hours of the morning.

B1 CLUB
Map p208 (entrance Sat ₩5000; Ⓜ Line 6 to Itaewon, Exit 1) On an alley just beyond the Hamilton Hotel is this newish lounge bar that morphs into a dance club on weekend nights. While not exclusively gay it's certainly gay-friendly.

⭐ ENTERTAINMENT

ALL THAT JAZZ JAZZ
p208 (☎795 5701; www.allthatjazz.kr; Itaewon; admission ₩5000; ☉8pm-midnight Sun-Thu, to 2am Fri & Sat; Ⓜ Line 6 to Itaewon, Exit 2) A fixture on the Seoul jazz scene since 1976, All That Jazz has a new, more spacious location closer to the subway. Top local musicians regularly perform here and table reservations are recommended for the weekend. The live music starts at 9pm except on Friday (8.30pm) and Saturday and Sunday (both 7pm).

WHITE BOX THEATRE THEATRE
Map p209 (www.probationarytheatre.com; tickets ₩15,000; Ⓜ Line 6 to Hyochang Park, Exit 2) This basement studio space is the home of the Probationary Theatre Company, dream project of Australian expat Desiree Munro. A different production plays each month, mainly on Friday, Saturday and Sunday, and they've tackled contemporary plays ranging from *Art* to *Who's Afraid of Virginia Woolf?*

SHOPPING

MILLIMETRE MILLIGRAM STATIONERY, BAGS
Map p208 (www.mmmg.net; Hannam-dong; Ⓜ Line 6 to Itaewon, Exit 3) Usually shortened to MMG, this is the spot to pick up quirky stationery and bags, including the Austrian brand Freitag. There's a cafe as well as a basement gallery/furniture store and, on the 3rd floor, the boutique art book and magazine shop **Post Poetics** (www.postpoetics.org; ☉1-8pm Tue-Fri, to 6pm Sat & Sun). There are also MMG shops near Anguk station in Insadong and on Garosugil.

YONGSAN ELECTRONICS MARKET ELECTRONICS
Map p209 (Yongsan; ☉9.30am-7.30pm, partly closed 1st & 3rd Sun; Ⓜ Line 1 Yongsan, Exit 3) If it plugs in you can find it at this geeky universe of high-tech marvels. Computer prices are usually marked but prices on other goods are lacking, so do what the locals do – check out the prices online before arriving. Leave the train station plaza via Exit 3, turn right, then right again and walk through the pedestrian overpass to enter the first building of Yongsan Electronics Town on the 3rd floor. If all this is too much try discount electronics chain E-Mart in the nearby I'Park Mall.

WHAT THE BOOK BOOKS
Map p208 (www.whatthebook.com; Itaewon-ro; ☉10am-8pm Mon-Sat, from noon Sun; Ⓜ Line 6 to

ITAEWON & YONGSAN-GU ENTERTAINMENT

LOCAL KNOWLEDGE

HANGING OUT IN HBC WITH SAM HAMMINGTON

Australian Sam Hammington is a comedian who regularly appears on the TV comedy show Gag Concert and co-hosts the Drive Time show on radio TBS 101.3FM in Seoul. Since arriving in Seoul in 2002 he has lived in Haebangchon (HBC).

'It used to be called the Ghetto,' says Hammington about HBC, which means 'liberation village' and was one of Seoul's original *daldongne* – a hillside tent village where Korean refugees lived in the 1950s and '60s. 'Together with Gyeongridan at the bottom of the hill, the area is now an arty enclave with a really diverse population.'

'You'll find some things here you won't find in other parts of Seoul,' says Hammington, such as the acoustic music **HBC Fest** (www.hbcfest.com) and a craft brewing and fermented foods festival, supported by local brewers Craftworks and Magpie Brewing.

To reach HBC take subway line 6 to Noksapyeong, head out of exit 2 and walk downhill, veering left at the kimchi pots. Hammington lists some of his favourite spots along this main drag going uphill towards Namsan.

Best Korean Barbecue
HBC Gogitjip (HBC고깃집; ☑796 5528; meals ₩10,000-25,000; ☺5-11pm Sun & Mon, 5pm-1am Tue-Sat; ☎) is my favourite galbi joint – I usually order the prime flower beef which isn't marinated. Each meal comes with plenty of side dishes and they have Dr Pepper BBQ sauce if you prefer instead of chilli paste.

Best Makgeolli
Damotori (다모토리; ☺6pm-1am Sun-Thu, to 2am Fri & Sat; ☎) serves around 30 types of *makgeolli* (Korean rice wine) including ones that are handmade with top quality natural ingredients.

Best Hang-outs
Phillies Pub is an institution, as are the brunch spot **Indigo** and above it, **The Orange Tree**, a bar which occasionally hosts comedy and improv nights.

Best Coffee
HBC is coffeeshop heavy. My favourite is **Le Cafe**; the owner roasts the coffee in the store so you can be sure it's fresh and tastes great. Across the road is the trendier-looking **Hackney**, which is also pet friendly.

Best Sandwich
Casablanca Sandwicherie (sandwiches ₩4000-5000; ☺5-10.45pm Tue-Sun) is always busy – no wonder as their Moroccan sandwiches served in crispy baguettes are incredible.

Itaewon, Exit 3) Itaewon's best bookshop sells new and secondhand English-language books as well as a wide range of American magazines.

TWO HEADS ARE BETTER
THAN ONE   FASHION
Map p208 (www.steveandyonip.com; Hannamdong; ☺11.30am-7.30pm; Ⓜ Line 6 to Hanganjin, Exit 3) The two heads collaborating on the super-fashionable streetware in this boutique are local designers Steve J and Yoni P. Their T-shirts, sweatshirts and colourful printed clobber is stocked by high-class boutiques around the world, but their flagship store is down this happening little street in Hannam-dong.

I'PARK MALL   MALL
Map p209 (www.iparkmall.co.kr; Yongsan; Ⓜ Line 1 to Yongsan, Line 4 to Sinyongsan, Exit 3 or 4) There's pretty much everything you need from brand-name fashion to digital goods at this mall that sprawls around the major overground Yongsan station. Up on the 9th floor is the e-Sports Stadium where e-game tournaments are staged.

THE BARBER SHOP   BARBER
Map p208 (Sobangseo-gil; haircuts from ₩7000; ☺10am-9pm Mon-Sat, noon-9pm Sun; Ⓜ Line 6 to

Itaewon, Exit 3) The English-speaking barber here learnt his trade at a branch of Vidal Sassoon's in London, and his skillful haircuts are an Itaewon bargain.

GOLDEN EELSKIN   LEATHER GOODS
Map p208 (Itaewon-ro; ⊙10am-8pm; MLine 6 to Itaewon, Exit 4) A good place to purchase eelskin handbags, belts, wallets and purses. Eelskin goods are an Itaewon speciality that make popular gifts. Owner Mr Kim is quietly persuasive but never hassles anyone. Purses start at ₩5000, belts at ₩12,000.

HAMILTON SHIRTS   FASHION
Map p208 (www.hs76.com; Itaewon-ro; MLine 6 to Itaewon, Exit 4) One of the larger and most reliable of the dedicated shirt makers that are clustered along Itaewon-ro; they also have a branch in Myeong-dong. A 100% cotton shirts start from ₩39,000.

DYNASTY TAILOR   FASHION
Map p208 (www.dynastytailor.com; off Itaewon-ro; ⊙10am-8pm; MLine 6 to Itaewon, Exit 4) The suits here are all handmade in the traditional way by expert tailors just a few doors down from the shop. Ask to see the workshop. Pure wool suits cost ₩350,000 to ₩400,000 and take about three days to make.

GALLERY GOLMOK   ART GALLERY
Map p208 (www.gallery-golmok.com; off Itaewon-ro; MLine 6 to Itaewon, Exit 4) Tucked away in an alley is this small gallery and cafe. It hosts a craft market every Sunday (noon to 6pm) and sometimes has performance-art events in the evening.

🏃 SPORTS & ACTIVITIES

DRAGON HILL SPA & RESORT   SAUNA
Map p209 (www.dragonhillspa.co.kr; Yongsan; day/night Mon-Fri ₩10,000/12,000, Sat & Sun all day ₩12,000; ⊙24hr; MLine 1 to Yongsan, Exit 1;

📞) This foreigner-friendly *jjimjil-bang* – a noisy mix of gaudy Las Vegas bling and Asian chic – is one of Seoul's largest, offering enough attractions over its seven floors to keep you entertained the 12 hours you can stay. In addition to the outdoor unisex pool, all manner of indoor saunas (including one shaped like a pyramid) and ginseng and cedar baths, there is a golf driving range, cinema, PC games room, beauty treatment rooms and multiple dining options. Show your Asiana Airlines ticket and you'll get in for half price.

HAMILTON HOTEL   GYM
Map p208 (해밀톤 호텔; http://hamilton.co.kr; MLine 6 to Itaewon, Exit 1) Quite the scene in the hot summer months, the Hamilton's **outdoor pool** (₩12,000 Mon-Fri, ₩16,000 Sat & Sun; ⊙10am-6pm late May-early Sep) is beloved by gay men and posturing Itaewon types. The **gym** (₩60,000; ⊙6.30am-11pm) is a decent workout option and there's a small **sauna** (₩7000, 10pm-5am ₩13,000; ⊙24hr).

ITAEWONLAND   SAUNA
Map p208 (📞749 4122; www.itaewonland.com; Hannam-dong; sauna ₩6000, 6pm-6am ₩8000; ⊙24hr; MLine 6 to Itaewon, Exit 2) This *jjimjil-bang* with a traditional gate facade is up a flight of steep steps from Itaewon-ro. A scrubdown is an extra ₩20,000, a massage ₩60,000.

BODY & SEOUL   GYM
Map p208 (📞749 2485; www.seoulmartialarts.com; Gyeongridan; classes ₩15,000-20,000; MLine 6 to Noksapyeong, Exit 2) Various martial arts and fitness classes are offered here by English-speaking trainers; it's above Craftworks pub.

JANKARA ARTSPACE   ART STUDIO
Map p208 (📞010-6227 4244; http://mstewartprintmaker.com/jankura.htm; Bogwang-dong; art classes from ₩10,000; MLine 6 to Itaewon, Exit 2) Regular drawing, life drawing and printing classes with tuition from expat Mike Stewart are held at this small artists-share studio.

Gangnam & South of the Han River

Neighbourhood Top Five

1 Pedal around the giant **Olympic Park** (p98), where there are the remains of 1700-year-old earth fortifications, the new Seoul Baekje Museum and over 200 quirky sculptures.

2 Join in the amusement-park fun of **Lotte World** (p100), with its thrill rides and fairy-tale carousel and castle.

3 Make a lotus lantern and sip tea with monks at the venerable temple **Bongeun-sa** (p99).

4 Pay your respects at **Seonjeongneung** (p99), the tombs of past Korean kings in Seolleung Park.

5 Head to **Seoul Grand Park** to enjoy the zoo, the amusement park and **National Museum of Contemporary Art** (p100).

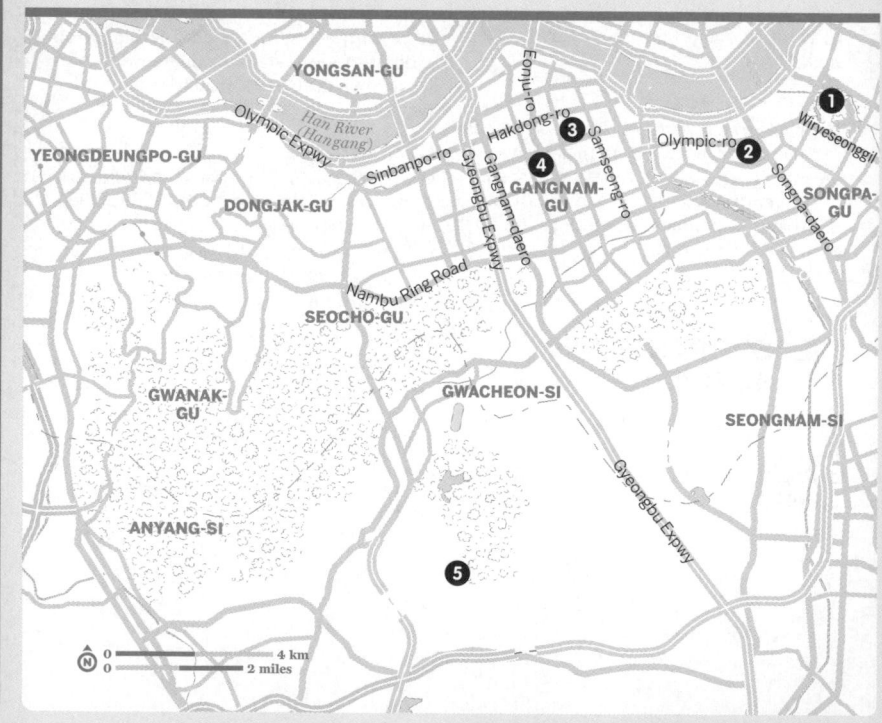

For more detail of this area, see Map p212 ➡

Explore Gangnam & South of the Han River

Meaning South of the River, Gangnam refers to an administrative area, Gangnam-gu, and the parts of Seoul that lie south of the Han. Looking at the ranks of tower blocks bisected by broad highways, it's hard to imagine that there wasn't much of the city here a few decades ago. The area saw much development for the 1988 Olympics, the legacy of which is Olympic Park. Built in the same location as the ancient fortress city Hanseong, this is one of the area's few bona-fide sights.

Another is the impressive Buddhist temple Bongeunsa; and Gangnam's wide open spaces allowed Lotte to create its giant indoor and outdoor theme park. But mainly this newer part of Seoul is a ritzy residential address, entertainment district and business hub with major company headquarters, such as Samsung D-Light, and the COEX complex with its convention centre and shopping mall.

Retail is as flash as it gets in upscale Apgujeong and Cheongdam. Checking out the eye-boggling design boutiques, with even more eye-boggling price tags on the merchandise, can be fun even if you lack the credit for purchases. More affordable is the shopping on nearby Garosu-gil.

Further south the Seoul Arts Centre promotes traditional and modern culture, Korean and Western, while in Gwacheon (technically outside the city limits), Seoul Grand Park is home to a huge zoo, major art gallery and a big amusement park.

Local Life

➡ **Shopping** Taxi hop between the designer boutiques of Apgujeong and Cheongdam – you wouldn't want to ruin your Jimmy Choo stilettos!

➡ **Clubbing** Sip cocktails and shimmy with the rich, celebs and wannabes at Seoul's flashiest nightspots such as Ellui and Club Eden.

➡ **Riverside Activities** Walk or cycle through the Han Riverside Park; and drop by the Banpo Bridge at night to see the Moonlight Rainbow Fountain and the illuminated Floating Islands.

Getting There & Away

➡ **Subway** The neighbourhood is too spread out for walking, so subway is the way to go.

➡ **Taxi** By road or in a boat along the Han River (www.pleasantseoul.com), hopping in a taxi can save time travelling around Gangnam.

Lonely Planet's Top Tip

The city has built several viewing cafes beside the bridges crossing the Han River. Two that are easy to access are **Dongjak Neoul Café** and **Dongjak Gureum Café** (M Line 4 Dongjak Station, Exit 1 or 2), a short walk from the subway exit.

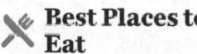 Best Places to Eat

➡ Jung Sikdang (p102)
➡ Gorilla in the Kitchen (p102)
➡ Samwon Garden (p102)

For reviews, p102 ➡

Best Places to Drink

➡ Platoon Kunsthalle (p103)
➡ Moon Jar (p103)
➡ Take Urban (p103)

For reviews, see p103 ➡

 Best Places to Shop

➡ 10 Corso Como Seoul (p105)
➡ D Cube City (p105)
➡ COEX Mall (p105)

For reviews, see p105 ➡

GANGNAM & SOUTH OF THE HAN RIVER

◎ TOP SIGHTS
OLYMPIC PARK

This large and pleasant park, a focus of the 1988 Olympics, also contains the remains of the Mongchon-toseong (Mongchon Fortress), an earth rampart surrounded by a moat, built in the 3rd century AD during the Baekje dynasty. Walk along the top of the old ramparts and learn more about them in a new museum.

History Museums

Olympic Park's (올림픽 공원) **Seoul Baekje Museum** (http://baekjemuseum.seoul.go.kr; admission free; ⊘9am-9pm Tue-Fri, 9am-6pm Sat & Sun) illuminates the history and culture of Hanseong (18 BC–AD 475), when this part of Seoul was the capital of the Baekje kingdom. Displays spread across three floors surround a full-scale model of workers constructing an earth rampart.

The **Mongchon Museum** (admission free; ⊘10am-8pm Tue-Fri, to 6pm Sat & Sun) has some precious golden relics of the Baekje kings and the usual dull pots.

Olympic Memorials

The **Olympic Museum** (www.88olympic.or.kr; admission free; ⊘10am-6pm Tue-Sun) has screens showing highlights of the 1988 Olympics, together with a brief history of the games. More interesting is the **SOMA Museum of Art** (www.soma museum.org; adult/child ₩3000/1000; ⊘10am-6pm Tue-Sun), with its display of Olympics-themed video art by Nam June Paik and five galleries for special exhibitions.

Scattered like buckshot around the park are over 200 quirky sculptures, the most prominent of which is the striking World Peace Gate, designed by Kim Jung-up for the Olympics.

DON'T MISS

➡ World Peace Gate
➡ Seoul Baekje Museum
➡ SOMA Museum of Art
➡ Mongchon-toseong

PRACTICALITIES

➡ Map p212
➡ Bang-dong, Songpa-gu
➡ admission free
➡ Ⓜ Line 8 to Mong-chontoseong, Exit 1 or Line 5 to Olympic Park Station, Exit 3

⦿ SIGHTS

OLYMPIC PARK   PARK
See p98.

SEONJEONGNEUNG   ROYAL TOMBS
Map p212 (선정릉; http://seonjeong.cha.go.kr; Seonjeongneung Park, Gangnam-gu; adult/teenager ₩1000/500; ⊙6am-5.30pm Tue-Sun Mar-Oct, 6.30am-8pm Tue-Sun Nov-Feb; MLine 2 or Bundang Line to Seolleung, Exit 8) The tombs of the Joseon kings and queens are scattered all around Seoul and the surrounding area. Seonjeongneung Park contains two main burial areas. The first is for King Seongjong (r 1469–94), who was a prolific author and father – he had 28 children by 12 wives and concubines. Go around the side and you can walk up to the tomb for a closer look. Nearby is the tomb of King Seongjong's second wife, Queen Jeonghyeon Wanghu.

A 10-minute walk further on through the thickly wooded park is the tomb of King Seongjong and Queen Jeonghyeon's second son, King Jeongjong (r 1506–44). Although he ruled for 38 years he was a weak king and court factions held the real power, as they often did during the Joseon period. At this tomb you can see the full layout – the gateway and the double pathway to the pavilion where memorial rites were carried out – but you can't go near the tomb.

COEX AQUARIUM   AQUARIUM
Map p212 (www.coexaqua.com; COEX, Yeong-dong-daero, Gangnam-gu; adult/child ₩17,500/11,000; ⊙10am-8pm, last entry 7pm; MLine 2 to Samseong, Exit 6) Seoul's largest aquarium exhibits thousands of fish and other sea creatures from around the world. You can see live coral, sharks, turtles, rays and evil-looking piranhas in their Amazonia World tanks. Exquisite small creatures such as pulsating jellyfish, glass fish and sea horses are also on display, as are the ever-popular penguins.

FREE BANPO BRIDGE & FLOATING ISLAND   ARCHITECTURE
Map p210 (http://hangang.seoul.go.kr/eng; Hanggan Riverside Park; MLine 3, 7 or 9 to Express Bus Terminal, Exit 8-1) At 1140m long, the world's longest fountain rains down in graceful arcs from the double-decker Banpo Bridge and is best viewed from Banpo Hangang Park. The 15-minute show usually happens

---

⦿ TOP SIGHTS
BONGEUN-SA

The shrines and halls of the Buddhist temple Bongeun-sa (봉은사) are spread over a forested hillside and have a secluded atmosphere. Founded in AD 794, the buildings have been rebuilt many times over the centuries.

Entry to the temple is through Jinyeomun (Gate of Truth), protected by four fierce guardians. On the left is a small hut where an English-speaking volunteer guide is usually available.

The main shrine, Daewungjeon is decorated inside and out with symbols and art that express Buddhist philosophy and ideals. A small 14th-century bell is hidden in one corner. On the right is the funeral hall, while behind are smaller shrine halls and a massive statue – the Maitreya (Future) Buddha.

Nearby is the oldest hall, Panjeon, constructed in 1856, which houses over 3000 150-year-old woodblocks with Buddhist scripture and art carved into them.

Visit on Thursday if you want to take part in the **Templelife program** (₩20,000/10,000; ⊙2-4pm Thu) which includes lotus-lantern making, *dado* (tea ceremony), a temple tour and Seon (Zen) meditation. Book three weeks in advance to take part in the overnight Templestay programs (₩70,000).

DON'T MISS
➡ Jinyeomun
➡ Daewungjeon
➡ Panjeon
➡ Templelife program

PRACTICALITIES
➡ Map p212
➡ ☑3218 4801
➡ www.bongeunsa.org
➡ Samseong-dong, Gangnam-gu
➡ MLine 2 to Samseong, Exit 6

between April and the end of August at noon, 8pm and 9pm Monday to Friday and noon, 6pm, 8pm, 8.30pm and 9pm on Saturday and Sunday. At night 200 coloured lights turn the water sprays into a rainbow, which explains its official name, the Moonlight Rainbow Fountain. Shows are cancelled if it's raining.

Just to the west of the bridge are three artificial floating islets, connected by pathways and anchored to the bottom of the river. Crowned by sculptural glass auditoria, the complex is called the Floating Island (www.floatingisland.com) and is a pretty sight, particularly when illuminated at night. However, it is yet another of the costly design white elephants from Seoul's previous city administration; most of the time nothing much happens here – there's not even a cafe.

Underneath the Banpo Bridge, the Jamsu Bridge has walking and cycle lanes leading across to the Hangang Park on the north side; uphill from here is Itaewon.

HORIM ART CENTER
MUSEUM

Map p210 (www.horimartcenter.org; dosan-daero, Apgujeong; adult/child ₩8000/5000; ⊙10.30am-6pm Tue & Thu-Sun, to 8pm Wed; MLine 3 to Apgujeong, Exit 3) Designed by Tehje Architecture Office, this is exactly the sort of stylish complex you'd expect to find in chic Apgujeong (but so often don't). The building's design was inspired by pottery and inside the lustrous walls is a museum devoted to this Korean art form.

FREE NATIONAL MUSEUM OF CONTEMPORARY ART
MUSEUM

(www.moca.go.kr; Seoul Grand Park, Gwacheon; special exhibition entry costs vary; ⊙10am-6pm Tue-Fri, to 9pm Sat & Sun Mar-Oct, 10am-5pm Tue-Fri, to 8pm Sat & Sun Nov-Feb; MLine 4 to Seoul Grand Park, Exit 4, then shuttle bus) The best reason for making the trip out to Seoul Grand Park is to visit this large and striking museum spread out over three floors and surrounded by a sculpture garden. The dazzling highlight is Nam June Paik's *The More the Better,* an 18m-tall pagoda-shaped video installation that uses 1000 flickering screens to make a comment on our increasingly electronic universe. Construction of an annex in Seoul's Samcheon-dong district is underway, scheduled for completion in 2013.

TOP SIGHTS
LOTTE WORLD

Kids *and* adults love the massive entertainment hub of Lotte World (롯데월드). The main attraction is **Lotte World Adventure & Magic Island** (adult/child ₩25,000/19,000, passport incl most rides adult/child ₩40,000/31,000; ⊙9.30am-10pm Mon-Thu, to 11pm Fri-Sun), a Korean version of Disneyland with the chipmunk-like Lotty and Lorry standing in for Mickey and Minnie.

Outdoor Magic Island is in the middle of Seokchon Lake and is closed in bad weather, but since much of the amusement park is based indoors over four floors this is not such a big deal. The beautifully decorated Camelot Carousel with 64 horses is a popular ride, and there's a 4D theatre.

On the third floor the **Folk Museum** (adult/child ₩5000/2000; ⊙9.30am-8pm) uses imaginative techniques like dioramas, scale models and moving waxworks to bring scenes from Korean history to life. Entrance is included in the day-passport ticket for Lotte World Adventure & Magic Island.

Other attractions include an **ice-skating rink** (B3 fl; per session adult/child ₩13,000/12,000, skate rental ₩4500; ⊙10am-10pm), theatre, multiplex cinema, department store, shopping mall, hotel and restaurants.

DON'T MISS

➡ Lotte World Adventure & Magic Island
➡ Folk Museum
➡ Ice-skating rink

PRACTICALITIES

➡ Map p212
➡ www.lotteworld.com
➡ Jamsil-dong, Songpa-gu
➡ MLine 2 or 8 to Jamsil, Exit 3

ROYAL TOMBS OF THE JOSEON DYNASTY

The 40-odd **royal tombs of the Joseon dynasty** (http://whc.Unesco.org/en/list/1319) are World Heritage listed and scattered across Seoul and Gyeonggi-do with a couple also in the North Korean city of Kaesong. In these tombs, each similarly arranged on hillsides according to the rules of Confucianism and feng shui, are buried every Joseon ruler right up to the last, Emperor Sunjong (r 1907–10). Tomb entrances are marked by a simple red-painted wooden gate, stone pathway and hall for conducting rites in front of the humped burial mounds decorated with stone statuary – typically a pair of civil officers and generals, plus horses and protecting animals such as tigers and rams.

The most central tomb in Seoul is **Seonjeongneung**. However, the largest and most attractive complex is **Donggureung** (동구릉; donggu.cha.go.kr; adult/child ₩1000/500; ☉6am-6.30pm Mar-Oct, to 5.30pm Nov-Feb) in Guri, around 20km northeast of central Seoul. Here lie seven kings and 10 queens, including the dynasty's founder King Taejo: in contrast to the other neatly clipped plots in this leafy park, his mound sprouts rushes from his hometown of Hamhung (now in North Korea) that – in accordance with the king's pre-death instructions – have never been cut. To reach the complex take subway Line 2 to Gangbyeon to connect with bus 1, 1-1 or 1115-6, around a two-hour trip from central Seoul.

SEOUL ZOO
ZOO

(http://grandpark.seoul.go.kr; Seoul Grand Park, Gwacheon; adult/child ₩3000/1000; ☉9am-7pm Mar-Oct, to 6pm Nov-Feb; Ⓜ Line 4 to Seoul Grand Park, Exit 2) One of the largest zoos in the world, this is home to a long list of exotic creatures including the popular African ones. It has a successful history of breeding, including tigers and pandas. Also here is an indoor botanic garden housing a forest of cacti, numerous orchids and carnivorous pitcher plants.

SEOUL LAND
AMUSEMENT PARK

(www.seoulland.co.kr; Seoul Grand Park, Gwacheon; day pass adult/child ₩31,000/24,000; ☉9.30am-10pm summer, to 6pm winter; Ⓜ Line 4 to Seoul Grand Park, Exit 2) Keep the children happy all day at this family amusement park with five themed areas, special shows and the main attraction: thrill rides and roller coasters that spin you like a top or drop you like a stone. Everland and Lotte World are better overall, but small kids will still be very happy here.

FREE SAMSUNG D'LIGHT
DIGITAL PLAYGROUND

Map p210 (www.samsungdlight.com; ☉10am-7pm Mon-Sat; Ⓜ Line 2 to Gangnam, Exit 8) Spread over three floors, one of which is devoted to selling the latest lines of gadgets, this showroom showcases the technology of the Korean electronics giant Samsung, whose headquarters are in the same building. Whether you're a techno geek or not, it's fun to play around with the various digital gizmos: watch as a video wall is lit up with a patchwork of your face, or have your photo imposed on a digital scroll which you can then email to yourself or loved ones.

PORORO PARK
AMUSEMENT PARK

(w&ww.dcubecity.com; D Cube City, Guro-gu; adult/child ₩16,000/6000; ☉10.30am-8.30pm Mon-Fri, 10.30am-10pm Sat & Sun; Ⓜ Line 1 or 2 to Sindorim, Exit 2) The bespectacled penguin Pororo and his Antarctic friends Patty, Krom, Rup Eddy, Harry and Poby (a polar bear in the Antarctic? Hey, let's not get picky!) are superstars to Korean small ones. Chances are your kids will love them too, at this colourful indoor theme park on the 4th floor of D Cube City mall.

FREE MUSEUM OF KOREAN TRADITIONAL MUSIC
MUSEUM

(www.gugak.go.kr; ☉9am-6pm Tue-Sun; Ⓜ Line 3 to Nambu Bus Terminal, Exit 5) Next door to the Seoul Arts Centre is this recently renovated museum, now with hi-tech displays. You can see and listen to traditional Korean musical instruments that are rarely heard today, such as the *eo*, shaped like a tiger and played by banging its head with a stick and then running the stick over the notches on its back.

FREE SEOUL CALLIGRAPHY ART MUSEUM
MUSEUM

(www.sac.or.kr; Seoul Arts Centre; ☉11am-7pm; Ⓜ Line 3 to Nambu Bus Terminal, Exit 5) The most unique of the three art galleries at the sprawling arts complex is devoted to hand-drawn *hangeul* (Korean phonetic alphabet) and Chinese characters, showcasing both traditional and contemporary examples of this art form. The others are the **Hangaram Design Museum** and **Hangaram Art Museum** both free and with same opening hours. To reach the complex, walk straight on from the subway exit and turn left at the end of the bus terminal, or else hop on bus 12 or grab a taxi.

KIMCHI FIELD MUSEUM
MUSEUM

Map p212 (B2, COEX, Yeongdong-daero, Gangnam-gu; adult/child ₩3000/1000; ⊗10am-6pm Tue-Sun; ⓂLine 2 to Samseong, Exit 6) If you love kimchi, seek out this small exhibition in the basement of COEX which sings the praises of pickled, peppery cabbage and its wondrous health benefits. To find it, go down the steps near the 7-Eleven convenience store.

✖ EATING

⟨TOP CHOICE⟩ JUNG SIKDANG
NEO KOREAN $$$

Map p210 (중식당; ☑517 4654; http://jungsik .kr; Sinsa-dong, Gangnam-gu; lunch/dinner menu from ₩40,000/70,000; ⓂLine 3 to Apgujeong, Exit 3) Neo-Korean cuisine hardly gets better than this Apgujeong outpost of the New York restaurant Jungsik named after creative chef Yim Jungsik. Expect inspired contemporary mixes of traditional ingredients and an amazing chocolate dessert on a bed of sugar straw. Book ahead and ask for a table with a view across Dosan Park.

GORILLA IN THE KITCHEN
FUSION $$$

Map p210 (☑3442 1688; www.gorillakitchen .co.kr; Sinsa-dong Gangnam-gu; mains ₩27,000-45,000; ⓂLine 3 to Apgujeong, Exit 2) This smart restaurant, facing the entrance to Dosan Park, focuses on health food. Unlike other places it has a firm handle on casual Euro dining, and most meals come up trumps. It's the perfect spot to chill over a lazy brunch at the weekend.

SAMWON GARDEN
KOREAN $$$

Map p210 (삼원가든; ☑548 3030; www.samwon garden.com; Sinsa-dong, Gangnam-gu; mains from ₩28,000; ⓂLine 3 to Apgujeong, Exit 2) Serving top-class *galbi* for over 30 years, Samwon is a Korean idyll, surrounded by beautiful traditional gardens including several water-

falls. It's one of the best places in the city for this kind of barbecued beef meal.

GRILL5TACO
MEXICAN $

Map p210 (www.grill5taco.com; Sinsa-dong, Gangnam-gu; taco from ₩7000; ⓂLine 3 to Sinsa, Exit 8) A business that started as a food truck has been so successful that it has a permanent base that caters perfectly to the on-the-go shoppers and hipsters mooching around Serosu-gil. The tacos filled with a choice of spare rib, spicy pork or spicy chicken hit the spot and if you're really hungry open your mouth very wide for the Monster Burrito.

QUEENS PARK
INTERNATIONAL $$$

Map p210 (☑542 4073; www.queens-park.co.kr; Cheongdam-dong, Gangnam-gu; mains ₩15,000-30,000; ⊗10am-midnight Mon-Fri, 8am-midnight Sat & Sun; ⓂLine 3 to Apgujeong, Exit 3) Opposite Boon the Shop, this is *the* place for fashionistas to see and be seen. Run by the bakery behemoth Paris Croissant, it has a classy bakery section and dining area with a soaring ceiling and great design. For late risers it's perfect as the brunch dishes, including an English breakfast, are available until 6pm daily.

HANMIRI
NEO KOREAN $$$

Map p210 (한미리; ☑569 7165; www.han miri.co.kr; 2nd fl, Human Starville, Nonhyeon-dong, Gangnam-gu; lunch/dinner from ₩30,000/50,000; ⊗noon-3pm & 6-10pm; ⓂLine 2 to Yeoksam, Exit 6) You'll be treated like royalty by *hanbok*-clad staff in this oasis of old-fashioned service and decor. The dozen well-presented dishes are a modernised version of royal cuisine.

NOLBOO YUHWANGORI JINHEUKGUI
DUCK $$$

Map p210 (놀부유황오리진흙구이; ☑452-5292; www.nolboo.co.kr; Bampo-dong, Seocho-gu; one duck ₩50,000; ⓂLine 3 or 7 to Express Bus Terminal, Exit 3) This restaurant cooks up a wonderful medicinal duck, packed with glutinous rice, red beans, ginseng, nuts and herbs. The duck is large with little or no fat and the taste is delicious. Try wrapping the meat, sauce and side dishes in the *daikon* slices – a Seoul version of Peking duck. Go up the escalator at Exit 3 and you can see the Nolboo signboard.

CINE DE CHEF
ITALIAN $$$

Map p210 (☑3446 0541; www.cinedechef .com; Sinsa-dong, Gangnam-gu; lunch/dinner

₩35,000/70,000; MLine 3 to Apgujeong, Exit 3) For the perfect lunch or dinner date, this classy Italian restaurant combines a three-course meal with watching a movie afterwards in one of two super-comfy screening rooms (the double movie ticket is ₩40,000 extra).

ALLÔ PAPERGARDEN
INTERNATIONAL $$$

Map p210 (☑541 6933; www.papergarden.co.kr; 520-9 Sinsa-dong, Gangnam-gu; meals ₩12,000-28,000; ⊘11am-1am; MLine 3 to Sinsa, Exit 8; ☜▣) Back a street from Garosu-gil you'll find this cafe and restaurant with an open courtyard and two levels. Apart from the usual salads, pasta and brunch items they do a refreshing *moca bingsoo,* a nice twist on the traditional Korean shaved-ice-and-red-bean dessert, spiced up with a shot of coffee.

FRESH HOUSE
BUFFET $$$

Map p212 (☑416 0606; www.freshhouse. co.kr; Olympic Park; lunch/dinner Mon-Fri ₩21,000/28,000, lunch & dinner Sat & Sun ₩30,000; ⊘11.30am-3pm & 5.30-10pm Mon-Fri, 11.30am-4pm & 5.30-10pm Sat & Sun; MLine 8 to Mongchontoseong, Exit 1) A great spread at a great price makes this a popular feeding option at Olympic Park. The cooks are constantly bringing in appetising, mainly Asian food but everyone is catered for. At weekends there are two lunch and dinner sittings limited to two hours each; kids eat at a discount Monday to Friday.

GOLDEN BURGER REPUBLIC
BURGERS $$

Map p210 (www.goldenburgerrepublic.com; Sinsa-dong, Gangnam-gu; burgers ₩8500-12,000; MLine 3 to Apgujeong, Exit 3; ☜▣) If you're hankering for a well-done burger and crispy fries while cruising Apgujeong's shops then this US-style place with an open terrace ticks the box perfectly.

🍷 DRINKING & NIGHTLIFE

TOP CHOICE **PLATOON KUNSTHALLE**
CLUB, BAR

Map p210 (☑3447 1191; www.kunsthalle.com; Nonhyeon-dong, Gangnam-gu; ⊘11am-1am Mon-Sat; MLine 3 to Apgujeong, Exit 3; ☜) What's not to love about this bar/gallery/events space created like a giant's Lego set from old shipping containers. Drinks and eats are affordable. Thursday night is open stage for live music performances and there's a wide variety of other events hosted here from the four-times-a-year Future Shorts (http://futureshorts.com) short film events to its annual Ink Bomb tattoo and body art convention.

MOON JAR
BAR

Map p210 (☑541 6118; MLine 3 to Apgujeong, Exit 3; ☜▣) Rustic charm meets Apgujeong chic at this convivial *magkeolli* bar and cafe spread over two floors. The menu has several different types of rice wine and there's some neat twists on the usual food accompaniments such as a five-coloured *tteok-boki* rice cake dish.

TAKE URBAN
CAFE

Map p210 (테이크어반; ☑519 0001; Bongeunsa-ro, Gangnam-gu; ⊘8am-midnight; MLine 9 to Sinnonhyeon, Exit 3) On the ground floor of a building that looks like a giant concrete beehive is this sophisticated and spacious cafe, with indoor and outdoor options, heaps of designer-style fresh bakery items and organic coffee.

COFFEE BAR K
COCKTAIL BAR

Map p210 (☑516 1970; Cheongdam-dong, Gangnam-gu; MLine 3 to Apgujeong, Exit 3) If you're into whisky then this swank bar is for you as it sports one of the largest selections of drams in the city. It's also famed for its cocktails and cigars – all of which come at a price; expect to pay at least ₩15,000 a drink.

OKTOBERFEST
BEER HALL

Map p210 (옥토버페스트; ☑3481 8881; off Scomyeong-gil, Gangnam; beers ₩4000; MLine 2 to Gangnam, Exit 9; ▣) It's much quieter than Oktoberfest at this long-running micro-brewery serving up four freshly produced brews in a large bare-brick and natural-wood cellar bar. German-style meats are served by frock-clad lasses. There's other branches around the city, including one in Hongdae.

ELLUI
CLUB

Map p212 (www.ellui.com; Cheongdam-dong, Gangnam-gu; admission Fri & Sat ₩30,000; MLine 7 to Cheongdam, Exit 13) Gangnam specialises in mega dance clubs and this industrial-chic place is one of the biggest, with a dazzling light and sound system, several dance spaces and plenty of room to move. Usually open only Friday and Saturday, but keep an eye out for one-off midweek events too.

EDEN
CLUB

Map p210 (www.eden-club.co.kr; Yeoksam-dong, Gangnam-gu; admission Sun, Tue-Thu ₩20,000, Fri & Sat ₩30,000; ⊘8.30pm-4am Sun, Tue-Thu, to 6am Fri & Sat; Ⓜ Line 9 to Sinnonhyeon, Exit 3) Lavish laser shows, leggy models, stratospheric drink prices and tons of security mark out Eden as the late-night haunt of Seoul's smart set.

CLUB MASS
CLUB

Map p210 (www.clubmass.net; admission ₩20,000; Gangnam-gu; ⊘8.30pm-6am Tue-Sun; Ⓜ Line 2 to Gangnam, Exit 5) A young, friendly crowd bops to electronic and house music in this spacious basement strafed by a dazzling lightshow.

☆ ENTERTAINMENT

SEOUL ARTS CENTRE
PERFORMING ARTS

(서울예술의전당; SAC; ☑580 1300; www.sac.or.kr; Nambusunhwan-ro, Seochu-gu; tickets from ₩10,000; Ⓜ Line 3 to Nambu Bus Terminal, Exit 5, then bus 12) The national ballet and opera companies are based at this sprawling arts complex, which sports a circular opera house with a roof shaped like a Korean nobleman's hat. It also houses a large concert hall and a smaller recital hall in which the national choir, the Korea and Seoul symphony orchestras and various drama companies stage shows. A couple more theatres and three art galleries complete the package. Check the website for the extensive program and to find out about free shows, which are often staged at weekends on the outdoor stage. To reach the SAC, walk straight on from the subway exit and turn left at the end of the bus terminal.

NATIONAL GUGAK CENTER
CLASSICAL MUSIC

(☑580 3333; www.gugak.go.kr; Nambusunhwan-ro, Seochu-gu; tickets from ₩10,000; Ⓜ Line 3 to Nambu Bus Terminal, Exit 5) Traditional Korean classical and folk music and dance are performed, preserved and taught at this centre, which is home to the Court Music Orchestra, the Folk Music Group, Dance Theatre and Contemporary Gugak Orchestra.

The main theatre, Yeak-dang, puts on an ever-changing program by leading performers every Saturday, usually at 4pm and 5.30pm, from early January to mid December. The 1½-hour show is a bargain and usually contains seven items including court dances, folk songs, *pansori, gayageum,* flute

---

GANGNAM ARCHI-TOUR

Given the generally blank historical canvas and wide-open spaces of Gangnam, architects have been able to push the envelope a bit more with their designs south of the river. Start this archi-tour opposite COEX. Hyundai Development Company commissioned Daniel Libeskind to work with Seoul-based firm Himma on its headquarters. The result, **Tangent** (Map p212; Ⓜ Line 2 to Samseong, Exit 6), is one of Seoul's boldest architectural statements, an enormous sculpture in glass, concrete and steel, reminiscent of a painting by Kandinsky.

A short walk south of COEX along Yeongdong-daero is **Kring** (Map p212; Ⓜ Line 2 to Samseong, Exit 1). Looking like a giant music speaker crossed with a slab of Swiss cheese, this incredible steel-clad building was designed by Unsangdong Architects; at the time of research the building was closed.

Take the subway to Gangnam where you won't miss the curvaceous stylings of the slinky **GT Tower** (Map p210; Ⓜ Line 2 to Samseong, Exit 9) beside the major crossing of Teheranno and Gangnam-daero. Re-dubbed U-Street, Gangnam-daero is lined with 12m-high, 1.4m-wide media poles displaying video art. Also here is the hulking brick edifice of **Kyobo Tower** (Map p210; Ⓜ Line 9 to Shinonhyeon, Exit 6), designed by Mario Botta. Above Shinonyheon Station is Urban Hive which looks like an enormous concrete beehive and has the cafe Take Urban on the ground floor.

Take a taxi to Apgujeong and the Horim Art Center. Between here and Dosan Park you'll find the **Ann Demeulemeester** (Map p210; Ⓜ Line 3 to Apgujeon, Exit 3) boutique, its facade a forest of greenery. Finish up the tour in front of the Galleria (West), its exterior covered with 4330 mother-of-pearl-like glass discs that shimmer in daylight and are a captivating canvas for dramatic LED lighting at night.

music and drumming. The centre is down the road from the Seoul Arts Centre.

LG ARTS CENTRE — PERFORMING ARTS

Map p210 (📞205 0114; www.lgart.com; Yeoksam-dong, Gangnam-gu; Ⓜ Line 2 to Yeoksam, Exit 7) Major local and international artists and companies perform at this multi-hall state-of-the-art venue. The seasonal CoMPAS program delivers the cream of contemporary performing arts from the around the world; the 2012 season included the likes of Ute Lemper, English physical theatre company DV8, a Peter Brooke–directed opera and Korean piano maestro Kim Sunwook.

ONCE IN A BLUE MOON — JAZZ

Map p210 (원스인어블루문; 📞549 5490; www.onceinabluemoon.co.kr; 85-1 Cheongdam-dong, Gangnam-gu; admission free; ⊙5pm-2am; Ⓜ Line 3 to Apgujeong, Exit 3) An intimate and classy club with live jazz from two groups of performers every night, each performing two sets between 7.30pm and 12.40am.

 # SHOPPING

TOP CHOICE D CUBE CITY — MALL

(www.dcubecity.com; Kyungin-ro, Guro-gu; Ⓜ Lines 1 & 2 to Sindorim, Exit 1) Seoul's shopping malls hardly come any more stylish than this new one in the previously industrial hub of Guro. The interior spaces surround a waterfall that cascades down seven floors and there's plenty of multilevel outdoor terraces on which to relax in fine weather. Also here is the D Cube Arts Centre with a concert hall and larger theatre for musicals, a very spiffy Sheraton Hotel (with fabulous views from all rooms), good restaurants and a superbly designed Korean food court in the basement.

10 CORSO COMO SEOUL — FASHION

Map p210 (www.10corsocomo.co.kr; Cheongdam-dong, Gangnam-gu; Ⓜ Line 3 to Apgujeong, Exit 3) Inspired by legendary London store Biba, this outpost of the fashion and lifestyle boutique is about as delicious as Seoul retail can get. The blend of fashion, art and design is seductive – if you can't afford the clothes, which include those of several local designers, there's a brilliant selection of international books and CDs to browse and a chic cafe for an espresso or glass of wine.

COEX MALL — MALL

Map p212 (www.coexmall.com; Samseoung-dong, Gangnam-gu; Ⓜ Line 2 to Samseong, COEX Exit) This vast subterranean maze of a mall is attached to a branch of Hyundai department store, three hotels, a multiplex cinema, the COEX Convention Centre and World Trade Centre. Among the scores of dining and shopping possibilities here is a branch of the bookshop Bandi & Luni's. Next door Evan Records is a good place to pick up K-Pop and K-Indie CDs as well as local movies and TV series on DVDs.

GALLERIA — DEPARTMENT STORE

Map p210 (http://dept.galleria.co.kr; Apgujeongno, Gangnam; Ⓜ Line 3 to Apgujeong, Exit 1) Department stores in Seoul don't get more luxurious than this. If you want to play Audrey Hepburn staring wistfully into Tiffany's, don a Helen Kaminski hat, try on a Stella McCartney dress or slip into a pair of Jimmy Choos; the east wing of fashion icon Galleria is the place to be. Dozens of top fashion-designer stores are packed into the two Galleria buildings, the west wing of which is covered in glass discs that turn psychedelic at night.

BOON THE SHOP — CLOTHING

Map p210 (www.boontheshop.com; Cheongdam-dong, Gangnam-gu; Ⓜ Line 3 to Apgujeong, Exit 2) There are two close-by branches of this multibrand boutique that's a byword for chic, high-end fashion. The original, worth a look if only for its gorgeous sculpture of a giant string of pearls hanging in the midst of an atrium, is the women's store. The newer men's store is a two-minute walk around the corner. Mainly exclusive niche designer brands from overseas are stocked; if you need to ask the price you can't afford to shop here.

DAILY PROJECTS — FASHION

Map p210 (http://dailyprojectsseoul.blogspot.com; Cheongdam-dong, Gangnam-gu; Ⓜ Line 3 to Apgujeong, Exit 3) Come here to find new creations from young local designers bursting with ideas and talent. You never know what you might come across at this ahead-of-the-game fashion store.

CENTRAL CITY MALL — MALL

Map p210 (www.centralcityseoul.co.kr; Gangnam; Ⓜ Line 3 or 7 to Express Bus Terminal, Exit 7) A branch of the department store Shinsegae anchors this popular mall next to the ex-

GANGNAM & SOUTH OF THE HAN RIVER SHOPPING

press bus terminal. You'll also find a food court and a six-cinema multiplex.

PUNGWOLDANG
MUSIC

Map p210 (www.pungwoldang.kr; Sinsa-dong, Gangnam-gu; ☉10am-9pm Mon-Sat; ⓜLine 3 to Apgujeong, Exit 3) On the 4th floor of a building tucked off the main street is this elegant, art nouveau–styled classical CD and DVD shop. Come here to find titles by the Korean composer Isang Yung or the operatic diva Hong Hei-kyung. Other pluses are the attached cafe where you can sip a free drink and small theatre for music and culture lectures and events.

ELORD HILLS
FASHION

Map p210 (www.elord.com/main.jsp; Nonheon-dong, Gangnam-gu; ⓜLine 3 to Apgujeong, Exit 3) This is where Korean golfers come when they want to look their most fashionable while teeing off on the course (or in the driving range). The boutique has a space-age design to offset the colourful, casual clothes and next door in the golf club section there's a free practice area with experts on hand to show you how to perfect your stroke.

🏃 SPORTS & ACTIVITIES

JAMSIL SPORTS COMPLEX
SPORTS

Map p212 (☎2240 8864; Jamsil-dong, Songpa-gu; ⓜLines 2 & 8 to Sports Complex, Exit 6) The professional baseball matches held at the stadium here are great entertainment; games kick off around 6.30pm. Also the location of the giant Olympic Stadium built for the 1988 games and still used for major events and pop concerts.

SPA LEI
SPA

Map p210 (☎545 4113; www.spalei.co.kr; Cresyn Bldg, Jamwong-dong, Seoch-gu; day/night ₩12,000/14,000; ☉24hr; ⓜLine 3 to Sinsa, Exit 5) Luxurious women-only spa providing excellent services in an immaculate, stylish environment. Staff are helpful and used to dealing with foreigners.

KUKKIWON
TAEKWONDO

Map p210 (☎563 3339; www.kukkiwon.or.kr; Yeoksam-dong, Gangnam-gu; ☉office 9am-5pm Mon-Fri; ⓜLine 2 to Gangnam, Exit 12) This *dojang* (practice hall) hosts a regular schedule of taekwondo displays, training courses and tournaments. Call (they speak English) to see when you might be able to see a training session by the world's best taekwondo demonstration team. Expect to see graceful movements, spectacular pine-board breaking and acrobatic high kicking.

OLYMPIC COLISEUM GOLF
GYM

Map p210 (☎514 7979; Seolleung-ro, Gangnam; ☉5am-10pm; ⓜLine 3 to Apgujeong, Exit 2) Not just for practicing your golf swing; at Olympic you can also use the gym and relax in the spa, all for ₩30,000 (70 minutes).

SEOUL RACECOURSE
RACECOURSE

(서울경마장; www.kra.co.kr; Gyeongmagong-won-daero, Gwacheon-si; ☉races Fri-Sun; ⓜLine 4 to Seoul Racecourse Park, Exit 2) Enjoy a day at the races where huge screens on the track show the odds, the races and close-ups of the horses. Short races around the sandy track take place every half-hour and bets are limited to ₩100,000. From the subway, the racecourse is a 10-minute walk under a covered walkway.

Dongdaemun & Eastern Seoul

Neighbourhood Top Five

1 Uncover layers of Seoul's history, from its foundation as the capital of the Joseon dynasty to its 21st-century incarnation, at the **Dongdaemun Design Plaza & Park** (p109).

2 Cruise the malls and buzzing streets of **Dongdaemun Market** (p110) into the early hours of the morning.

3 Cycle around **Seoul Forest** (p109), past the wetlands, the riverside and Sika deer.

4 Explore the **Seoul Art Space Sindang** (p109) in the underground arcade beneath Jungang Market.

5 Learn about your yin and yang and the traditional Korean approach to medicine at the **Seoul Yangnyeongsi Herb Medicine Museum** (p109).

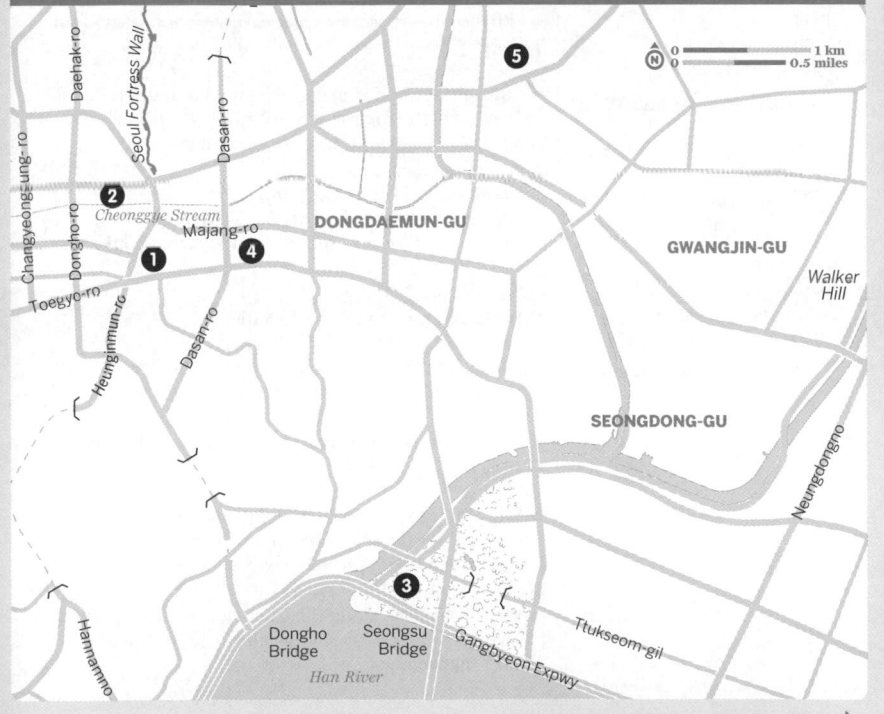

For more detail of this area, see Map p214 ➡

Lonely Planet's Top Tip

Gwangjang Market, a great place to eat in the evening, is well worth exploring by day too. Search out the upstairs arcade in the northwestern corner packed with stalls selling second-hand and vintage clothing.

 Best Places to Eat

➡ Gwangjang Market (p110)

➡ Woo Rae Oak (p110)

➡ My Friend & Ala-Too (p110)

For reviews, p110 ➡

 Best Places to Shop

➡ Doota (p111)

➡ Seoul Folk Flea Market (p111)

➡ Dapsimni Antiques Market (p111)

For reviews, see p110 ➡

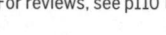 **Best Parks**

➡ Seoul Forest (p109)

➡ Children's Grand Park (p110)

➡ Cheong-gye-cheon (p110)

For reviews, see p109 ➡

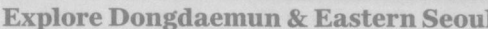

Explore Dongdaemun & Eastern Seoul

Taking its name from the Great East Gate (Heunginji-mum) to the city, Dongdaemun – an area synonymous for centuries with shopping in Seoul – is now famous for the Zaha Hadid–designed Dongdaemun Design Plaza & Park (DDP), an architectural showpiece so complex that it wasn't ready in time for Seoul's stint as World Design Capital in 2010.

With the DDP now fully formed, it's fascinating to explore the ribbon of indoor markets that stretch around it and along either side of Cheong-gye-cheon, spilling out into side streets where you can find anything and everything from succulents and sewing-machine parts to every hue of zipper and variety of kimchi. Much of the action is wholesale, with traders haggling over deals until the break of dawn, but there's also plenty of retail, particularly in fashion goods.

Further east there are more interesting markets to discover, including ones devoted to herbal medicines, antiques and second-hand goods. There's also the Jun-gang Market, an evocative, old-school food market, beneath which lies the Seoul Art Space Sindang, where up-and-coming artists and young creatives hone and display their craft. A couple of big green spaces – Seoul Forest Park and the Children's Grand Park – provide natural relief from the commercial activity.

Local Life

➡ **Late-night shopping** Join fashion bargain-hunters as they trawl the high-rise malls of Migliore, Cerestar, Hello APM and Doota into the wee hours.

➡ **Local delicacies** Sample spicy rice cake stews at **Sindang-dong Tteobokki Town** (신당동 떡볶이 타운; ⏱9am-10pm Mon-Sat; ⓂLine 2 or 6 to Sindang, Exit 7 or 8) or marinated pigs feet (*jokbal*) at **Jangchung Jokbal Alley** (장충족발길; Map p214; Heunginmun-ro; ⓂLine 3 to Dongguk University, Exit 3).

➡ **Herbal remedies** Natural medicines, such as arrowroot by the cup, are downed at Seoul Yangnyeongsi (p111). They taste pretty bad, but the *maesil* (plum) one is said to improve blood pressure.

Getting There & Away

➡ **Subway** Hop off at either Dongdaemun or Dongdaemun History & Culture Park stations for the Dongdaemun area. The subway is also the best way to access the markets and parks further east.

➡ **Walk** The paths along the Cheong-gye-cheon provide pleasant strolling access between Dongdaemun and Seoul Yangnyeongsi.

 **SIGHTS**

FREE SEOUL FOREST   PARK

off Map p214 (http://parks.seoul.go.kr; ☉24hr; ⓜLine 2 to Ttukseom, Exit 8) A hunting ground in Joseon times, this park makes a very pleasant area to enjoy some time in natural surroundings. It's big; to see it all it's best to hire a bicycle (₩3000 per hour) or a pair of rollerblades (₩4000 per hour) from the **rental stall** (☉9am-10pm) by Gate 1. Among the trees and lakes are deer enclosures, eco areas, an insect exhibition, a plant nursery and fountains. You can also cycle through a tunnel down to the Han and along the cycleway that follows the river.

FREE SEOUL ART

SPACE SINDANG   ARTISTS' STUDIO

off Map p214 (http://eng.seoulartspace.or.kr; Dongdaemun; ☉9am-10pm; ⓜLine 2 to Sindang, Exit 1 or 2) In the arcade that runs under the Jungang Market is this colourful collection of 40 design and art studios, part of a city-wide project to foster up-and-coming artists. The arcade itself has been turned into a gallery of the artists' work, some of whom collaborated with the existing stallholders –

including many raw-fish cafes and the traders from the atmospheric wet market above, which was once one of the most important food markets in the city.

FREE SEOUL YANGNYEONGSI

HERB MEDICINE MUSEUM   MUSEUM

(http://museum.ddm.go.kr; B2 Donguibogam Tower, Jeji-dong; ☉10am-5pm Tue-Sun; ⓜLine 1 to Jeji-dong, Exit 3) Learn about the history and practice of traditional Korean medicine at this imaginative museum in the basement of the building with a big Korean flag on it (look for the entrance hood at the corner of the street). The displays have plenty of English, and the kindly ladies here will give you herbal tea and allow you to work out which 'Sasang' constitution you have.

HEUNGINJIMUM

(DONGDAEMUN)   HISTORIC BUILDING

Map p214 (Dongdaemun; ⓜLine 1 or 4 to Dongdaemun, Exit 6) The Great East Gate to Seoul's fortress has been rebuilt several times in its 700-year history and was under wraps again for another major renovation at the time of research. Stranded in a

 TOP SIGHTS
DONGDAEMUN DESIGN PLAZA & PARK

Dongdaemun Design Plaza (동대문; DDP) is architect Zaha Hadid's sleek concept dubbed the 'Metonymic Landscape'. The building, a curvaceous concrete structure with a silvery facade partly coated with lawns that rise up on to its roof, is planned to be a showcase for Korean and international design. The attached **Dongdaemun History & Culture Park** is already open, and includes event halls and exhibition spaces that highlight past uses of this area, such as a 16th-century military camp.

During the site's excavation, major archaeological remains from the Joseon dynasty were uncovered, including original sections of Seoul's fortress wall. The remains have been incorporated into the park and include the arched floodgate Yigansumun. The **Dongdaemun History Museum** (free; ☉10am-9pm) imaginatively displays the pick of the 2575 artefacts from the site and provides the historical background to the ancient foundations preserved outside. Look for the patterned section of pavement made from clay tiles. The **Dongdaemun Stadium Memorial** (free; ☉10am-9pm) re-lives key moments from the stadium's history and includes video clips.

DON'T MISS

➡ Dongdaemun Design Plaza

➡ Dongdaemun History Museum

➡ Dongdaemun Stadium Memorial

➡ Dongdaemun History & Culture Park

PRACTICALITIES

➡ Map p214

➡ 🖉2266 7077

➡ http://ddp.seoul.go.kr

➡ Dongdaemun

➡ ⓜLine 1 & 4 to Dongdaemun, Exit 7

traffic island, it's not possible to enter inside the gate; view it from the remains of the fortress walls that snake uphill to Naksan Park.

FREE CHEONG-GYE-CHEON MUSEUM
MUSEUM

(www.cgcm.co.kr; Cheong-gye-cheon-no; ⊙9am-9pm Tue-Fri, to 6pm Sat & Sun; MLine 2 to Yongdu, Exit 5) To fully comprehend what a mammoth and expensive effort it was to resurrect Seoul's long-covered-over Cheong-gye-cheon watercourse, pay a visit to this well-designed museum. It's a good aiming point for a walk along the riverside park; you'll know you're there when you see the reconstruction of wooden shacks that used to line the river back in the 1950s.

CHILDREN'S GRAND PARK
PARK

(☏2290 6114; www.childrenpark.or.kr; admission free; ⊙5am-10pm; MLine 5 & 7 to Children's Grand Park, Exit 1) Let your little ones run wild in this enormous playground which includes a **zoo** (admission free; ⊙10am-6pm) with pony and camel rides. There's also a botanical garden, with cacti up one end and a tropical jungle and bonsai trees at the other end. Other features include a wetland eco area, amusement rides and a giant musical fountain.

✖ EATING

TOP CHOICE GWANGJANG MARKET
KOREAN $

Map p214 (광장시장; Jongno-5ga; dishes ₩4000-10,000; ⊙5am-10pm Mon-Sat; MLine 1 to Jongno-5ga, Exit 5) Also spelled 'Kwangjang', this market feels like it's been frozen in time; during the day you'll find food and fabrics sold here as well as a great section specialising in second-hand clothes (accessed by the stairs to the upper floor outside exit 5, open until 7pm). The best time to visit. though. is the evening, when the end towards Dongdaemun morphs into Seoul's largest food alley (or *meokjagolmok*), with some 200 stalls specialising in dishes such as crispy, thick *nokdu bindaetteok* (mung-bean pancake; ₩5000) that are big enough to be shared by two. Pair them up with healthy bowls of *bibimbap* or *boribap* (mixed rice and barley topped with a selection of veggies).

TOP CHOICE WOO RAE OAK
NOODLES, BARBECUE $$

Map p214 (☏2265 0151; Jugyo-dong; mains ₩11,000-43,000; ⊙11.30am-9.30pm Tue-Sun; MLine 2 or 4 to Euljiro 4ga, Exit 4; 🖰) Tucked away in the sewing-machine parts section of Dongdaemun's sprawling market is this elegant old-timer specialising in *bulgogi* and *galbi* (barbecued beef; from ₩29,000, could feed two). But it's the delicious *naengmyeon* (buckwheat cold noodles) that are the best and a great lunch with the delicious kimchi.

GULMAEUL NAKJICHON
KOREAN $

(굴마을 낙지촌; ☏959 3004; www.gulgul.co.kr; Jegi-dong; mains ₩6500-8000; ⊙10.30am-10pm; MLine 1 to Jegi-dong, Exit 2; 🖰) This sit-on-the-floor place, specialising in good-value oyster and octopus dishes served either with rice or in spicy soups, is a fine option if you're browsing the medicinal herb market. Find it heading towards the river, south of, but on the same side of the road as, Shinhan Bank.

MY FRIEND & ALA-TOO
CENTRAL ASIAN $$

Map p214 (⊙9am-10pm Mon-Sat; MLine 1 or 4 to Dongdaemun History & Culture Park, Exit 5; 🖰) Cyrillic script on the buildings signal the location of Dongdaemun's 'Central Asian' village where you'll find Russian speaking traders from the 'stans, Mongolia and Russia hanging out, enjoying *shashlyk* (barbecue meat), *plov* (a meaty pilaf dish) and *lagman* (soup noodles). A good place to join in the party is this spacious, friendly joint.

🛍 SHOPPING

TOP CHOICE DONGDAEMUN MARKET
MARKET

Map p214 (Dongdaemun; ⊙24hr; MLine 1 or 4 to Dongdaemun, Exit 5 or 7) Take Seoul's commercial pulse at this colossal retail and wholesale market, which sprawls across a wide area on both sides of the Cheong-gye-cheon and where the bargaining never stops. The wholesale sections operate mainly through the night, but even during the day it's a buzz to wander the network of buildings and streets. You can buy practically anything, although it's mainly fashion that drags in the punters.

TOP CHOICE **DOOTA** DEPARTMENT STORE

Map p214 (Dongdaemun; www.doota.com; ⊙10.30am-5am Tue-Sat, to 11pm Sun, 7pm-5am Mon) Cut through Dongdaemun's commercial frenzy by heading to its leading fashion mall full to the brim with domestic brands. Ten floors above and below ground are dedicated to clothing, accessories, beauty items and souvenirs. When you start flagging, there's plenty of cafes and a good food court on the 7th floor.

SEOUL YANGNYEONGSI

HERB MEDICINE MARKET TRADITIONAL MEDICINE

(www.seoulya.com; Jegi-dong; ⊙8am-6.30pm; MLine 1 to Jegi-dong, Exit 2) Also known as Gyeongdong Market, Korea's biggest Asian medicine market runs back for several blocks from the traditional gate on the main road and includes thousands of clinics, retailers, wholesalers and medicine makers. If you're looking for a leaf, herb, bark, root, flower or mushroom to ease your ailment, it's bound to be here.

At Shinhan Bank on the corner go first right, and on the left is a 2nd-floor arcade with stalls piled high with ginseng and honey products. Underneath and nearby are hundreds more food-cum-medicine stalls, including some selling nuts and dried fruit.

SEOUL FOLK FLEA MARKET FLEA MARKET

(Sinseol-dong; ⊙10am-6pm, closed 2nd & 4th Tue of month; MLine 1 or 2 to Sinseol-dong, Exit 6 or 10) Spilling out of a two-storey building into the surrounding area, here you'll find a fascinating collection of artworks, collectables and general bric-a-brac from wooden masks and ink drawings to Beatles LPs and valve radios.

DAPSIMNI ANTIQUES MARKET ANTIQUES

(⊙10am-4.30pm Mon-Sat; MLine 5 to Dapsimni, Exit 2) It's 'out with the old and in with the new' in Seoul, so ever wondered what happens to all the old stuff? It ends up here, stuffed inside scores of small antique shops in three separate arcades where you can browse through old dusty treasures – from *yangban* (aristocrat) pipes and horsehair hats to wooden shoes, fish-shaped locks and embroidered status insignia.

At the subway exit walk over to the orange-tiled **Samhee 6** building behind the car park. A similar arcade on the left is **Samhee 5**. After visiting them, walk back to Exit 2 and go left along the main road for 10 minutes to reach a brown-tiled arcade, **Janganpyeong**, with another section behind it. You can't miss them with all the stonework stored permanently outside.

SPORTS & ACTIVITIES

JANGCHUNG GYMNASIUM SPORTS STADIUM

Map p214 (Dongguk University; www.jangchung gym.co.kr; MLine 3 to Dongguk University, Exit 5) Major *ssireum* (Korean wrestling) competitions are held at this 7000-seat indoor arena, which looks like a huge cooking pot.

Northern Seoul

Neighbourhood Top Five

1 Hike up **Bukaksan**, the tallest of Seoul's four guardian mountains, following the most intact sections of the city's original **Fortress Walls** (p114).

2 Learn about horrors of the Japanese colonial period at the **Seodaemun Prison History Hall** (p115).

3 Witness ancient shamanistic ceremonies at atmospheric **Inwangsan Guksadang** (p117).

4 Go on a Templestay at serene **Gilsang-sa** (p115) in leafy Seongbuk-dong.

5 Hang out in Buam-dong, taking in an exhibition at the **Whanki Museum** (p117).

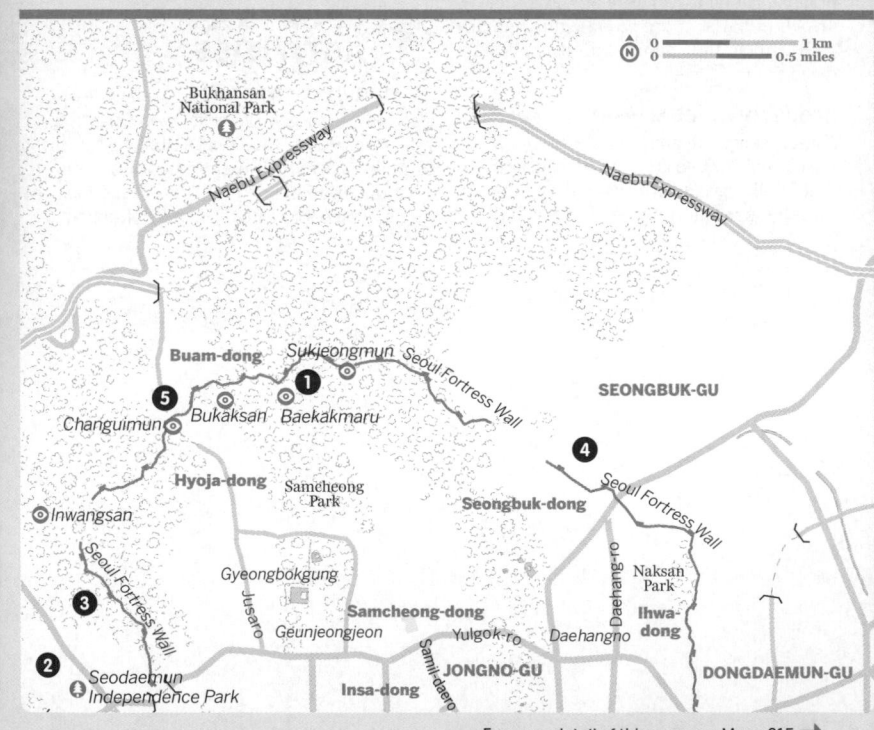

For more detail of this area, see Map p215 ➡

Explore: Northern Seoul

The city's northern districts seldom figure prominently on international tourist itineraries, which is a pity as they are home to some of Seoul's most charming neighbourhoods and some fascinating sights, not least of which are the best sections of the Fortress Walls. Start exploring in the university district of Daehangno, a performing-arts hub with scores of theatres ranging from intimate fringe-style venues to major auditoria such as the Arko Art Theatre.

Hike to Naksan Park and follow the Fortress Wall northwest over to Seongbuk-dong, a leafy mountainside community known as the Beverly Hills of Seoul because of its grand mansions, many of them home to ambassadors and CEOs. Here you'll find the Buddhist temple Gilsang-sa, charming cafes and the *hanok* teahouse Suyeon Sanbang.

It's a stiff climb, but views of the city from the summit of Mt Bukaksan repay the effort of getting there. Come down to Buan-dong where the high-security trappings of Bukaksan are replaced by relaxed teahouses, cafes and galleries.

The Fortress Trail will eventually lead you to Inwangsan (White Tiger Mountain) with its weirdly eroded rocks, temples and Guksadang shrine. The area has a special atmosphere because of the outdoor shamanist ceremonies that invoke the spirits of the departed. At the foot of the mountain is the large Seodaemun Independence Park, with monuments that celebrate Korea's march towards nationhood, free from the interference and colonisation of China and Japan. The haunting displays at the Seodaemun Prison History Hall provide a sobering end to this tour which can occupy several days of your time in Seoul.

Local Life

➡ **Hiking** Naksan is popular for relaxing. Part of the Fortress Wall hiking trail runs along the back of the park.
➡ **Cafe Society** Buy coffee beans from around the world at Club Espresso in Buam-dong or chill out in the cafes and teahouses of Seongbuk-dong.
➡ **Street Theatre** Check out the free performances by musicians, dancers, comedians and other dramatic hopefuls that take place most weekend afternoons at Daehangno's Marronnier Park.

Getting There & Away

➡ **Bus** Numbers 1020, 7022, 7212 for Buam-dong, 1111 or 2112 for Seongbuk-dong.
➡ **Subway** Daehangno and Seodaemun are easily accessed by the metro.
➡ **Walking** All areas covered in this chapter can be accessed from the Fortress Walk hiking route.

Lonely Planet's Top Tip

For info on what's showing at the 100-plus venues in Daehangno ,and discounts on tickets of up to 50%, go the **Theatre Ticket Office** (Map p215; ⊘2-7.30pm Tue-Sun), next to Marronnier Park, or the **Seoul Theatre Centre** (Map p215; www.e-stc.or.kr; ⊘1-8pm Tue-Fri, 11am-8pm Sat, 11am-7pm Sun; Ⓜ Line 4 to Hyehwa, Exit 4), next to the subway exit.

NORTHERN SEOUL

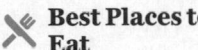 **Best Places to Eat**

➡ Jaha Sonmandoo (p117)
➡ Deongjang Yesool (p117)
➡ Serious Deli (p117)

For reviews, p117 ➡

 **Best Places to Drink**

➡ Suyeon Sanbang (p118)
➡ Sanmotoonge (p118)
➡ Hakrim (p118)

For reviews, see p118 ➡

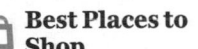 **Best Places to Shop**

➡ Dolsilnai (p119)
➡ Hyojae (p119)
➡ Mono Collection (p119)

For reviews, see p119

GREGORY CURLEY / GETTY IMAGES ©

TOP SIGHTS
BUKAKSAN & SEOUL'S FORTRESS WALLS

In 1968 North Korean agents launched an assassination attempt on then-president Park Chung-hee by climbing over Bukaksan and into the presidential compound of Cheongwadae. From then until 2006 the mountain was off limits to the public. Security is still tight but the 342m peak is now open, on a steep hike along the most spectacular section of Seoul's Fortress Walls.

High Security Area

Unlike other remaining sections of the walls, military security is very evident around Bukaksan. You need to show your passport or other photo ID and register when you enter at Changuimun, the old sub-gate in Buam-dong, or Sukjeongmun, the main north gate, which can be accessed from Samcheong Park; there's no need to register in advance as mentioned on the website. This section of the wall is also open only during daylight hours and photography is allowed at designated spots only, such as Baekakmaru, the summit viewpoint. The wall is in excellent condition and with plenty of soldiers and CCTV cameras, there's a vivid sense of its original purpose as the city's last line of defence.

History of Seoul Fortress

By the late 14th century an 18.6km wall encircled Seoul, linking up the peaks of Bukaksan, Naksan (125m), Namsan (262m) and Inwangsan (338m) and punctuated by four major gates facing north, south, east and west. Over time parts of the wall were demolished and today only 10.5km of it remains. The city has been restoring some of the missing sections, such as stretches that are part of Dongdaemun Design Plaza & Park and across Mt Namsam. A hiking route around the original fortress is detailed in the free English-language booklet *Walking Along the Fortress Wall of Seoul*, available from tourist information offices.

DON'T MISS

➡ Baekakmaru
➡ Changuimun
➡ Sukjeongmun

PRACTICALITIES

➡ Map p215
➡ www.bukak.or.kr
➡ admission free
➡ ⊘9am-3pm Apr-Oct, 10am-3pm Nov-Mar
➡ 🚌1020, 7022 & 7212 to Changuimun

SIGHTS

SEODAEMUN INDEPENDENCE PARK PARK
(서대문독립공원; Seodaemun; ⓜLine 3 to Dong-nimmun, Exit 4) Apart from the former prison, this park (dedicated to those who fought for Korean independence) also features Dongnimmun, an impressive granite archway modelled after the Arc de Triomphe. Built by the Independence Club in 1898, it stands where envoys from Chinese emperors used to be officially welcomed to Seoul. A tribute of gold, tiger skins, green tea, ginseng, horses, swords, *ramie* cloth, straw mats and eunuchs would be handed over by the Koreans. This ritual symbolised Chinese suzerainty over Korea, which only ended when King Gojong declared himself an emperor in 1897.

GILSANG-SA TEMPLE
Map p215 (길상사; ☏3672 5945; www.gilsangsa.or.kr; Seongbuk-dong; ◷10am-6pm Mon-Sat; ⓜLine 4 to Hangsung University, Exit 6) This delightful hillside temple once housed the elite restaurant Daewongak, where *gisaeng* (female entertainers accomplished in traditional arts) performed. In 1997 the property was donated by its owner, a former *gisaeng*, to a Buddhist monk to be turned into a temple. It's beautiful to visit at any time of year, but particularly in May when the grounds are festooned with lanterns for Buddha's birthday. There's a small teahouse and the temple offers an overnight Templestay program on the fourth Saturday and Sunday of the month; see p26 for details. A shuttle bus runs to the temple from near the subway exit at 8.30am, 9.20am, 9.40am, 10am, noon, 1pm, 3pm and 4.30pm.

FREE CHOI SUNU HOUSE HOUSE
Map p215 (최순우 옛집; Seongbuk-dong; ◷10am-4pm Tue-Sat Apr-Nov; ⓜLine 4 to Hangsung University, Exit 6, then bus 1111 or 2112) The charming *hanok* home of a former director of the National Museum of Korea and academic on Korean arts is now looked after by the National Trust of Korea. Built in the 1930s, it follows a traditional pattern with a box of outer walls containing the L-shaped inner and outer wings of the home and gardens. Find it off the main road behind some flower shops near the cafe Chocolate Con Churros.

NORTHERN SEOUL SIGHTS

TOP SIGHTS
SEODAEMUN PRISON HISTORY HALL

Now a museum, Seodaemun Prison History Hall (서대문형무소 역사관) was built by the colonial Japanese in 1908 to house 500 prisoners. Up to 3500 were packed inside during the height of the 1919 anti-Japanese protests. The factories where prisoners were forced to make bricks and military uniforms have gone, but some of the prison-made bricks with Chinese characters on them have been used to make pavements, and the whole complex has been expertly restored.

In the main exhibition hall chilling tableaux display the various torture techniques employed on Korean patriots. Photographs of the prison are on view along with video footage, and you can go into cells in the central prison building. The most famous victim was Ryu Gwan-sun, an 18-year-old Ewha high school student, who was tortured to death in 1920. You can see the underground cell where this happened, as well as a separate execution building where other prisoners were killed and the tunnel where their bodies were secretly removed. What you won't see are details of how the prison continued to be used by Korea's various dictatorships in the postwar years right up until its closure in 1987.

DON'T MISS
➡ Exhibition hall
➡ Central prison building
➡ Ryu Gwan-sun's cell

PRACTICALITIES
➡ Map p215
➡ www.sscmc.or.kr/culture2/foreign/eng/eng01.html
➡ adult/child ₩1500/500
➡ ◷9.30am-6pm Tue-Sun Mar-Oct, to 5pm Tue-Sun Nov-Feb
➡ ⓜLine 3 to Dongnimmun, Exit 5

START ENTRANCE GATE
END SEODAEMUN PRISON
DISTANCE 3-4KM
DURATION 3 HOURS

Neighbourhood Walk
Inwangsan Shamanist Walk

On this hillside walk you can see Seoul's most famous shamanist shrine, small Buddhist/shamanist temples and part of Seoul's medieval Fortress Walls, as well as enjoy a bird's-eye view of Seoul from Inwangsan. Treat the area and people with respect, and remember that taking a photograph could interfere with an important ceremony.

To get here, take subway line 3 to Dongnimmun station. From the subway exit 2, turn down the first small alley on your left. At the five-alley crossroads, fork right up the steps and you'll soon reach the colourful ❶ **entrance gate** to the shamanist village.

Turn left where the houses and small temples are terraced up the rocky hillside. Most are decorated with colourful murals of birds and blossom on their outside walls, and wind chimes clink in the breeze.

On the main path is a temple, ❷ **Seonamjeong** and, up the steps, the shamanistic shrine ❸ **Inwangsan Guksadang**. Walk left and up some steps to the extraordinary ❹ **Seonbawi** (Zen Rocks), so called because they are thought to look like giant monks in prayer. A path continues up around the Dali-esque rocks and you can climb to higher ❺ **giant boulders** for expansive views across the city.

Inwangsan's peak, a little higher up, was off limits at the time of research; instead head back to Guksadang and follow the metal fence up the gully to where it meets a rope fence on the right. Take this path along the mountain ridge, just beneath the old Fortress Walls until you reach the road. Turn left and you'll soon reach the renovated ❻ **Seoul Fortress Wall**. Stride alongside the wall to where it ends, and turn right along the road for 10 minutes until you reach ❼ **Dongnimmun**, and Seodaemun Independence Park across the road. Finish your walk by having a look around the ❽ **Seodaemun Prison History Hall**.

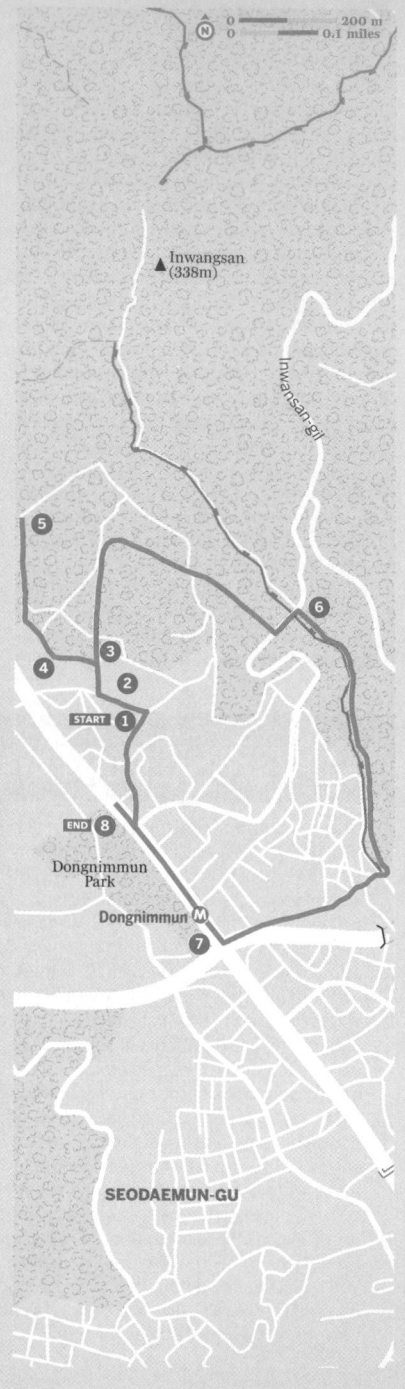

INWANGSAN GUKSADANG
SHRINE

(인왕산 국사당; Seodaemun; MLine 3 to Dongnimmun, Exit 2) Originally located on Namsan and used to make sacrifices and to perform exorcisms, this is Seoul's most famous shamanist shrine. The Japanese demolished it in 1925, so Korean shamanists rebuilt it here. The shrine is above the temple Seonamjeong, marked by a bell pavilion and gates painted with a pair of traditional door guardians.

WHANKI MUSEUM
MUSEUM

(환기미술관; www.whankimuseum.org; Buam-dong; adult/student ₩3000/2000, extra for special exhibitions; ☉10am 6pm Tue Sun; ☐1020, 7022, 7212) This attractive museum, surrounded by sculptures, showcases works by Kim Whan-ki (1913–74), a local pioneer of modern abstract art who is known as the 'Picasso of Korea'. Apart from some of Kim's works, the gallery also hosts various exhibitions, some of which have cutting-edge themes and include interesting installations.

FREE ARKO ART CENTRE
GALLERY

Map p215 (하르코미술관; www.arko.or.kr; Marronnier Park, Daehangno; ☉11am-7pm; MLine 4 to Hyehwa, Exit 2) Interesting avant-garde art is assembled in three large galleries, run by the Arts Council Korea. The big red-brick complex (designed by Kim Swoo Geun, one of Korea's most famous postwar architects) overlooks Marronnier Park, which was being renovated at the time of research.

LOCK MUSEUM
MUSEUM

Map p215 (쇳대박물관; www.lockmuseum.org; Daehangno; adult/child ₩5000/2000; ☉10am-6pm Tue-Sun; MLine 4 to Hyehwa, Exit 2) One of Seoul's quirkier private collections makes for a surprisingly absorbing exhibition. It focuses on the artistry of locks, latches and keys of all kinds, mainly from Korea but also with international examples, including a gruesome-looking chastity belt. The Corten steel-clad building contrasts nicely with a colourful wall mural nearby.

✖ EATING

TOP CHOICE JAHA SONMANDOO
KOREAN $

(자하손만두; www.sonmandoo.com; Buam-dong; mains ₩7000-10,000; ☉11am-9.30pm; ☐1020, 7022, 7212; ▥) Seoulites flock to

STREET ART IN IHWA-DONG

Ihwa-dong (이화동), on the west side of Naksan between the Fortress Walls and Marronier Park in Daehangno, was one of Seoul's old *daldongnae*. Literally 'moon village', these were where refugees lived in poor conditions after the Korean War: the euphemistic name alluded to the fact that residents had a great view of the moon from their hovels high on the hillside.

In 2006 a public art project involving 46 artists and the community was carried out to beautify this area; the imaginative results are still around to be seen on Ihwa-dong's steep stairways and alleys where you may encounter quirky sculptures and wall and floor murals. It's a great area for casual wandering, with views of the city as you go higher up Naksan.

this mountainside dumpling house for the steamed and boiled vegetable and beef and pork parcels. One plate is enough of these whoppers; the sweet cinnamon tea to finish is free.

DEONGJANG YESOOL
KOREAN $

Map p215 (된장예술; ☎745 4516; meals ₩8500; ☉9am-11pm; MLine 4 to Hyehwa, Exit 3) Serves a tasty fermented bean paste and tofu stew with a variety of nearly all vegetarian side dishes at bargain prices – no wonder it's well patronised by the area's student population. Look for the stone carved lions flanking the door.

SERIOUS DELI
PIZZA $$

Map p215 (☎070 7723 9686; Seongbuk-dong; mains ₩15,000-19,000; ☉10.30am-10.30pm; MLine 4 to Hangsung University, Exit 6, then bus 1111 or 2112; ▥▥) They are serious about pizza at this busy, rustic space, its walls lined with shelves of tinned goods. The super-crispy thin-crust pies come with a variety of toppings; they also serve pasta dishes and chunky homemade burgers.

LE GOURMET
BAKERY $$

Map p215 (www.woodnbrick.com; Seongbuk-dong; ₩7000-16,000; ☉8am-10pm; MLine 4 to Hangsung University, Exit 6, then bus 1111 or 2112; ▥▥) Sandwiches, bakery and deli items to go; good brunch dishes including a full American-style breakfast – either way you can't go wrong. Should you want something fancier there's the posh European restaurant Pavillion upstairs.

SLOW GARDEN INTERNATIONAL $$

Map p215 (www.sloowgarden.co.kr; Seongbuk-dong; mains ₩7000-15,000; ⊙9am-11.30pm; MLine 4 to Hangsung University, Exit 6, then bus 1111 or 2112; 🛜📶) Chandeliers, stained glass and recycled wood make up the shack-chic decor of this pleasant self-serve cafe where you can have brunch, grab a sandwich or waffle or just sip wine or coffee.

🍷 DRINKING & NIGHTLIFE

TOP CHOICE SUYEON SANBANG TEAHOUSE

Map p215 (수연 산방; Seongbuk-dong; ⊙11.30am-10pm; MLine 4 to Hangsung University, Exit 6, then bus 1111 or 2112) Seoul's most charming teahouse is based in a 1930s *hanok* that was once the home of novelist Lee Tae-jun; you'll find his portrait and books in one section of the house that flanks a peaceful garden. Apart from a range of medicinal teas and premium quality wild green tea, they also serve traditional sweets; the salty-sweet pumpkin soup with red bean paste is a taste sensation. Find it around the corner from the Seongbuk Museum of Art and avoid weekend afternoons when it gets busy.

SANMOTOONGE CAFE

(산모퉁이; www.sanmotoonge.co.kr; Buam-dong; ⊙11am-10pm; 📶1020, 7022, 7212) Being featured in a Korean TV drama can do wonders for your business, but customers would still come to Sanmotoonge regardless for the wonderful views from its outdoor terraces and quirky interior design. Order drinks and snacks at the counter.

HAKRIM CAFE

Map p215 (www.hakrim.pe.kr; Daehangno; ⊙10am-midnight; MLine 4 to Hyehwa, Exit 3; 🛜📶) Little has changed in this retro Seoul classic since the place opened in 1956, save for the price of drinks. Apart from coffee they also serve tea and alcohol. The cosy wooden booths and dark corners make it popular with couples.

CLUB ESPRESSO COFFEE ROASTERS

(www.clubespresso.co.kr; Buam-dong; ⊙9am-6pm; 📶1020, 7022, 7212) The choice of coffee-lovers for the fine range of roasted beans from around the world. You can sample some of the brews before buying. They also serve sugary snacks, which along with the caffeine should give you the energy to climb nearby Bukaksan.

MINTO CAFE

Map p215 (www.minto.co.kr; Maronie 2-gil, Daehangno; ⊙10am-midnight; MLine 4 to Hyehwa, Exit 2; 📶) This cute, youth-orientated cafe chain has two pleasant locations in Daehangno. This one, spread over five floors, offers masses of different zones and hideaway spots, each with its own decor and furniture.

COMFORT ZONE BAR

Map p215 (Daehangno; MLine 4 to Hyehwa, Exit 4) A spacious cafe-bar that lives up to its title with comfy sofas on two colourfully decorated levels and a large outdoor area. Happy hour with half-price draught beers runs from 5pm to 8pm.

☆ ENTERTAINMENT

CHUNNYUN JAZZ

Map p215 (천년동안도; 📞743 5555; www.chunnyun.com; Maronie 2-gil, Daehangno; admission ₩7000; ⊙5pm-3am; MLine 4 to Hyehwa, Exit 2) Enjoy two or three sessions every evening in this spacious jazz haven with black decor subtly blended with blue neon. Look for the English sign Live Jazz Club.

HANGUK PERFORMING ARTS CENTRE THEATRE

Map p215 (📞3668 0007; www.hanpac.or.kr; Marronnier Park, Daehangno; MLine 4 to Hyehwa, Exit 2) In this large red-brick complex, designed by Kim Swoo-geun, are the main and small halls of both the Arko Art Theatre and Daehangno Arts Theatre. Come here for a varied dance-oriented program of events and shows.

DONGSOONG ARTS CENTRE THEATRE

Map p215 (📞766 3390; www.dsartcenter.co.kr; Dongsung-gil, Daehangno; MLine 4 to Hyehwa, Exit 1) Major theatre complex, where you can see Korean and international performance arts in a variety of genres. The centre includes a puppet theatre, smaller performances spaces and a museum devoted to *kokdu* (wooden dolls and effigies with spiritual properties).

 # SHOPPING

DOLSILNAI   FASHION
Map p215 (돌실나이; www.dolsilnai.co.kr; Myeongryun-dong; ☺10.30am-8pm; ⓜLine 4 to Hyehwa, Exit 1) Produces beautifully designed, casual *hanbok* (traditional Korean clothing) made from natural fabrics in a variety of soft natural and pastel colours. Many of the garments for men and women are discounted and are of a far superior quality than what you'll find in the tourist shops of Insa-dong.

HYOJAE   TRADITIONAL FABRICS
Map p215 (효재; Seongbuk-dong; ☺10am-6pm Mon-Sat; ⓜLine 4 to Hangsung University, Exit 6)

Opposite Gilsang-sa, this gift shop with a sign in Chinese characters sells pretty *bojagi* (Korean wrapping cloths), embroidered pillowcases, placemats, clothes and other trinkets; they're pricey, but good quality.

MONO COLLECTION   TRADITIONAL FABRICS
(www.monocollection.com; Buam-dong; ☺10am-6pm Mon-Sat; ☐1020, 7022, 7212) Chang Eung Bong creates exquisite fabrics used for fashion and soft furnishings, including gorgeous quilts, pillows and contemporary spins on *hanbok*. Browse the collection in this tiny shop near the Fortress Walls and opposite Club Espresso.

FILIPINO SUNDAY MARKET   MARKET
Map p215 (Daehangno; ☺9am-6pm Sun; ⓜLine 4 to Hyehwa, Exit 1) Seoul's Filipino community gathers every Sunday to shop, meet, chat and eat Filipino food. Street stalls sell tropical treats such as coconut drinks, cassava cakes and fried bananas on a stick, as well as various tinned and dried goods and international telephone calling cards.

NORTHERN SEOUL SHOPPING

Day Trips from Seoul

The DMZ & JSA p121

For history buffs and collectors of weird and unsettling experiences, a visit to the DMZ buffer zone between North and South Korea is not to be missed; in the JSA you can straddle the line between the two countries.

Heyri & Paju Book City p122

The art and culture village of Heyri is a charming place to browse galleries and while away time in cafes; Paju Book City has premium outlet shopping and another observation post across into North Korea.

Suwon p124

Stride around the World Heritage–listed 18th-century Fortress Walls of the City of Filial Piety, drop by the restored Joseon-dynasty temporary palace and enjoy the charms of the Korean Folk Village.

Incheon p127

Korea opened up to the world at the end of the 19th century in this port city where you'll find a colourful Chinatown, creative Art Platform and pleasant beaches on nearby islands.

The DMZ & JSA

Explore

The DMZ (Demilitarised Zone) is a 4km-wide and 240km-long buffer splitting North from South Korea. Lined on both sides by tank traps, electrical fences, landmines and two armies in full battle readiness, it is one of the scariest places on earth. It is also one of the most surreal since it has become a major tourist attraction with several observatories allowing you to peek into North Korea.

The key sight is the Joint Security Area (JSA), inside of which is the truce village of Panmunjeom – there's nowhere else in South Korea where you can get so close to North Korea (and its soldiers) without being arrested or shot, and the tension is palpable. The only way in this heavily restricted area is on an organised tour.

The Best...

➡ **Sight** JSA (Panmunjeon)
➡ **Sight** Dora Observatory (p122)
➡ **Sight** Third Infiltration Tunnel (p122)

Top Tip

Book at least two weeks in advance for the popular USO tour, which includes the JSA. If booking other tours, check that they include the JSA. Also ask whether time will be filled out with shopping stops, and find out about refund rescheduling options if a tour is cancelled – this can very occasionally happen.

Getting There & Away

Tour The USO tour is run by **Koridoor Tours** (Map p209; ☑02 795 3028; www.koridoor.co.kr; cash US$80, credit card ₩96,000; ⊙office 8am-5pm Mon-Sat; Ⓜ Line 1 to Namyeong, Exit 2). The times are usually Saturday and Sunday from 7.30am to 3.30pm, with occasional additional tours on Wednesday, 12.30pm to 7.40pm. Bring a packed lunch, or budget around ₩10,000 for lunch at the restaurant stop. Plenty of other tour companies offer DMZ tours but they are more expensive (around ₩135,000 for ones that include the JSA); try **Panmunjom Travel Center** (www.panmunjomtour.com).

Need to Know

➡ **Location** 55km north of Seoul
➡ **Rules** Citizens of certain countries are not allowed on tours that include the JSA. There are also strict dress and behavioural codes.

SIGHTS

The following describes the major stops on the tour offered by the USO. Dora Observatory and the Third Tunnel are both in Imjingak and can be visited independently of going on a tour; for more details see http://en.paju.go.kr.

JSA (PANMUNJEOM)   MILITARY AREA

Tours kick off with a rapid-fire briefing by the soldier guides at Camp Bonifas. Though your tour will likely be a quiet one, the soldier will remind you that this frontier is no stranger to violent incidents, one of the most notorious being in 1976 when two US soldiers were hacked to death with axes by North Korean soldiers after the former had tried to chop down a tree obstructing the view from a watch tower. Camp Bonifas, the joint US-ROK army camp just outside the DMZ, is named after one of the slain soldiers.

Next you will board specially designated buses to travel into the JSA towards the collection of blue-painted UN buildings that constitute Panmunjeom. Official meetings are still sometimes held here, and in the main conference room mikes on the tables constantly record everything said. Straddling the ceasefire line, this is the only place where you can safely walk into North Korea. South Korean soldiers stand guard inside and out in a modified taekwondo stance – an essential photo op – and their North Korean counterparts keep a steady watch, usually, but not always, from a distance.

Back on the bus you'll be taken to one of Panmunjeom's lookout posts from where you can see the two villages within the DMZ: Daeseong-dong in the South and Gijeong-dong in the North; Gijeong-dong is also known by the South as Propaganda Village because virtually all the buildings are empty or just facades.

DORA OBSERVATORY · OBSERVATORY

(use of binoculars ₩500; ☉10am-5pm Tue-Sun)
Peer through binoculars from here for a
closer look at Kaesong city and Kaesong
Industrial Complex in North Korea, where
cheap North Korean labourers are employed by South Korean conglomerates.
At the foot of the mountain, Dorasan train
station, currently the northern terminus of
South Korea's rail line, is a symbol of the
hope for the eventual reunification of the
two Koreas.

THIRD INFILTRATION TUNNEL · TUNNEL

(제3땅굴; ☉9am-5pm Tue-Sun) Since 1974
four tunnels have been found running under the DMZ, dug by the North Koreans so
that their army could launch a surprise attack. Walking along 265m of this 73m-deep
tunnel is not for the claustrophobic or the
tall: creeping hunched over to reach the
coiled barbed wire at the triple-concrete
wall-blocked end of the tunnel, you'll re-
alise why they issue hard hats to protect
heads from knocking the low ceiling. The
guide will point out how the North Koreans
painted the rocks black so they might claim
it was a coal mine!

Heyri & Paju Book City

Explore

Less than 10km south of the DMZ, Heyri
(헤이리) is a charming village of small-
scale contemporary buildings that couldn't
be more of a contrast to the heavily fortified, doom-laden border. Conceived as a
'book village' connected to the nearby publishing centre of Paju Book City, it has blos-
somed into a community of artists, writers,
architects and other creative souls. There

WORTH A DETOUR

EVERLAND RESORT

Set in lush hillsides 40km south of Seoul, the mammoth amusement park **Everland Resort** (www.everland.com) offers more than just thrill rides and fairy floss.

The main theme park **Everland** (adult/teenager/child ₩40,000/34,000/31,000; ☉9.30am-10pm Sep-Jun, to 11pm Jul & Aug) is filled with fantasy buildings, fairground attractions, impressive seasonal gardens and live music and parades. Lit up at night, the park takes on a magical atmosphere and there are always fireworks.

Next door is **Caribbean Bay** (adult/child from ₩35,000/27,000; ☉10am-5pm Sep-Jun, 9.30am-11pm Jul & Aug), a superb indoor and outdoor water park. The outdoor sec-tion is usually open from June to September (there's a higher entrance charge to the park in July and August) and features a huge wave pool that produces a mini-tsunami every few minutes and water-based thrill rides.

A free shuttle bus runs from Everland's main entrance to the **Hoam Art Museum** (http://hoam.samsungfoundation.org; adult/child ₩4000/3000, free with Everland ticket; ☉10am-6pm Tue-Sun) and you are well advised to take it. The serenely beautiful **Hee Won** traditional Korean gardens induce a calm frame of mind so that visitors can fully appreciate the gorgeous art treasures inside the museum, including traditional paint-ings, screens and celadon pottery.

There's so much to see here that staying over is worth considering. There are two accommodation options: **Home Bridge Hillside Hostel** (☏031 320 8849; r & ondol from ₩50,000; ❄@) is the older but quite acceptable property, while **Home Bridge Cabin Hostel** (☏031 320 9740; r from ₩130,000; ❄@) offers Swiss-style log cabins and hotel rooms, the most expensive with balconies overlooking the park. Rates at both places are higher on Saturday nights and during July and August. On Sundays, rates are slashed in half. Bookings can be made via the Everland website and guests can use their one-day park passes over two days.

To get here from Seoul take bus 5002 (₩2000, 50 minutes, every 15 minutes) from Gangnam. From outside Suwon's train station, hop on bus 66 or 66-4 (₩1700, one hour, every 30 minutes).

SLEEPING IN HEYRI

Rates for accommodation usually rise for Friday and Saturday nights when many people visit from Seoul.

➡ **Yonaluky** (☎031 959 1122; www.yonaluky.com; Gate 8; d ₩350,000; ❄🛜) Each of the seven massive, elegantly contemporary rooms at this gallery-cum-hotel have a broad outdoor private courtyard with sunken granite bath. Rates include breakfast.

➡ **Motif #1** (☎031 949 0901; www.motif1.co.kr; Gate 1; d from ₩150,000; ❄🛜) This guesthouse is packed with art, a library of 10,000 books and beautifully designed en suite rooms that are worthy of a boutique hotel. Guests can use the kitchen.

➡ **Forest Garden** (☎031 8071 0127, 010 4363 2660; www.forestgarden.kr; Gate 1; d from ₩200,000; ❄🛜) An award-winning home that climbs up the hillside, with rooms that are very comfortable and come with TV, DVD and fridge.

---

are scores of small art galleries, cafes, boutique shops and quirky private collections turned into mini museums.

The Best...

➡ **Sight** Heyri

➡ **Place to Eat** Café Between (p124)

➡ **Place to Stay** Yonaluky

Top Tip

At Heyri's tourist office you can pick up a good English guidebook (₩2000) that details the many places to see in the village.

Getting There & Away

Bus Express Bus 2200 (₩2000, 45 minutes) and local bus 200 (₩1800, one hour 20 minutes) both leaves from stop 16, near Hapjeong station on subway Lines 2 and 6 in Seoul. Both pass through Paju on the way to Heyri; the local bus also stops near Odusan and the Premium Outlet Mall in Paju.

Need to Know

➡ **Area Code** ☎031

➡ **Location** 48km north of Seoul

➡ **Tourist Office** ☎031 946 8551; www.heyri.net; Gate 1; ⊙10am-6pm

 **SIGHTS**

HEYRI   ARTS CENTRE

Just wandering around the village is a pleasure. Interesting pieces of architecture and sculpture abound, most created with materials that reflect and fit in with the natural environment. **Bikes** (per hr/day ₩5000/13,000; ⊙10.30am-6.30pm) can be hired near Gate 3.

Among the many small museums and galleries is the **Han Hyang Lim Onggi Museum** (www.heyrimuseum.com; Gate 7; admission ₩3000; ⊙10am-7pm Tue-Fri, 10am-8pm Sat & Sun; 🛜), with a fine collection of traditional Korean pottery including many giant kimchi pots. There's also a colourful **playground area** (Gate 5; www.dalki.com) that's devoted to the cartoon character Dalki, created by the Ssamzie accessories brand.

PAJU BOOK CITY   NEIGHBOURHOOD

(www.pajubookcity.org) Contemporary architecture and original building concepts are also abundant in Paju Book City, 10km south of Heyri. Check out the **Asia Publication Culture & Information Centre** (www.jijihyang.org), partly clad in rusting steel that picks up the colours of the environment and juxtaposed with a beautiful example of a *hanok* (traditional house), dating from 1834 and transported here from the province of Jeollabuk-do.

Paju is also known for its shopping, and is home to a couple of fashion malls, **Premium Outlets** (www.premiumoutlets.co.kr) and **Lotte Outlets** (http://paju.lotteoutlets.com).

Between Heyri and Paju, the **Odusan Unification Observatory** (오두산통일전망대; www.jmd.co.kr; adult/teenager/child ₩3000/1600/1000; ⊙9am-5.30pm Apr-Sep, to 5pm Oct-Mar, to 4.30pm Nov-Feb) provides another chance to gaze across the DMZ into North Korea.

✕ EATING & DRINKING

The following are in Heyri, where you'll find scores more cafes and restaurants.

CAFÉ BETWEEN
CAFE, PIZZERIA **$$**

(Gate 3; pizza ₩15,000-22,000; ◷10am-11pm; 📶🐕) On the 2nd floor is a brick oven producing crispy pizzas while on the ground is a pleasant cafe – both have outdoor terrace seating with a view of the heart of the village.

LACHEM
NEO KOREAN **$$**

(Gate 1; meals ₩10,000-26,000; ◷11am-9.30pm; 📶🍴🐕) Beside the gallery Jin Art is this stylish restaurant serving tasty and nicely presented modern takes on Korean dishes. The ₩10,000 set meal is all vegetarian.

FORESTA
CAFE **$**

(www.heyribookhouse.co.kr; Gate 3; drinks from ₩5000; ◷noon-9pm; 📶🐕) Inside the Hangil Book House and overlooking a leafy glade in the midst of Heyri is this appealing cafe with plenty of beverages, including freshly made coffee and smoothies. Light meals include sandwiches and cakes.

Suwon

It was King Jeongjo, the 22nd Joseon dynasty ruler, who had the idea of moving the national capital from Seoul to Suwon, 48km south, in 1794. The fortress walls that surrounded the original city were constructed but the king died and power stayed in Seoul. Named Hwaseong, Suwon's impressive World Heritage–listed fortifications remain the best reason for visiting the city, where you'll also find the faithfully restored palace Hwaseong Haenggung. Suwon is also close to the Korean Folk Village and Everland Resort and can be used as a base to visit both.

The Best...

→ **Sight** Hwaseong
→ **Place to Eat** Yeonpo Galbi (p126)
→ **Place to Stay** Hwaseong Guest House (p125)

Top Tip

At the Yeonmudae **archery centre** (Map p126; 10 arrows ₩2000; ◷9.30am-5.30pm, every 30min) you can practise a traditional sport in which Koreans often win Olympic medals.

Getting There & Away

Subway Line 1 connects Seoul to Suwon (₩1850, one hour) but make sure you're on a train that heads to the city before the line splits at Guro.

Train KTO trains from Seoul are speedier (from ₩4600, 30 minutes) but not as frequent.

Need to Know

→ **Area Code** ☎031
→ **Location** 48km south of Seoul
→ **Tourist Office** ☎031 228 4673; www.suwon.ne.kr; outside Suwon station, on the left; ◷9am-6pm Mar-Oct, to 5pm Nov-Feb
→ There's also an information booth near Paldamun and in Suwon Cultural Foundation next to Hwaseong Haenggung.

◎ SIGHTS

HWASEONG
FORTRESS WALLS

(화성; Map p126; http://ehs.suwon.ne.kr; admission ₩1000; ◷24hr) Suwon's fortress wall, with its command posts, observation towers, entrance gates and fire-beacon platform, was innovative for its time and makes for a fascinating two-hour historical walk. Faced with large stone blocks and grey bricks, the wall stretches for 5.7km, nearly all of which has been restored. Walk outside the wall for at least part of the way, as the fortress looks much more impressive the way an enemy would see it.

Start at **Paldalmun**, also known as Nammun (South Gate), and follow the steep steps off to the left up to the **Seonam Gangu**, an observation point near the peak of **Paldalsan** (143m). Near the command post, **Seojangdae** is the large Hyowon Bell you can toll (₩1000), and **Seonodae**, a tower that was used by crossbow archers.

On the wall's north side is **Hwahongmun**, a watergate over a stream, and the **archery centre**. Nearby is **Dongbukgong-**

SLEEPING IN SUWON

Although Suwon is an easy day trip from Seoul, there are several good places to stay should you choose to make it a base for seeing other sights in the region.

➡ **Hwaseong Guest House** (📞031 245 6226; www.hsguesthouse.com; dm/r ₩15,000/25,000; 🕸@📶) Run by friendly English-speaking folk, this backpackers has rooms decorated with a variety of flowery wallpapers, all of which share communal bathrooms. To find it turn left at Compador Bakery on Jeongjo-ro north of Paldamun.

➡ **Suwon Hwaesong Sarangchae** (수원화성 사랑채; 📞031 245 5555; www.sarangchae.org; d, tw or ondol from ₩30,000; 🕸📶) Tucked behind the Suwon Cultural Foundation is this professionally run place, more of a guesthouse than a hostel (you need to be a party of four to take advantage of its four-bed dorm rooms). The spacious *ondol* rooms, with private bathrooms, are particularly nice and good value.

➡ **Ramada Plaza Hotel Suwon** (📞031 230 0031; www.ramadaplazasuwon.com; d or tw from ₩200,000; 🕸@📶) About five minutes by taxi east of the fortress, the Ramada is a stylish affair with contemporary rooms and top-grade facilities, including a gym, a deli and a couple of restaurants.

simdon, another watchtower but with a unique design – a high, tapering structure with rounded corners, a stone base and a brick tower. Further on are the **Bongdon beacon towers**, which were used to send messages around the country – the number of lit beacons signified different messages. From here the wall dips down to cross the Suwon-cheon where it breaks for the **Jidong market** (where you can buy fresh produce, clothing and homewares), coming back to Paldamun.

HWASEONG HAENGGUNG   PALACE
(화성행궁; Map p126; admission ₩1500; ⊘9am-5pm) King Jeongjo's palace, destroyed during the Japanese occupation, has meticulously been reconstructed and is worth exploring. Find out how detailed court records aided the reconstruction process and see how the area used to look at the **Suwon Cultural Foundation** (admission free; ⊘9.30am-6pm Mar-Oct, 9.30am-5pm Nov-Feb) on the south side of the plaza in front of the palace.

From March to November, various traditional performances are held at the palace, including a **changing of the guard ceremony** (⊘2pm Sun) and a **martial arts display** (⊘11am Tue-Sun). Every October a grand **royal procession** is re-enacted as part of Suwon's annual festival.

KOREAN FOLK VILLAGE   ARCHITECTURAL PARK
(한국 민속촌; www.koreanfolk.co.kr; adult/teenager/child ₩15,000/12,000/10,000; ⊘9am-6.30pm Mar-Oct, to 5pm Nov-Feb) Around 260 thatched and tiled traditional houses and buildings from around the country make up this attractive folk village that takes at least half a day to look around. Artisans wearing *hanbok* (traditional Korean clothing) create pots, make paper and weave bamboo, while other workers tend to vegetable plots, and livestock.

Throughout the day traditional musicians, dancers, acrobats and tightrope walkers perform, and you can watch a staged wedding ceremony. Other attractions, including an amusement park and horse riding, cost extra. The village also has several rustic restaurants and a food court.

A free shuttle bus leaves Suwon's main tourist information centre (30 minutes, every hour from 11am to 3pm). The last shuttle bus leaves the folk village at 4.30pm (5pm on weekends). After that time, walk to the far end of the car park and catch city bus 37 (₩1300, one hour, every 20 minutes) back to Suwon station.

🍴 EATING & DRINKING

Suwon is renowned for its *galbi* (beef) dishes, including *galbitang,* meaty bones in a broth. There are plenty of restaurants near the fortress walls, but the main place to meet carousing locals is close by Suwon station: lively bars cluster along and around the pedestrian street that starts between Face Shop and Paris Baguette.

Hwaseong & Haenggung

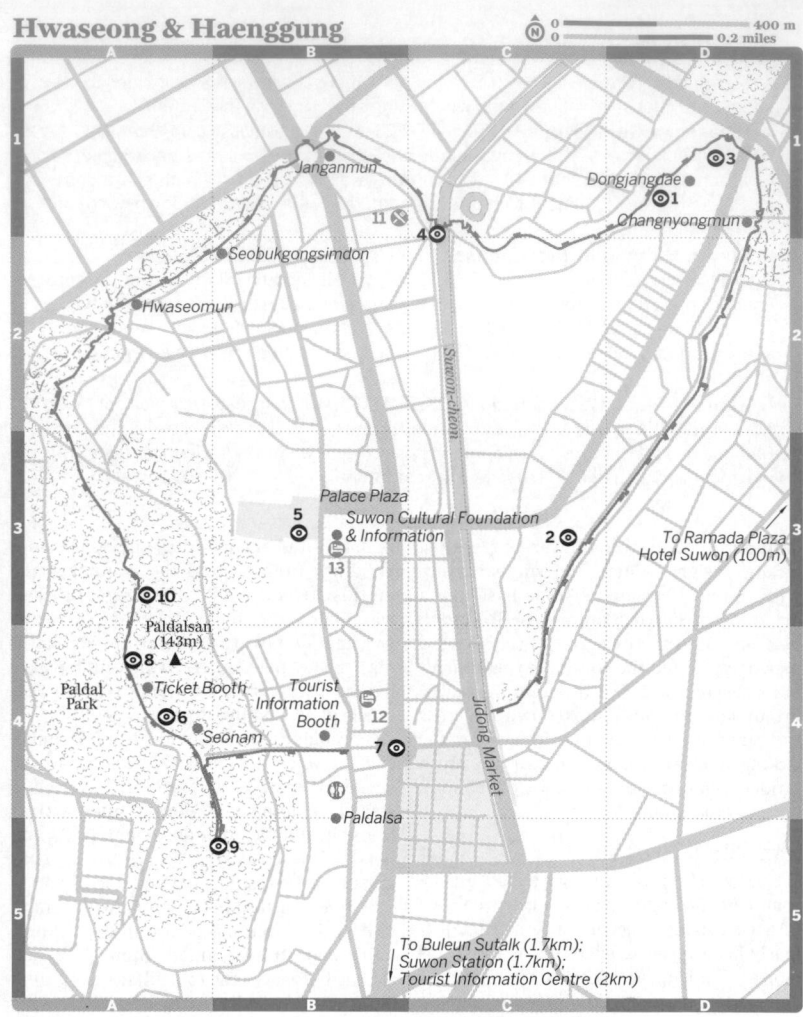

YEONPO GALBI   KOREAN **$**

(연포갈비; Map p126; meals ₩8000-35,000; ⊙11.30am-10pm) Down the steps from Hwahongmun, this famous restaurant serves up its special Suwon version of *galbitang* – chunks of meat and a big rib in a seasoned broth with noodles and leeks. Look for the building with a facade of logs.

JONDONGCHAJIP   TEASHOP **$**

(전통찻집; Map p126; teas from ₩6000; ⊙10am-10pm) Rest your feet, sip local teas and nibble sweet rice cakes in this antique-style teashop above the archery centre. You can

also order spicy snail noodles and Korean-style savoury pancakes (₩1300).

BULGEUN SUTALK   BAR

(붉은수탉; off Map p126; ⊙5pm-3am) Look for the iron rooster marking the entrance to this bohemian fantasy bar, with rose petals scattered on the stairs, mammoth melted candles, crystal chandeliers and plenty of scatter cushions, where you can enjoy a chilled evening with Suwon's hipsters. It's five minutes' walk northeast of the station along Maesanno on the corner where you'll find SK Telekom.

Hwaseong & Haenggung

Incheon

This major port is where Korea opened up to the world in the 1880s, ending centuries of self-imposed isolation. The layers of history here are fascinating and include memorials to the daring landing behind enemy lines of UN forces led by US General Douglas MacArthur in 1950. Its colourful Chinatown, Korea's largest such community, is next to the Open Port area with Japanese colonial era buildings and the brick warehouses transformed into a contemporary arts centre. Incheon can also be used as a stepping stone to the West Sea islands and their beaches.

The Best...

➡ **Sight** Incheon Art Platform
➡ **Place to Eat** Mandabok (p130)
➡ **Place to Stay** Harbor Park Hotel

Top Tip

Don't miss the tiny car-free island of **So-Muuido** (admission ₩1000) connected by footbridge to Muuido's southeastern tip; the island's charming fishing village couldn't be more of a contrast to 21st-century Seoul.

Getting There & Away

Subway Line 1 connects Seoul to Incheon (₩1850, one hour 15 minutes) but make sure you're on a train that heads to the city before the line splits at Guro.

Need to Know

➡ **Area Code** ☏032
➡ **Location** 36km west of Seoul
➡ **Tourist Office** ☏777 1330; http://english.incheon.go.kr; Incheon subway station; ☺9am-6pm

◉ SIGHTS

`FREE` **INCHEON ART PLATFORM** ARTS CENTRE (www.inartplatform.kr; Open Port; ☺10am-6pm Sun-Thu, 10am-8pm Fri & Sat) An attractive complex of 1930s and '40s brick warehouses has been turned over to the Incheon Foundation for Arts and Culture, which has created gallery spaces and art residency studios that are worth exploring. Performances and events are also held here.

SLEEPING IN INCHEON

The following are located within walking distance of Incheon subway station.

➡ **Hong Kong Motel** (☏777 9001; r ₩30,000; ❋ @) Steps from the station, this love hotel is clean and well maintained and has friendly staff.

➡ **Paradise Hotel** (☏762 5181; www.paradisehotel.co.kr; d from ₩253,000; ❋ @ ☎) Located on a hill overlooking the port; rates at this long-established upmarket hotel with a spa and gym can dip significantly if you book online or ask for a walk-in discount.

➡ **Harbor Park Hotel** (☏770 9500; www.harborparkhotel.com; r from ₩242,000; ❋ @ ☎) Sporting a sleek contemporary design both inside and out, with floor-to-ceiling windows providing great views of the harbour and hillsides from every woodtone-decorated room.

Incheon

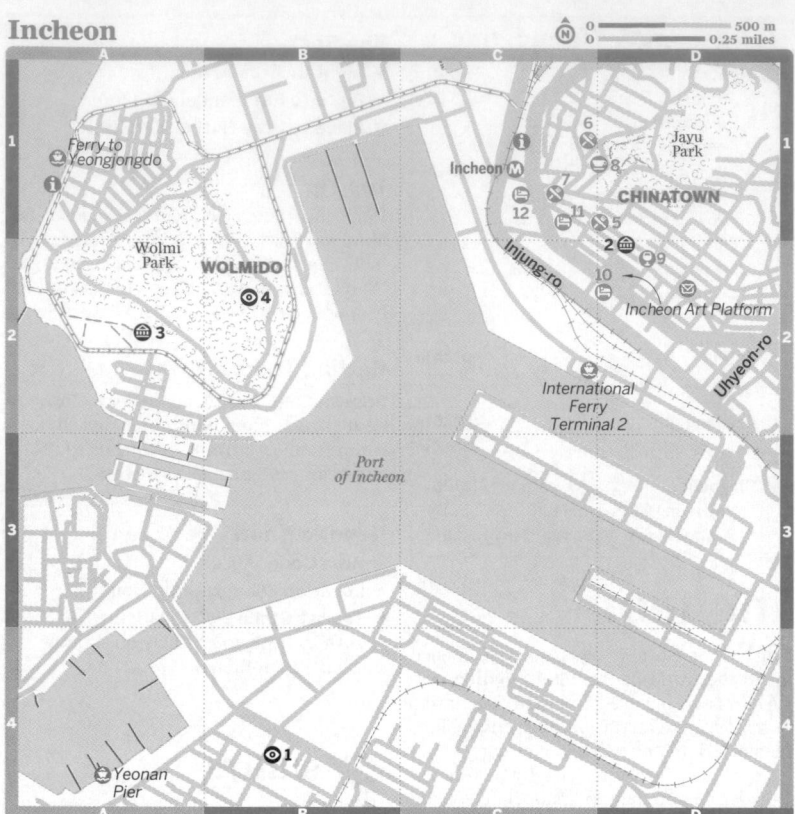

Incheon

JAYU PARK
PARK

Map p128 (Open Port; Ⓜ Line 1 to Incheon) Jayu means freedom and this hillside park, designed by a Russian civil engineer in 1888, is a good spot to catch the breeze. It contains the monument for the centenary of Korea-USA relations and a statue of General MacArthur.

INCHEON GRAND FISHERY MARKET
MARKET

(www.asijang.co.kr; Yeonan; ⊙4.30am-9pm) Even if you've already visited Noriyangjin in Seoul, this fish and seafood market is still worth seeing. It's a more intimate, brightly lit place displaying hundreds of types of marine products, all of which you can eat on the spot at several small restaurants and cafes.

INCHEON OPEN PORT MUSEUM
MUSEUM

(인천개항박물관; www.icjgss.or.kr/open_port; Open Port; adult/teenager/child ₩500/300/200;

9am-6pm Tue-Sun) One of three former Japanese bank buildings along the same street has been turned into this interesting museum about the area's distinctive architecture, which dates back to the 1890s.

FREE WOLMI PARK   PARK

(월미도; wolmi.incheon.go.kr; Wolmido; park 5am-10pm, garden 9am-8pm, museum 9am-6pm Tue-Sun, observatory 7am-10pm) Crafted from a former military base and site of the Incheon Landing Operation during the Korean War, this attractive park includes a replica of a traditional palace garden, walking trails shaded by leafy trees, a museum on the history of Korean emigration, and the hilltop **Wolmi Observatory** (admission free), offering views across the port and towards Yeongjongdo.

FREE INCHEON LANDING OPERATION MEMORIAL HALL   MUSEUM

(인천 상륙 작전 기념관; www.landing915.com; Songdo; 9am-6pm Tue-Sun) Some 70,000 UN and South Korean troops took part in the surprise landing in Incheon in 1950, supported by 260 warships. Find out about this daring attack at this sombre, strikingly designed museum. The displays include newsreel films of the Korean War.

INCHEON METROPOLITAN CITY MUSEUM   MUSEUM

(인천광역시립박물관; Songdo; adult/child ₩400/free; 9am-6pm Tue-Sun) Next to the Incheon Landing Memorial Monument Hall is the city's main museum, offering an excellent collection of celadon pottery and some interesting historical displays.

✖ EATING & DRINKING

In Chinatown you can sample local variations of Chinese cuisine including *jjajangmyeon* (noodles in a savoury-sweet blackbean sauce), *jjampong* (noodles in a spicy seafood soup) and *onggibyeong* (crispy meat or veg dumplings baked inside large clay jars). Wolmido's promenade also offers plenty of touristy seafood restaurants; better-value feasts are available at Yeonan's fish market, where a raw fish platter big enough to feed four is around ₩40,000.

DAY TRIPS FROM SEOUL INCHEON

YEONGJONGDO & MUUIDO

Also part of Incheon's municipality are the 100-plus islands scattered off the coast including **Yeongjongdo**, home to Incheon International Airport and connected to the mainland by bridges, train lines or a brief ferry ride from Wolmido (adult/child ₩3000/1000, 7am to 9pm). Buses run from the island ferry terminal to **Eulwangri Beach** on the island's western tip, a popular spot with plenty of motels and pensions, decent sand and lovely sunsets.

The cheapest self-catering rooms at the swank **Golden Sky International Resort** (032 745 5000; www.goldensky.co.kr; apt from ₩200,000;) have sufficient space for four people (two in the bed and two on mattresses on the *ondol* floor). There's an attached spa and pool complex. Across the road up on the hill is **Caffe Ora** (10am-11pm), a modernist piece of architecture housing a high-class cafe and restaurant.

Nicer than Yeongjongdo is **Muuido**, which can be reached via a five-minute ferry trip (₩3000 return, half-hourly until 7pm, until 6pm in winter) from Jamjindo, a tiny islet connected by a causeway to the southwest tip of Yeongjongdo. On Muuido, **Hanagae Beach** (하나개 해수욕장; 032 751 8833; www.hanagae.co.kr; adult/child ₩2000/1000) and **Silmi Beach** (실미 해수욕장; 032 752 4466; adult/child ₩2000/1000) are top relaxation spots where you can either camp or stay in inexpensive cabins.

Muuido has plenty of *minbak* (homestays) and pensions. An excellent one is **Lifou** (032 747 0053, 011 269 4224; www.lifou.kr; r from ₩70,000;), a hillside self-catering complex with both *ondol* and Western-style rooms and English-speaking owners who are a lot of fun.

Note that accommodation prices on the islands are higher on weekends and during July and August.

PUNGMI
CHINESE $

(풍미; ☎772 2680; Chinatown; meals ₩5000-10,000; ⊙11am-9.30pm) In business for over half a century, this is a good place to sample *jjajangmyeon* or other tasty, inexpensive dishes such as seafood fried rice.

MANDABOK
CHINESE $$

(만다복; ☎773 3838; www.mandabok.com; Chinatown; mains ₩7000-30,000; ⊙11am-10pm) Guarded by a pair of terracotta warriors, this is one of Chinatown's fanciest restaurants, with a refined interior and top-notch cuisine. Try the sweet-and-sour pork (₩20,000).

FOG CITY INTERNATIONAL CAFÉ
INTERNATIONAL $$

(☎766 9024; www.fogcitycafe.com; Open Port; meals ₩15,000-30,000; ⊙8.30am-midnight) If you're tired of Korean or Chinese food, drop by this appealing modern all-day cafe serving a mix of sandwiches, salads, pizza and pasta. Get there early if you want to try the *makgeolli* bread, as it usually sells out.

CAFÉ CASTLE
CAFE

(www.cafecastle.com; Chinatown; ⊙11.30am-midnight) Enjoy coffee, tea, cocktails and snacks at this intimate cafe festooned with greenery. There's a fantastic harbour view from its rooftop garden.

MIN
BAR

(민; ⊙7pm-1am) With a painting of a smiling tiger on its outside wall, this cosy bar, part of a row of colonial-era shophouses, is a hang-out for students from the local art college who sip beers and *soju* and tuck into cheap savoury pancakes.

Sleeping

Seoul has a wide selection of accommodation including many budget backpacker guesthouses. There's also no shortage of top-end hotels. In the mid range, if you're looking for somewhere memorable rather than bland, your options will be narrowed to Bukchon's charming hanok guesthouses and a handful of design-conscious operations scattered around the city.

Backpacker Guesthouses

Seoul has many small, friendly backpacker guesthouses that cater to budget-conscious foreigners of all ages; most are concentrated in Myeong-dong and Hongdae. Rooms – dorms and doubles – tend to be tiny, but are nearly always en suite. The young helpful staff speak English. Communal facilities usually include a satellite TV and DVD lounge, a kitchen, a free basic breakfast, free use of a washing machine and internet access.

Hanok Guesthouses

Traditional *hanok* (Korean one-storey wooden houses) are increasingly being turned into guesthouses. Staying in one is a unique and memorable experience. Rooms are small and you'll sleep on *yo* (padded quilts and mattresses) on the floor, but underfloor heating systems (*ondol*) keep them snug in winter. At cheaper *hanok* you'll share the bathroom, but many guesthouses offer en suite rooms too. Rates often include breakfast. For more about *hanok* guesthouses, see the KTO site **Hanokstay** (www.hanokstay.or.kr). Jongno-gu also runs a **hanok homestay program** (http://homestay.jongno.go.kr/homestayEngMain.do).

Motels, Love Motels & Hotels

Thousands of small, family-run budget hotels are scattered throughout Seoul. The rooms are always on the small size but they are packed with facilities – en suite, TV, DVD, telephone, fridge, drinking water, air-con and heating, toiletries, and even computers. However, staff rarely speak any English.

Love motels cater for couples seeking some by-the-hour privacy, but they also accept conventional overnight guests. They're easy to spot by the plastic curtains shielding the parked cars from prying eyes. Don't be put off, as they can be an excellent option; some of the extravagantly decorated rooms are a bargain compared with what you'd pay for similar facilities at a top-end hotel.

Seoul's top hotels rate with the best anywhere in terms of facilities and services. However, hotels with character and style are rare and there are relatively few places that could truly be described as 'boutique'.

Homestays

These are the best way to experience Korean food, customs and family life at close quarters. Some families offer pick-ups and dinner, and rates are greatly reduced if you stay long-term. The charge for bed and breakfast per night can be as low as ₩30,000 per person.

Serviced Apartments & Longer-Term Rentals

Even if you're not staying long-term in Seoul, serviced apartments can often be a great option, offering more home conveniences such as kitchen and laundry facilities than a regular hotel. Renting an apartment can be tricky because of the traditional payment system that involves paying a huge deposit to the landlord and/or having to pay all your rent up front. Browse real-estate websites www.nicerent.com or www.nearsubway.com for what's on offer.

NEED TO KNOW

Price Ranges
$ less than ₩61,000
$$ ₩61,000-250,000
$$$ over ₩250,000

Breakfast
Some hostels and *hanok* guesthouses include a simple breakfast in their rates; most hotels don't.

Taxes & Service Charges
Budget and midrange places usually include a VAT of 10% in their rates. All top-end hotels will slap a service charge of 10% on the bill as well as VAT (so a total of 21% over the quoted rate); rates listed in this guide include all taxes.

Tipping
Not expected.

Transport
Only a handful of top-end hotels are not near a subway station; those that aren't provide shuttle buses. Alternatively, use a taxi.

Wi-Fi
Often free, but sometimes only in the hotel lobby. If wi-fi is not available in guest rooms, the alternative will be connection to the internet via LAN cable. Top-end hotels can charge as much as ₩35,000 a day for internet access.

Lonely Planet's Top Choices

La Casa (p140) Chic boutique hotel close to the trendy boutique, cafes and bars of Garosu-gil.

Chi-Woon-Jung (p134) *Hanok* guesthouses don't come any more luxurious than this beauty.

V Mansion (p137) Connect with artists at this spacious backpackers near the Han River.

Fraser Suites (p134) Top-class serviced apartments in Insa-dong

Park Hyatt Seoul (p140) Sophisticated contemporary design hotel overlooking COEX.

Best By Budget

$
Inside Backpackers (p142)
V Mansion (p137)
Bebop House (p137)

$$
Hotel Sunbee (p134)
Hotel Tria (p140)
Metro Hotel (p136)

$$$
Banyan Tree Club & Spa (p135)
Grand Hyatt Seoul (p138)
The Plaza (p135)

Best Hanok Guesthouses

Rak-Ko-Jae (p134)
Eugene's House (p141)
Seoul Guesthouse (p134)

Best Love Motels

Jelly Hotel (p140)
Hotel D'Oro (p138)
Princess Hotel (p141)

Best Serviced Apartments

Marriott Executive Apartments (p138)
Han Suites (p136)
Euljiro Co-Op Residence (p139)

Best Accommodation Booking Sites

Lonely Planet (www.hotels.lonelyplanet.com)
Korean Hotel Reservation Center (www.khrc.com)
Benikea (www.benikea.com)
Agoda (www.agoda.com)

Best Homestay Options

Koreastay (www.koreastay.or.kr)
Go Homestay (www.gohomestay.com)
Homestay Korea (www.homestaykorea.com).
Lex (www.lex.or.kr)

Where to Stay

Neighbourhood	For	Against
Gwanghwamun & Jongno-gu	Ideal for exploring city on foot with the palaces, Insa-dong and Bukchon on your doorstep. Plenty of characterful *hanok* guesthouses and homestays.	Light on top-end hotels. Parts of Insa-dong and Bukchon are very heavily trafficked with tourists.
Myeong-dong & Jung-gu	Central location and direct access to Mt Namsan and shopping in Myeong-dong and Namdaemun. Good selection of accommodation at all levels.	Streets in heart of Myeong-dong are perpetually busy – not a place for those seeking peace and tranquillity.
Western Seoul	Best for budget travellers who want to party with the hipsters in Hongdae, Sinchon and Edae. Yeouido is recommended only if you have business on the island.	You will spend a fair amount of time on the subway to get to the major sights.
Itaewon & Yongsan-gu	Reasonably central location close to some major sights. Perfect if you want to take full advantage of Itaewon's plentiful dining and nightlife options.	The most 'Western' area of Seoul. You'll be catching taxis or taking the subway to major sights north of Namsan.
Dongdaemun & Eastern Seoul	Shopping nirvana, particularly for those who love markets. Night owls will be thrilled by the 24-hour activity.	Hotels on Walker Hill are a long drive from the city and not close to the subway either.
Gangnam & South of the Han River	For those who will settle for nothing less than major top-end brands. There's buzzing nightlife in Apgujeong and Gangnam. Handy for COEX if you're visiting for a convention there.	Very light on budget options. The grid-like layout, barrelling highways and dearth of historical sights make it way less appealing than north of the Han.
Northern Seoul	Handy for theatre district of Daehangno.	Most areas here are not accessible by subway.

Gwanghwamun & Jongno-gu

CHI-WOON-JUNG TOP CHOICE HANOK GUESTHOUSE $$$

Map p195 (취운정; ☎765 7400; www.chiwoonjung.co.kr; 31-53 Gahoe-dong; s/d from ₩500,000/1,000,000; ❄@☞) The *hanok* as an exclusive luxury experience doesn't get much finer than this stunning property that has just four elegant guestrooms, all en suite with beautifully tiled bathrooms and pine-wood tubs. Completely remodelled since Korean president Lee Myung Bak once lived there, it is decorated with beautiful crafts and has a Zen calm garden wrapped around it. Rates include breakfast and dinner, which is a sumptuous royal banquet served by the charming staff dressed in floaty *hanbok*.

FRASER SUITES TOP CHOICE SERVICED APARTMENTS $$$

Map p198 (☎6262 8888; www.frasershospitality.com; 272 Nakwon-dong; 1/2/3-bedroom apt ₩330,000/440,000/550,000; ❄@☞) These fully equipped serviced apartments are modern, light and spacious, great for a long-term stay for which major discounts are available. Staff try hard to make this a home-away-from-home and its location, steps away from Insadong-gil, can't be beat. A buffet breakfast is included in the rates.

RAK-KO-JAE HANOK GUESTHOUSE $$$

Map p195 (락고재; ☎742 3410; www.rkj.co.kr; 98 Gyeo-dong; s/d ₩198,000/275,000; ❄Line 3 to Anguk, Exit 2; ❄@) This beautifully restored *hanok*, with an enchanting garden is modelled after Japan's ryokan. The guesthouse's mud-walled sauna is included in the prices, as is breakfast, dinner, traditional tea ceremony and copious amounts of house-made alcohol. The en-suite bathrooms are tiny though.

HOTEL SUNBEE HOTEL $$

Map p198 (호텔썬비; ☎730 3451; www.hotelsunbee.com; 198-11 Gwanhun-dong; d/tw/ondol ₩100,000/120,000/140,000; ❄Line 3 to Anguk, Exit 6; ❄@☞) This hotel has a great location close to Insadong-gil. The double beds are huge and the rooms are decorated tastefully. Many rooms come with a widescreen TV and computer. Breakfast is coffee, toast and orange juice in your room.

SEOUL GUESTHOUSE HANOK GUESTHOUSE $$

Map p195 (서울게스트하우스; ☎745 0057; www.seoul110.com; 135-1 Gye-dong; s/d/f ₩50,000/70,000/120,000; ❄Line 3 to Anguk, Exit 3; ❄@☞) This wooden *hanok* has a charming courtyard garden, and the English-speaking owners (who have an adorable shaggy dog, Ssari) are helpful hosts. It's a delightful place to stay, but as with other *hanok*, rooms are small, bathrooms are cramped (but modern), and you sleep on a *yo* (padded quilt) mattress on an *ondol*-heated floor. Except in the more expensive rooms, the computers, TV lounge, washing machine and kitchen facilities are all shared. They also rent out a separate *hanok* sleeping six for ₩230,000.

MOON GUEST HOUSE HANOK GUESTHOUSE $$

Map p198 (☎745 8008; www.moonguesthouse.com; 87-1 Unni-dong; s/d from ₩60,000/80,000; ❄Line 3 to Anguk, Exit 4; ❄☞) There are seven rooms at this 50-year-old *hanok* which has been newly renovated to a high standard. Rooms are tiny and the cheapest have shared bathrooms, but breakfast is included and various traditional cultural experiences are offered to guests.

SOPHIA GUEST HOUSE HANOK GUESTHOUSE $$

Map p195 (☎720 5467; www.sophiagh.com; 157-1 Sogyeok-dong; s/d from ₩50,000/70,000; ❄Line 3 to Anguk, Exit1; ❄☞) Rooms surround a pretty courtyard at this place run by hospitable Sophia. The main *hanok* has nine rooms (all of which share bathrooms) and there's five more rooms in an annex building around the corner. It has an antique feel but there are TVs in the rooms and rates include breakfast.

ANGUK GUESTHOUSE HANOK GUESTHOUSE $$

Map p195 (안국게스트하우스; ☎736 8304; www.anguk-house.com; 72-3 Anguk-dong; s/d ₩50,000/70,000; ❄Line 3 to Anguk, Exit1; ❄@) Down a quiet alley, the four varnished-wood guest rooms at this *hanok* are spread around a courtyard. All have en-suite bathrooms as well as a computer, and beds rather than *yo* mattresses. The kitchen can be used to make a DIY breakfast. Owner Mr Kim speaks English.

DOO GUESTHOUSE HANOK GUESTHOUSE $$

Map p195 (☎3672 1977; www.dooguesthouse.com; 15-6 Gye-dong; s/d/tr/f ₩50,000/60,000/80,000/120,000; ❄Line 3 to Anguk,

Exit 3; ✳@🛜) Mixing old and new is this enchanting *hanok* in a garden setting that has a very traditional-style room where breakfast is served. The shared bathrooms are high quality, with bidets and walk-in showers. The rooms have TVs and DVD players.

NOBLE HOTEL
HOTEL $$

Map p198 (☎742 4025; www.noblehotel.co.kr; 19 Unni-dong; d/tw ₩70,000/80,000; ⓂLine 3 to Anguk, Exit 4; ✳@) Looking for just a nice room? In a good location? Want a computer in it? And a giant LCD TV? And a whirlpool bath? And free drinks? Free body lotions? All at a cheap price? Look no further than this midrange hotel that is a cut above the average.

YMCA TOURIST HOTEL
HOTEL $$

Map p198 (☎734 6884; www.ymca.or.kr/hotel; Jongno 2-ga 9; s/d/tw/tr ₩71,500/88,000/99,000/143,000; ✳🛜) We can't guarantee whether it's fun to stay at the YMCA, but this 8th-floor hotel in a very central location offers a decent range of clean, simply furnished rooms with friendly service. Breakfast is included and it's served in the popular coffee shop on the ground floor.

SAERIM HOTEL
HOTEL $

Map p198 (세림 호텔; ☎739 3377; Eorumgol-gil, Insa-dong; r ₩50,000; ⓂLine 3 to Anguk, Exit 6) Flatscreen TVs as large as the double beds feature in this excellent-value, quiet and clean hotel. Facility-filled rooms are as good as they get in the heart of Insa-dong at this price, and everything works. The wallpaper designs are quite flash. Some rooms have computers at no extra cost.

INN DAEWON
HANOK GUESTHOUSE $

Map p200 (대원여관; ☎787 4308; 26 Dangju-dong; dm/s/d ₩19,000/27,000/35,000; ⓂLine 3 to Gyeongbokgung, Exit 4) As lovable as a scruffy dog, this long-running inn has the cheapest *hanok*-style accommodation, built around a covered courtyard. Everything is cramped, and guests sleep on floor mattresses, except in the dorm, reached up a steep flight of stairs. Toilets and showers are shared. Daewon's greatest asset is the owner, Mr Kim; he and his wife (they live next door) are brimful of kindness.

BEEWON GUESTHOUSE
GUESTHOUSE $

Map p198 (비원장; ☎765 0677; www.beewonguesthouse.com; 28-2 Unni-dong; dm/d/tr ₩19,000/50,000/60,000; ⓂLine 3 to Anguk, Exit 4; ✳@🛜) Combining facility-filled motel-style rooms (some with *ondol* options) with free, guesthouse-style communal facilities, the clean and tidy Beewon is generally quiet and friendly, plastered with photos of happy past guests. Look for an orange-tiled building. Add ₩5000 to rates for stays on Friday and Saturday.

GUESTHOUSE KOREA
BACKPACKERS $

Map p198 (게스트하우스 코리아; ☎3675 2205; www.guesthouseinkorea.com; 155-1 Gwonnong-dong; dm/s/d from ₩19,000/33,000/44,000; ⓂLine 3 to Anguk, Exit 4; ✳@🛜) The large communal living room is furnished with comfy armchairs, free computers, a breakfast area and even a bar. Newcomers to Seoul and solo travellers can mix in and mingle easily even when there's no party raging. The rooms and dorms have air-con and modern en suites; private rooms also have a TV and fridge. It can be messy, but is also a friendly place to park your pack.

Myeong-dong & Jung-gu

BANYAN TREE CLUB & SPA
HOTEL $$$

off Map p202 (☎2256 6677; www.banyantreeclub.net; 60 Jang Chang Dan-ro; r from ₩550,000; ⓂLine 3 to Beotigogae, Exit 1; ✳♨@🛜) Billing itself a 'sanctuary for the senses', the Banyan Tree occupies a hilltop tower designed by feted local architect Kim Swoon Guen, and offers just four rooms per floor. Calmly decorated and coolly sophisticated, each has a giant relaxation pool and amazing views. Guests have access to the darkly luxurious club with its leisure facilities. In summer there's big outdoor pool surrounded by private cabanas; in winter it becomes a skating rink.

THE PLAZA
HOTEL $$$

Map p202 (☎771 2200; www.hoteltheplaza.com; 23 Taepyeong-ro 2-ga; r from ₩387,200; ⓂLine 1 or 2 to City Hall, Exit 6; ✳♨@🛜) Opposite the rising glass edifice of the new City Hall, you couldn't get more central than the Plaza, which was given a striking makeover inside and out in 2010. Rooms now sport a trendy design with giant anglepoise lamps, circular mirrors and crisp white linens contrasting against dark carpets. It also has some chic restaurants and a good fitness club with a 20m pool.

WESTIN CHOSUN
HOTEL $$$

Map p202 (☑771 0500; www.westin.com/seoul; 87 Sogong-dong; r from ₩410,000; Ⓜ Line 2 to Euljiro 1-ga, Exit 4; ✻✻@☎) Not Seoul's most spectacular hotel, but the relaxing atmosphere and the conscientious staff keep it a cut above the rest. Each stylish room decorated in soft caramel tones comes with a rent-free mobile phone and choice of 10 types of pillows. Note though that free entrance to the sports club and pool is only for executive-floor guests and those staying in suites.

LOTTE HOTEL
HOTEL $$$

Map p202 (☑771 1000; www.lottehotelseoul.com; 30 Eulji-ro; r from ₩423,500; Ⓜ Line 2 to Euljiro 1-ga, Exit 8; ✻✻@☎) The natural extension to its Myeong-dong shopping empire, this twin-towered hotel with over 1000 rooms has a marble-lined lobby long enough for Usain Bolt training runs. The new wing's standard rooms are bigger than those in the old but don't have as modern a design. There's also a ladies-only floor with a book-lined lounge. Renowned French chef Pierre Gagnaire's new restaurant is on the 35th floor.

METRO HOTEL
HOTEL $$

Map p202 (메트로호텔; ☑752 1112; www.metrohotel.co.kr; 199-33 Euljiro 2-ga; s/d from ₩115,500/126,500; Ⓜ Line 2 to Euljiro 1-ga, Exit 6; ✻@☎) This small, professionally run hotel has boutique aspirations. Splashes of style abound, beginning with the flashy, metallic lobby and its laptops. Room size and design vary – ask for one of the larger ones with big windows (room numbers which end in 07). Prices include a Western breakfast.

HOTEL PRINCE
HOTEL $$

Map p202 (프린스호텔; ☑752 7111; www.princeseoul.com; Toegye-ro, Myeong-dong; d/tw/ondol ₩143,000/170,500/220,000; Ⓜ Line 4 to Myeong-dong, Exit 2; ✻@☎) Rooms at this well-located business hotel are smallish but sparkling, with some bright primary colours to alleviate the otherwise all-white regime. Online booking discounts can make the Prince an excellent deal, and the

rates include a buffet breakfast and free wi-fi.

PACIFIC HOTEL
HOTEL $$

Map p202 (퍼시픽호텔; ☑777 7811; www.thepacifichotel.co.kr; 31-1 Namsan-dong 2-ga; d/tw ₩150,400/178,200; Ⓜ Line 4 to Myeong-dong, Exit 3; ✻@☎) Bell boys in caps greet you at this hotel that exudes old-fashioned elegance. Light neutral colours, greenery and a natural-wood effect are the design style. Bathrooms are a tad cramped, but there's a big sauna and spa bath in the building, as well as a small rooftop garden.

HAN SUITES
APARTMENT $$

Map p202 (☑2280 8000; www.hansuites.com; 2-19 Yeajang-dong; studio/1-bedroom apt from ₩88,000/231,000; Ⓜ Line 3 or 4 to Chungmuro, Exit 4; ✻@☎) A great location, friendly and professional service and reasonable rates make this one of the best serviced apartment options for short or long stays. Rooms are plainly furnished but have everything you need. Note that many of the cheaper studios have windows onto an internal light well, so can be rather gloomy.

ASTORIA HOTEL
HOTEL $$

Map p202 (☑2268 7111; astoria1959@naver.com; Toegye-ro, Myeong-dong; d/tw from ₩143,000/165,000; Ⓜ Line 3 or 4 to Chungmuro, Exit 4; ✻@☎) White and pine decor make for pleasant rooms. They're reasonably sized, but a faded look is creeping in at this old timer, dating to 1959. Ask for a room with a Namsan view and keep your eyes on that. The attached Italian restaurant and cafe adds a dash of contemporary style.

NAMSAN GUESTHOUSE
BACKPACKERS $

Map p202 (남산게스트하우스; ☑752 6363; www.namsanguesthouse.com; 33-3 Namsan-dong 2-ga; d & tw from ₩45,000; Ⓜ Line 4 to Myeong-dong, Exit 2; ✻@☎) Now in two locations on the slopes of Namsan, this long-running backpacker guesthouse is a good budget choice. The newer location, lower down the mountain opposite a wedding hall, offers the better rooms and some breezy terraces that allow you to mingle with fellow guests. A free basic breakfast is included in the rates.

ALPS SEOUL
GUESTHOUSE $$

Map p202 (☑754 5111; www.alpsseoul.com; 37-1 Namsan-dong 2-ga; r from ₩70,000; Ⓜ Line 4 to

Myeong-dong, Exit 2; ✵ @ ⎙) If you're looking for somewhere central and with a bit more space to spread out than at the backpacker lodges, then this place in a large house may be your answer. There's a kitchen and big bathrooms and some antique style to the rooms. The company also has several other short-stay apartments around the city for rent.

SEOUL BACKPACKERS
BACKPACKERS $

Map p202 (서울백팩커스; ☏3672 1972; www.seoulbackpackers.com; 205-125 Namchang-dong; s/d/f ₩50,000/60,000/75,000; Ⓜ Line 4 to Hoehyeon, Exit 4) There are no dorms, but the cramped motel-style en-suite rooms are brightly decorated and have TVs. There's scant communal areas beyond the lobby and tiny kitchen. From the subway exit take the first alley on the left and then walk down the second alley.

YUN GUEST HOUSE
BACKPACKERS $

Map p202 (☏070 8117 8668; www.yunguest.com; 45-7 Namsan-dong 2-ga; s/d from ₩50,000/60,000; Ⓜ Line 4 to Myeong-dong, Exit 3; ✵ @ ⎙) Fake flowers around the entrance and some real ones in the garden make this 11-room Namsan-slope backpackers a little more distinctive and pretty than others in the district. Mr Kim the manager is very friendly. Pricier rooms have *ondol*, while some have no windows. A basic breakfast is offered.

INTERNATIONAL SEOUL YOUTH HOSTEL
HOSTEL $

Map p202 (☏319 1318; www.seoulyh.go.kr; 100-250 San 4 5 Yejang dong; tw/d/q ₩60,000/100,000/120,000; Ⓜ Line 4 to Chungmuro, Exit 4; ✵ @ ⎙) The slightly isolated position, 10 minutes' walk up Namsan from the subway exit, is compensated for at this modern hostel by huge rooms, *ondol* option, a large kitchen for self-catering and a delightful rooftop garden. There's also a restaurant.

BANGARANG HOSTEL
BACKPACKERS $

off Map p202 (☏6414 224; www.bangranghostel.com; 397-14 Jungnim-dong; dm/s/tw/d from ₩18,000/30,000/45,000/50,000; Ⓜ Line 2 or 5 to Chungjeongno, Exit 5; ✵ @ ⎙) On the western edge of Jung-gu in an interesting local area, this backpacker lodge is more stylish than most and has a pleasant communal area with kitchen (where you can make

your simple breakfast, included in the rates), TV lounge and outdoor terrace.

Western Seoul

TOP CHOICE V MANSION
BACKPACKERS $

Map p204 (☏010 9627 6898; www.bvseoul.com; 262-2 Sansu-dong, Mapo-gu; dm/s/d with shared bathroom ₩27,000/50,000/80,000; s/d with private bathroom ₩70,000/100,000; Ⓜ Line 6 to Sangsu, Exit 3; ✵ @ ⎙) The lovely Aram Kim, after travelling around the world for a decade, decided to start a guesthouse to welcome people to Korea. She did that successfully with Jaam, and now has this second venture, created with a couple of her friends. It offers something quite unexpected in a Seoul backpackers – space and a big garden! Converted from a 1960s restaurant, within a minute's walk of the Han River park in trendy Sangsu, this is a blissful place to chill. There are plans to host exhibitions of local artists and various arty events here to help visitors connect with Seoul's more creative spirits. Rates include breakfast.

TOP CHOICE JAAM GUESTHOUSE
GUESTHOUSE, APARTMENT $$

Map p204 (☏010 9627 6898; www.jaamguesthouse.net; 601 MJ Bldg, 400-10 Seokyo-dong, Mapo-gu; d/apt from ₩70,000/150,000; Ⓜ Line 2 or 6 to Hapjeong, Exit 4; ✵ @ ⎙) Aram Kim's first guesthouse is exactly the colourful, groovy kind of pad where you'd want to stay in Hongdae. The place sleeps up to six in three rooms and can be rented out as one apartment.

BEBOP HOUSE
BACKPACKERS $

Map p204 (☏8261 4835; http://bebop-guesthouse.com; 464-50 Seogyo-dong, Mapo-gu; dm/d/tw/tr from ₩20,000/60,000/75,000/75,000; Ⓜ Line 2 Hongik University, Exit 1; ✵ @ ⎙) A little tricky to find (check the website for directions) but a real gem that captures the youthful, arty buzz of Hongik. The white-washed house used to be an architect's office and is decorated with very funky wall-papered walls and tons of posters. Food is provided in the kitchen for you to make breakfast.

LEE & NO GUESTHOUSE
GUESTHOUSE $

Map p204 (리앤노게스트하우스; ☏336 4878; www.lnguesthouse.com; Hongdae; dm/s/d from

₩22,000/55,000/60,000; MLine 2 to Hongik University, Exit 2; ✳@🛜) This four-room guesthouse is run by laidback former backpacker Mr Lee and his wife. Bathrooms are shared but there's a patio and breakfast included. They also have two more appealing guesthouses in the area, **Namu** and **Studio 41st**. From Exit 2, take the second left, then cross over the road to Hana Bank and walk straight for five minutes. Turn right at Grazie Espresso, and it's on your left.

SEOKYO HOTEL
HOTEL $$

Map p204 (☑330 7777; www.hotelseokyo.co.kr; 165 Yanghwa-ro, Mapo-gu; r from ₩200,000; Line 2 to Hongik University, Exit 1; ✳🛜) Next to the airport bus stop, this business hotel is patronised by airline cabin crews and is super convenient for partying in the Hongik area. Not all rooms have been upgraded so ask to see a few; also note wi-fi is only available in the lobby. The gym and spa/sauna are a plus and you can grab breakfast in the lobby cafe.

MARRIOTT EXECUTIVE APARTMENTS
APARTMENT $$$

Map p207 (☑2090 8000; www.measeoul. com; Yeouido Park Center, 28-3 Yeouido-dong, Yongdeungpo-gu; studio/1-bed apt from ₩326,700/363,000; ✳✳@🛜) If you're going to stay on Yeouido then these top-grade, beautifully decorated serviced apartments are the way to go. The complex, which faces onto a park on the south of the island, also has a gym, pool and the fancy bakery-cafe Paul.

LEXINGTON HOTEL
HOTEL $$

Map p207 (☑6670 7000; www.thelexington. co.kr; 13-3 Yeouido-dong, Yongdeungpo-gu; r from ₩236,500; ✳@🛜) Very handy for the Yeouido Full Gospel Church, this fine but old-fashioned midrange hotel takes its theme seriously with various facilities named after NYC landmarks, such as the Broadway buffet restaurant and Yanks & Mettz sports bar. Corridors are decorated with past *Time* magazine covers and they offer free mobile-phone rental to guests.

BLU: HOME GUEST HOUSE
BACKPACKERS $

Map p204 (☑4065 7218; www.bluguesthouse. com; 464-52 Seogyo-dong, Mapo-gu; dm/s/d from ₩22,000/55,000/65,000; MLine 2 or 6 Hapjeong, Exit 8; @🛜) Decked out in plenty

of blue paint, and in two locations close to Hongdae and one in Sinchon, this is another appealing backpackers lodge with all the usual facilities, friendly staff and a free basic breakfast thrown into the bargain. Long-term residency is a possibility here too.

COME INN
BACKPACKERS $

Map p204 (☑070 8958 7279; www.comeinnkorea. com; 358-91 Seogyo-dong, Mapo-gu; dm/s/d/tr from ₩19,000/43,000/58,000/76,000; MLine 2 or 6 Hapjeong, Exit 9; ✳@🛜) You could hardly get more central to Hongdae than this compact 3rd-floor guesthouse offering the usual mix of dorms and private rooms, all of which share common bathrooms. There's a comfy lounge and a broad outdoor terrace with views across the area. Rates include breakfast.

Itaewon & Yongsan-gu

GRAND HYATT SEOUL
HOTEL $$$

Map p208 (☑797 1234; www.seoul.grand.hyatt. com; Hamman-dong; r/ste from ₩363,000/ 550,550; MLine 6 to Hangangjin, Exit 1; ✳✳@🛜) Making the most of its hilltop views, the Grand Hyatt oozes class. Rooms are a bit smaller than at rivals but all have been freshly renovated and sport a contemporary look. Pamper yourself in the spa, dance the night away at popular club JJ Mahoney's or swim in the excellent outdoor pool which, come winter, is turned into an ice rink.

IP BOUTIQUE HOTEL
HOTEL $$$

Map p208 (☑3702 8000; www.ipboutique hotel.com; 731-32 Hamman-dong; s & d from ₩262,200; MLine 6 to Itaewon, Exit 2; ✳✳@🛜) Trying a bit too hard to be hip with bold contemporary artworks and quirky interior-design choices, this boutique wannabe slightly misses the mark. Still, it has a great location and in a city with a dearth of these kinds of places it certainly stands out.

HOTEL D'ORO
LOVE HOTEL $$

Map p208 (디오로호텔; ☑749 6525; 124-3 Itaewon, Yongsan-gu; d from ₩88,000; MLine 6 to Itaewon, Exit 2; ✳@🛜) This above-average love motel has some style and attitude, verging on the hip. It offers modern equipment and furnishing, and free soft drinks rather than an expensive minibar. About the best value you're going to get to be within stumbling distance of Itaewon's bars and clubs. The entrance is up the hill off the main road.

HAMILTON HOTEL
HOTEL $$

Map p208 (해밀톤호텔; ☎3786 6000; www.hamilton.co.kr; 179 Itaewon-ro; s/d ₩106,900/132,000; ☀@☎) This workhorse of the Itaewon strip has zero style, with mainly old-fashioned, although pretty spacious, rooms. In its favour is its location, and facilities such as a sauna, gym and outdoor pool (all available to inhouse guests for 50% off the regular rates).

KAYA HOTEL
HOTEL $

Map p209 (☎798 5101; www.kayahotel.net; 98 11 Garwol dong, Yongsan-gu; d/tw from ₩53,000/63,000; ☀Line 1 to Namyeong, Exit 1; ☀@☎) Near the US army's Yongsan base, convenient for USO tours to the DMZ, this basic, old-fashioned hotel is nothing special but it's clean, has some *ondol* rooms and the staff are used to dealing with foreigners. Rates go up by ₩6000 on Friday and Saturday nights.

Dongdaemun & Eastern Seoul

W SEOUL WALKERHILL
HOTEL $$$

(☎465 2222; www.whotels.com/seoul; Walkerhill-ro, Gwangjin-gu; r from ₩363,000; ☀Line 5 to Gwangnaru, Exit 2; ☀@☎☂) One of the city's best-designed hotels, with spectacular public areas and generally fablicious rooms with striking colour schemes and splendid river or mountain views. The spa, pool, gym, trendy restaurants and happening Woobar are so nice you probably won't want to stray far, which is just as well as it's distant from most sights. There's a free shuttle bus to Gwangnaru station every 10 to 20 minutes, as well as another one to Itaewon and Myeong-dong each hour from 10am to 7.10pm. The W shares Walker Hill with the Sheraton Grande Walkerhill and its 14 convention halls, meaning this place can get very busy during major events.

EULJIRO CO-OP RESIDENCE
APARTMENTS $$

Map p214 (☎2269 4600; http://rent.co-op.co.kr; 32 Euljiro 6-ga, Jung-gu; studios from ₩90,000; ☀Line 2, 4 or 5 to Dongdaemun History & Culture Park, Exit 12; ☀@☎) These smart, white studio apartments provide a chic little nest high above the 24-hour hurly-burly of Dongdaemun Market. Everything is bright, modern, stylish and mini-sized – not much elbow room. Slightly more space and better facilities, including a gym, are provided at the same company's nearby **Western Co-Op Residence**, where rates start at ₩120,000.

TOYOKO INN SEOUL DONGDAEMUN
HOTEL $$

Map p214 (☎2267 1045; www.toyoko-inn.com; 73 Gwanghui-dong 2-ga, Jung-gu; s/d/tw from ₩60,500/77,000/88,000; ☀Lines 2, 4 & 5 to Dongdaemun History & Culture Park, Exit 4; ☀@) You've got to hand it to this Japanese business hotel group for bagging a prime spot close to the Dongdaemun Design Plaza & Park. The small, clean and well-equipped rooms here (with plenty of single ones) are great value, with rates including a simple breakfast.

HOTEL SHILLA
HOTEL $$$

Map p214 (신라호텔; ☎2230 3310; www.shilla. net/en; Jangchung-dong 2-ga, Jung-gu; r/ste from ₩544,500/968,000; ☀Line 3 to Dongguk University, Exit 5; ☀@☎☂) A dependable level of luxury is offered by the elegant, classic-style Shilla which stands aloof on a hill near Namsan. There's a regular shuttle bus to get you up here from the subway exit. The outdoor pool is open from May to August, but they also have an indoor one next to the gym.

DONGDAEMUN HOSTEL
BACKPACKERS $

Map p214 (☎070 7785 8055; www.dongdaemun hostel.com; 43-1 Gwanghui-dong 2-ga, Jung-gu; r ₩42,000; ☀Lines 2, 4 & 5 to Dongdaemun, Exit 4; ☎) A lot is crammed into the nicely decorated tiny single rooms at this backpackers guesthouse, including computers, desk and a shower/toilet cubicle. Staff are helpful and there's also a tiny shared kitchen. A basic breakfast is included.

HOTEL PJ
HOTEL $$

Map p214 (☎070 7785 8055; www.hotelpj. co.kr; 73-1 Inhyung-dong, Jung-gu; d/tw/tr/ste ₩220,000/242,000/308,000/385,000; ☀@☎) Standing for prestige and joy, the PJ occupies a more modern block in the gargantuan Jinyang stretch of buildings dating from the 1960s. It's a solid midrange hotel with larger rooms than average, all including spacious sit-out balconies that provide great cityscape views, and generous amenities. Also offers a women-only floor.

Gangnam & South of the Han River

TOP CHOICE LA CASA · HOTEL $$

Map p210 (☎546 0088; www.hotellacasa. kr; Sinsa-dong, Gangnam-gu; r/ste from ₩193,600/471,900; Ⓜ Line 3 to Sinsa, Exit 6; ❄@ ⑤) The first venture into the hospitality business by classy Korean furniture and interior design store Casamia packs plenty of chic style. The rooms are attractive and spacious with quirky details such as the travel-themed pillow cases. Rates include a buffet breakfast in their restaurant. It's also very handy for Garosu-gil.

TOP CHOICE PARK HYATT SEOUL · HOTEL $$$

Map p212 (☎2016 1234; www.seoul.park.hyatt. com; Daechi 3-dong, Gangnam-gu; r/ste from ₩407,000/572,000; ❄@ ⑤✉) A discreet entrance – look for the rock sticking out of the wall – sets the Zen minimalist tone for this gorgeous property. Each floor only has 10 rooms with spot-lit antiquities lining the hallways. Spacious rooms ingeniously combine the high-tech with the traditional, and come with luxurious bathrooms that have quite rightly been classed among the best in Asia.

HOTEL TRIA · HOTEL $$

Map p210 (☎553 2471; www.hoteltria.co.kr; Yeoksam-dong, Gangnam-gu; r/ste from ₩95,000/150,000; Ⓜ Line 2 to Yeoksam, Exit 8; ❄@ ⑤) Very affordable for this end of town, the 50-room boutiquey Hotel Tria has lots going for it. Opt for any room above standard and you'll get a whirlpool bath. The hotel is tucked away in the streets behind the Renaissance Hotel, a five-minute walk from the subway exit.

JELLY HOTEL · LOVE MOTEL $$

Map p210 (젤리호텔; ☎553 4737; www.jellyho tel.com; Yeoksam-dong, Gangnam-gu; r ₩70,000-280,000; Ⓜ Line 2 to Gangnam, Exit 12; @ ⑤) The corridors are as dark as a coalmine (safeguarding guests' anonymity), but the more expensive rooms at this hip love motel are spacious, exotic and classy. Every room is different and you can check them out on the lobby screen. The most spectacular and expensive room has a full-sized pool table, a heart-shaped spa, two huge TV screens, his and hers computers, a gilt mirror and black armchairs.

RITZ CARLTON · HOTEL $$$

Map p210 (리츠칼튼호텔; ☎3451 8000; www. ritzcarltonseoul.com; Yeoksam-dong, Gangnam-gu; r from ₩423,500; Ⓜ Line 9 to Shinnonhyeon, Exit 4; ❄@ ⑤✉) Traditional but not old-fashioned, the Ritz Carlton wraps guests in soothing luxury with high levels of service, plenty of facilities and a European atmosphere stretching from the furniture to the food. Some rooms have huge balconies (a soccer team could sunbathe there), but all have some warm colours to contrast with the pervasive white.

JW MARRIOTT HOTEL SEOUL · HOTEL $$$

Map p210 (☎6282 6262; www.marriott.com; 19-3 Banpo-dong, Seocho-gu; r from ₩319,000; Ⓜ Line 3, 7 or 9 to Express Bus Terminal, Exit 7; ❄@ ⑤✉) The Marriott is a feel-good hotel that's classy and comfortable, with top facilities everywhere. Rooms and bathrooms here are spacious compared with other top Seoul hotels. Other plusses is that it sits above three subway lines and is attached to a major shopping mall.

MERCURE AMBASSADOR SODOWE · HOTEL $$

Map p210 (☎2050 6000; www.mercureseoul. com; 642 Yeoksam-dong, Gangnam-gu; r from ₩308,000; Ⓜ Line 2 to Yeoksam, Exit 4; ❄@ ⑤) This brand-new property off the main road is decorated in candy colours and has arty flourishes in the rooms. It's well designed for business and includes a laundry, gym and sauna (extra ₩20,000)

LOTTE WORLD HOTEL · HOTEL $$$

Map p212 (☎419 7000; www.lottehotel world.com; Olympic-ro, Songpa-gu; r/ste from ₩314,600/450,000; Ⓜ Line 2 or 8 to Jamsil, Exit 4; ❄@ ⑤✉) Next to the theme park Lotte World, this luxury hotel is typical of Lotte's version of 'euro palatial'. Natural wood and pastel shades make the rooms less flamboyant than the public areas. Two floors have corridors and rooms gaily decorated with colourful cartoon characters as well as PlayStations.

HOTEL BLUE PEARL
HOTEL $$

Map p212 (블루펄호텔; ☎3015 7777; www.
hotelbluepearl.com; 129-3 Cheongdam-dong,
Gangnam-gu; d/tw ₩143,000/159,000; ⓜLine
7 to Cheongdam, Exit 13, ✳@⑩) Although it
could do with some touching up here and
there, the Blue Pearl remains a stylish mid-
range hotel that is easy on the wallet for
this pricey end of town. Ask for a room on
the side away from the main road as they're
quieter. Rooms have blinds and computers,
and breakfast is included.

M CHEREVILLE
APARTMENTS $$

Map p210 (☎532 9774; www.mchereville.net;
Seomyeong-gil, Gangnam; studio/1-/2-bedroom
apt from ₩110,000/132,000/165,000; ⓜLine 2
to Gangnam, Exit 9) Chuck grubby socks into
the washer/dryer, shove dirty crocks into
the dishwasher and soothe tired muscles in
the steam sauna showers. All that's needed
is artwork on the walls, and a bit of touching up to keep the decor and furnishings up
to scratch. Reception is in room 607.

DORMY INN SEOUL
APARTMENTS $$

Map p210 (도미인서울; ☎6474 1515; www.
dormy.co.kr; 205-8 Nonhyeon-dong, Gangnam-gu;
studios from ₩132,000; ⓜLine 9 to Sinnonhyeon,
Exit 3; ✳@⑩) These light, modern studio
apartments have all the conveniences of
home and are reasonably priced. Toilets
are cramped but there is a walk-in show-
er. Don't expect anything special and you
won't be disappointed. Buffet breakfast is
₩11,000.

POPGREEN HOTEL
HOTEL $$

Map p210 (☎544 6623; www.popgreenhotel.com;
614-1 Sinsa-dong, Gangnam-gu; d/tw incl breakfast ₩128,840/138,820; ⓜLine 3 to Apgujeong,
Exit 2; ✳@⑩) Light, modern and reasonably
sized rooms and bathrooms are on offer at
Popgreen. There are touches of style here
and there from the colourful prints in the
lobby and the desk staff in red and gold uni-
form. Rooms vary so check out more than
one.

BEST WESTERN PREMIER
GANGNAM
HOTEL $$

Map p210 (☎6474 2000; www.bestwesterngang
nam.com; 205-9 Nonhyeon-dong, Gangnam-gu;
s/d ₩154,800/193,600; ⓜLine 9 to Sinnonhyeon,
Exit 3; ✳@⑩) A few arty features brighten
up this otherwise bland modern business
hotel. Big windows provide great views

from the higher rooms. The staff are help-
ful and wi-fi is included in the rates.

ELLUI
HOTEL $$

Map p212 (☎514 3535; 129 Cheongdam-dong,
Gangnam-gu; r from ₩200,000; ⓜLine 7 to
Cheongdam, Exit 13) Dashes of style, such as
a glass-view elevator, an outside waterfall
and a trendy club next door, raise hopes for
the Ellui. However, the spacious rooms are
old-fashioned and the location is traffic-
dominated. Ask for a room with a river view
(no extra cost).

PRINCESS HOTEL
LOVE MOTEL $$

Map p210 (프린세스호텔; ☎544 0366; Apgu-
jeong; r from ₩80,000; ⓜLine 3 to Apgujeong,
Exit 2; ✳@) If you need to be close to Apgu-
jeong's shopping action, this easy-to-locate
love motel with English-speaking reception
staff is just the ticket.

SEOUL OLYMPIC PARKTEL
HOTEL $

Map p212 (☎421 2114; www.kyha.or.kr; Olympic
Park, 88-8 Bang-dong, Songpa-gu; dm ₩22,000;
ⓜLine 8 to Mongchontoseong, Exit 1; ✳@) If
you're a youth hostel member you can stay
in this functional business hotel at a youth-
hostel rate. Inside Olympic Park, it's a long,
long way from most sights, but the dorms,
with two double bunks and two pull-out
beds, have big windows with park views.
Unless you need to be in the area for some
reason you'll find more convivial budget
accommodation elsewhere. The regular
double rooms here kick off at an overpriced
₩198,000.

Northern Seoul

EUGENE'S HOUSE
HANOK GUESTHOUSE $$

Map p215 (☎741 3338; www.eugenehouse.co.kr;
5-43 Hyehwa-dong; s/tw with shared bathroom
₩60,000/110,000, s/d with private bathroom
from ₩90,000/110,000; ⓜLine 4 to Hyehwa,
Exit 1; ✳⑩) The friendly family who run
this *hanok* homestay (named after their
daughter) speak English and have another
hanok around the corner where they also
conduct various cultural experi-ences.
These homes have larger courtyards than
similar places in Bukchon, and a pleasing,
lived-in quality. The rooms are all different and uniquely furnished. Rates include
breakfast.

INSIDE BACKPACKERS BACKPACKERS **$**
Map p215 (☎3672 1120; www.backpackersinside.
com; 2nd fl 112 Myeongryun 2-ga; dm/s/d with
shared bathroom ₩16,000/27,000/44,000, s/d
with private bathroom ₩42,000/60,000; Ⓜ Line
4 to Hyehwa, Exit 4; @ 🛜) The best of several
backpacker hostels in the Daehangno area,
this is a friendly, clean place with plenty
of character and room options. Apart from
the main hostel, they also have rooms in a
character-filled *hanok* closer to the subway
exit.

Understand Seoul

Seoul Today

When Park Won-soon, a former human-rights lawyer and independent candidate, was elected Seoul's mayor in October 2011, it was a watershed moment not only for Korean politics but also for the city itself. Under the previous two mayors, top of the agenda had been construction-led growth that resulted in flashy, expensive projects. Park's winning mandate promises to shift the focus to greater welfare spending for Seoul's citizens.

Best on Film

The Host (2006) Seoul-based classic monster movie that juggles humour, poignancy and heart-stopping action.
The King and the Clown (2005) Courtly politics and relationships in the Joseon dynasty, with a homosexual subtext.
JSA (2001) Gripping thriller about a friendship between soldiers on opposite sides of the DMZ and its tragic outcome.

Best in Print

Please Look After Mother (Shin Kyung-sook; 2011) Emotional drama ensues as family members search for their mother after she goes missing on the Seoul subway.
Meeting Mr Kim (Jennifer Barclay; 2008) Seoul has changed since the author's experiences here in 2000, but overall this is an amusing, easy read with fresh insights.
Korea Bug (J Scott Burgeson; www.kingbaeksu.com; 2005) Seoul 'zine turned book, featuring interviews with a fascinating set of characters.

New Mayor, New Policies

After the South Korean president, the mayor of Seoul is the second most powerful job in the country, so it was something of a wake-up call for both of Korea's major political parties – the currently governing Saenuri Party (a conservative party formerly known as the Grand National Party) and the liberal opposition Democratic United Party (DUP) – when the previously unelected and politically unaffiliated Park won the election. Known for promoting a chain of thrift shops for the poor, Park portrayed himself as the nation's first 'welfare mayor' (South Korea has a minimal social safety net and the gap between rich and poor is widening).

Opinion polls indicated that Park benefited from a wave of support from younger voters disillusioned with traditional politics, where the needs of the people have come second to those of big-business conglomerates (the so-called *jaebeol*), such as Samsung and Hyundai. In a press briefing soon after his election, Park claimed his predecessors did not listen to the people. He has called a halt to the mega construction projects favoured by his predecessors and started pushing populist ideas such as urban farms.

The Presidential Race

In February 2012, Park affiliated himself with the DUP. However, in the National Assembly elections in April 2012, the beleaguered Saenuri Party, dogged by a series of scandals and corruption cases involving President Lee Myung-bak's aides and relatives, held on to its majority status in the country's parliament. Much of that victory was put down to the relentless campaigning of the party's interim leader Park Geun-hye, daughter of South Korea's former dictator, Park Chung-hee.

Attention subsequently shifted to the presidential poll, which is set for December 2012. At the time of writing, Park Geun-hye is the likely Saenuri Party candidate (Lee Myung-bak will be stepping down, as South Korean presidents can only serve one four-year term in office). Other presidential hopefuls include the DUP's Moon Jae-in and the unaffiliated Ahn Cheol-soo, a professor and IT businessman who was a major supporter of Park Won-soon to become Seoul's mayor.

Racial Issues

A night out in Itaewon might suggest otherwise, but Seoul, like the rest of Korea, is very monocultural. According to the Korean Immigration Service, foreigners accounted for 2.8% of the nation's population in 2012, with most of these being Chinese of Korean ethnicity (known as *Joseonjok*). Seoul has just 360,000 foreign residents and it is not uncommon for them to face discrimination and xenophobia.

Following the 2012 National Assembly election, Jasmine Lee, born in the Philippines and the country's first elected MP who is also a naturalised citizen, faced a barrage of racial attacks from a small but vocal group of Korean 'netizens'. 'Now there will be illegal immigrants doing what they want and more sham marriages', wrote one person on an internet forum. There are nearly 200,000 marriage immigrants in Korea. The attacks on Lee came in the wake of public outrage over the murder by a Chinese immigrant worker of a girl in Suwon. In 2009 Amnesty International reported that migrant workers in Korea are exposed to abusive work conditions, including discrimination, and verbal and physical abuse.

Despite the racial issues, travellers should feel safe and are unlikely to encounter anything other than friendly locals as they travel around Seoul.

Foes in the North?

Less than 50km from the border, Seoul is literally on the front line with North Korea. Events such as the bombing of Yeonpyeongdo in November 2010, the death of North Korean leader Kim Jong-il in December 2011, and the failed launch of a North Korean rocket in April 2012 are inevitably taken very seriously in Seoul. Not for nothing was the city chosen as the venue for the 2012 Nuclear Security Summit (www.thenuclearsecuritysummit.org). US president Barack Obama chose that occasion to make a visit to the DMZ and speak of his country's continued military support for South Korea against aggression from the North. However, most of the time the only indication you'll have of heightened tensions with the North is if there's increased security mounted around central Seoul and the Blue House, official home of the president.

population per sq km

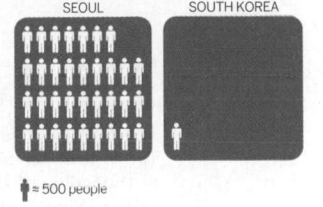

SEOUL   SOUTH KOREA

♦ ≈ 500 people

ethnic groups

(% of population)

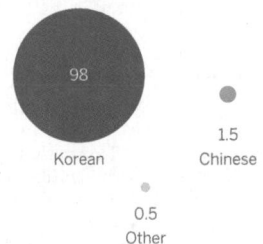

98
Korean

1.5
Chinese

0.5
Other

if Seoul were 100 people

93 would own a mobile (cell) phone
7 would not own a mobile (cell) phone

History

The mighty walls of Korea's modern capital rose in 1394, when King Taejo, founder of the Joseon dynasty, settled the government seat in the valley of Hanyang – later to become Seoul. At the new city's centre, King Taejo built Gyeongbokgung, the Palace of Shining Happiness. Seoul's social geography has changed little since. The presidential seat of power – Cheongwadae (the Blue House) – rests behind Gyeongbokgung, with the capital's central axis (Sejongno) spread before it.

JAPANESE COLONISATION

Korean geomancy (feng shui, or pungsu-jiri in Korean, meaning the study of the patterns of wind and water) decreed Seoul's location: the Han River supplied yin force and access to the sea, and the Bukhan mountain range supplied yang energy and protection from the north.

Since recorded time, external forces have cast designs upon Korea, a small peninsula among giants – Japan to the east, China and Mongolia to the west. Brutal invasions – many lasting and painful – comprise the fabric of Korean history. None weighs as heavily on the Korean psyche as the annexation by Japan just after the turn of the 20th century.

Japan long had its sights on the strategic peninsula. So when a large-scale peasant rebellion raged uncontrollably in Korea in 1894, Japan stepped in to 'help'. One year later, Japanese assassins would fatally stab Queen Min, King Gojong would abdicate in 1907, and in 1910 the cession would be complete.

This period marked the subjugation, and attempted eradication, of Korean identity. Locals were made to take Japanese names and were forbidden to speak their national tongue. As Japan exploited Korea's resources, only 20% of Koreans were able to even start elementary school. Though some Koreans collaborated with their colonial rulers and reaped great profit, most were unable to rise above second-class citizenship in their own land.

KOREAN VERSUS KOREAN

While external powers continued to knock on Korea's door, there was no shortage of internal conflict, either. The Three Kingdoms period, preced-

TIMELINE	1392	1394	1796
	Having overthrown the Goryeo dynasty, General Yi Seong-gye ascends the throne, naming himself King Taejo and establishing the Joseon dynasty that will rule Korea for 500 years.	King Taejo decrees Hanyang (Seoul) as the capital of the Joseon kingdom, mobilising some 200,000 labourers to surround the city with a great wall, remnants of which still remain.	King Jeongjo moves the royal court to Suwon to be closer to his father's grave, and builds the Hwaseong fortress (now a World Heritage site) to protect the new palace.

KING SEJONG'S GIFT

As the seat of government, Seoul has born the brunt of bad policies during periods of lacklustre rule, but has reaped the fruits of the thinking of its wisest leaders. The greatest of these leaders was King Sejong (r 1418–50), a scholar-king of unmatched abilities who sponsored many cultural projects, consolidated border defences and served as a model of Confucian probity. At his direction, court scholars devised the phonetic *hangeul* alphabet, a simple system of writing the Korean language that made it possible for anyone to learn to read. King Sejong's alphabet is one reason why Korea enjoys universal literacy today.

ing the Goryeo dynasty, was marked by continual feuds, and peasant rebellions were commonplace throughout the Joseon era. The Korean War (1950–53) represents another such conflict along internally riven lines – the more agrarian south had always resented the wealthier north, and vice versa.

When the nation was at last returned to Korea with the Allied victory in 1945, the decision to divide the country into protectorates – the north overseen by the USSR and the south by the US – soon led to rival republics. On 25 June 1950, under the cover of night, the North Korean army marched over the mountains that rim Seoul, marking the start of the brutal civil war.

Seoul's sudden fall to the North caught the populace by surprise; the government of President Syngman Rhee fled southward, destroying the only Han River highway bridge and abandoning the remaining population to face the communists. During its 90-day occupation of the city, North Korea's army arrested and shot many who had supported the Rhee government.

In September 1950, UN forces led by US and South Korean troops mounted a counterattack. After an amphibious landing at Incheon, they fought their way back into Seoul. During a series of bloody battles, whole districts of the capital were bombed and burned in the effort to dislodge Kim Il Sung's Korean People's Army. When at last UN forces succeeded in reclaiming the city, much of it lay in smouldering ruins.

Later that year, as UN forces pushed northward, the Chinese Army entered the war on the North Korean side and pushed back down into Seoul. This time the invaders found a nearly empty city. Even after the UN regained control in March 1951, only a fraction of Seoul's population returned during the two years of war that raged along the battle-front until the armistice in July 1953. Instead, they holed up in rural villages and miserable camps, slowly trickling back into the shattered

Korea was unified in AD 918 with the start of the Goryeo dynasty (from which comes the name 'Korea'). The unification would persevere – with Seoul at the centre – until the country's division following WWII, solidified by the Korean War.

1910	1948	1950–53	1960–61
After gradually increasing its power and forcing King Gojong to abdicate to Seoul's Russian legation three years earlier, Japan annexes Korea, beginning 35 years of colonial rule.	The Republic of Korea is founded in the southern part of the peninsula, while Kim Il Sung sets up the Democratic People's Republic of Korea in the north.	North Korean forces occupy Seoul for 90 days before UN forces led by US and South Korean troops mount a counterattack. An armistice ends the Korean War three years later.	Popular protests oust President Syngman Rhee. Attempts at democratic rule fail – a military coup topples the unstable elected government and installs General Park Chung-hee into power.

capital that was once their home. Most would never hear from their northern relatives again, whether living or lost to the war.

MIRACLE ON THE HAN

Immediately following the war, as Seoul's population slowly returned to pick up the pieces, they found little to give them hope. Widespread hunger, disease, crime and misery comprised daily life for hundreds of thousands. On the slopes of Namsan a wretched village called Hae-bang-chon (Liberation Town) housed tens of thousands of war refugees, widows and beggars. Prostitutes lined up at the gates of the US military bases in Yongsan in a desperate effort to earn a few dollars. Even a decade after the war, average male life expectancy hovered barely above 50.

When General Park Chung-hee forcibly took the reins of the government in 1961, he quickly went to work defining national economic goals. He often followed patterns set by Imperial Japan, such as fostering big businesses (*zaibatsu* in Japanese, *jaebeol* in Korean) as engines of growth. Conglomerates such as Hyundai and Samsung achieved – and still retain – incredible economic influence.

Under Park, fear and brutal efficiency combined to deliver results. Wages were kept artificially low to drive exports, and by the mid-1970s Seoul was well on its way to becoming a major world city. Slums were bulldozed, and the city spread in all directions. Expressways, ring roads and a subway network connected these new districts. Modernity had arrived in Seoul, but at an undeniable cost.

MILITARY RULE

Historically, Seoul never possessed an egalitarian social set-up. Social inequality continued through the Japanese colonial period, and after the Korean War dictatorships sprang up in the South.

The Syngman Rhee regime (1948–60) rigged its own re-election (by mass arrests of opposition leaders and changes to the constitution) several times until 19 April 1960, when a popular rebellion led by unarmed students sought to overthrow the president. Police opened fire on the group, which had gathered in downtown Seoul; by dusk, nearly 200 people lay dead. Rhee's right-hand man, Gibung Lee, committed suicide, as did his family. Rhee resigned a few days later and was spirited away to exile in Hawaii by the US Air Force.

What came to be known as the April Revolution resulted in eight months of democracy under a cabinet system of government led by prime minister Chang Myon. However, on 16 May 1961, the civilian gov-

History Books

The Dawn of Modern Korea (Andrei Lankov)

Korea's Place in the Sun (Bruce Cumings)

The Korean War (Max Hastings)

During the Joseon dynasty, a rigid hereditary class system sharply limited social mobility. A registry from the mid-1600s suggests that perhaps three quarters of Seoul's citizens were slaves.

1979

After surviving a couple of assassination attempts (one of which had killed his wife), Park is finally shot dead by the trusted head of his own Central Intelligence Agency.

1987

Following sweeping national protests, Korea's last military dictatorship, under Chun Doo-hwan, steps down to allow democratic elections.

BETTMANN / CORBIS ©

Former president Chun Doo-hwan

ernment was replaced by a military junta led by Major General Park Chung-hee. In 1963 Park was narrowly elected South Korea's president.

Park held an iron grip on power for 16 years, during which scores of political dissidents were executed or disappeared, and he created an internal police system complete with a Central Intelligence Agency that quelled any antigovernment or pro-North movements.

DEMOCRACY – AT LONG LAST

Following Park's assassination in 1979, another general – Chun Doo-hwan – crushed pro-democracy uprisings all over the country (most notoriously in the southwestern city of Gwangju). But by 1987 the world was watching and the tide of popular protest was too strong. Chun stepped down and allowed democratic elections.

The sea of change finally rolled all the way in when former dissident Kim Dae-jung, a 'radical' who had survived several assassination attempts during the Park Chung-hee reign, became president in 1998. Once in power, Kim worked to achieve détente with North Korea. His presidency was followed by that of equally liberal Roh Moo-hyun.

South Korea's 17th president (and former Seoul mayor), Lee Myung-bak, was a fascinating change from the previous two administrations. Formerly the hard-nosed CEO of the Hyundai construction *jaebeol* (huge, often family run, corporations), he is nicknamed 'the bulldozer' – derisively by those who loathe him, glowingly by his supporters – for his penchant for ramming through his policies. It was under Lee's tenure as mayor that the Cheong-gye-cheon stream project was begun.

INTERNATIONAL RECOGNITION

Seoulites continue to generate excellent ideas in order to build their future, while also trying to work out their differences with North Korea and adjusting to the emerging order in East Asia. In 2010, the city was appointed a Unesco City of Design in recognition of its cultural heritage and promotion of strong design policies.

At the same time, the face of Seoul – long one of the most homogenous cities in the world – is changing, with a recent influx of immigrants from China, South and Southeast Asia, and the Middle East. Host to major international events including the World Cup in 2002, the G-20 Economic Summit in 2010 and the Nuclear Security Summit in 2012, it would seem that Seoul, for centuries the centre of Korea's world, is now getting used to being a major centre of the world at large.

Seoul, meaning 'capital' in Korean, has only been the official name of the city since 1945. Before the Joseon dynasty it was known as Hanyang, afterwards Hanseong. During Japanese rule it was called Keijo in Japanese, Gyeongseong in Korean.

In the modernisation of Seoul, 1969 was a big year. The completion of the Hannam Bridge kicked off the city's major expansion south of the Han River, and Namsan Tower (now N Seoul Tower) was erected.

1988	2002	2010	2011
Seoul hosts the Summer Olympic Games, building a huge Olympic Park and major expressway. International showcase leads to increased trade and diplomatic relations for Korea.	Seoul serves as one of the host cities for the World Cup, with the opening game of the soccer tournament held at the new World Cup Stadium.	Seoul hosts the G-20 Economic Summit and becomes World Design Capital, but its centrepiece – Dongdaemun Design Plaza & Park, by architect Zaha Hadid – remains uncompleted.	Independent candidate and former human-rights lawyer Park Won-soon is elected Seoul's mayor. He puts the brakes on major construction projects and focuses on welfare spending.

Food & Drink

So you thought Korean cuisine was mainly about kimchi and barbecued beef? A few days in Seoul will swiftly bring you up to speed. Prepare to be blown away by the amazing diversity and spicy deliciousness of the nation's cuisine, ranging from rustic stews and tasty street snacks to glorious royal banquets involving elaborate preparation and presentation. The leisurely sampling of soothing traditional teas and herbal infusions is also one of Seoul's great pleasures, as is the chance to sample a variety of local alcoholic beverages.

FOOD

A traditional Korean meal (either breakfast, lunch or dinner) typically consists of meat, seafood or fish served at the same time as soup, rice and a collection of dipping sauces and *banchan*, the ubiquitous cold side dishes. The fermented kimchi cabbage or radish is the most popular side dish, but there are many others, such as bean sprouts, black beans, dried anchovy, spinach, quail eggs, shellfish, lettuce, acorn jelly and tofu. It's a healthy and balanced approach to eating – no wonder Korean cooks refer to food as 'medicine'.

The pinnacle of Korean dining is *jeongsik* or *hanjeongsik*. These banquets that cover the table with food include fish, meat, soup, *dubu jjigae* (spicy tofu stew), *doenjang jjigae* (soybean-paste stew), rice, noodles, steamed egg, shellfish and lots of cold vegetable side dishes, followed by a cup of tea. It's invariably too much to eat and it's meant to be – don't feel obliged to eat everything put in front of you. When going for such a set meal, it's a good idea to choose the one with the least number of courses.

Specialities

Barbecue

The many barbecue restaurants have a grill set into the tables on which to cook slices of beef *(bulgogi)*, beef ribs *(galbi)*, pork *(samgyeopsal)*, chicken *(dak)*, seafood or vegetables. The server often helps out with the cooking. The inexpensive *samgyeopsal* is bacon and can be fatty. These meals are usually only available in servings for two or more.

Bulgogi, galbi and *samgyeopsal* are served with a bunch of *sam,* typically lettuce and sesame leaves. Take a leaf in one hand (or combine two leaves for different flavours) and with your other hand use your chopsticks to load it with meat, side-dish flavourings, garlic and sauces. Then roll it up into a little package and eat it in one go.

Rice Dishes

Bibimbap is a tasty mixture of rice, vegetables and minced beef, often with a fried egg on top. Add *gochujang* (red-chilli paste) to taste and thoroughly mix it all together with a spoon before digging in. *Sanchae bibimbap* is made with mountain-grown greens; *dolsot bibimbap* is served in a stone hotpot, which makes some of the rice nicely crispy. *Boribap* is rice with barley mixed in.

Similar to sushi rolls, but not exactly the same, are *gimbap* – rice rolled in dried seaweed with strips of carrot, radish, egg and ham in the centre. 'Nude' *gimbap* has no dried seaweed wrap. There are also *samgak gimbap*, triangular-shaped rice parcels filled with beef, chicken, tuna or kimchi, wrapped in *gim* (dried seaweed). Sold mainly in convenience stores, it's a tasty snack once you've mastered the art of taking it out of the plastic.

Traditional, slow-cooked rice porridge *(juk)* is mixed with a wide choice of ingredients and is popular as a healthy, well-being food that is not spicy.

Joseon kings and queens used to scoff specially prepared *juk* (rice porridge) with abalone, pine nuts and sesame seeds as a pre-breakfast meal.

FOOD & DRINK FOOD

Chicken

Samgyetang is a small whole chicken stuffed with glutinous rice, red dates, garlic and ginseng root, and boiled in broth. *Dakgalbi* is pieces of spicy chicken, cabbage, other vegetables and finger-sized pressed rice cakes, all grilled at your table. *Jjimdak* is a spiced-up mixture of chicken pieces, transparent noodles, potatoes and other vegetables. Many informal *hof* (pubs) serve inexpensive barbecued or fried chicken to accompany the beer. Street stalls offer chicken kebabs with various sauces.

Fish & Seafood

Fish *(saengseon)* and other seafood *(haemul)* is generally served broiled, grilled or in a soup, while *hoe* is raw fish like *sashimi*. Fish are usually served whole with both the head and guts. Visit Noryangjin Fish Market or the West Sea islands such as Muuido to indulge in raw fish, steamed crab, grilled prawns or barbecued shellfish feasts. *Nakji* (octopus) is usually served in a spicy sauce; if you're brave try the raw version of *sannakji* (baby octopus) – the chopped-up tentacles still wriggle on the plate when brought to the table. *Haemultang* is a seafood soup containing so much chilli that even locals have to mop their brows.

Royal palace cuisine, a style of cooking now replicated in fancy restaurants for the general public, requires elaborate preparation and presentation. It includes dishes such as *gujeolpan* (snacks wrapped in small pancakes) and *sinseollo* (hotpot).

Soups & Stews

Soups *(tang* or *guk)* are a highlight of Korean cuisine. 'A meal without soup is like a face without eyes', goes a traditional saying. They vary from spicy seafood and tofu soups to bland broths such as *galbitang* and *seolleongtang*, made from beef bones; the latter is a Seoul speciality. *Gamjatang* is a spicy peasant soup with meaty bones and a potato. Tip: if a soup is too spicy, mix in some rice.

Stews *(jjigae)* are usually served sizzling in a stone hotpot with plenty of spices. Popular versions are made with tofu *(dubu jjigae),* soybean

---

SEOUL'S SWEET SNACKS

A director of O'ngo Food Communications (www.ongofood.com), Daniel Gray is a food journalist who writes the blog Seoul Eats and a column in the monthly magazine *Seoul*. He recommends sampling the following street snacks on your meanders through Insa-dong.

➡ *hotteok* – deep-fried dough pancakes, usually with a brown-sugar-and-crushed-nut filling (although you can also get savoury vegetable-filled versions). Look also for the *oksusu* (corn) *hotteok*, which are really, really huge.

➡ *delimanjoo* – minicakes filled with custard or red bean, freshly baked on the street.

➡ *kkultarae* – superfine threads of honey and cornflour wrapped around crushed nuts (formerly a royal sweet). The young guys making them at several stalls along Insa-dong-gil put on a fun show.

paste *(doenjang jjigae)* and kimchi. *Beoseotjeongol* is a less spicy but highly recommended mushroom hotpot.

Kimchi

Traditionally, kimchi was made to preserve vegetables and ensure proper nutrition during the harsh winters, but it's now eaten year-round and adds zest, zip and a long list of health benefits to any meal. A cold side dish of the spicy national food is served at nearly every Korean meal, whether it's breakfast, lunch or dinner.

Generally made with pickled and fermented cabbage seasoned with garlic and red chilli, it can be made from cucumbers, white radish or other vegetables. Note, kimchi is not always vegetarian as it can have anchovies added. *Mul* kimchi is a cold, gazpacho-type minimalist soup, and is not spicy.

Dumplings, Noodles & Pancakes

Mandu are small dumplings and *wangmandu* are large ones; both can be filled with minced meat, seafood, vegetables and herbs. They are often freshly made to a special recipe by restaurant staff during quiet times. Fried, boiled or steamed, they make a tasty snack or addition to a meal. *Manduguk* is *mandu* in soup with seaweed and makes a perfect light lunch.

There's a whole range of *guksu* (noodles) to sample. A much-loved Pyongyang speciality is *naengmyeon,* chewy buckwheat noodles in an icy, sweetish broth, garnished with shredded vegetables and topped with half a hard-boiled egg – add red-chilli paste or *gyeoja* (mustard) to taste. Popular in summer, it is often eaten after a meat dish like *galbi.* Use the scissors provided to cut up the noodles so they're easier to eat.

Kalguksu is thick, hand-cut noodles usually served in a bland clam-and-vegetable broth. *Ramyeon* is instant noodles often served in a hot chilli soup. Seoulites believe in fighting fire with fire and claim it's a good cure for hangovers.

Pajeon are thick, savoury pancakes the size of pizzas, often filled with spring onions and seafood. *Bindaetteok* are just as big and even more filling, made from ground mung beans with various fillings and fried until a crispy, golden brown – they're best eaten at Gwangjang Market.

Desserts & Confectionary

Desserts are not common in traditional Korean restaurants, but sometimes a piece of fruit, coffee or traditional tea is served at the end of the meal. Ice cream, yogurt and waffle parlours are springing up everywhere, not to mention all the cafes and bakeries.

Tteok (pronounced 'dock') are traditional rice cakes, a bland, unsweetened and healthy alternative to sugary Western cakes, flavoured with dried fruit, nuts and beans.

Dining Etiquette

If you're invited out by Korean colleagues or friends, it's difficult or impossible to pay the bill or even contribute towards it. Arguing about who should have the honour of paying the restaurant bill is a common scene at the cashier's desk.

Meals are usually eaten communally, so dishes are placed in the centre of the table and diners put a little from each common dish in their own dish or bowl.

At some traditional restaurants, customers sit on cushions on the floor (the *ondol,* an underfloor heating system, is beneath). Before stepping up, always remove your shoes.

Strict rules govern the types of foods prepared for display during Confucian ancestral rite ceremonies. The first row includes rice-cake soup and glasses of rice wine. The second row, fried foods; the third, stews; the fourth, side dishes including kimchi; the fifth, piles of fruit.

Budae jjigae (or *Johnsontang*) is a unique Seoul dish that originated in the hungry years after the Korean War. At this time tins of ham, sausages and baked beans from American army bases (such as Yongsan) were bought on the black market and mixed with noodles and vegetable scraps to make a meal.

RULES OF KOREAN DINING

➡ Take off your shoes in traditional restaurants where everyone sits on floor cushions.

➡ Pour drinks for others if you notice that their glasses are empty. It's polite to use both hands when pouring or receiving a drink. Don't pour drinks for yourself (unless you're alone).

➡ Ask for *gawi* (scissors) if you're trying to cut something and your spoon won't do it.

➡ Place the chopsticks and spoon back in their original position at the end of the meal.

➡ Don't start or finish your meal before your seniors and elders.

➡ Don't touch food with your fingers, except when handling *ssam* (salad leaves used as edible wrapping for other foods).

➡ Use a spoon rather than chopsticks to eat rice.

➡ Don't leave your chopsticks or spoon sticking up from your rice bowl. This is taboo, only done with food that is offered to deceased ancestors.

➡ Don't blow your nose at the table.

Koreans usually call out to attract a server's attention, so don't be shy to call out *'ajumma!'* or *'ajeossi!'* (which literally mean 'middle-aged woman' or 'middle-aged man' – sounds impolite but it's not). Nearly every restaurant in Seoul serves bottled or filtered water free of charge when you first arrive.

DRINKS

Bottled and canned soft drinks are everywhere. Some uniquely Korean choices are grape juice with whole grapes inside, and *sikhye,* rice punch with rice grains inside. Health tonics, made with fibre, vitamins, ginseng and other medicinal herbs, are available in shops and pharmacies; many claim to boost your virility, vitamin levels and alertness, or cure (or prevent) a hangover!

Tea

Tea *(cha)* is a staple, with the term also used to describe drinks brewed without tea leaves. The most common leaf tea is *nokcha* (green tea). Black tea *(hongcha)* is harder to find. Non-leaf teas include the ubiquitous *boricha* (barley tea), *daechucha* (red-date tea), *omijacha* (five-flavour berry tea), *yujacha* (citron tea) and *insamcha* (ginseng tea). They may be served hot or cold.

Alcoholic Beverages

Koreans drink enough *soju* – a highly potent mix of ethanol mixed with water and flavouring – that the Jinro-brand *soju* (you'll see the green bottles everywhere) is the top-selling brand of spirits *worldwide.* The size of the *soju* bottle is calculated to fill only seven shot glasses. The stuff might go down easily, but it can induce a killer hangover the next day. Go for the higher-quality stuff distilled from grain (try Andong Soju or Jeonju Leegangju); it offers a far more delicate flavour, but can have an alcohol content of up to 45%.

Makgeolli is a traditional farmer's brew made from unrefined, fermented rice wine. Generally much lower in alcohol content than *soju,* it has a cloudy appearance and a sweetish yogurty flavour. It is

Japchae is a Chinese-style dry dish of transparent noodles stir-fried in sesame oil with strips of egg, meat and vegetables. It's sometimes served as a side dish or by royal-cuisine restaurants.

traditionally served in a brass kettle and poured into shallow brass bowls, although Seoul has several bars now where higher-quality styles of *makgeolli,* akin to the range of Japanese sake, are served and savoured.

A host of sweetish traditional spirits are brewed or distilled from grains, fruits and roots. Many are regional or seasonal. *Bokbunjaju* is made from wild raspberries, *meoruju* from wild fruit, *maesilju* from green plums and *insamju* from ginseng.

Religion & Culture

It was once divided strictly along nearly inescapable class lines and hierarchical distinctions, but Seoul's sensibility is now much like any modern city. People often hold loyalties to school, company and church, but egalitarianism has given way to greater individualism. The concept of family is rapidly changing as well: nuclear rather than extended families are the norm, and birth rates are among the lowest in the developed world. Still, there linger strong traces of Korea's particular identity. Remnants of its Confucian past coexist alongside 'imported' spiritual beliefs, denting the myth that modernisation necessitates secularisation.

THE MAIN BELIEF SYSTEMS

Of the four streams of spiritual influence in Korea, Confucianism and Buddhism are the most important. Christianity, which first made inroads into Korea in the 18th century, also plays a major role in the lives of many, while the ancient superstitions of shamanism persist as well.

Confucianism

The state religion of the Joseon dynasty, Confucianism still lives on as a kind of ethical bedrock (at least subconsciously) in the minds of most Koreans, especially the elderly.

The Chinese philosopher Confucius (552–479 BC) devised a system of ethics that emphasised devotion to parents and family, loyalty to friends, justice, peace, education, reform and humanitarianism. He also urged that respect and deference should be given to those in positions of authority – a philosophy exploited by Korea's Joseon-dynasty ruling elite. Confucius firmly believed that men were superior to women and that a woman's place was in the home.

These ideas led to the system of civil service examinations (*gwageo*), where one could gain position through ability and merit, rather than from noble birth and connections (though it was, in fact, still an uphill battle for the commonly born). Confucius preached against corruption, war, torture and excessive taxation. He was the first teacher to open his school to all students solely on the basis of their willingness to learn.

As Confucianism trickled into Korea, it evolved into neo-Confucianism, which combined the sage's original ethical and political ideas with the quasi-religious practice of ancestor worship and the idea of the eldest male as spiritual head of the family.

Buddhism

When first introduced during the Koguryo dynasty in AD 370, Buddhism coexisted with shamanism. Many Buddhist temples have a *samseionggak* (three-spirit hall) on their grounds, which houses shamanist deities such as the Mountain God.

The religion was persecuted during the Joseon period, when its temples were tolerated only in the remote mountains. It suffered another sharp

Visit the spirit shrines of Joseon royalty at the splendid Jongmyo. A grand Confucian ceremony honouring the deceased is held there every May.

About 90% of Korean Buddhist temples belong to the Jogye order (www.koreanbud dhism.net). Buddha's birthday is a national holiday, which includes an extravagant lantern parade in Seoul.

decline after WWII as Koreans pursued more worldly goals. But South Korea's success in achieving developed-nation status, coupled with a growing interest in spiritual values, is encouraging a Buddhist revival. Temple visits have increased and large sums of money are flowing into temple reconstruction.

Korean Buddhism is also building international attention by operating a Templestay program for travellers at facilities across the country. Many Koreans take part in these temple stays, regardless of whether they are Buddhist or not, as a chance to escape societal pressures and clear their minds.

Culture Books

Notes on Things Korean (Suzanne Crowder Han)

Understanding Koreans and their Culture (Choi Joon-sik)

Korea Bug (J Scott Burgeson)

The 48 Keywords that Describe Korea (Kim Jin-woo & Lee Nam-hoon)

Christianity

Korea's first exposure to Christianity was in the late 18th century. It came via the Jesuits from the Chinese imperial court when a Korean aristocrat was baptised in Beijing in 1784. The Catholic faith took hold and spread so quickly that it was perceived as a threat by the Korean government and was vigorously suppressed, creating the country's first Christian martyrs (see p78).

Christianity got a second chance in the 1880s, with the arrival of American Protestant missionaries who founded schools and hospitals, and gained many followers – so many, in fact, that today Christianity is the nation's second most popular religion after Buddhism.

Shamanism

Historically, shamanism influenced Korean spirituality. It's not a religion but it does involve communication with spirits through intermediaries known as *mudang* (female shamans). Although not widely

THE CONFUCIAN MINDSET

Confucianism is a social philosophy, a prescription for achieving a harmonious society. Not everyone follows the rules, but Confucianism does continue to shape the Korean paradigm. Some of the key principles and practices:

➡ Obedience and respect towards seniors – parents, teachers, the boss, older brothers and sisters – is crucial. Heavy penalties (including physical punishment) are incurred for stepping out of line.

➡ Seniors get obedience, but they also have obligations. Older siblings help out younger siblings with tuition fees, and the boss always pays for lunch.

➡ Education defines a civilised person. Despite having built a successful business, a high-school graduate would still feel shame at their lack of scholastic credentials.

➡ Men and women have separate roles. A woman's role is service, obedience and management of household affairs. Men don't do housework or look after children.

➡ Status and dignity are critical. Every action reflects on the family, company and country.

➡ Everything on and beyond the earth is in a hierarchy. People never forget who is senior and who is junior to them.

➡ Families are more important than individuals. Everyone's purpose in life is to improve the family's reputation and wealth. No one should choose a career or marry someone against their parents' wishes – a bad choice could bring ruin to a family. Everyone must marry and have a son to continue the family line. For these reasons homosexuality is considered a grossly unnatural act.

➡ Loyalty is important. A loyal liar is a virtuous person.

➡ Be modest and don't be extravagant. Only immoral women wear revealing clothes. Be frugal with praise.

FORTUNE-TELLING

These days most people visit one of the city's street-tent fortune-tellers for a bit of fun, but no doubt some take it seriously. For a *saju* (reading of your future), inform the fortune-teller of the date, including the hour, of your birth; another option is *gunhap* (a love-life reading), when a couple gives their birth details and the fortune-teller pronounces how compatible they are. Expect to pay ₩10,000 for *saju* and double that for *gunhap*. If you don't speak the language, you'll also need someone to translate.

practised today, shamanist ceremonies are held to cure illness, ward off financial problems or guide a deceased family member safely into the spirit world.

Ceremonies involve contacting spirits who are attracted by lavish offerings of food and drink. Drums beat and the *mudang* dances herself into a frenzied state that allows her to communicate with the spirits and be possessed by them. Resentments felt by the dead can plague the living and cause all sorts of misfortune, so their spirits need placating. For shamanists, death does not end relationships. It simply takes another form.

On Inwangsan in northwestern Seoul, ceremonies take place in or near the historic Inwangsan Guksadang shrine.

COMPETITIVE LIVES

The country's recovery from the ashes of the Korean War, construction workers on the job seven days a week, or computer-game addicts: they're all strands cut from the same cloth, the country's tenacious, pitbull spirit. Once Koreans lock onto something, it's difficult to break away. Life is competitive and everything is taken seriously, be it tenpin bowling, hiking or overseas corporate expansion.

'A person without education is like a beast wearing clothes' is a proverb that nails Korea's obsession with education. Though everyone complains about this manic pursuit, it is a system hard to shake. To get into one of the top Korean universities (nearly all of which are in Seoul), high-school students go through a gruelling examination process, studying 14 hours a day, often in private cram schools at night, for their one annual shot at the college entrance test.

Koreans are also fanatical about health. The millions of hikers who stream into the mountains on weekends are not only enjoying nature but also keeping fit. Thousands of health foods and drinks are sold in markets and pharmacies, which stock traditional as well as Western medicines. Nearly every food claims to be a 'well-being' product or an aphrodisiac – 'good for stamina' is the local phrase.

Koreans give their family name first, followed by their birth name, which is typically two syllables, ie Lee Myung-bak. There are less than 300 Korean family names, with Kim, Lee (or Yi) and Park accounting for 45% of the total.

CONTEMPORARY & TRADITIONAL CULTURE

Driven by the latest technology and fast evolving trends, Seoul can sometimes seem like one of the most cutting-edge cities on the planet. On subway trains and the streets, passengers tune into their favourite TV shows via their smartphones and tablet computers. In PC *bang* (computer-game rooms), millions of diehard fans battle at online computer games, while in *noraebang* (karaoke rooms), wannabe K-Popsters belt out the latest hit tunes.

General fashions tend to be international and up to the moment, too. However, it's not uncommon to see some people wearing *hanbok,*

MINDING YOUR KOREAN MANNERS

Most locals understand that visitors do not mean disrespect when they commit a minor social faux pas. But you'll be even more warmly received when it is obvious that you've gone out of your way to burnish your graces, Korean style.

Shoes Off
In any residence, temple, guesthouse or Korean-style restaurant, leave your shoes at the door. And socks are better than bare feet.

Artful Bow
Though you may see members of the royal court drop to the ground to greet the king on Korean TV dramas, don't get inspired. A quick, short bow – essentially a nod of the head – is most respectful for meetings and departures.

All Hands on Deck
Give and receive any object using both hands – especially name cards (essential for any formal and many informal meetings), money and gifts.

Giving Gifts
When you visit someone at their home, bring along a little token of your appreciation. The gift can be almost anything – flowers, chocolates, fruit, a book, a bottle of liquor or wine, tea or something from your home country. It's also a nice gesture to gift-wrap your offering.

Your host may at first strongly refuse your gift. This is a gesture of graciousness. Keep insisting, and they will accept it 'reluctantly'. For the same reason, your host will not open the package immediately.

Paying the Bill
Fighting to pay the bill is a common phenomenon, though the quid pro quo is that one person pays this time and the other fights a little harder to pick up the cheque next time. If a Korean takes you under their wing, it's difficult to pay for anything.

Get Over Here
Don't beckon someone using your forefinger. Place your hand out, palm down (palm up is how you call your pet) and flutter all your fingers at once.

Loss of Face
In interpersonal relations, the least desirable outcome is to somehow 'lower the harmony (gibun)'. A mishandled remark or potentially awkward scene should be smoothed over as soon as possible, and if you sense someone actively trying to change the subject, go with the flow. An argument or any situation that could lead to embarrassment should be avoided at all costs.

Smile, You're Embarrassed
Often, potential loss of face – say, when someone realises they are clearly in the wrong – will result in an unlikely reaction: a wide smile. No, you're not being mocked; you've just been told 'I'm sorry'. So if a taxi almost mows you down, only to roll down his window and flash you a big grin, he's not off his rocker – he's showing his embarrassment, which is both a form of apology and a gesture of sympathy.

the striking traditional clothing that follows the Confucian principle of unadorned modesty. Women wear a loose-fitting short blouse with long sleeves and a voluminous long skirt, while men wear a jacket and baggy trousers. Today *hanbok* is worn mostly at weddings or special events, and even then it may be a more comfortable 'updated' version. Everyday *hanbok* is reasonably priced, but formal styles, made of colourful silk and intricately embroidered, are objects of wonder and cost a fortune.

Architecture

Seoul's skyline – dominated by skyscrapers and endless high-rise apartments – at first suggests no building has survived the war and economic modernisation. But examples of architecture from all periods of Seoul's history do remain, resulting in a juxtaposed hotchpotch that at times finds a quirky harmony. Explore the city and you'll discover not only fortress walls, grand palaces and decorative temples, but also charming early-20th-century hanok (traditional wooden homes) and dramatic contemporary structures, such as the new City Hall and Dongdaemun Design Plaza.

TRADITIONAL ARCHITECTURE

There are three main types of traditional architecture found in Seoul: palaces, temples and homes. They are all primarily made of wood, with no nails used – a system of braces and brackets holds the elements together. They were (and often still are) heated using an ingenious system of circulating underfloor smoke tunnels called *ondol*.

Palaces

During the Joseon era (1392–1897), five main palaces were constructed in the royal capital. These were cities unto themselves, massive complexes with administrative offices, residences, pleasure pavilions and royal gardens, all hemmed in by imposing walls. A prominent feature is the roof of these structures, which is made from heavy clay tiles with dragons or other mythical beasts embossed on the end tile. The strikingly bold, predominantly green-and-orange paintwork under the eaves is called *dancheong*. Ceilings are often intricately carved and coloured.

Because of centuries of invasion and war, Seoul's palaces have all been painstakingly rebuilt countless times, sometimes changing their shape altogether.

Temples, Shrines & Royal Tombs

Korean temples, like palaces, are painted in natural colours. Outside murals depict the life of Buddha or parables of self liberation; inside the shrines are paintings of Buddhist heavens – and occasionally hells. Look for intricately carved lattice in the Buddhist shrines, and for a *sansingak*, or Mountain God Hall, which contains an image of the deity in question and represents the accommodation of Korean Buddhism to Korea's preexisting shamanist beliefs.

Also visually striking in their command of space and use of natural materials are the royal shrines and burial tombs of the Joseon dynasty, 40-odd of which are on the Unesco World Heritage list. In these tombs, each similarly arranged on hillsides according to the rules of Confucianism and feng shui, are buried every Joseon ruler right up to the last, Emperor Sunjong (r 1907–10). Tombs are marked by a simple red-painted wooden gate, from which a stone pathway leads to a hall for conducting rites in front of the humped burial mounds decorated with stone statuary – typically a pair of civil officers and generals, plus horses and protecting animals.

Constructed around the 1st century AD, the Mongchon-toseong (Mongchon Clay Fortress) was built on the southern banks of the Han River during the kingdom of Baekje (18 BC–AD 475). It's still there in Olympic Park.

Top Traditional Buildings

Gyeongbokgung

Bosingak pavilion

Jongmyo

Sajikdan

Sungnyemun (Namdaemun)

Hanok

Traditional houses, or *hanok,* are complex in design yet masterfully understated. These one-storey homes are crafted entirely from wood, save for the clay tiled roofs, insulated with mud and straw. The windows are made of a thin translucent paper that allows daylight to stream in. They're heated by the underfloor system called *ondol.*

One of the programs of the National Trust of Korea (www. nationaltrust. or.kr), an NGO charged with helping to protect the country's environment and national relics, focuses on the preservation of *hanok.*

Unlike the ostentatious manor homes of Europe, even an aristocrat's lavish *hanok* was designed to blend with nature; they are typically left unpainted, their brown and tan earth tones giving off a warm, intimate feel. All of the rooms look onto a courtyard (or *madang*), which usually includes a simple garden. Life was lived on the floor, so all the furniture was low-slung, and people sat and slept on mats rather than chairs and beds.

Social rank dictated the decorations, beam size, roof pitch and number of rooms – these rules were not relaxed until the 1930s. The traditional home was also divided into two sections: the *sarangchae* for men and the *anchae* for women. In larger homes, these comprised different buildings, surrounded by walls and gates. In the *anchae,* the women of the family raised children, did the cooking and ran the household. The *sarangchae* housed the library, an ancestral shrine and rooms in which to receive guests, who seated themselves on comfortable low cushions and enjoyed a tea service.

With South Korea's modernisation, desire to live in *hanok* waned. Their thin walls prevented privacy. There was no easy space to install

SAVING THE HANOK

'Thirty-five years ago there were around 800,000 *hanok* in South Korea; now there are less than 10,000', says Peter Bartholomew, an American expat in Korea. For over 40 years Bartholomew has been battling the predominant view among Koreans that such traditional houses are an anachronism in their modern country, unworthy of preserving.

Bartholomew has lived in *hanok* since he first came to Korea in 1968 as a Peace Corps volunteer and has owned one in the Dongsomun-dong area of northern Seoul since 1974. He bought an adjacent property in 1991. In 2009 Bartholomew and his neighbours won a two-year legal battle against the city over plans to redevelop the area. 'I deplore the assumption that these old houses are irreparable, dirty and unsanitary', he says, pointing out that traditional *hanok* are very easy to modernise in just the same way that centuries-old homes across the West have been adapted to contemporary life.

The proof of this lies in the Bukchon area, where some 900 *hanok* remain, the bulk concentrated in a few streets in Gahoe-dong (also transliterated as Kahoi-dong). 'The preservation program has only been achieved by the government providing financial incentives to owners for repairs and maintenance', says Bartholomew. However, according to some local residents, even in Bukchon the *hanok* as a private home is under threat. Kahoi-dong 'is being relentlessly destroyed', says David Kilburn, author of Preservation of Kahoi-dong (www.kahoidong.com), a website that documents the abuses of the preservation system over the past decade.

Contemporary Seoulites may shun *hanok* as places to live, but tourists clearly love them if the increasing number of *hanok* guesthouses is anything to go by. Ahn Young-hwan, owner of Rak-Ko-Jae, a *hanok* guesthouse in Bukchon, was one of the first people to suggest that *hanok* be used in this way. 'People thought I was crazy', he says, 'but now many more people are doing it'.

For Ahn, *hanok* are the 'vessels that contain Korean culture' and a way of experiencing the joys of an analogue life in an increasingly digital society. It's a view that Bartholomew underlines when he says that living in his *hanok* has 'filled my life with peace and beauty'.

indoor toilets. Rooms were small, and living on the floor had its inconveniences. In comparison, Seoul's modern high-rises offered amenities galore. Recently, however, Seoul has seen a revival of interest in traditional homes, with increased efforts to preserve their unique character.

Bukchon has Seoul's largest concentration of *hanok*, mostly dating from the 1930s. To see larger-scale *hanok* in a more traditional setting, visit Namsangol Hanok Village at the foot of Namsan.

EARLY MODERN & COLONIAL ARCHITECTURE

In the late 19th century, Western and Japanese missionaries, traders and diplomats flooded into the Hermit Kingdom. The architecture of this period is often regarded as 'colonial', although some of it purely represents Korean attempts to modernise along Western lines.

Churches were usually designed by French, American or British missionaries, including wonderful examples of Gothic and Romanesque styles, but much of Seoul's early modern architectural heritage was built by the Japanese, who destroyed significant chunks of the capital's traditional buildings (particularly palaces) in the process.

Japanese colonial architects often emulated Western Renaissance and neo-baroque architectural styles, although you'll also find the occasional art nouveau or other modernist style thrown in.

MODERN ARCHITECTURE 1950S–80S

Though the needs of post–Korean War reconstruction required a focus on more utilitarian concerns, much of Korea's modern architecture is distinct, usually following one of two trajectories: either an attempt to reinterpret traditional Korean architecture in concrete and steel, or to communicate Seoul's cutting-edge technological prowess.

First and perhaps foremost of Korea's post-independence architects was Japanese-trained Kim Swoo-geun, whose early work reflected the influence of Le Corbusier and Kenzo Tange. He is responsible for the curving lines of the Olympic Stadium and the ivy-clad Kyungdong Presbyterian Church (1981). Among other local architectural greats are Kim Chung-up, whose work includes the soaring Peace Gate at Olympic Park, and Kim Joong-up, responsible for the 31-storey smoked-glass Samil Building (1969), Seoul's first International-style skyscraper.

CONTEMPORARY ARCHITECTURE

Spurred on by its winning bid to be the World Design Capital in 2010, the city government and major construction firms went on a building spree, hiring such luminaries as Zaha Hadid for the Dongdaemun Design Plaza and Park, and Daniel Libeskind for Archipelago 21, part of the US$28 billion redevelopment of the Yongsan International Business District.

The work of these celebrated international architects shouldn't overshadow that of local talents, who have imposed their creative visions on a series of both small- and large-scale projects adding to Seoul's built beauty. The shopping complex Ssamziegil in Insa-dong (designed by Choi Moon-gyu and Gabriel Kroiz) and Bae Dae-young's Why Butter building in Hongdae (housing KT&G SangsangMadang) are both fine examples of contemporary buildings with a strong point of view.

Top Early Modern & Colonial Buildings

Cheondogyo

Myeong-dong Cathedral

Former Bank of Korea HQ

Former Seoul Station (Culture Station Seoul 284)

Seodaemun Prison

Architecture Books

Hanoak – Traditional Korean Houses (various authors)

Joseon Royal Court Culture (Shin Myung-ho)

Seoul's Historic Walks (Cho In-Souk & Robert Koehler)

City as Art: 100 Notable Works of Architecture in Seoul (Yim Seock-jae)

Arts

Seoul has long been the nexus of Korea's spectacular range of arts. Rich, colourful costumes set the scene for passionate traditional pansori operas. Folk dances such as samullori, with its whirling dervish of dancers, seamlessly meld the cacophonous and melodic. Artisans preserve the ancient art of calligraphy with their silken strokes. Seoul takes national pride of place in the modern arts, too. Korea's film directors are regularly feted at international festivals. The city's art museums and galleries burst with contemporary works. And Asia goes gaga for Korean pop (K-Pop).

A fascinating traditional Korean art form is *hanji* (handmade paper). Often dyed soft colours, *hanji* can be pressed and lacquered so that it can serve as a waterproof cup or plate.

VISUAL ART

Traditional

Stone Buddhist statues and pagodas such as the one in Tapgol Park are among the oldest artworks in Seoul. Some marvellous examples of cast-bronze Buddhas can be seen in the National Museum of Korea. Zen-style Buddhist art can be seen inside and outside Seoul's temples, Jogye-sa and Bongeun-sa, and you'll find stone and wooden effigies of shamanist spirit guardians outside the National Folk Museum in the grounds of the main palace, Gyeongbokgung.

Chinese influence is paramount in traditional Korean painting. The basic tools (brush and water-based ink) are those of calligraphy, which influenced painting in both technique and theory. The brush line, which varies in thickness and tone, is the most important feature. Traditional landscape painting is meant to surround the viewer, and there is no fixed viewpoint as in traditional Western painting. A talented artist who painted everyday scenes was Kim Hong-do (1745–1816). Court ceremonies, portraits, flowers, birds and traditional symbols of longevity – the sun, water, rocks, mountains, clouds, pine trees, turtles and cranes – were popular subjects.

Major modern Korean artists include Nam June Paik (1932–2006), who has some imaginative installations in the National Museum of Contemporary Art, and Kim Tschang Yeul, whose work can be seen at the Leeum Samsung Museum of Art.

Modern & Contemporary

Seoul has a thriving contemporary art scene with the best of local artists incorporating Korean motifs and themes, and sometimes traditional techniques, with a modern vision. Insa-dong, Bukchon, Samcheong-dong and Tongui-dong are all packed with small galleries, often with free shows; you'll also find major galleries south of the river in Cheongdam.

The city is fostering up-and-coming artists through its Seoul Art Space project (http://eng.seoulartspace.or.kr); visit one of the gallery spaces beneath the Jungang Market in Sindang. Another interesting movement to check out is Seoul Urban Art Project (SUP; http://sup-project.com), a collective of 14 local and international artists who create 'real art in the real streets'. Zoning in on areas under threat of development, such as Buk Ahyeon-dong west of Myeong-dong, the artists have painted bright murals on the decaying streets. They've also jazzed up parts of Itaewon with a street art attack.

CERAMICS & POTTERY

Archaeologists have unearthed Korean pottery that dates back some 10,000 years, although it wasn't until the early 12th century that the art form reached a peak, with skilled potters turning out wonderful celadon pottery with a warm-green tinge. Visit the National Museum of Korea for one of the best displays. Original celadon fetches huge sums at auctions, but modern copies are widely available.

Sadly, after the 13th-century Mongol invasion the art was lost, and Koreans started to produce *buncheong*-ware, less refined pottery decorated with simple folk designs. But it was much admired by the Japanese, and during the Imjin War in the 1590s entire families and villages of Korean potters were abducted and resettled in Japan to produce *buncheong* for their new masters. Some are still there.

MUSIC

Korean traditional music *(gugak)* is played on stringed instruments, most notably the *gayageum* (12-stringed zither) and *haegum* (two-stringed fiddle) as well as on chimes, gongs, cymbals, drums, horns and flutes. Court music *(jeongak)* is slow and stately, while folk music such as *samullori* is fast and lively.

Similar to Western opera is *changgeuk,* which can involve a large cast of characters. An unusual type of opera is *pansori*. It features a solo storyteller (usually female) singing to the beat of a drum, while emphasising dramatic moments with a flick of her fan. The singing is strong and sorrowful: some say if *pansori* is done correctly, the performer will have blood in her mouth upon finishing. Only a few *pansori* dramas have survived; *Chunhyang,* the story of a woman's faith and endurance, is the most popular.

K-Pop

Fans of Korean pop (K-Pop) will have ample opportunity to enjoy tunes – both recorded and live – by their favourite singers and bands in Seoul. Among solo singers, few have attained the level of commercial success of BoA (www.boaamerica.com) and her male counterpart Rain (www.rain-jihoon.com), one of Korea's most versatile entertainers, who can sing, dance, act and run a company.

At the park in front of Jongmyo you may see pensioners dancing to 'trot' music. Short for 'foxtrot', this musical form combines Korean scales with Western harmonies and sounds similar to Japanese enka music.

ARTS CERAMICS & POTTERY

SEOUL IN LITERATURE

Seoul has always been a city of writers. Part of the Joseon-era government-service exam *(gwageo)* involved composing verse. During the Joseon dynasty, literature meant *sijo,* short nature poems that were handwritten (using a brush and ink) in Chinese characters, even after the invention of *hangeul* (the Korean phonetic alphabet) in the 15th century.

In the 20th century, however, there was a sharp turn away from Chinese (and Japanese) influence of any kind. Western ideas and ideals took hold, and existentialism and other international literary trends found footing, but through a unique and pervasive Korean lens. A fascinating example is *Three Generations,* a novel by Yom Sang-seop, originally written as a serialisation in the newspaper *Chosun Ilbo* in 1931. It follows the soap opera-ish and ultimately tragic lives of the wealthy Jo family under the Japanese occupation of the time.

Bang up to date is Kim Young-ha's *I Have The Right To Destroy Myself,* which delves into alienation in contemporary Seoul and has been described as both Korean Noir and Kafkaesque.

Other successful artists include cute boy-band Bigbang (www.yg family.com), the 13-member group Super Junior (http://superjunior. smtown.com), Wonder Girls (www.wondergirlsworld.com), five bubbly young women, and the nine-piece Girls' Generation (www.girlsgenera tionusa.com), currently Korea's top pop group.

Koreanfilm.org (www.koreanfilm. org) is a top resource covering all aspects of the industry and features numerous reviews. The bookshop Seoul Selection has a great selection of Korean DVDs.

CINEMA

Seoul's Chungmuro neighbourhood has long been the heart of the nation's vibrant and critically acclaimed film industry, which has been at the forefront of *hallyu* or the Korean Wave of popular culture sweeping across Asia and the world.

Directors haven't shied away from major issues, such as the Korean War with *Taegukgi* (2004) and its turbulent political aftermath in *The President's Last Bang* (2005). Pervasive social issues in modern Seoul – such as the blistering pace of city life and the shifting notion of family – are tackled in films like *The Way Home* (2002) and *Family Ties* (2006), both quietly touching. The horror films *Memento Mori* (1999) and *A Tale of Two Sisters* (2003) provide gruesome shocks for the genre aficionado, and for an action-revenge flick – something Korea excels at – nothing tops the jaw-dropping *Old Boy* (2003).

Filmmaking used to be a boys' club. No longer: superb films by female directors are receiving greater recognition. These include Jeong Jae-eun's *Take Care of My Cat* (2001), the pitch-perfect story of five girls coming of age in the suburbs outside of Seoul, and Yim Soon-rye's *Waikiki Brothers* (2001), a sobering exploration of those left behind by Korea's economic rise. Yim's *Forever the Moment* (2008) follows the Korean women's handball team into the 2004 Olympics, offering a more reflective take than is the genre standard.

Elegant court dances, accompanied by an orchestra and dating back 600 years, are performed in front of Jongmyo on the first Sunday of every May.

THEATRE & DANCE

Seoul's thriving theatre scene is based mainly around Daehangno, where more than 50 small theatres put on everything from rock musicals and satirical plays to opera and translations of Western classics. Nearly all shows are in Korean. More accessible are the many nonverbal shows such as *Nanta* and *Jump*.

Korean folk dances include dynamic *seungmu* (drum dances), the satirical and energetic *talchum* (mask dances) and solo improvisational *salpuri* (shamanist dances). Most popular are *samullori* dance troupes, who perform in brightly coloured traditional clothing, twirling a long tassel from a cap on their heads at the same time as they dance and beat a drum or gong.

Survival Guide

Transport

GETTING TO SEOUL

Most likely you'll arrive at Incheon International Airport. If flying from within Korea, it's possible that your arrival point will be Gimpo International Airport, Seoul or Yongsan stations (for rail journeys) or one of the long-distance bus stations. Ferries to Incheon, west of Seoul, connect the country with China. Flights, tours and rail tickets can all be booked online at www.lonelyplanet.com/bookings.

Airlines

The following airlines have offices in Seoul:

Air Busan (☑1666 3060; www.airbusan.com)

Air Canada (☑757 9181; www.aircanada.com)

Air China (☑774 6886; www.airchina.kr)

Air France (☑3483 1033; www.airfrance.com)

Asiana Airlines (☑1588 8000; www.flyasiana.com)

Cathay Pacific Airways (☑311 2800; www.cathaypacific.com)

Japan Airlines (☑757 1711; www.kr.jal.com)

Jeju Air (☑1599 5000; www.jejuair.net)

Jin Air (☑1600 6200; www.jinair.com)

KLM Royal Dutch Airlines (☑3483 1133; www.klm.com)

Korean Air (☑1588 2001; www.koreanair.com)

Lufthansa Airlines (☑2019 0180; www.lufthansa.com)

Malaysia Airlines (☑775 0952; www.malaysiaairlines.com)

Singapore Airlines (☑755 1226; www.singaporeair.com)

United Airlines (☑751 0300; www.united.com)

Incheon International Airport

The main international gateway is **Incheon International Airport** (☑032 1577 2600; www.airport.kr), 52km west of central Seoul on the island of Yeongjongdo. This top-class operation also has a few domestic connections

Bus

City limousine buses Take around an hour to reach central Seoul (₩10,000, 5.30am to 10pm, every 10 to 30 minutes) depending on traffic.

KAL deluxe limousine buses (www.kallimousine.com) Run along four routes (₩15,000), dropping passengers at over 20 top hotels around Seoul.

Taxi

Regular taxis charge around ₩65,000 for the 70-minute journey to downtown Seoul, but the price can rise if traffic is jammed; meters run on a time basis when the taxis are not moving. From midnight

CLIMATE CHANGE & TRAVEL

Every form of transport that relies on carbon-based fuel generates CO_2, the main cause of human-induced climate change. Modern travel is dependent on aeroplanes, which might use less fuel per kilometre per person than most cars but travel much greater distances. The altitude at which aircraft emit gases (including CO_2) and particles also contributes to their climate change impact. Many websites offer 'carbon calculators' that allow people to estimate the carbon emissions generated by their journey and, for those who wish to do so, to offset the impact of the greenhouse gases emitted with contributions to portfolios of climate-friendly initiatives throughout the world. Lonely Planet offsets the carbon footprint of all staff and author travel.

to 4am regular taxis charge 20% extra.

Train

A'REX express trains (www.arex.or.kr) To Seoul station costs ₩13,800 (43 minutes); the commuter trains cost ₩3850 (53 minutes).

Gimpo International Airport

The bulk of domestic flights (and a handful of international ones) arrive at **Gimpo International Airport** (☑660 2114; http://gimpo.airport.co.kr; West Seoul), 18km west of the city centre.

Bus

City/KAL limousine buses Run every 10 minutes to central Seoul (₩5000/7000, around 40 minutes to Seoul station, depending on traffic).

Subway

Lines 5 and 9 connect the airport with the city (₩1250, 35 minutes).

Train

A'REX Trains Run to Seoul station (₩1300, 15 minutes).

Taxi

A taxi costs around ₩35,000 to the city centre and takes from 40 minutes to an hour.

Seoul Station

Seoul station (Map p202) is the hub of the domestic rail network operated by **Korean National Railroad** (☑1544 7788; www.korail.go.kr). Tickets can be bought up to one month in advance at many travel agents, as well as at train stations or online. Booking ahead is advised. If you plan to travel by train a lot over a short period, con-

---

CITY AIR TERMINALS

If you're flying Korean Air, Asiana or Jeju Air, you can check in your luggage and go through immigration at **KARST** (http://english.arex.or.kr/jsp/eng/index.jsp) at Seoul station (Map p202), then hop on the A'REX train to Gimpo or Incheon. If you're south of the river, a similar service operates from **CALT** (Map p210; www.calt.co.kr; ◷5.30am-6.30pm; Ⓜ Line 2 to Samseong, Exit 5) at the COEX Mall and includes Qatar Airways, Singapore Airlines Qantas, Air Canada and Philippine Airlines. From here limousine buses run to either airport.

---

sider buying a 'KR pass' (see the website for details).

The fastest train is the KTX (Korea Train Express). A grade down are *saemeaul* services, which also only stop in major towns. *Mugunghwa* trains are also comfortable and fast, but stop more often.

Bus & Taxi

City buses and taxis depart from the east side of the station.

Subway

Lines 1 and 4 connect Seoul station with the city.

Yongsan Station

Some long-distance trains from the south of Korea terminate at Yongsan station (Map p202); many others pass through on their way to Seoul station.

Bus & Taxi

City buses and taxis depart from the east side of the station.

Subway

Line 4 and the Jungang line connect Yongsan Station with the city.

Seoul Express Bus Terminal

Long-distance buses arrive at this major **bus station** (Map p210; ☑536 6460; www.

kobus.co.kr, www.hticket.co.kr) split across two separate buildings. **Gyeongbu-Gumi-Yeongdong Terminal** serves mainly the eastern region, and **Honam Terminal** serves the southwestern region.

It's only necessary to buy tickets in advance for holidays and weekends. Deluxe-class buses have more leg room and cost more than ordinary buses. Buses that travel after 10pm have a 10% surcharge and are generally deluxe. Children go half price.

Subway

Lines 3, 7 and 9 connect the bus terminal with the city; use exit 1 for Gyeongbu-Gumi-Yeongdong Terminal, exit 7 for Honam Terminal.

Dong-Seoul Bus Terminal

This **terminal** (Map p212; ☑455 3161; www.ti21.co.kr) in Jamsil serves the eastern part of Korea (1st floor) and major cities (2nd floor).

Subway

Line 2 to Gangbyeon, Exit 4.

Nambu Bus Terminal

Located in Gangnam, this **terminal** (Map p210; ☑521 8550; www.nambuterminal.co.kr) serves destinations south of Seoul.

Subway

Line 3 to Nambu Bus Terminal, Exit 5.

Incheon Port

Ferries connect Incheon, west of Seoul, with a dozen port cities in China. Journey times vary from 12 to 24 hours. One-way fares start at ₩115,000 to most destinations but prices double for the more private and comfortable cabins. To reach Incheon's port (ferries leave from Yeonan Pier or International Terminal 2), take subway line 1 to Incheon station and then take a taxi (around ₩4000).

Ferries to a number of Japanese cities leave from the southern city of Busan. See www.korail.com for details of a Seoul-Japan rail-and-ferry through ticket.

GETTING AROUND SEOUL

Bus, subway, taxi and train fares can all be paid using the rechargeable touch-and-go **T-Money card** (http://eng.t-money.co.kr), which gives you a ₩100 discount per trip. The basic card can be bought for a nonrefundable ₩3000 at any subway station booth, bus kiosks and convenience stores displaying the T-Money logo; reload it with credit at any of the aforementioned places and get money refunded that hasn't been used (up to ₩20,000 minus a processing fee of ₩500) at subway machines and participating convenience store before you leave Seoul.

Subway

Seoul has an excellent, user-friendly **subway system** (www.smrt.co.kr; ⊙5.30am-midnight) which connects up with destinations well beyond the city borders, including Suwon and Incheon. The minimum fare of ₩1150 (₩1050 with a T-Money card) takes you up to 12km. In central Seoul the average time between stations is just over two minutes, so it takes around 25 minutes to go 10 stops. Some top-end hotels and a few sights are a 15-minute walk from a subway station but you can hail taxis from the closest station.

Most subway stations have lifts or stair lifts for wheelchairs. Escalators are common, but you'll do a fair amount of walking up and down stairs and along corridors. Neighbourhood maps, including ones with digital touch screens, inside the stations help you figure out which of the subway exits to take. The closest station and exit number is provided for all listings.

Taxi

Regular taxis are a good deal for short trips. The basic fare for 2km is ₩2400 and rises ₩100 for every 144m or 35 seconds after that if the taxi is travelling below 15km/h. A 20% surcharge is levied between midnight and 4am. Deluxe taxis are black with a yellow stripe and cost ₩4500 for the first 3km and ₩200 for every 164m or 39 seconds, but they don't have a late-night surcharge.

Few taxi drivers speak English, but most taxis have a free interpretation service whereby an interpreter talks to the taxi driver and to you by phone. Orange **International Taxi** (☑1644 2255; www.internationaltaxi.co.kr) have English-speaking drivers; these can be reserved in advance for 20% extra on the regular fare and can be chartered on an hourly or daily basis for longer journeys. All taxis are metered, tipping is not required.

Bus

Seoul has a comprehensive and reasonably priced **bus system** (☑414 5005; www.bus.go.kr; ⊙5.30am-midnight). Some bus stops have some bus route maps in English, and most buses have their major destinations written in English on the outside and a taped announcement of the names of each stop in English, but few bus drivers understand English.

Using a T-Money card saves ₩100 on each bus fare and transfers between bus and subway are either free or discounted. Put your T-Money card to the screen as you exit as well as when you get on a bus, just as you do on the subway.

BUS JOURNEYS FROM SEOUL

DESTINATION	EXPRESS/DELUXE (₩)	DURATION
Busan	22,000/32,800	4hr 20min
Gyeongju	19,500/29,000	4hr 30min
Sokcho	17,000	2hr 40min
Gongju	7700/8600	1hr 50min
Mokpo	19,600/29,000	4hr
Gwangju	16,900/29,200	3hr 30min
Jeonju	12,200/17,900	2hr 45min
Gongju	8600	2hr
Chuncheon	6300	1hr 10min
Buyeo	14,400	2hr 40min

Red buses Long-distance express run to the outer suburbs

Green buses Link subways within a district

Blue buses Run to outer suburbs

Yellow buses Short-haul buses that circle small districts

Bicycle

Cycling the busy main streets of the city is not recommended but a pedal along the cycling lanes beside the Han River and through several parks can be a pleasure. Bicycles can be rented at several parks along the Han River including on Yeouido, Ttukseom Resort, Seoul Forest Park and Olympic Park. Rental is ₩3000 per hour and you'll need to leave some form of ID as a deposit.

Water Taxi

Reservations need to be made for **water taxis** (☑1588 3960; www.pleasantseoul.com) which can be boarded at 12 stations along the Han River: Jamsil Pier, Ttukseom Resort, Seoul Forest, Jamweon Pier, Ichon Geobukseon Naruteo, Yeoui 119, Yeouinaru Station, Yanghwa Dangsan Station, Yanghwa Ferry, Seonyu-do, Mangwon and Nanji.

Commuter services run between Yeouido and Ttsukseom and Yeouido and Jamsil (₩5000; ⊙7am to 8.30am and 6.30pm to 7.30pm) on weekdays. The taxis can also be hired for private tours (for up to seven passengers) ranging from ₩50,000 to ₩130,000 for trips of 20 minutes to one hour.

Car & Motorcycle

Driving is on the right, but due to the traffic jams, the impatience and recklessness of other drivers and the lack of street names, directional signs and parking, we recommend first-time visitors to Seoul give driving a miss. Public transport and taxis are cheap and convenient.

Hire

To rent a car you must be over 21 and have both a driving licence from your own country and an International Driving Permit. The latter must be obtained abroad as they're not available in Korea. Incheon International Airport has a couple of car-rental agencies. Try **KT Kumho** (www.kumhorent.com) or **Avis** (www.avis.com). Daily rates start at ₩80,000.

Directory A-Z

Business Hours

Exceptions to the following general hours are listed in reviews.

Banks 9am to 4pm Monday to Friday, ATMs 7am to 11pm

Bars 6pm to 1am, longer hours Friday and Saturday

Cafes 7am to 10pm

Post offices 9am to 6pm Monday to Friday

Restaurants 11am to 10pm

Shops 10am to 8pm

Customs Regulations

Visitors must declare all plants, fresh fruit, vegetables and dairy products that they bring into South Korea. Meat is not allowed without a certificate. Log on to www.customs.go.kr for further information. Antiques of national importance are not allowed to be exported.

Discount Cards

Korea Pass (www.koreapass.or.kr) is a prepaid card, available in denominations from ₩50,000 to ₩500,000 and available at Incheon and Gimpo International Airports, that provides discounts on a range of goods and services.

See p168 for information on the T-Money transport card.

Embassies

Australia (Map p200; ☑2003 0100; www.southkorea.embassy.gov.au; 19th fl, Kyobo Bldg, Jongno 1-ga, Jongno-gu)

Canada (Map p200; ☑3783 6000; www.canadainternational.gc.ca/korea-coree/; 21 Jeong-dong-gil, Jung-gu)

China (Map p200; ☑738 1038; www.chinaemb.or.kr; 54 Hyoja-dong, Jongno-gu)

France (off Map p202; ☑3149 4300; www.ambafrance-kr.org; 30 Hap-dong, Seodaemun-gu)

Germany (Map p208; ☑748 4114; www.seoul.diplo.de; 308-5 Dongbinggo-dong, Yongsan-gu)

Ireland (Map p200; ☑774 6455; www.embassyofireland.or.kr; 13th fl, Leema Bldg, 146-1 Susong-dong, Jongno-gu)

Japan (Map p200; ☑2170 5200; www.kr.emb-japan.go.jp; 18-11 Junghak-dong, Jongno-gu)

New Zealand (Map p200; ☑3701 7700; www.nzembassy.com/korea; 15th fl, Kyobo Bldg, Jongno 1-ga, Jongno-gu)

UK (Map p202; ☑3210 5500; http://ukinkorea.fco.gov.uk; 24 19-gil, Sejong-daero, Jung-gu)

PRACTICALITIES

Daily Newspapers

➧ **Korea Times** (www.koreatimes.co.kr)

➧ **Korea Herald** (www.koreaherald.co.kr)

➧ **Korea JoongAng Daily** (http://joongangdaily.joins.com)

Monthly Magazines

➧ **Seoul** (www.seoulselection)

➧ **Bridge** (www.bridgezine.com)

➧ **10 Magazine** (www.10mag.com)

➧ **Groove Korea** (www.groovekorea.com)

TV & Radio

➧ **KBS World** (http://world.kbs.co.kr) News and features.

➧ **Radio Gugak** (ww.gugakfm.co.kr) Traditional Korean music.

➧ **TBS** (http://tbsefm.seoul.kr) Music and news.

USA (Map p200; ☎397 4114; http://seoul.usembassy.gov; 32 Sejong-ro, Jongno-gu)

Emergency

If no English-speaking staff are available, ring the 24-hour tourist information and help line ☎1330.

Ambulance (☎119)

Fire Brigade (☎119)

Police (☎112)

Gay & Lesbian Travellers

Korea has never passed any laws that mention homosexuality, but this shouldn't be taken as a sign of tolerance or acceptance. Some older Koreans insist that there are no gay people in Korea – even though there are at least several very high-profile ones such as the TV personality/Seoul restauranter Hong Seok-chun and transgender celebrity Ha Ri-su.

Attitudes are changing, especially among young people, but virtually all of the local gay population (called *ivan* in Korean) chooses to stay firmly in closet. Gay and lesbian travellers who publicise their sexual orientation should be prepared for some less than positive reactions. This said, there are openly gay areas of Seoul where few will bat an eyelid at your behaviour; see p31 for more information.

At the end of May, Seoul pins up its rainbow colours for the **Korean Queer Cultural Festival** (www.kqcf. org), usually held in conjunction with the **Seoul LGBT Film Festival** (www.selff. com). Don't miss the parade along the Cheong-gye-cheon.

Useful resources:

Chungusai (Between Friends; chingusai.net) Korean GLBT human-rights group.

Utopia (www.utopia-asia. com) Check the Korea section.

iShap (www.ishap.org) Gay HIV/AIDS awareness project; produces a free Korean guidebook to gay bars and clubs – ask for it at bars such as Barcode in Nagwon-dong.

Electricity

South Korea is on the 220V standard at 60Hz and uses two round pins with no earth.

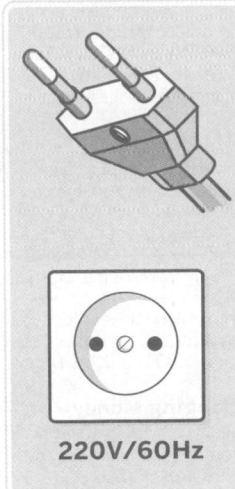

220V/60Hz

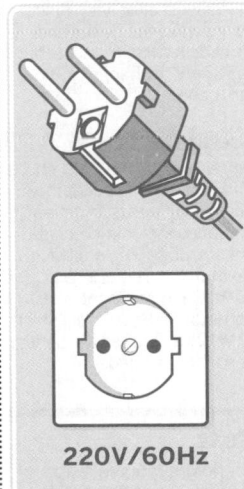

220V/60Hz

Health

The quality of medical care in Seoul is high. You need a doctor's prescription to buy most medications, and it may be difficult to find the exact medication you use at home, so take extra. A letter from your physician outlining your medical condition and a list of your medications (using generic names) could be useful.

There are no special vaccination requirements for visiting Korea, but you should consider vaccination against hepatitis A and B. Most people don't drink the tap water, but those who do seem to come to no harm. Filtered or bottled water is served free in most restaurants.

The **World Health Organisation** (WHO; www.who. int/ith) publishes the annually revised booklet *International Travel & Health*, available free online.

Internet Access

Wi-fi is universal and often free. Nearly all hotels offer it, too; if they don't they will have LAN cables for wired access in rooms. Check charges, which vary from free to around ₩30,000 per day at top-end hotels.

If you need a computer, look for places with a 'PC 방' sign, which charge around ₩2000 per hour and are invariably packed with teenager online gamers. The KTO Tourist Information Centre also offers free internet access.

The major phone companies offer USB dongle devices to rent, in the same way as mobile phones, to connect to the internet anywhere around Korea.

Maps

The Korean Tourism Organisation (KTO) and Seoul Metropolitan Government publish numerous free brochures and maps of Seoul, which are fine for most purposes. **Chungang Atlas** (Map p200; Sambong-gil, Insadong; ⊘9am-6pm Mon-Sat; Ⓜ Line 1 to Jonggak, Exit 2) has some hiking maps with a bit of English.

Medical Services

Seoul has medical-care standards equal to those of other developed countries. Hospitals normally require cash upfront, which you should be able to claim back from your insurance company, if you have appropriate cover.

Clinics

Asan Medical Centre (Map p212; ☑3010 5100; http://eng.amc.seoul.kr; Songpa-gu; ⊘international clinic 9am-5pm Mon-Fri; Ⓜ Line 2 to Seongnae, Exit 1) A 10-minute walk from the subway exit.

Severance Hospital (Map p204; ☑2228 5800; www.yuhs.or.kr; Sinchon, Seodaemun-gu; ⊘international clinic 9.30-11.30am & 2-4.30pm Mon-Fri, 9.30am-noon Sat; Ⓜ Line 2 to Sinchon, Exit 3) A 15-minute walk from the subway exit.

International Clinic (Map p208; ☑790 0857; www.internationalclinic.co.kr; Hannam Bldg, Itaewon-ro, Itaewon; ⊘9am-6.30pm Mon-Wed & Fri, 9am-4pm Sat; Ⓜ Line 6 to Itaewon, Exit 2) Appointments are a must.

Pharmacies

Almost all pharmacies stock at least some Western medicines. Pharmacists often know some English but it may help them if you write down your symptoms or the medicine you want on a piece of paper. If you have a language problem and a mobile phone, dial ☑1330, explain what you want in English, and ask the interpreter to explain in Korean to the pharmacist.

Sudo Pharmacy (Map p198; ☑732 3336; Insadong-gil, Insadong; ⊘8.30am-7.45pm Mon-Sat, noon-7pm Sun; Ⓜ Line 3 to Anguk, Exit 6)

Money

The South Korean unit of currency is the won (₩), with ₩10, ₩50, ₩100 and ₩500 coins. Notes come in denominations of ₩1000, ₩5000, ₩10,000 and ₩50,000.

See www.xe.com for up-to-date exchange rates.

ATMs

ATMs that accept foreign cards are common: look for one that have a 'Global' sign or the logo of your credit-card company. ATMs often operate only from 7am to 11pm, but some are 24-hour. Restrictions on the amount you can withdraw vary. It can be as low as ₩100,000 per day.

Changing Money

Many banks in Seoul offer a foreign exchange service. There are also licensed moneychangers, particularly in Itaewon, that keep longer hours than the banks and provide a faster service, but may only exchange US dollars cash.

Credit Cards

More upmarket hotels, shops and restaurants accept foreign credit cards, but plenty of places including budget accommodation, stalls and restaurants require hard cash. Cash payment is still common in Seoul, so a stash of ₩10,000 notes will almost certainly be needed.

Post

For postal rates refer to the website of **Korea Post** (www.koreapost.go.kr); offices are fairly common and have a red/orange sign.

Central Post Office (Map p202; Sogong-ro, Myeong-dong; ⊘9am-8pm Mon-Fri, to 1pm Sat & Sun)

Public Holidays

Eight Korean public holidays are set according to the solar calendar and three according to the lunar calendar, meaning that they fall on different days each year. Restaurants, shops and tourist sights stay open during most holidays, but may close over the three-day Lunar New Year and Chuseok (harvest-festival) holidays. School holidays mean that beaches and resort areas are busy in August.

New Year's Day (1 January)

Lunar New Year (12 February 2013, 31 January 2014, 19 February 2015) Korea grinds to a halt during this three-day holiday when many people return to their hometown and visits relatives. Trains and planes are booked up months ahead and expressways are one long traffic jam.

Independence Movement Day (1 March) The anniversary of the day in 1919 when nationwide protests against Japanese colonial rule began.

Children's Day (5 May) Take the darlings out for the day and load them up with gifts.

Buddha's Birthday (17 May 2013, 6 May 2014, 25 May 2015) Colourful lanterns decorate all the Buddhist temples and overflow into the streets.

Memorial Day (6 June) Honours those who died fighting for their country.

Constitution Day (17 July) Commemorates the founding of the Republic of South Korea in 1948.

Liberation Day (15 August) Celebrates the day the

Japanese surrendered to Allied forces in 1945, marking the end of their 35-year rule of Korea.

Chuseok (19 September 2013, 8 September 2014, 27 September 2015) The Harvest Moon Festival is a three-day holiday when families get together, eat crescent-shaped rice cakes and visit their ancestors' graves. Avoid travelling at this time.

National Foundation Day (3 October) Dangun, the legendary founder of the Korean nation, was supposedly born on this day in 2333 BC.

Christmas Day (25 December)

Safe Travel

Seoul is a safe city, except when it comes to traffic. Drivers tend to be impatient; many routinely go through red lights. For those on foot, don't be the first or last person to cross over any pedestrian crossing and don't expect any vehicles to stop for you. Watch out for motorcyclists who routinely speed along pavements and across pedestrian crossings.

Drunks in Seoul are better behaved than in the West, so walking around at 3am shouldn't pose a problem.

There's always an exception, of course, and as always it's best not to antagonise people who have been drinking.

Visitors are often surprised to see police in full riot gear, carrying large shields and long batons, streaming out of blue police buses that have their windows covered in protective wire. Student, trade-union, anti-American, environmental and other protests occasionally turn violent. Keep well out of the way of any confrontations that may occur.

Telephone

Gyeonggi-do code (☏031) This province surrounds Seoul.

Incheon city and airport code (☏032)

International access code KT (☏001)

Seoul code (☏02) Do not dial the zero if calling from outside Korea.

South Korea country code (☏82)

Tourist Phone Number (☏1330 or ☏02-1330 from a mobile)

Mobile Phones

Korea uses the CDMA network system, which few

other countries use, so you will probably have to rent a mobile (cell) phone while you're in Seoul. The best place to do this is at Incheon International Airport as soon as you arrive, although some top-end hotels will have phones available for guests, and discount electronic stores in Itaewon also sell a range of new and used phones. Mobile-phone hire is available from four companies, which all have counters at Incheon's arrivals floor:

KT (http://roaming.kt.com/eng/index.asp)

LG Telecom (www.uplus.co.kr)

SK Telecom (www.skroaming.com)

S'Roaming (www.sroaming.com)

Each company offers similar, but not identical schemes; you'll pay more for smartphone rentals. Online discounts can cut daily rental fees. Incoming calls are free and outgoing domestic calls cost around ₩600 a minute, while calls to the US, for example, cost ₩900 a minute. Check that prices quoted include the 10% VAT.

Korean mobile phone numbers have three-digit area codes, always beginning with 01, eg ☏011 1234 5678. When you make a call from your cell phone you always

---

FINDING AN ADDRESS

Seoul is divided up into 25 districts (*gu*, eg Jongno-gu) with these districts further divided into subdistricts (*dong*, ie Insa-dong). Under an old system of addresses, buildings were then numbered according to their chronology within the subdistrict. It was all pretty confusing, so the city has decided to move over to a new address system of logically numbered buildings on named streets (*gil*).

However, until the end of 2013 the old address system will exist alongside the new one. In this guide the practical details for sights, restaurants, hotels etc provide the basic address information that will help you most easily locate a business, typically the *dong* and, if the area in a chapter covers more than one *gu* then also the *gu*. If a place is on a well-known street (ie Itaewon-ro) or on a clearly marked new street address (ie those off Insa-dong-gil), then that information is included too, along with the number you'll find on the building.

If you have the correct full address (either system) these can be used by satellite navigation in taxis or on phones to locate where you are going. For more information on the address changeover see www.juso.go.kr/openEngPage.do.

TRANSLATION & COUNSELLING SERVICES

If you need interpretation help or information on practically any topic, any time of the day or night, you can call either of the following:

➡ **Tourist Phone Number** ☎1330 or ☎02-1330 from a mobile phone

➡ **BBB** ☎1588 5644; http://bbbkorea.org

Also very useful is the **Seoul Global Center** (Map p202; ☎2075-4180; http://global.seoul.go.kr; 3rd fl, Korea Press Center, 124 Sejong-daero, Jung-gu; ☺9am-6pm Mon-Fri; Ⓜ Line 1 or 2 to City Hall, Exit 4), a comprehensive support centre for foreign residents in Seoul; they have volunteers who speak a range of languages as well as full-time staff who can assist on a range of issues. Language and culture classes are also held here.

input the area code, even if you're in the city you're trying to reach. For example, in Seoul when calling a local Seoul number you would dial ☎02-123 4567.

Public Phones & Phonecards

With practically everyone having a mobile phone, it's increasingly rare to find public pay phones; the best place to look are subway stations. Ones accepting coins (₩50 or ₩100) are even rarer. Telephone cards usually give you a 10% bonus in value and can be bought at convenience stores. There are two types of cards, so if your card does not fit in one type of pay phone, try a different looking one. The more squat pay phones accept the thin cards. A few public phones accept credit cards. Local calls cost ₩70 for three minutes.

Time

South Korea is nine hours ahead of GMT/UCT (London) and does not have daylight saving. When it is noon in Seoul, it's 7pm the previous day in San Francisco, 10pm the previous day in New York and 1pm the same day in Sydney.

Toilets

Seoul nowadays has plenty of clean, modern and well-signed *hwajangsil* (public toilets). Virtually all toilets are free of charge, some are decorated with flowers and artwork, and a few even have music. Toilet paper is usually outside the cubicles. As always, it's wise to carry a stash of toilet tissue around with you just in case. Asian-style squat toilets are losing their battle with European-style ones, but there are still a few around. Face the hooded end when you squat.

Tourist Information

There are scores of tourist information booths around the city. In major tourist areas such as Insa-dong and Namdaemun, look for red-jacketed city tourist guides who can also help with information in various languages. Handy tourist information centres:

Cheong-gye-cheon Tourist Information Centre (Map p200; Sejong-daero, Gwanghwamun; ☺9am-10pm; Ⓜ Line 5 to Gwanhwamun, Exit 6)

Gyeongbokgung Tourist Information Centre (Map p200; Gwanghwamun; ☺9am-6pm; Ⓜ Line 3 to Gyeongbokgung, Exit 5)

Insa-dong Tourist Information Centre (Map p198; ☎734 0222; Insa-dong; ☺10am-10pm; Ⓜ Line 3 to Anguk, Exit 6) Two more centres are at the south and north entrances to Insadong-gil.

Itaewon Subway Tourist Information Centre (Map p208; ☎3785 2514; Itaewon; ☺9am-9pm; Ⓜ Line 6 to Itaewon)

KTO Tourist Information Centre (Map p200; ☎1330; www.visitkorea.or.kr; Cheonggye-cheon-ro, Jung-gu; ☺9am-8pm; Ⓜ Line 1 to Jonggak, Exit 5; @) The best information centre; knowledgeable staff, free internet and many brochures and maps.

Myeong-dong Tourist Information Centre (☎757 0088; Myeong-dong; ☺9am-6pm; Ⓜ Line 2 to Euljiro 1-ga, Exit 6)

Namdaemun Market Tourist Information Centre (Map p202; ☎752 1913; Namdaemun Market; ☺9am-6pm; Ⓜ Line 4 to Hoehyeon, Exit 5) You'll find two info kiosks within the market.

Seoul Center for Culture & Tourism (Map p202; ☎3789 7961; 5th fl, M Plaza Bldg, Myeong-dong; Ⓜ Line 4 to Myeong-dong, Exit 6; @) Offers guide services, free internet, culture and language programs.

Travellers with Disabilities

Seoul is slowly getting better at catering for disabled people. Many subway stations now have stair lifts and elevators, and new toilets for disabled people have been built. A few hotels have specially adapted rooms. Tourist attractions, especially government-run ones, offer generous discounts or even free entry for disabled people and a helper. For more information see http:// english.visitkorea.or.kr/enu/ GK/GK_EN_2_5_2.jsp.

Visas

Tourist Visas

With a confirmed onward ticket, visitors from the USA, nearly all West European countries, New Zealand, Australia and around 30 other countries receive 90-day permits on arrival. Visitors from a handful of countries receive 30 day permits, while 60 day permits are given to citizens of Italy and Portugal. Canadians receive a six-month permit.

About 30 countries – including the Russian Federation, China, India and Nigeria – do not qualify for visa exemptions. Citizens from these countries must apply for a tourist visa, which allows a stay of 90 days.

Visitors cannot extend their stay beyond 90 days except in situations such as a medical emergency. More info is at www.mofat.go.kr and www.moj.go.kr.

Work Visas

Applications for a work visa can be made inside South Korea, but you must leave the country to pick up the visa. Most applicants fly (or take the Busan ferry) to Fukuoka in Japan, where it usually takes two days to process the visa. You can also apply for a one-year work visa before entering South Korea but it can take a few weeks to process. Note that the visa authorities will want to see originals (not photocopies) of your educational qualifications. This a safeguard against fake degree certificates.

You don't need to leave South Korea to renew a work visa as long as you carry on working for the same employer. But if you change employers you must normally apply for a new visa and pick it up outside Korea.

If you are working or studying in South Korea on a long-term visa, it is necessary to apply for an alien registration card (ARC) within 90 days of arrival, which costs ₩10,000. This is done at your local immigration office.

Seoul Immigration Head Office (✆2650 6212; http://seoul.immigration. go.kr; Mok-dong; ☉9am-6pm Mon-Fri; ⓜLine 5 to Omokgyo, Exit 7) is always busy, so take something to read. To reach it, carry straight on from the subway exit and walk along the road until it ends, where you'll see a white-tiled building on your left with a big blue sign in English. An Immigration Office in the **Seoul Global Centre** can help with issues related to D8 and any C-type visa.

Volunteering

Volunteers are always needed to teach English and entertain children who live in orphanages. Koreans are very reluctant to adopt children, partly because of the huge educational costs and partly because of the traditional emphasis on blood lines. Charities working in this area include US-based **Korean Kids & Orphanage Outreach Mission** (http:// kkoom.org) and **HOPE** (Helping Others Prosper through English; www.alwayshope. or.kr), a Korean-based non-profit run by foreign English teachers that helps out at orphanages, assists low-income and disadvantaged children with free English lessons and serves food to the homeless.

In Seoul, the Seoul Global Center is a good place to start looking for other volunteer possibilities. More charities and organisations

with volunteer opportunities include the following:

Amnesty International (www.amnesty.or.kr/index. htm) Works mainly on raising awareness in Korea about international human-rights issues.

Cross-Cultural Awareness Program (CCAP; http://ccap.Unesco.or.kr/) Volunteer activities for this Unesco-run program include presenting a class about your own culture to Korean young people, in a Korean public school, or on a weekend trip to a remote area.

Korea Women's Hot Line (KWHL; ✆02 2269 2962; http://eng.hotline.or.kr) Nationwide organisation with 25 branches that also runs a shelter for abused women.

Korean Federation for Environmental Movement (KFEM; ✆735 7000; http://english.kfem.or.kr) Offers volunteer opportunities on various environmental projects and campaigns.

Korean Unwed Mothers' Families Association (KUMFA; www.facebook.com /groups/kumfa) Provides support to single mums.

Seoul International Women's Association (www.siwapage.com) Organises fundraising events to help charities across Korea.

Seoul Volunteer Center (http://volunteer.seoul.go.kr) Opportunities to teach language and culture, take part in environmental clean-ups and help out at social welfare centres.

World Wide Opportunities on Organic Farms (WWOOF; ✆723 4510; www. wwoofkorea.co.kr) Welcomes volunteer workers to farms across Korea to work five to seven hours a day, five to six days a week in return for free board and lodging.

Women Travellers

Korea is a relatively crime-free country for all tourists including women, but the usual precautions should be taken. Korea is a very male-dominated society, although it is becoming less so. See Volunteering for some contact details of women's organisations, including the very active Seoul International Women's Association.

Work

Although a few other opportunities are available for work (particularly for those with Korean language skills), the biggest demand is for English teachers. Koreans have an insatiable appetite for studying English and the country is a deservedly popular place for English-language teachers to find work.

Native English teachers on a one-year contract can expect to earn around ₩2.5 million or more a month, with a furnished apartment, return flights, 50% of medical insurance, 10 days paid holiday and a one-month completion bonus all included in the package. Income tax is very low (around 4%), although a 4.5% pension contribution (reclaimable by some nationalities) is compulsory.

Most English teachers work in a *hagwon* (private language school) but some are employed by universities or government schools. Company classes, English camps and teaching via the telephone are also possible, as is private tutoring, although this is technically illegal. Teaching hours in a *hagwon* are usually around 30 hours a week and are likely to involve split shifts, and evening and Saturday classes.

A degree in any subject is sufficient as long as English is your native language. However, it's a good idea to obtain some kind of English-teaching qualification before you arrive, as this increases your options and you should be able to find (and do) a better job.

Some *hagwon* owners are less than ideal employers and don't pay all that they promise, so check out the warnings on the ATEK website at the end of this section before committing yourself. Ask any prospective employer for the email addresses of foreign English teachers working at the *hagwon*, and contact them for their opinion and advice. One important point to keep in mind is that if you change employers, you will usually need to obtain a new work visa, which requires you to leave the country to pick up your new visa. Your new employer may pick up all or at least part of the tab for this.

The best starting point for finding out more about the English-teaching scene is the **Association for Teachers of English in Korea** (ATEK; www.atek.or.kr).

Doing Business

Investor Korea (www.investkorea.org) can help with visas, legal formalities, customs and tax. Seoul Global Centre has brochures and advice about doing business in Seoul, including taxation. Immigration staff are on hand and can help with some issues and paperwork.

Language

Korean belongs to the Ural-Altaic language family and is spoken by around 80 million people in the world. The standard language of South Korea is based on the dialect of Seoul.

Korean script, Hangul, is simple and accessible, as each character represents a sound of its own. There are a number of competing Romanisation systems in use today for Hangul. Since 2000, the government has been changing road signs to reflect the 'new' Romanisation system, so you may encounter signs, maps and tourist literature with at least two different Romanisation systems.

Korean pronunciation should be pretty straightforward for English speakers, as most sounds are also found in English or have a close approximation. If you follow the coloured pronunciation guides we provide, you'll be understood. Korean distinguishes between aspirated consonants (formed by making a puff of air as they're pronounced) and unaspirated ones (pronounced without a puff of air). In our pronunciation guides, aspirated consonants (except for s and h) are immediately followed by an apostrophe ('). Syllables are pronounced with fairly even emphasis in Korean.

BASICS

Hello.	안녕하세요.	an·nyŏng ha·se·yo
Goodbye. (when leaving/ staying)	안녕히 계세요/ 가세요.	an·nyŏng·hi kye·se·yo/ ka·se·yo
Yes./No.	네./아니요.	né/a·ni·yo

WANT MORE?

For in-depth language information and handy phrases, check out Lonely Planet's *Korean Phrasebook*. You'll find it at **shop.lonelyplanet.com**, or you can buy Lonely Planet's iPhone phrasebooks at the Apple App Store.

Excuse me.	실례합니다.	shil·le ham·ni·da
Sorry.	죄송합니다.	choé·song ham·ni·da
Thank you.	고맙습니다./ 감사합니다.	ko·map·sŭm·ni·da/ kam·sa·ham·ni·da

How are you?
안녕하세요?   an·nyŏng ha·se·yo

Fine, thanks. And you?
네. 안녕하세요?   ne an·nyŏng ha·se·yo

What is your name?
성함을 여쭤봐도   sŏng·ha·mŭl yŏ·tchŏ·bwa·do
될까요?   doélk·ka·yo

My name is ...
제 이름은 ...입니다. che i·rŭ·mŭn ...·im·ni·da

Do you speak English?
영어 하실 줄   yŏng·ŏ ha·shil·jul
아시나요?   a·shi·na·yo

I don't understand.
못 알아 들었어요.   mot a·ra·dŭ·rŏss·ŏ·yo

ACCOMMODATION

Do you have a ... room?	... 룸 있나요?	... rum in·na·yo
single	싱글	shing·gŭl
double	더블	tŏ·bŭl
How much per ...?	...에 얼마예요?	...·é ŏl·ma·ye·yo
night	하룻밤	ha·rup·pam
person	한 명	han·myŏng
air-con	냉방	naeng·bang
bathroom	욕실	yok·shil
toilet	화장실	hwa·jang·shil
window	창문	ch'ang·mun

Is breakfast included?
아침 포함인가요?   a·ch'im p'o·ha·min·ga·yo

DIRECTIONS

Where's a/the ...?
... 어디 있나요?　　... ŏ·di in·na·yo

What's the address?
주소가 뭐예요?　　chu·so·ga mwŏ·ye·yo

Could you please write it down?
적어 주시겠어요?　　chŏ·gŏ ju·shi·gess·ŏ·yo

Please show me (on the map).
(지도에서) 어디인지　　(chi·do·e·sŏ) ŏ·di·in·ji
가르쳐 주세요.　　ka·rŭ·ch'ŏ ju·se·yo

EATING & DRINKING

Can we see the menu?
메뉴 볼 수 있나요?　　me·nyu bol·su in·na·yo

What would you recommend?
추천　　ch'u·ch'ŏn
해 주시겠어요?　　hae·ju·shi·gess·ŏ·yo

Do you have any vegetarian dishes?
채식주의 음식　　ch'ae·shik·chu·i ŭm·shik
있나요?　　in·na·yo

I'd like ..., please.
... 주세요.　　... ju·se·yo

Cheers!
건배!　　kŏn·bae

That was delicious!
맛있었어요!　　ma·shiss·ŏss·ŏ·yo

Please bring the bill.
계산서 가져다　　kye·san·sŏ ka·jŏ·da
주세요.　　ju·se·yo

I'd like to	... 테이블	... t'e·i·bŭl
reserve a	예약해	ye·ya·k'ae
table for ...	주세요.	ju·se·yo
(eight) o'clock	(여덟) 시	(yŏ·dŏl)·shi
(two) people	(두) 명	(tu)·myŏng

KEY PATTERNS

To get by in Korean, mix and match these simple patterns with words of your choice:

When's (the next bus)?
(다음 버스) 언제　　(ta·ŭm bŏ·sŭ) ŏn·jé
있나요?　　in·na·yo

Where's (the train/subway station)?
(역) 어디예요?　　(yŏk) ŏ·di·ye·yo

I'm looking for (a hotel).
(호텔) 찾고　　(ho·t'el) ch'ak·ko
있어요.　　iss·ŏ·yo

Do you have (a map)?
(지도) 가지고　　(chi·do) ka·ji·go
계신가요?　　kye·shin·ga·yo

Is there (a toilet)?
(화장실) 있나요?　　(hwa·jang·shil) in·na·yo

I'd like (the menu).
(메뉴) 주세요.　　(me·nyu) ju·se·yo

I'd like to (hire a car).
(차 빌리고)　　(ch'a pil·li·go)
싶어요.　　shi·p'ŏ·yo

Could you please (help me)?
(저를 도와)　　(chŏ·rŭl to·wa)
주시겠어요?　　ju·shi·gess·ŏ·yo

How much is (a room)?
(방) 얼마예요?　　(pang) ŏl·ma·ye·yo

Do I need (a visa)?
(비자) 필요한가요?　　(pi·ja) p'i·ryo·han·ga·yo

snack	간식	kan·shik
spicy (hot)	매운	mae·un
spoon	숟가락	suk·ka·rak

Key Words

bar	술집	sul·chip
bottle	병	pyŏng
bowl	사발	sa·bal
breakfast	아침	a·ch'im
chopsticks	젓가락	chŏk·ka·rak
cold	차가운	ch'a·ga·un
dinner	저녁	chŏ·nyŏk
fork	포크	p'o·k'ŭ
glass	잔	chan
hot (warm)	뜨거운	ddŭ·gŏ·un
knife	칼	k'al
lunch	점심	chŏm·shim
market	시장	shi·jang
plate	접시	chŏp·shi
restaurant	식당	shik·tang

Meat & Fish

beef	쇠고기	soé·go·gi
chicken	닭고기	tak·ko·gi
duck	오리	o·ri
fish	생선	saeng·sŏn
herring	청어	ch'ŏng·ŏ
lamb	양고기	yang·go·gi
meat	고기	ko·gi
mussel	홍합	hong·hap
oyster	굴	kul
pork	돼지고기	twae·ji·go·gi
prawn	대하	tae·ha
salmon	연어	yŏ·nŏ
seafood	해물	hae·mul
tuna	참치	ch'am·ch'i
turkey	칠면조	ch'il·myŏn·jo
veal	송아지 고기	song·a·ji go·gi

Fruit & Vegetables

apple	사과	sa·gwa
apricot	살구	sal·gu
bean	콩	k'ong
capsicum	고추	ko·ch'u
carrot	당근	tang·gŭn
corn	옥수수	ok·su·su
cucumber	오이	o·i
eggplant	가지	ka·ji
fruit	과일	kwa·il
legume	콩류	k'ong·nyu
lentil	렌즈콩	ren·jŭ·k'ong
lettuce	양상추	yang·sang·ch'u
mushroom	버섯	pŏ·sŏt
nut	견과류	kyŏn·gwa·ryu
onion	양파	yang·p'a
orange	오렌지	o·ren·ji
pea	완두콩	wan·du·k'ong
peach	복숭아	pok·sung·a
pear	배	pae
plum	자두	cha·du
potato	감자	kam·ja
pumpkin	늙은 호박	nŭl·gŭn ho·bak
spinach	시금치	shi·gŭm·ch'i
strawberry	딸기	ddal·gi
tomato	토마토	t'o·ma·t'o
vegetable	야채	ya·ch'ae
watermelon	수박	su·bak

Other

bread	빵	bbang
cheese	치즈	ch'i·jŭ
egg	계란	kye·ran
honey	꿀	ggul
noodles	국수	kuk·su
rice (cooked)	밥	pap
salt	소금	so·gŭm
soup	수프	su·p'ŭ
sugar	설탕	sŏl·t'ang

Drinks

beer	맥주	maek·chu
coffee	커피	k'ŏ·p'i
juice	주스	jus·sŭ
milk	우유	u·yu
mineral water	생수	saeng·su
red wine	레드 와인	re·dŭ wa·in
soft drink	탄산 음료	t'an·san ŭm·nyo
tea	차	ch'a
water	물	mul
white wine	화이트 와인	hwa·i·t'ŭ wa·in

EMERGENCIES

Help!	도와주세요!	to·wa·ju·se·yo
Go away!	저리 가세요!	chŏ·ri ka·se·yo
Call ...!	... 불러주세요!	... pul·lŏ·ju·se·yo
a doctor	의사	ŭi·sa
the police	경찰	kyŏng·ch'al

I'm lost.
길을 잃었어요. ki·rŭl i·rŏss·ŏ·yo

Where's the toilet?
화장실이 어디예요? hwa·jang·shi·ri ŏ·di·ye·yo

I'm sick.
전 아파요. chŏn a·p'a·yo

It hurts here.
여기가 아파요. yŏ·gi·ga a·p'a·yo

I'm allergic to ...
전 ...에 알레르기가 chŏn ...·é al·le·rŭ·gi·ga
있어요. iss·ŏ·yo

SHOPPING & SERVICES

I'm just looking.
그냥 구경할게요. kŭ·nyang ku·gyŏng halk·ke·yo

Do you have (tissues)?
(휴지) 있나요? (hyu·ji) in·na·yo

How much is it?
얼마예요? ŏl·ma·ye·yo

Can you write down the price?
가격을 써 ka·gyŏ·gŭl ssŏ
주시겠어요? ju·shi·gess·ŏ·yo

Signs

영업 중	Open
휴무	Closed
입구	Entrance
출구	Exit
... 금지	... Prohibited
금연 구역	No Smoking Area
화장실	Toilets
신사용	Men
숙녀용	Women

Can I look at it?
보여 주시겠어요? po·yŏ ju·shi·gess·ŏ·yo

Do you have any others?
다른 건 없나요? ta·rŭn·gŏn ŏm·na·yo

That's too expensive.
너무 비싸요. nŏ·mu piss·a·yo

Please give me a discount.
깎아 주세요. ggak·ka·ju·se·yo

There's a mistake in the bill.
계산서가 이상해요. kye·san·sŏ i·sang·hae·yo

ATM	현금인출기	hyŏn·gŭ·min·ch'ul·gi
internet cafe	PC방	p'i·shi·bang
post office	우체국	u·ch'e·guk
tourist office	관광안내소	kwan·gwang an·nae·so

TIME & DATES

What time is it?
몇 시예요? myŏs·shi·ye·yo

It's (two) o'clock.
(두) 시요. (tu)·shi·yo

Half past (two).
(두) 시 삼십 분이요. (tu)·shi sam·ship·pu·ni·yo

morning	아침	a·ch'im
afternoon	오후	o·hu
evening	저녁	chŏ·nyŏk
yesterday	어제	ŏ·jé
today	오늘	o·nŭl
tomorrow	내일	nae·il

Monday	월요일	wŏ·ryo·il
Tuesday	화요일	hwa·yo·il
Wednesday	수요일	su·yo·il
Thursday	목요일	mo·gyo·il
Friday	금요일	kŭ·myo·il
Saturday	토요일	t'o·yo·il
Sunday	일요일	i·ryo·il

TRANSPORT

A ... ticket (to Daegu), please.
(대구 가는) ... 표 주세요. (tae·gu ka·nŭn) ... p'yo chu·se·yo

1st-class	일등석	il·dŭng·sŏk
one-way	편도	p'yŏn·do
return	왕복	wang·bok
standard class	일반석	il·ban·sŏk
standing room	입석	ip·sŏk

Which ...	어느 ...이/가	ŏ·nŭ ...i/·ga
goes to (Myeongdong)?	(명동)에 가나요?	(myŏng·dong)·é ka·na·yo
boat	배	pae
bus	버스	bŏ·sŭ
metro line	지하철 노선	chi·ha·ch'ŏl no·sŏn
train	기차	ki·ch'a

When's the ... (bus)?	... (버스) 언제 있나요?	... (bŏ·sŭ) ŏn·jé in·na·yo
first	첫	ch'ŏt
last	마지막	ma·ji·mak

platform	타는 곳	t'a·nŭn·got
ticket machine	표 자판기	p'yo cha·pan·gi
timetable display	시간표	shi·gan·p'yo
transportation card	교통카드	kyo·t'ong k'a·dŭ

At what time does it get to (Busan)?
(부산)에 언제 도착하나요? (pu·san)·é ŏn·jé to·ch'a·k'a·na·yo

Does it stop at (Gyeongju)?
(경주) 가나요? (kyŏng·ju) ka·na·yo

Please tell me when we get to (Daejeon).
(대전)에 도착하면 좀 알려주세요. (tae·jŏn)·é to·ch'a·k'a·myŏn chom al·lyŏ·ju·se·yo

Please take me to (Insa-dong).
(인사동)으로 . 가 주세요 (in·sa·dong)·ŭ·ro ka·ju·se·yo

Numbers
Use pure Korean numbers (first option below) for hours when telling the time, for counting objects and people, and for your age. Use Sino-Korean numbers (second option below) for minutes when telling the time, for dates and months, and for addresses, phone numbers, money and floors of a building.

1	하나/일	ha·na/il
2	둘/이	tul/i
3	셋/삼	set/sam
4	넷/사	net/sa
5	다섯/오	ta·sŏt/o
6	여섯/육	yŏ·sŏt/yuk
7	일곱/칠	il·gop/ch'il
8	여덟/팔	yŏ·dŏl/p'al
9	아홉/구	a·hop/ku
10	열/십	yŏl/ship

GLOSSARY

-am – monastery

anju – bar snacks

banchan – side dishes

bang – room

bong – peak

buk – north

buncheong – Joseon-era pottery decorated with simple folk designs

cheon – stream

Chuseok – Thanksgiving holiday

-daero – major road, boulevard

DMZ – the Demilitarized Zone that separates North and South Korea

-do – province

do – island

-dong – ward, subdivision of a *gu*

dong – east

DVD bang – minicinemas that show DVDs

-eup – town

-ga – section of a long street

gang – river

geobukseon – 'turtle ships'; iron-clad warships

-gil – small street

-gu – urban district

-gun – county

gung – palace

gugak – traditional Korean music

gwageo – Joseon-era civil-service examination

hae – sea

hagwon – private schools where students study after school or work

hanbok – traditional Korean clothing

hangeul – Korean phonetic alphabet

hanji – traditional Korean handmade paper

hanok – traditional Korean one-storey wooden house with a tiled roof

hansik – Korean food

ho – lake

hof – bar or pub

insam – ginseng

jaebeol – huge conglomerate business, often family run

jeon – hall of a temple

jeong – pavilion

jjimjil-bang – luxury sauna and spa

KTO – Korea Tourism Organisation

KTX – Korean bullet train

maeul – town

minbak – a private home in the countryside with rooms for rent

mudang – shaman, usually female

mugunghwa – limited-stop express train

mun – gate

-myeon – township

nam – south

neung – tomb

noraebang – karaoke room

ondol – underfloor heating

ondol room – traditional, sleep-on-a-floor-mattress hotel room

pansori – traditional Korean opera with a soloist and a drummer

PC bang – internet cafe

pojenmacha – tent bar on street

pungsu – Korean geomancy or feng shui

pyeong – a unit of measurement equal to 3.3 sq m

ramie – see-through cloth made from pounded bark

-ri – village

-ro (sometimes -no) – large street, boulevard

ROK – Republic of Korea (South Korea)

ru – pavilion

-sa – temple

saemaeul – luxury express train

samullori – farmer's percussion music and dance

-san – mountain

seo – west

Seon – Korean version of Zen Buddhism

si – city

sijo – short, Chinese-style nature poetry

ssireum – Korean-style wrestling

taekwondo – Korean martial arts

tap – pagoda

USO – United Service Organizations; it provides leisure activities for US troops and civilians

yangban – aristocrat

yo – padded quilt or futon mattress for sleeping on the floor

MENU DECODER

Fish & Seafood Dishes

chobap (초밥) – raw fish on rice

garibi (가리비) – scallops

gwang-eohoe (광어회) – raw halibut

hongeo (홍어) – ray, usually served raw

jangeogui (장어구이) – grilled eel

kijogae (키조개) – razor clam

kkotgejjim (꽃게찜) – steamed blue crab

modeumhoe (모듬회) – mixed raw-fish platter

nakji (낙지) – octopus

odeng (오뎅) – processed seafood cakes in broth

ojingeo (오징어) – squid

saengseongui (생선구이) – grilled fish

saeugui (새우구이) – grilled prawns

ureok (우럭) – rockfish

Gimbap (김밥)

chamchi gimbap (참치김밥) – tuna gimbap

modeum gimbap (모듬김밥) – assorted gimbap

Kimchi (김치)

baechu kimchi (배추김치) – cabbage kimchi; the classic spicy version

kkakdugi (깍두기) – cubed radish kimchi

mul kimchi (물김치) – cold kimchi soup

Meat Dishes

bossam (보쌈) – steamed pork with kimchi, cabbage and lettuce wrap

bulgogi (불고기) – barbecued beef slices and lettuce wrap

dakgalbi (닭갈비) – spicy chicken pieces grilled with vegetables and rice cakes

dwaeji galbi (돼지갈비) – pork ribs

galbi (갈비) – beef ribs

heukdwaeji (흑돼지) – black pig

jjimdak (찜닭) – spicy chicken pieces with noodles

jokbal (족발) – steamed pigs' feet

kkwong (꿩) – pheasant

metdwaejigogi (멧돼지고기) – wild pig

neobiani/tteokgalbi (너비아니/떡갈비) – large minced-meat patty

samgyeopsal (삼겹살) – barbecued (bacon-like) streaky pork belly

tangsuyuk (탕수육) – Chinese-style sweet-and-sour pork

tongdakgui (통닭구이) – roasted chicken

yukhoe (육회) – seasoned raw beef

Noodles

bibim naengmyeon (비빔냉면) – cold buckwheat noodles with vegetables, meat and sauce

bibimguksu (비빔국수) – noodles with vegetables, meat and sauce

jajangmyeon (자장면) – noodles in Chinese-style black-bean sauce

japchae (잡채) – stir-fried 'glass' noodles and vegetables

kalguksu (칼국수) – wheat noodles in clam-and-vegetable broth

kongguksu (콩국수) – wheat noodles in cold soybean soup

makguksu (막국수) – buckwheat noodles with vegetables

naengmyeon (물냉면) – buckwheat noodles in cold broth

ramyeon (라면) – instant noodles in soup

Rice Dishes

bap (밥) – boiled rice

bibimbap (비빔밥) – rice topped with egg, meat, vegetables and sauce

bokkeumbap (볶음밥) – Chinese-style fried rice

boribap (보리밥) – boiled rice with steamed barley

daetongbap (대통밥) – rice cooked in bamboo stem

dolsot bibimbap (돌솥비빔밥) – bibimbap in stone hotpot

dolsotbap (돌솥밥) – hotpot rice

dolssambap (돌쌈밥) – hotpot rice and lettuce wraps

gulbap (굴밥) – oyster rice

hoedeopbap (회덮밥) – bibimbap with raw fish

honghapbap (홍합밥) – mussel rice

jeonbokjuk (전복죽) – rice porridge with abalone

juk (죽) – rice porridge

pyogo deopbap (표고덮밥) – mushroom rice

sanchae bibimbap (산채비빔밥) – bibimbap with mountain vegetables

sinseollo (신선로) – meat, fish and vegetables cooked in broth

ssambap (쌈밥) – assorted ingredients with rice and wraps

Snacks

beondegi (번데기) – boiled silkworm larvae

bungeoppang (붕어빵) – fish-shaped waffle with red-bean paste

dakkochi (닭꼬치) – spicy grilled chicken on skewers

gukhwappang (국화빵) – flower-shaped waffle with red-bean paste

hotteok (호떡) – wheat pancake with sweet or savoury filling

jjinppang (찐빵) – giant steamed bun with sweet-bean paste

norang goguma (노랑고구마) – sweet potato strips

nurungji (누룽지) – crunchy burnt-rice cracker

patbingsu (팥빙수) – shaved-iced dessert with *tteok* and red-bean topping

tteok (떡) – rice cake

tteokbokki (떡볶이) – pressed rice cakes and vegetables in a spicy sauce

Soups

bosintang (보신탕) – dog-meat soup

chueotang (추어탕) – minced loach-fish soup

dakbaeksuk (닭백숙) – chicken in medicinal herb soup

dakdoritang (닭도리탕) – spicy chicken and potato soup

galbitang (갈비탕) – beef-rib soup

gamjatang (감자탕) – meaty bones and potato soup

haejangguk (해장국) – bean-sprout soup ('hangover soup')

haemultang (해물탕) – spicy assorted seafood soup

hanbang oribaeksuk (한방 오리백숙) – duck in medicinal soup

kkorigomtang (꼬리곰탕) – ox tail soup

maeuntang (매운탕) – spicy fish soup

manduguk (만두국) – soup with meat-filled dumplings

oritang (오리탕) – duck soup

samgyetang (삼계탕) – gin-seng chicken soup

seolnongtang (설렁탕) – beef and rice soup

Stews

budae jjigae (부대찌개) – 'army stew' with hot dogs, Spam and vegetables

dakjjim (닭찜) – braised chicken

doenjang jjigae (된장찌개) – soybean-paste stew

dubu jjigae (두부찌개) – spicy tofu stew

galbijjim (갈비찜) – braised beef ribs

gopchang jeongol (곱창전골) – tripe hotpot

kimchi jjigae (김치찌개) – kimchi stew

nakji jeongol (낙지전골) – octopus hotpot

Other

bindaetteok (빈대떡) – mung-bean pancake

donkkaseu (돈까스) – pork cutlet with rice and salad

dotorimuk (도토리묵) – acorn jelly

gujeolpan (구절판) – eight snacks and wraps

hanjeongsik (한정식) – Korean-style banquet

jeongsik (정식) – set menu or table d'hôte, with lots of side dishes

mandu (만두) – filled dump-lings

omeuraiseu (오므라이스) – omelette with rice

pajeon (파전) – green-onion pancake

sangcharim (상차림) – ban-quet of meat, seafood and vegetables

sigol bapsang (시골밥상) – countryside-style meal

sujebi (수제비) – dough flakes in shellfish broth

sundae (순대) – noodle and vegetable sausage

sundubu (순두부) – uncurdled tofu

twigim (튀김) – seafood or vegetables fried in batter

wangmandu (왕만두) – large steamed dumplings

Nonalcoholic Drinks

boricha (보리차) – barley tea

cha (차) – tea

daechucha (대추차) – red-date tea

hongcha (홍차) – black tea

juseu (주스) – juice

keopi (커피) – coffee

mukapein keopi (무카페인 커피) – decaffeinated coffee

mul (물) – water

nokcha (녹차) – green tea

omijacha (오미자차) – five-flavour berry tea

saengsu (생수) – mineral spring water

seoltang neo-eoseo/ppaego (설탕 넣어½/빼고) – with/without sugar

sikhye (식혜) – rice punch

sujeonggwa (수정과) – cin-namon and ginger punch

uyu (우유) – milk

uyu neo-eoseo/ppaego (우유 넣어½/빼고) – with/without milk

yujacha (유자차) – citron tea

Alcoholic Drinks

bokbunjaju (복분자주) – wild berry liquor

dongdongju/makgeolli (동동주/막걸리) – fermented rice wine

insamju (인삼주) – ginseng liquor

maekju (맥주) – beer

maesilju (매실주) – green plum liquor

soju (소주) – vodka-like drink

Behind the Scenes

SEND US YOUR FEEDBACK

We love to hear from travellers – your comments keep us on our toes and help make our books better. Our well-travelled team reads every word on what you loved or loathed about this book. Although we cannot reply individually to postal submissions, we always guarantee that your feedback goes straight to the appropriate authors, in time for the next edition. Each person who sends us information is thanked in the next edition – and the most useful submissions are rewarded with a selection of digital PDF chapters.

Visit **lonelyplanet.com/contact** to submit your updates and suggestions or to ask for help. Our award-winning website also features inspirational travel stories, news and discussions.

Note: We may edit, reproduce and incorporate your comments in Lonely Planet products such as guidebooks, websites and digital products, so let us know if you don't want your comments reproduced or your name acknowledged. For a copy of our privacy policy visit lonelyplanet.com/privacy.

OUR READERS

Many thanks to the travellers who used the last edition and wrote to us with helpful hints, useful advice and interesting anecdotes:

Rebecca Barnshaw, Nicholas Bremer, Christian Cantos, Logan Drury, George Edat, Yungsuk Jung, Tracy Lassiter, Takis Markopoulos, Alex Miletich, Lesley Miller, Magnus Olsson, Brendan O'Rourke, Wlodzimierz Rakowski, Jim Rogers, Patricia Skully, Catharina Treber, Daniel Wörtz and Yelena Yaskova.

AUTHOR THANKS

Simon Richmond

Many thanks to the following: Maureen O'Crowley, Kim Heesun, Park Seo-young, Daniel Gray, Elly Kim, Matt Kelly, Sam Hammington, Aram Kim, Hassan Haider, Shin Haein, Ray Kang, David Kilburn, Zhang Ki Chul, Shin Ok-ja, Jesse Lord, Angela Hong and the great staff at Han Suites. Also thanks to Neil for enduring my absence with such good grace and keeping my creative juices flowing.

ACKNOWLEDGMENTS

Cover photograph: Downtown Seoul. Mark Barnes/Getty Images.

THIS BOOK

This 7th edition of Lonely Planet's *Seoul* guidebook was researched and written by Simon Richmond. The previous four editions were written by Martin Robinson with assistance from Jason Zahorchak on edition 6. This guidebook was commissioned in Lonely Planet's Melbourne office, and produced by the following:

Commissioning Editor Glenn van der Knijff

Coordinating Editors Michelle Bennett, Kate James

Coordinating Cartographer Jolyon Philcox

Coordinating Layout Designer Carlos Solarte

Managing Editors Bruce Evans, Martine Power

Senior Editor Susan Paterson

Managing Cartographers Mark Griffiths, Corey Hutchison, Diana Von Holdt

Managing Layout Designer Chris Girdler

Assisting Editors Kate Daly, Trent Holden, Helen Yeates

Assisting Cartographers Katalin Dadi-Racz, Karusha Ganga

Cover Research Naomi Parker

Internal Image Research Aude Vauconsant

Language Content Branislava Vladisavljevic

Thanks to Shahara Ahmed, Anita Banh, Lucy Birchley, David Connolly, Barbara Delissen, Ryan Evans, Jonathan Hilts, Annelies Mertens, Trent Paton, Anthony Phelan, Kirsten Rawlings, Gerard Walker

BEHIND THE SCENES

Index

See also separate subindexes for:

- **EATING P189**
- **DRINKING & NIGHTLIFE P190**
- **ENTERTAINMENT P191**
- **SHOPPING P191**
- **SLEEPING P191**
- **SPORTS & ACTIVITIES P192**

☕ DRINKING & NIGHTLIFE

INDEX ENTERTAINMENT

Seoul Maps

Map Legend

Sights

- Beach
- Buddhist
- Castle
- Christian
- Hindu
- Islamic
- Jewish
- Monument
- Museum/Gallery
- Ruin
- Winery/Vineyard
- Zoo
- Other Sight

Eating

- Eating

Drinking & Nightlife

- Drinking & Nightlife
- Cafe

Entertainment

- Entertainment

Shopping

- Shopping

Sports & Activities

- Diving/Snorkelling
- Canoeing/Kayaking
- Skiing
- Surfing
- Swimming/Pool
- Walking
- Windsurfing
- Other Sports & Activities

Sleeping

- Sleeping
- Camping

Information

- Bank
- Embassy/Consulate
- Hospital/Medical
- Internet
- Police
- Post Office
- Telephone
- Toilet
- Tourist Information
- Other Information

Transport

- Airport
- Border Crossing
- Bus
- Cable Car/Funicular
- Cycling
- Ferry
- Monorail
- Parking
- S-Bahn
- Taxi
- Train/Railway
- Tram
- Tube Station
- U-Bahn
- Underground Train Station
- Other Transport

Routes

- Tollway
- Freeway
- Primary
- Secondary
- Tertiary
- Lane
- Unsealed Road
- Plaza/Mall
- Steps
- Tunnel
- Pedestrian Overpass
- Walking Tour
- Walking Tour Detour
- Path

Boundaries

- International
- State/Province
- Disputed
- Regional/Suburb
- Marine Park
- Cliff
- Wall

Geographic

- Hut/Shelter
- Lighthouse
- Lookout
- Mountain/Volcano
- Oasis
- Park
- Pass
- Picnic Area
- Waterfall

Hydrography

- River/Creek
- Intermittent River
- Swamp/Mangrove
- Reef
- Canal
- Water
- Dry/Salt/Intermittent Lake
- Glacier

Areas

- Beach/Desert
- Cemetery (Christian)
- Cemetery (Other)
- Park/Forest
- Sportsground
- Sight (Building)
- Top Sight (Building)

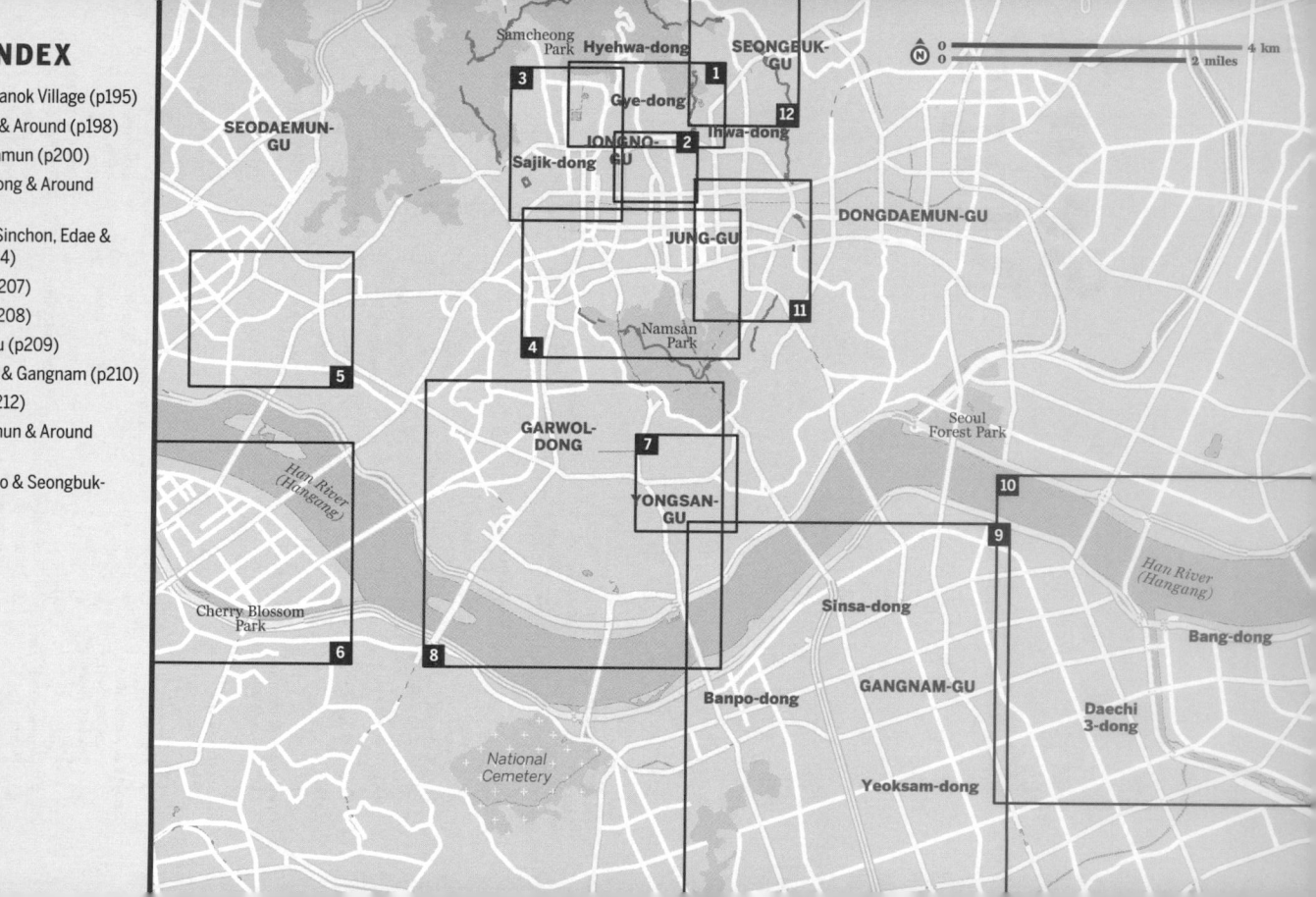

MAP INDEX

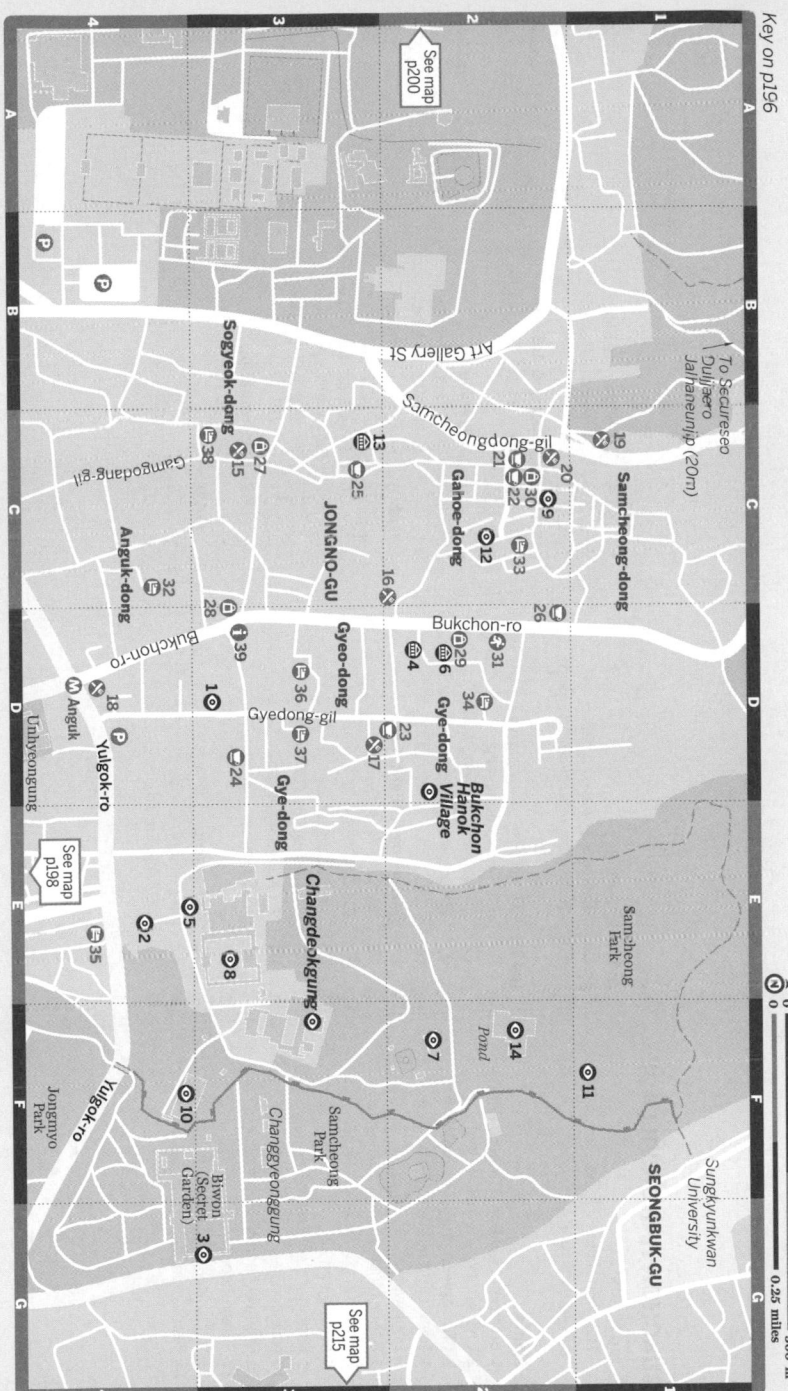

Key on p196

BUKCHON HANOK VILLAGE

See map p200

See map p198

See map p215

To Seocureseo
Duljjaero
Jalhaneunjip (20m)

Art Gallery St

Samcheongdong-gil

Sogyeok-dong

Gamgodang-gil

JONGNO-GU

Gahoe-dong

Samcheong-dong

Anguk-dong

Bukchon-ro

Bukchon-ro

Gyeodong-gil

Gyedong-gil

Gye-dong

Gye-dong

Gye-dong Village

Bukchon Hanok Village

Anguk

Yulgok-ro

Unhyeongung

Changdeokgung

Changgyeonggung

Samcheong Park

Sam-cheong Park

Pond

SEONGBUK-GU

Sungkyunkwan University

Jongmyo Park

Yulgok-ro

Yulgok-ro

Biwon (Secret Garden)

0.25 miles

500 m

BUKCHON HANOK VILLAGE *Map on p195*

INSA-DONG & AROUND *Map on p198*

INSA-DONG & AROUND

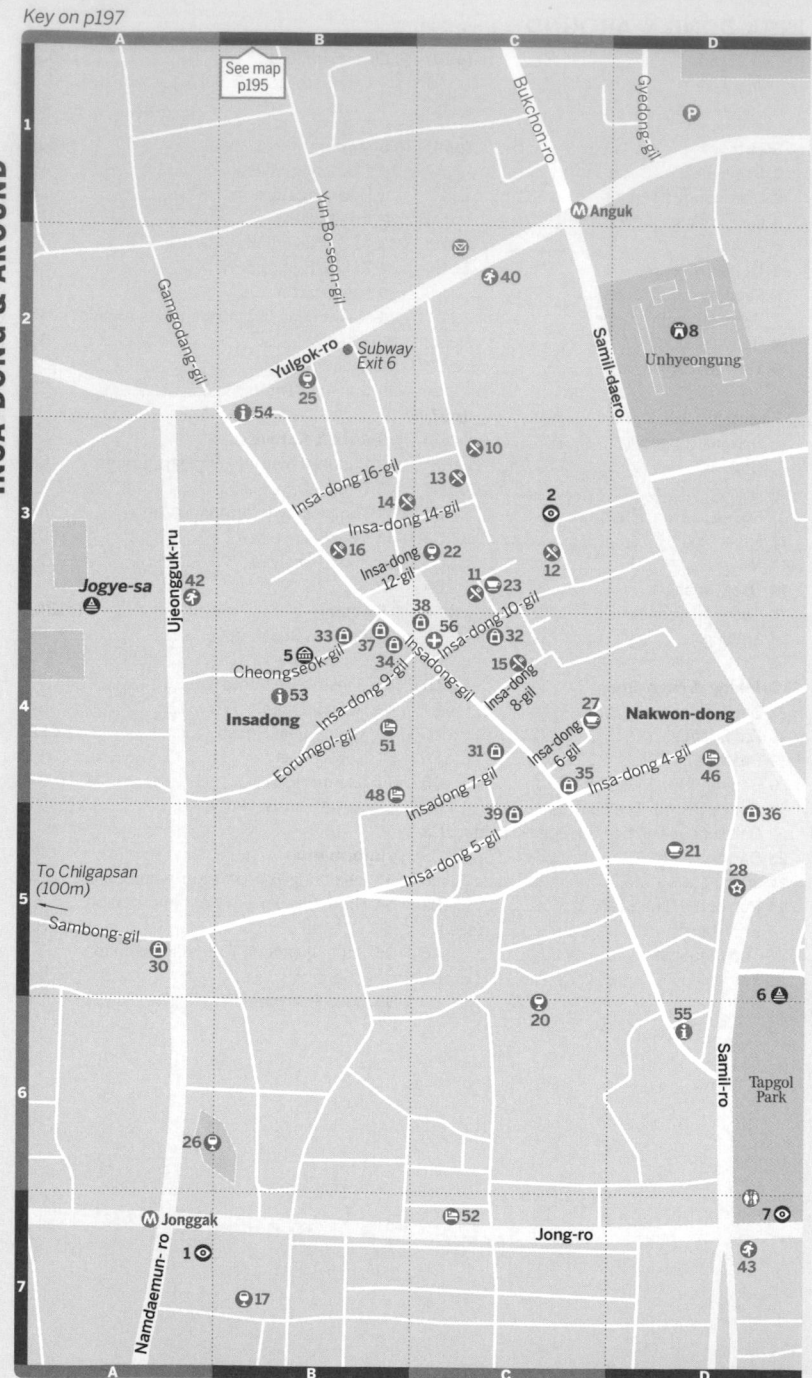

See map
p195

Bukchon-ro

Gyedong-gil

P

M Anguk

✈ 40

⚑ 8

Samil-daero

Unhyeongung

Yun Bo-seon-gil

Gamgodang-gil

Yulgok-ro ● Subway
Exit 6

🏠 25

ℹ 54

✈ 10

Insa-dong 16-gil

✈ 13

✈ 14

Insa-dong 14-gil

2 ◉

✈ 16

Insa-dong
12-gil

🍴 22

✈ 12

11 🍴 23

Ujeongguk-ru

Jogye-sa 🏠 42

38

56

🍴 32

Insa-dong 10-gil

5 🏠 33 ⊞ 37

34

Cheongseok-gil

15 ✈

Insa-dong
8-gil

27

Nakwon-dong

ℹ 53

Insadong

Insa-dong 9-gil

Insadong-gil

Insa-dong
6-gil

🍴 51

31 🔒

Eorumgol-gil

35

Insa-dong 4-gil

⊞ 46

48 🍴

Insadong 7-gil

39 🔒

🔒 36

Insa-dong 5-gil

🍴 21

28
★

To Chilgapsan
(100m)

Sambong-gil

🔒 30

6 🏠

🍴 20

55
ℹ

Samil-ro

**Tapgol
Park**

26 🍴

🚻 7 ◉

M Jonggak

⊞ 52

Jong-ro

Namdaemun-ro

1 ◉

🍴 17

43

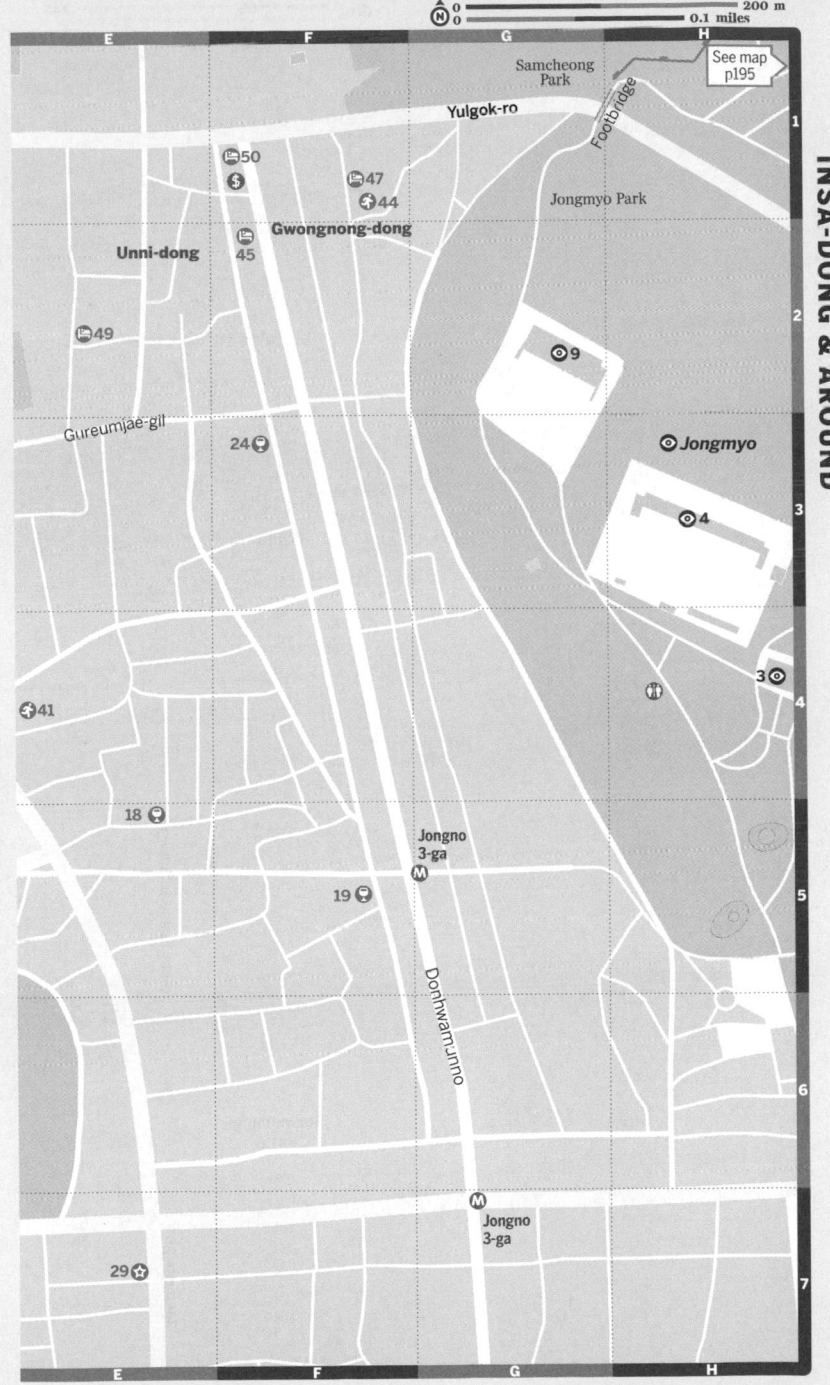

GWANGHWAMUN

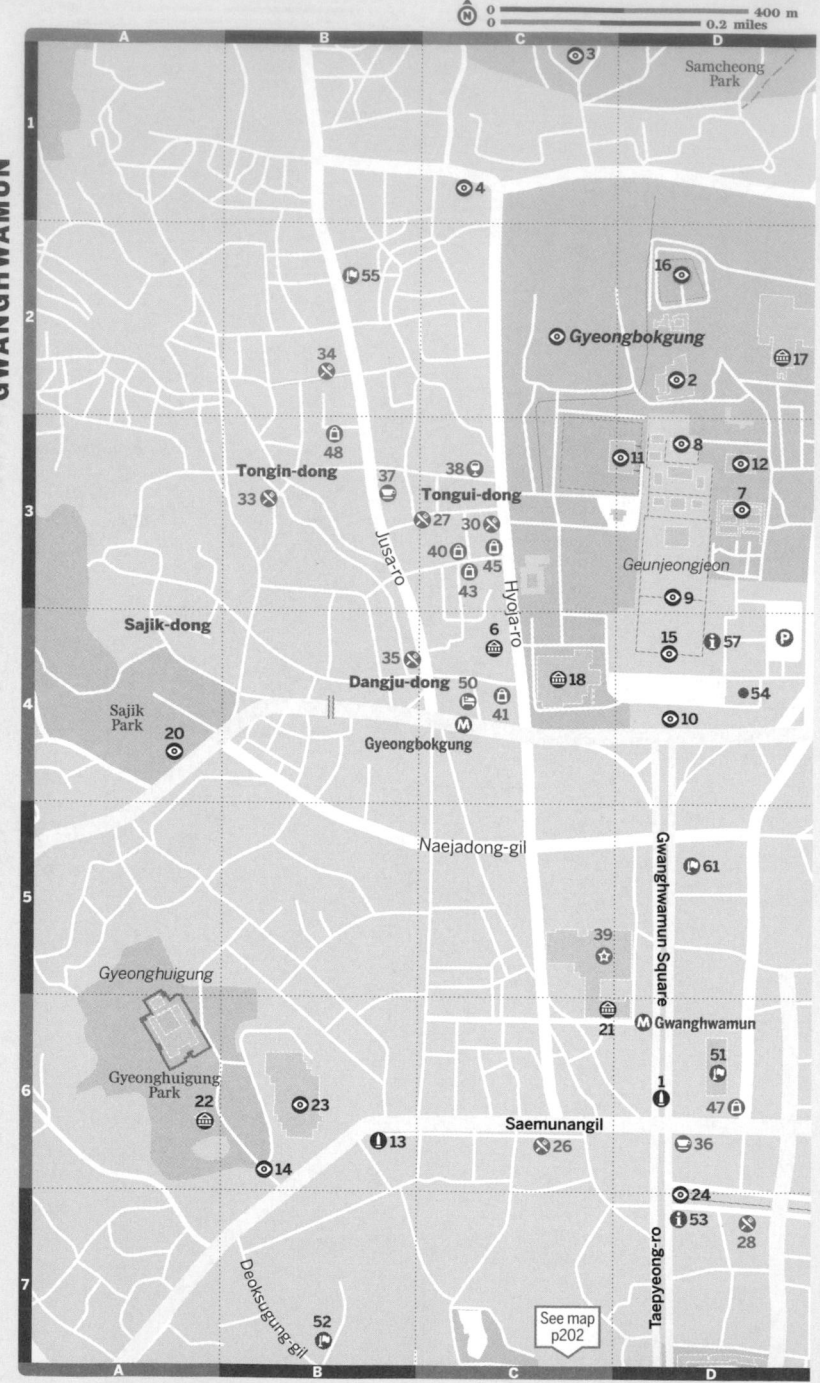

0 ————— 400 m
0 ————— 0.2 miles

3

Samcheong Park

4

55

16

34

Gyeongbokgung

17

2

48

Tongin-dong

37

38

11

8

12

Tonguid-dong

7

33

27

30

Jusa-ro

40

45

Geunjeongjeon

43

Sajik-dong

Hyoja-ro

9

35

6

15

57

P

Dangju-dong

50

18

Sajik
Park

41

54

20

M

10

Gyeongbokgung

Naejadong-gil

61

Gyeonghuigung

39

Gwanghwamun Square

21

M Gwanghwamun

*Gyeonghuigung
Park*

51

22

23

1

47

14

13

Saemunangil

36

26

24

53

28

Taepyeong-ro

Deoksugung-gil

52

See map
p202

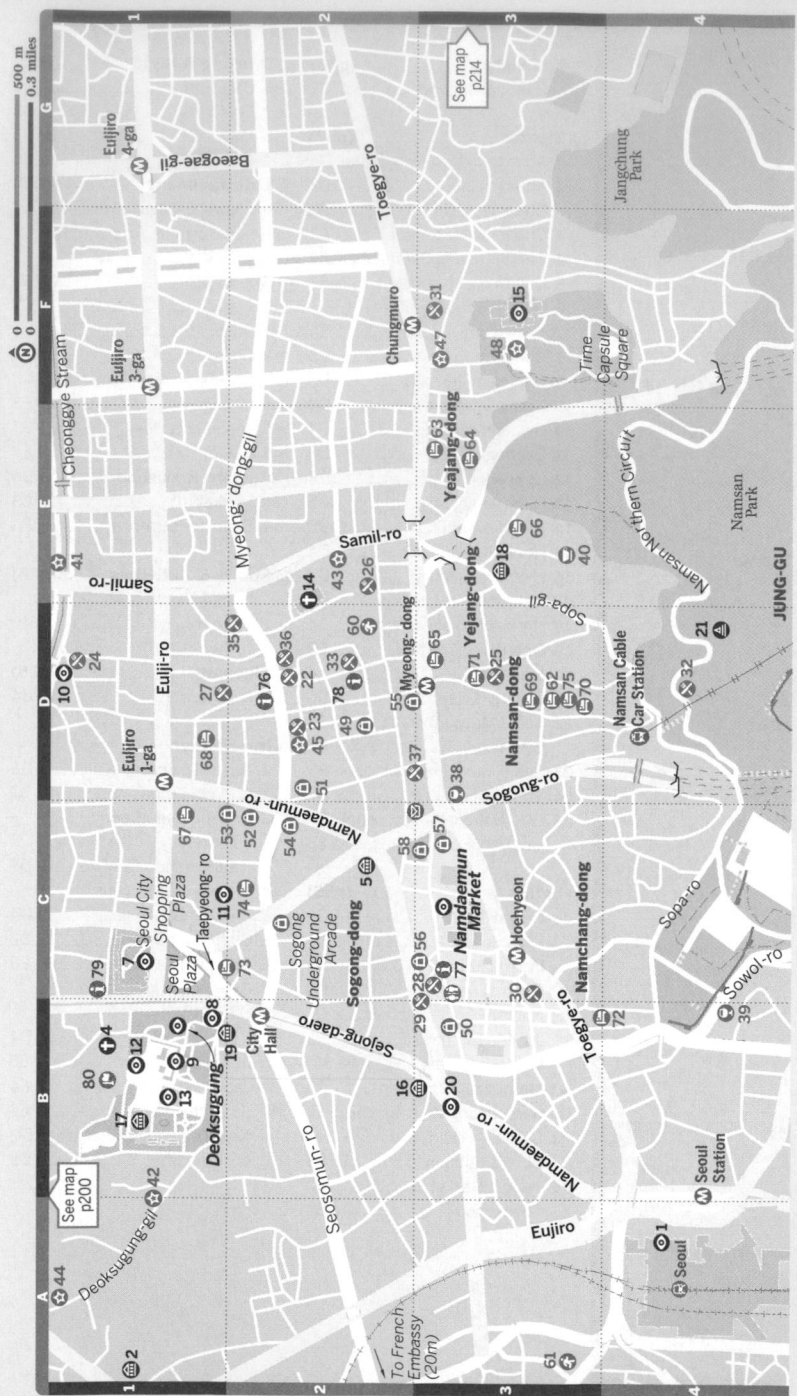

MYEONG-DONG & AROUND

MYEONG-DONG & AROUND

203

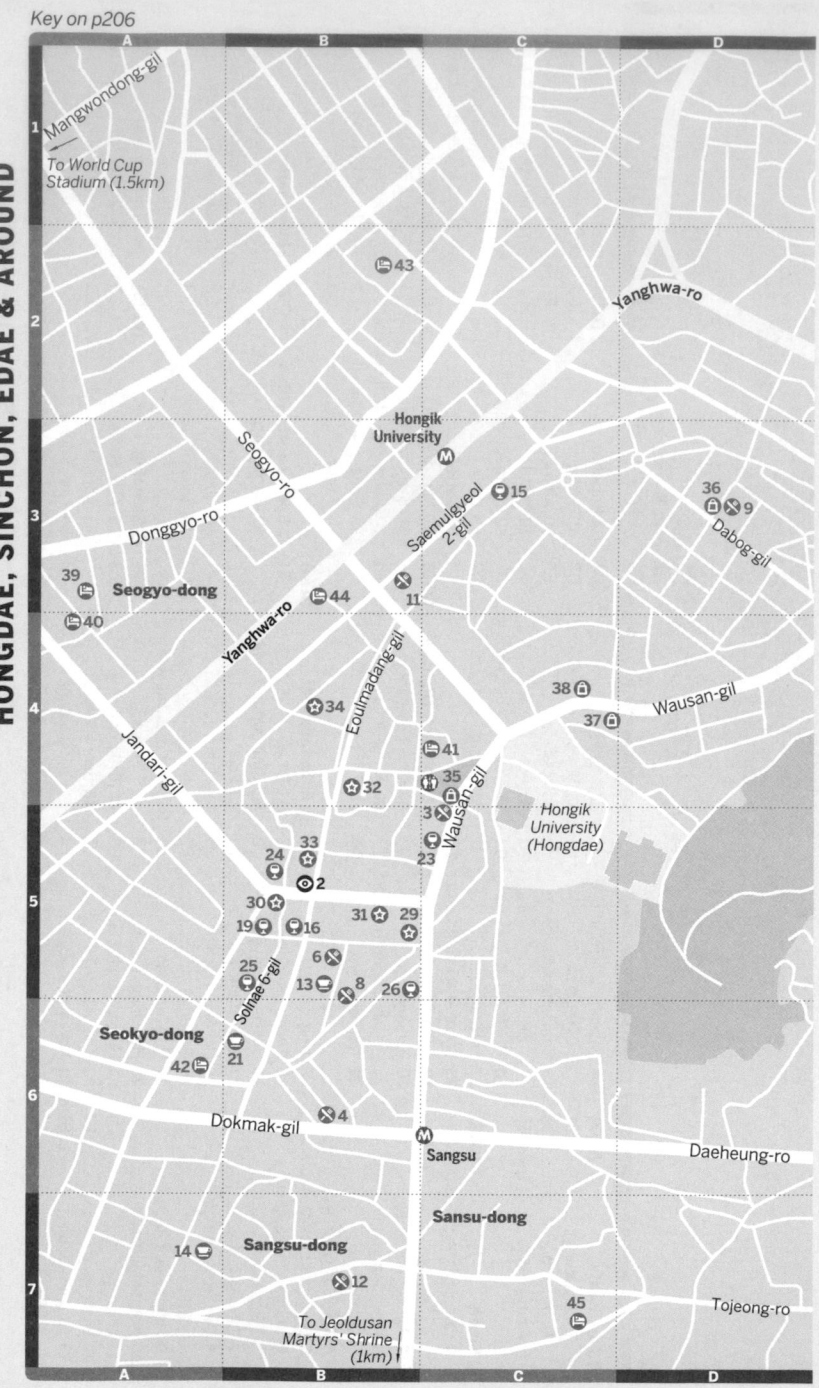

0   500 m
0   0.25 miles

46

*To Ewha Womans
University Museum;
Arthouse Momo (50m)*

Seongsanno

5   7

22
27

10

20

Yanghwa-ro

Ⓜ Sinchon

28   18

17

1

Sogang
University

Seogangno

Gwangheungchang
Ⓜ

Daeheung Ⓜ

Taehiungno

HONGDAE, SINCHON, EDAE & AROUND *Map on p204*

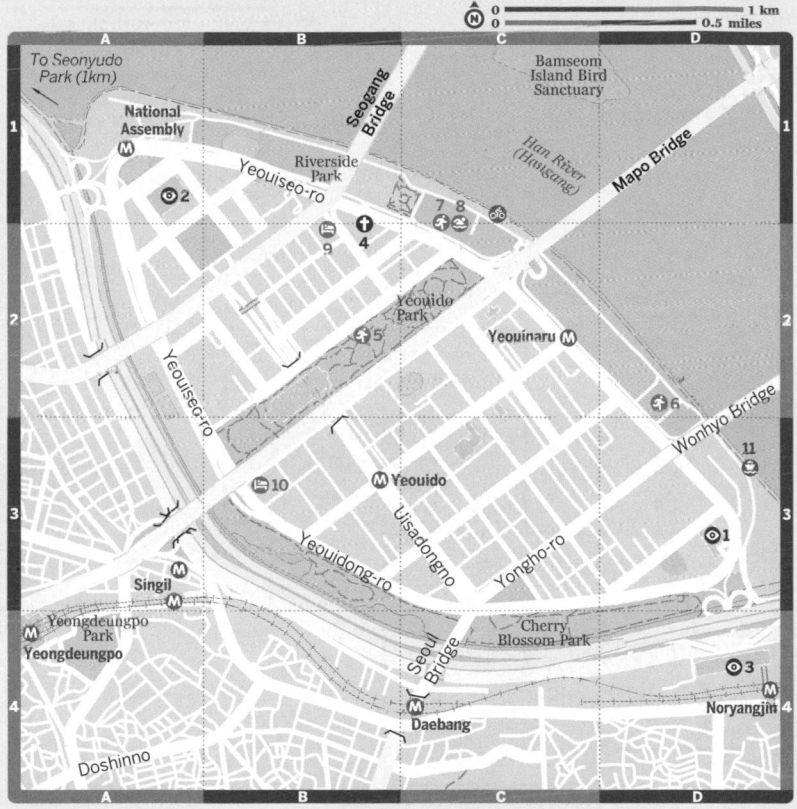

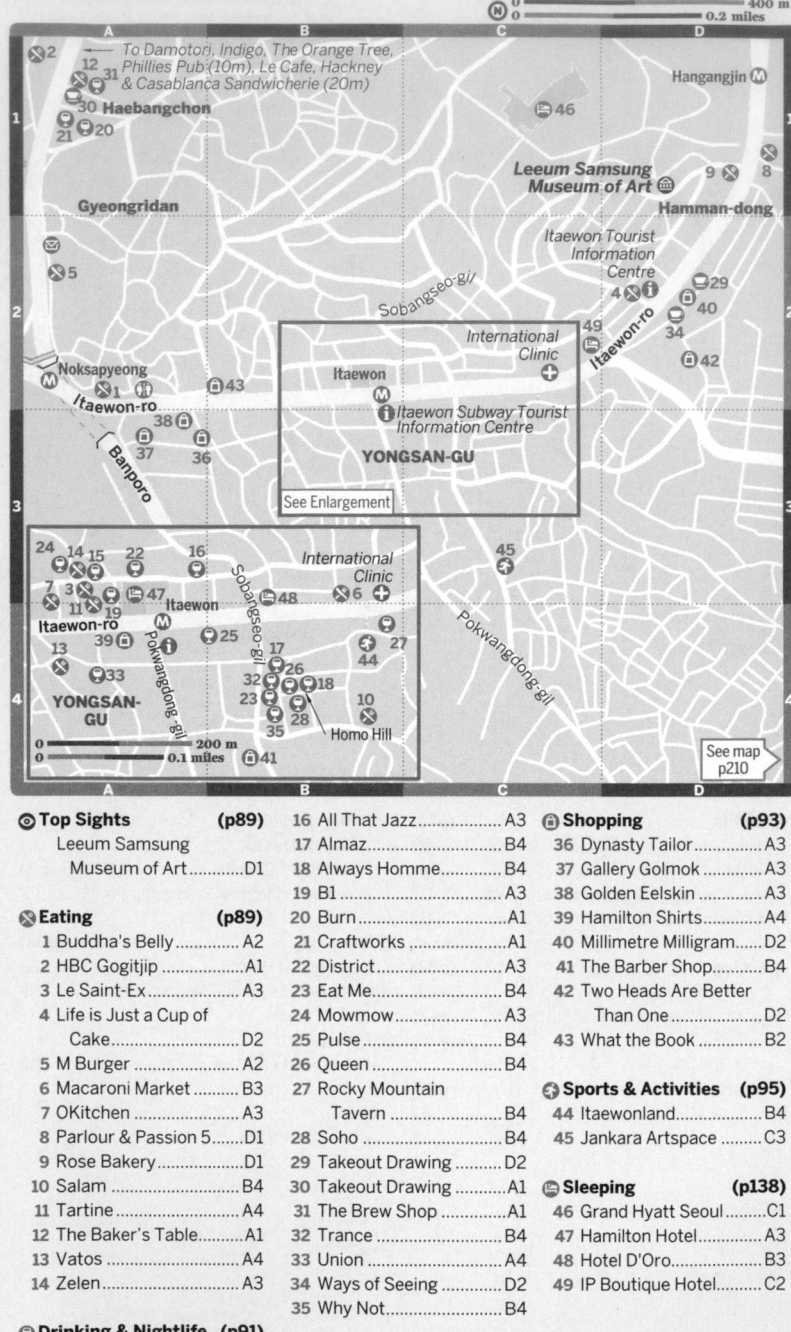

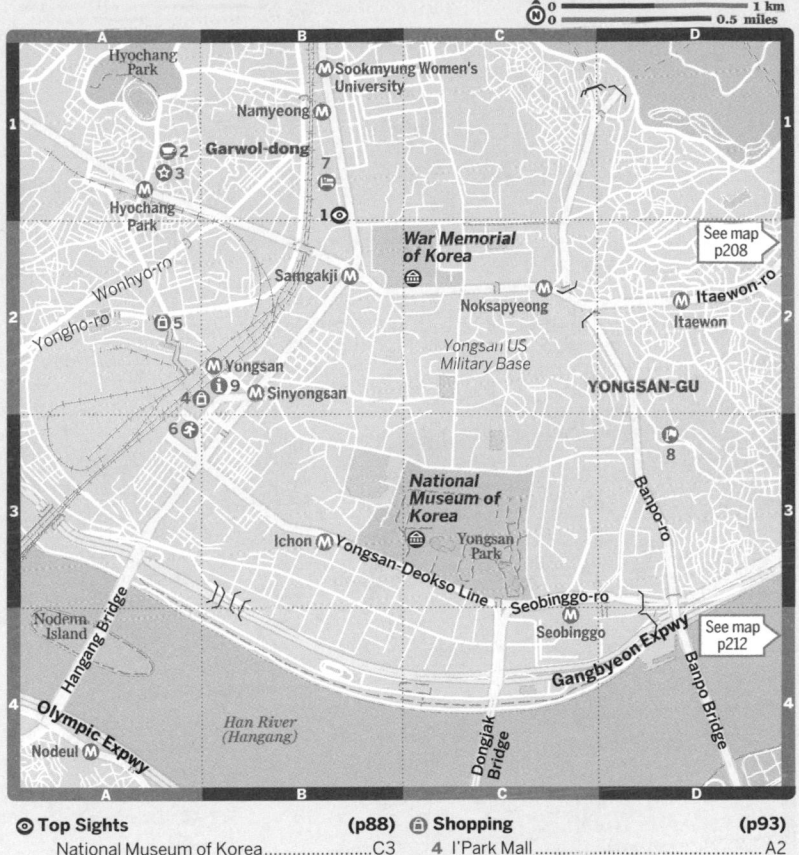

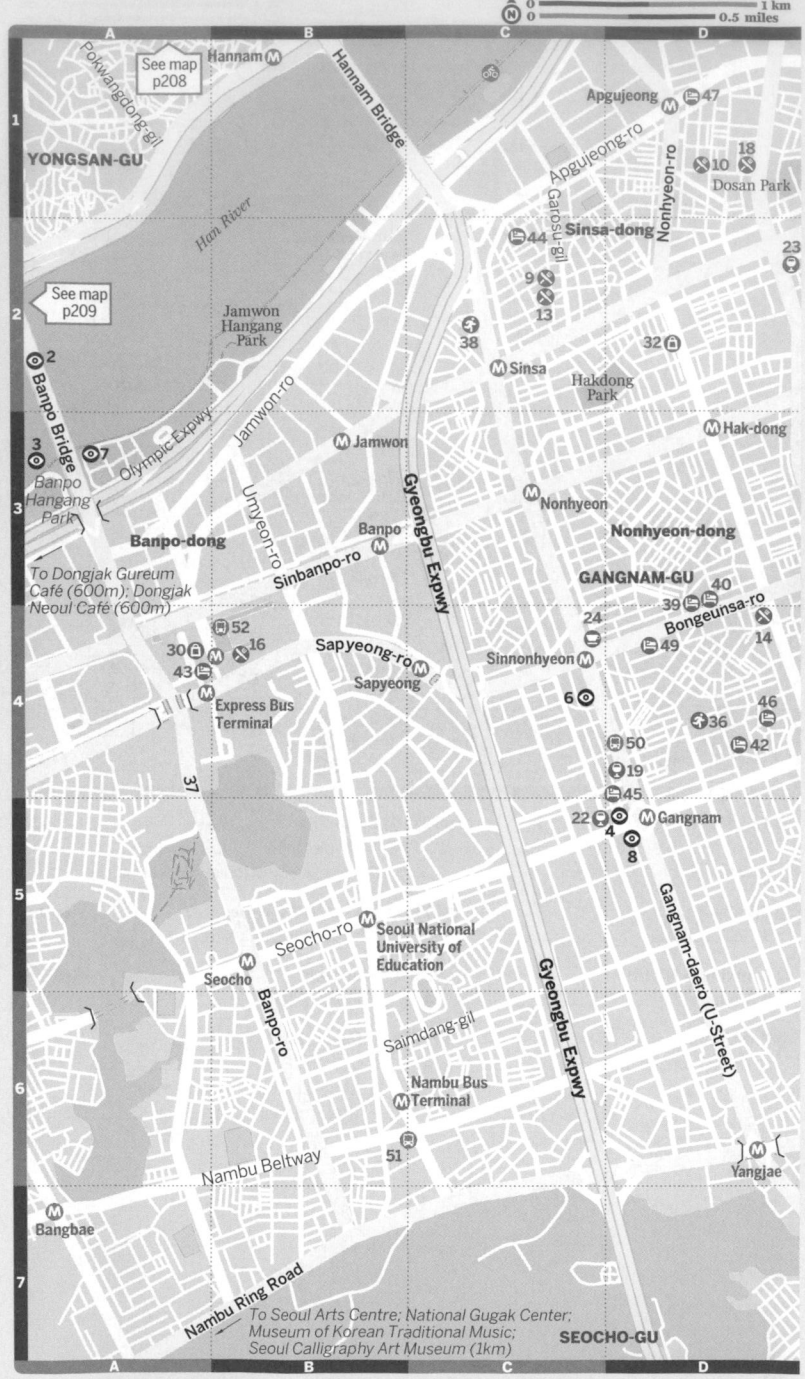

YONGSAN-GU

Han River

Pokwangdong-gil

See map
p208

Hannam

Hannam Bridge

Apgujeong

Apgujeong-ro

Nonhyeon-ro

47

18

10

Dosan Park

23

Sinsa-dong

44

Garosu-gil

9

13

38

Sinsa

Hakdong
Park

32

Hak-dong

See map
p209

Jamwon
Hangang
Park

Banpo Bridge

2

3

7

Banpo
Hangang
Park

Olympic Expwy

Umyeon-ro

Jamwon-ro

Jamwon

Gyeongbu Expwy

Banpo

Nonhyeon

Nonhyeon-dong

Banpo-dong

Sinbanpo-ro

To Dongjak Gureum
Café (600m); Dongjak
Neoul Café (600m)

GANGNAM-GU

24

40

39

Bongeunsa-ro

14

49

Sinnonhyeon

6

36

46

52

30

16

43

Express Bus
Terminal

Sapyeong-ro

Sapyeong

50

19

45

22

4

8

42

Gangnam

37

Seocho-ro

Seoul National
University of
Education

Seocho

Banpo-ro

Saimdang-gil

Gangnam-daero (U-Street)

Nambu Bus
Terminal

51

Nambu Beltway

Yangjae

Bangbae

Nambu Ring Road

To Seoul Arts Centre; National Gugak Center;
Museum of Korean Traditional Music;
Seoul Calligraphy Art Museum (1km)

SEOCHO-GU

1 km
0.5 miles

APGUJEONG & GANGNAM

JAMSIL

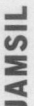

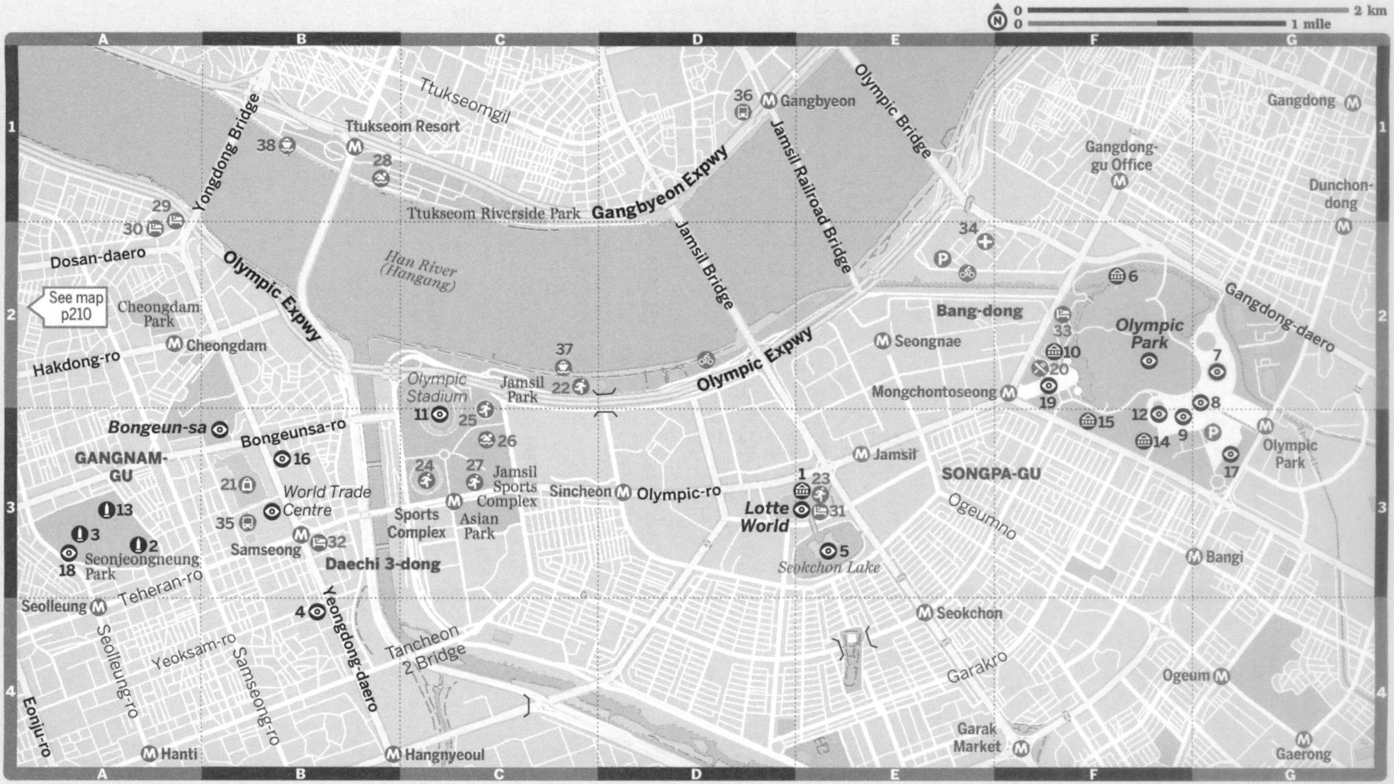

0 2 km
0 1 mile
A B C D E F G
1 2 3 4
Ttukseomgil
Ttukseom Resort
Yongdong Bridge
Gangbyeon
Olympic Bridge
Jamsil Railroad Bridge
Gangbyeon Expwy
Jamsil Bridge
Ttukseom Riverside Park
Han River (Hangang)
Gangdong
Gangdong-gu Office
Dunchon-dong
Dosan-daero
Olympic Expwy
See map p210
Cheongdam Park
Cheongdam
Hakdong-ro
Olympic Stadium
Jamsil Park
Bang-dong
Seongnae
Olympic Park
Gangdong-daero
Mongchontoseong
Bongeun-sa
Bongeunsa-ro
GANGNAM-GU
World Trade Centre
Jamsil Sports Complex
Sports Complex
Asian Park
Sincheon
Olympic-ro
Jamsil
SONGPA-GU
Lotte World
Seokchon Lake
Ogeumno
Bangi
Seonjeongneung Park
Samseong
Daechi 3-dong
Teheran-ro
Seolleung
Seolleung-ro
Yeoksam-ro
Samseong-ro
Yeongdong-daero
Tancheon 2 Bridge
Seokchon
Garakro
Ogeum
Garak Market
Gaerong
Eonju-ro
Hanti
Hangnyeoul

JAMSIL

DONGDAEMUN & AROUND

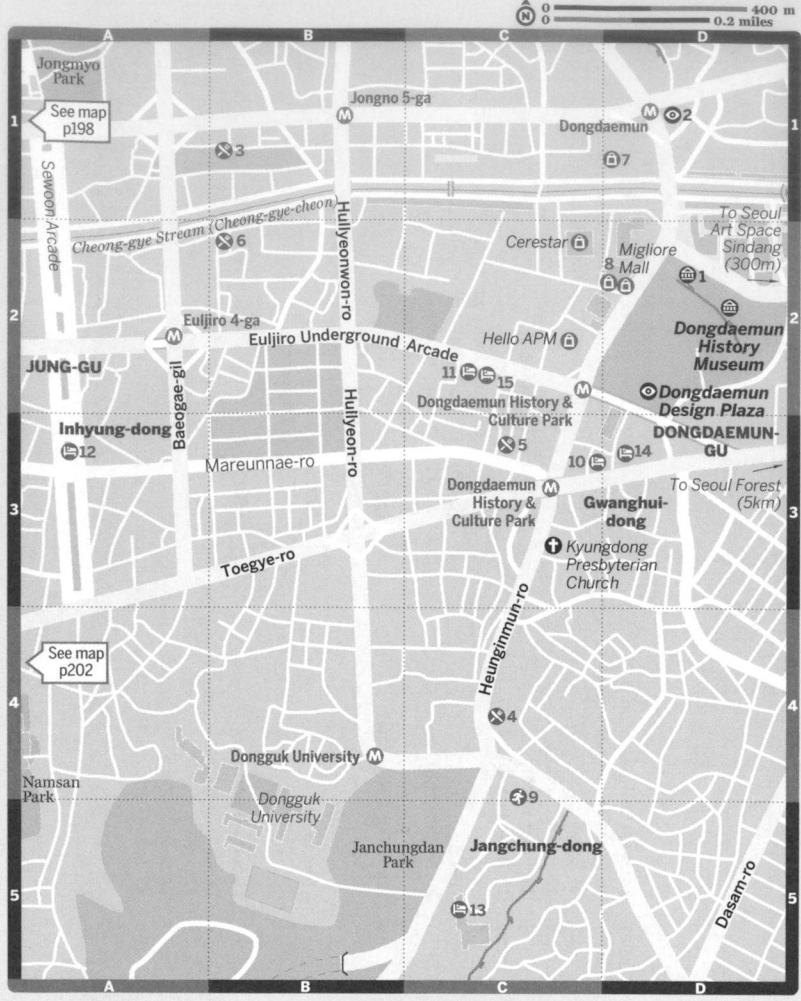

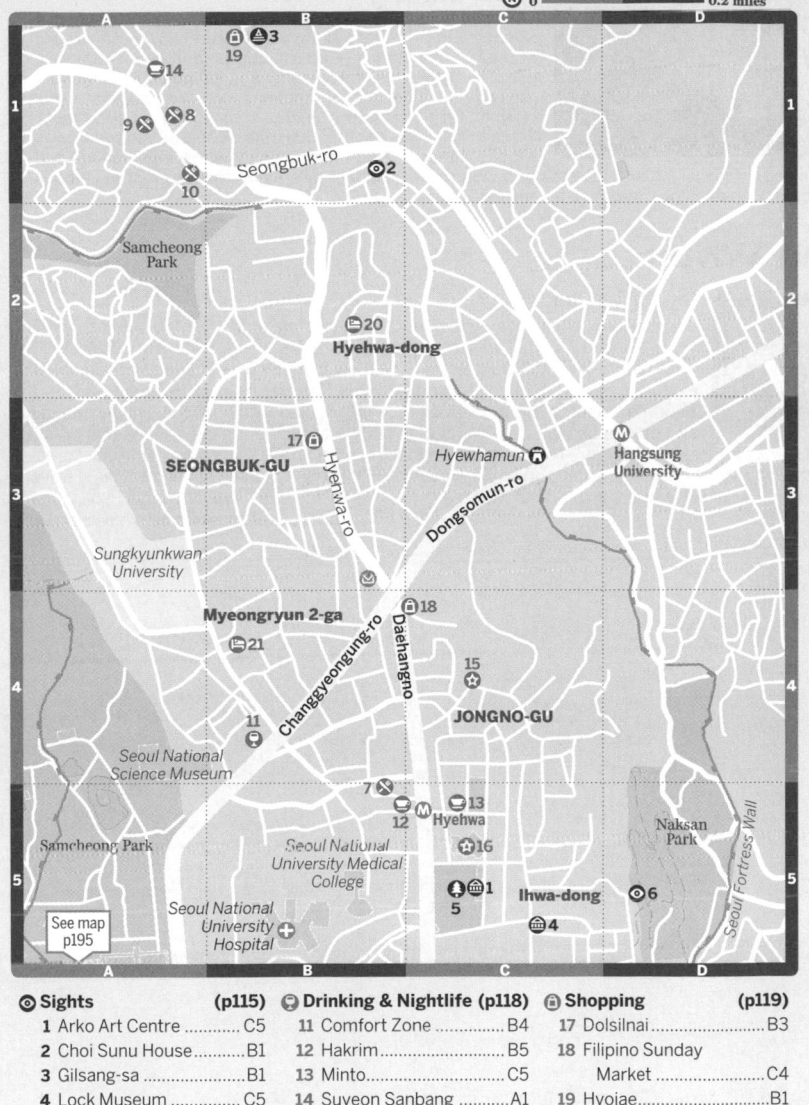

0   400 m
0   0.2 miles

Our Story

A beat-up old car, a few dollars in the pocket and a sense of adventure. In 1972 that's all Tony and Maureen Wheeler needed for the trip of a lifetime – across Europe and Asia overland to Australia. It took several months, and at the end – broke but inspired – they sat at their kitchen table writing and stapling together their first travel guide, *Across Asia on the Cheap*. Within a week they'd sold 1500 copies. Lonely Planet was born.

Today, Lonely Planet has offices in Melbourne, London and Oakland, with more than 600 staff and writers. We share Tony's belief that 'a great guidebook should do three things: inform, educate and amuse'.

Our Writer

Simon Richmond

Long before he became a travel writer and photographer, Simon spent several years living in Japan. It was from there that he first visited Seoul in 2004. He next returned in 2009 to coordinate Lonely Planet's *Korea*, spending six weeks exploring Seoul and the surrounding areas. The two months he spent living in Seoul to research this guidebook took him deeper into both the heavily touristed and off-the-beaten-track parts of the city – a fascinating experience that continues to leave him hungry for more (of the delicious food, in particular!). Simon has written scores of other titles for Lonely Planet and other publishers, and has contributed features to many travel magazines and newspapers around the world.

Read more about Simon at:
lonelyplanet.com/members/simonrichmond

Published by Lonely Planet Publications Pty Ltd
ABN 36 005 607 983
7th edition – Dec 2012
ISBN 978 1 74179 674 2
© Lonely Planet 2012   Photographs © as indicated 2012
10 9 8 7 6 5 4 3 2 1
Printed in China